Pension Systems and Retirement Incomes across OECD Countries

Pension Systems and Retirement Incomes across OECD Countries

Edited by

Richard Disney

University of Nottingham and Institute for Fiscal Studies

Paul Johnson

Chief Economist, Department for Education and Employment

Edward Elgar

Cheltenham, UK • Northampton, MA, USA

Published by
Edward Elgar Publishing Limited
Glensanda House
Montpellier Parade
Cheltenham
Glos GL50 1UA
UK

Edward Elgar Publishing, Inc.
136 West Street
Suite 202
Northampton
Massachusetts 01060
USA

A catalogue record for this book
is available from the British Library

Library of Congress Cataloguing in Publication Data

Pension systems and retirement incomes across OECD countries / [edited by] Richard Disney and Paul Johnson.
        p. cm.
    Includes index.
    1. Old age pensions—OECD countries—Case studies—Congresses.
2. Pensions—OECD countries—Case studies—Congresses. 3. Social security—OECD countries—Case studies—Congresses. 4. Aged—Economic conditions—OECD countries—Statistics—Congresses. 5. Retirement income—OECD countries—Statistics—Congresses. I. Disney, Richard II. Johnson, Paul, 1967–

HD7105.3 .P458 2001
331.25'2'091821—dc21   2001023722

ISBN 1 84064 563 6

Printed and bound in Great Britain by MPG Books Ltd, Bodmin, Cornwall

Contents

Figures

Tables

Contributors

Affiliations at time of writing

Hans Bækgaard	National Centre for Social and Economic Modelling, University of Canberra
Axel Börsch-Supan	Department of Economics, University of Mannheim Centre for Economic Policy Research, London National Bureau of Economic Research, Cambridge, Massachusetts
Agar Brugiavini	Dipartimento di Scienze Economiche, Università Ca' Foscari di Venezia
Bev Dahlby	Department of Economics and Institute of Public Economics, University of Alberta
Klaas de Vos	CentER Applied Research, Tilburg University
Richard Disney	School of Economics, University of Nottingham Institute for Fiscal Studies, London
Carl Emmerson	Institute for Fiscal Studies, London
Elsa Fornero	Dipartimento di Scienze Economiche 'G.Prato' and Centre for Research on Pensions and Welfare Policies, Università di Torino
Ann Harding	National Centre for Social and Economic Modelling, University of Canberra
Michael Hoffman	Department of Economics and Institute of Public Economics, University of Alberta
Paul Johnson	Chief Economist, Department for Education and Employment
Alain Jousten	Université de Liège CORE
Arie Kapteyn	CentER, Tilburg University
Anthony King	National Centre for Social and Economic Modelling, University of Canberra
Nadine Legendre	Division Revenus et Patrimoine des Ménages, Institut National de la Statistique et des Etudes Economiques, Paris
Louis-Paul Pelé	Division Redistribution et Politiques Sociales, Institut National de la Statistique et des Etudes Economiques, Paris

Anette Reil-Held	Department of Economics, University of Mannheim
Reinhold Schnabel	Department of Economics, University of Essen
Susan St John	Department of Economics, University of Auckland

Preface

This book is a comparative analysis of pension systems in nine OECD countries. It draws on the work of experts from each of those countries, with specific chapters on each country prepared according to a common approach or 'template'. This commonality permits meaningful cross-country comparisons of pension systems and of pensioners' incomes, and comparisons of this type are included in the editorial introduction. In particular, calculations concerning pensioner income distributions have been made for each country using household data and every effort has been made to ensure that they use comparable data and methods. Nevertheless, differences in the availability of data in different countries and in definitions and conventions mean that full comparability is, as always, elusive. Even so, full confidence can be placed in the general patterns of similarities and differences indicated.

The editors, and authors of the individual country chapters, have many debts of thanks, which are acknowledged in the respective chapters. The editors and authors also thank the other participants at the conference held in March 1998 at the Institute for Fiscal Studies to discuss this project, especially to the discussants of the papers – James Banks, Andrew Dilnot, Stephen Jenkins, David Miles, Susann Rohwedder, Sarah Smith and Bill Tuck. We are also indebted to the UK National Association of Pension Funds for funding that conference and especially to the Institute of Chartered Accountants of Australia (ICAA) for funding the main part of the project. An extended survey and summary of the results was published on behalf of the ICAA (Johnson, 1998).

Last but not least, our thanks to Nigel Foster for his skill and patience in reproducing the graphs and to Judith Payne who carried out the task of copy-editing and correcting our mistakes with her usual efficiency and good humour.

REFERENCE

Johnson, P. (1998), *Older Getting Wiser*, Sydney: Institute of Chartered Accountants in Australia.

1. An Overview

Richard Disney and Paul Johnson

1.1 INTRODUCTION

Pension systems around the world are in a state of flux. Change, driven by cost increases and adverse demographic circumstances, is widespread (OECD, 1998; Disney, 2000a). And if there is a common theme to that change – more private funded provision and cuts in future unfunded public provision – the starting-points, the rate of change and the size of the change are dramatically different across different countries.

Though many of the problems faced by countries in considering how to design and reform their pension systems are similar – ageing populations, expensive state provision, difficulties in regulating and appropriately taxing private provision – there is remarkably little sharing of knowledge and experience between them. In part this just reflects the difficulty involved in gathering information on and understanding what are always complex arrangements. But the losses from not learning where appropriate from the experiences and mistakes of other countries are potentially very great.

This book is intended to go some way towards remedying that deficiency. Contributions from scholars in nine major OECD countries (Australia, Canada, France, Germany, Italy, the Netherlands, New Zealand, the United Kingdom and the United States)[1] are used to explain and assess pension systems in a variety of institutional settings.[2] Two aspects of pension systems are central to the analysis – the incomes that pensioners actually receive, and the future cost and financial sustainability of different systems, which determine what pensioners will receive in the future. The two aspects are clearly related, depending both on the economic and legislative frameworks and on system design. The purpose of this book is to describe how the pension systems in these countries work and to draw out the links between the structures and the two great tests of the systems – their capacity to provide reasonable incomes to all pensioners and their future macroeconomic sustainability.

Each chapter of the book is written by an academic expert or group of experts in that country according to a common 'template' or thematic structure. These themes are:

- How has each country's pension and retirement system developed? What has been the driving force behind institutional change?
- What are the main conditions determining eligibility for public pension benefits? What other sources of public income (for example means-tested benefits, healthcare, housing support and so on) are available to the elderly? How have benefit levels changed over time?
- What is the extent of coverage by private pension schemes? Will private pensions provide a greater share of pensioner income in the future? How are private pensions treated for tax purposes?
- Is the current pension system in each country sustainable? What are the projected surpluses and deficits of schemes, and future benefit and contribution levels? Are these projections plausible?
- What has happened to labour market activity rates, both just before and after state pension age? Have pension schemes played a part in changes in economic activity rates over time?
- How do the incomes of pensioners compare with those of non-pensioners? Is the income distribution of pensioners more or less unequal than that of non-pensioners, and how is it changing over time? What are the sources of pensioner income, and how are these sources evolving over time?
- What are the current policy issues in each country and how might each system evolve in the future?

In examining pensioner income distributions, each country contributor has utilised appropriate household expenditure datasets for the late 1990s to derive the relevant distributional measures. Pension benefit levels, both now and in the future, are also looked at on a standardised basis across countries in order to facilitate comparisons. Inevitably there are measurement issues and differences in definitions across countries, and these are explored briefly below. But we believe that on a consistency basis the results are largely robust. Furthermore, as described previously, each chapter provides a comprehensive treatment not just of *current* pension incomes but also of *projected* pensioner incomes given existing eligibility criteria, demographic forecasts and policy reform. Typically other studies focus on either one of these issues but not both.[3]

In the remainder of this overview we summarise some of the main findings concerning the operation of public pension schemes in the 10 countries

(Section 1.2) and examine the issue of sustainability and reform of the public systems (Section 1.3). In Section 1.4 we switch attention to the provision of pension schemes in the private sector. Section 1.5 summarises some of the most important comparative findings from the country-specific chapters concerning the distribution of pensioner incomes relative to workers' incomes in the different countries. A brief conclusion completes the picture.

1.2 PUBLIC PENSION BENEFITS

1.2.1 Replacement Rates of Public Benefits and Public Pension Expenditures

The countries in the study can be grouped into a small number of broad categories. France, Germany and Italy have generous earnings-related public (state) schemes that provide high levels of benefits to most pensioners on the basis of a comprehensive system of social insurance. The US, the UK, Japan and Canada also contain earnings-related components in their public pension schemes, but in the case of the two North American countries these are explicitly redistributive and provide much lower replacement rates to high earners than to low earners. In the case of the UK there is an earnings-related state pension, but it is of recent origin and is relatively small by comparison with the main flat basic pension. Japan also has a mixed system with a flat pension and an earnings-related pension on top. New Zealand and the Netherlands both have purely flat public pension schemes, with the pension paid on the basis of past residence in the country, not on the basis of a contributory record. Finally Australia is unique among the countries studied here in that the public pension system consists entirely of a means-tested benefit for pensioners.

The projected generosity of these various public systems, in terms of incomes of pensioners relative to workers, is illustrated in Table 1.1. These figures can be gleaned from the country-specific chapters or are obtained in some cases from supplementary analyses by the editors. We also include comparable data from Japan, taken from Takayama (1996). The table shows for each country the pension that a single person would receive, expressed as four different proportions:

- the person's net pension as a proportion of his or her previous net earnings ('net replacement', column 1);
- the gross pension relative to own previous gross earnings ('gross replacement', column 2);

Table 1.1   Alternative Measures of Replacement Rates of Public Pension Benefits by Relative Income Level (%)

	(1) Net replacement	(2) Gross replacement	(3) Net over net average	(4) Gross over gross average
Australia[a]				
Half	n.a.	n.a.	33	25
Average	n.a.	n.a.	33	25
Twice	n.a.	n.a.	33	25
Canada				
Half	76	59	48	35
Average	44	31	49	37
Twice	25	15	49	37
France				
Half	84		48	39
Average	84		95	79
Twice	73		165	136
Germany				
Half	67 (79)[b]	48	34 (40)[b]	24
Average	72	45	72	45
Twice	75	40	150	80
Italy				
Quarter	103	103	32	24
Average	90	78	82	72
Three times	85	70	192	193
Japan				
Half	77	68		36
Average	56	49		49
Twice	43	36		72
Netherlands				
Half	73	63	41	32
Average	43	32	41	32
Twice	25	16	41	32
New Zealand				
Half	75	66	38	33
Average	38	33	38	33
Twice	19	15	38	33
UK				
Half	72	63	25	19
Average	50	44	34	26
Twice	35	33	48	39
US				
Half	64.6	47.2		
Average	54.6	37.5		
Twice	32.3	20.8		

Notes to Table 1.1:
^aThe figures for Australia are for the maximum benefit. Replacement rates are not really relevant in this means-tested system.
^bThe figures in parentheses for Germany include social assistance.

- the net pension as a proportion of national average net earnings ('net over net average', column 3);
- the gross pension as a proportion of national average gross earnings ('gross over gross average', column 4).

These figures are calculated on three bases – for someone on half average earnings during his or her life, someone on average earnings and someone on twice average earnings. Naturally this is a simplification in that there are an infinite variety of possible earnings histories which will result in an infinite variety of eventual pension payments, but the figures provide good illustrations of the nature and generosity of the various systems.[4]

The results are as might be expected given the pension regimes. Italy, France and Germany all have very high replacement rates at all the levels of income considered. Note also that in these countries, pensioners with histories of high earnings earn pensions from the state that provide them with an income that is higher than the average earnings of current workers. In contrast, despite having important earnings-related elements, the UK, US, Japanese and Canadian systems provide lower replacement rates for higher earners than for lower earners. Indeed the Canadian system, at these earnings levels, almost collapses to a flat-rate system. Naturally the flat-rate Dutch, New Zealand and Australian systems provide the same cash level of benefits whatever the previous earnings history and as such appear quite redistributive.

The high levels of public pensions in some of the countries relative to others obviously come at some relative cost. Table 1.2 shows public pension spending as a percentage of GDP in each country around the mid-1990s. By spending, the division into two camps is clear. The French, Germans and Italians all spend more than 11 per cent of national income on their public pension programmes, and this is primarily because they offer similar replacement rates at all income levels (see Table 1.1, columns 1 and 2). Spending in most of the other countries is nearer 5 per cent of GDP, depending on exactly what is included in pension spending, with the Dutch and Japanese somewhere between the two. The lower spending in these countries arises because replacement rates decline at higher levels of pre-retirement income, as again demonstrated in Table 1.1. The individual country chapters discuss the various benefit calculations and eligibility conditions in some detail.

There are also variations in the treatment of different expenditures and benefit categories across countries. In the UK, for instance, spending on the main pension system is 4.2 per cent of GDP, but additional spending on means-tested and other benefits raises that to 5.2 per cent. In the US the treatment of the Medicare programme makes a major difference. The figure for the Netherlands includes payment of retirement and disability pensions to those under normal state pensionable age. All the calculations exclude the costs to the government of tax reliefs given to encourage individuals to have private pensions.

Table 1.2   Pension Spending as a Share of GDP (% of GDP)

	Public pension spending as a % of GDP (year)
Australia	3.3 (1990)
Canada	5.4 (1994)
France	12.1 (1998)
Germany	11.1 (1995)
Italy	16.0 (including 2.1% on disability pensions) (1997)
Japan	6.6 (1995)
Netherlands	6.4 (1995)
New Zealand	5.6 (gross) (1995)
UK	5.2 (1998)
US	4.6 (plus 3.5% on Medicare and means-tested programmes) (1996)

Sources: Authors' calculations in text. Japan: see Takayama (1996).

1.2.2   Treatment of Spouses

It is common, as in the exposition so far, to look at pension systems from the point of view of a single recipient. This basis of comparison ignores the calculation of benefits for couples and gives no basis for understanding the difference in the effective treatments of men and women. Not that any of the countries sets out to treat men and women differently within the rules of the systems – except in some cases with respect to pensionable ages – but given their different working patterns women inevitably end up with a different pension from that of men.

In Australia for example the situation is straightforward. A couple is entitled to 67 per cent more benefit than a single person; otherwise the benefit calculation is just as it would be for a single person. The income and assets tests are done on a joint basis, as occurs in the British and Canadian means-tested benefit systems. Indeed it is an almost inevitable part of a large-scale means-tested system that couples should be treated as a single unit.

The Dutch and New Zealand systems, providing universal benefits on a non-work-related basis, are probably best placed to treat men and women separately and a couple as two individuals rather than as a single unit. This indeed is what happens, although that does *not* mean that couples between them receive twice what a single person would get. In New Zealand a single person receives 60 per cent of the amount that a couple would receive and there is a separate living-alone rate of 65 per cent of the married rate. In the Netherlands the scheme operates such that each individual is entitled to a benefit worth half the minimum wage with a supplement of 20 per cent of this figure for single people – so effectively the single rate is 70 per cent of the married rate. Being non-contributory systems, there is no issue about inheriting basic pension rights in Australia, New Zealand and the Netherlands.

An interesting point is that in both New Zealand and Canada there have been clawback systems or surcharges on the universal basic pension in an effort to recoup some of the cost of paying a universal benefit to higher-income pensioners. In each case the surcharge has been explicitly levied on the basis of *individual* income and not family income. There seems to be a difference in practice, though it is not clear what the difference is in principle, between the treatment of couples in assessment for means-tested benefits and their treatment for clawbacks of, or surcharges on, universal benefits.

Earnings-related components are treated differently: 60 per cent of the earnings-related part of the Canadian pension can be inherited when a spouse dies. Similarly (under the 1986 legislation) half of the SERPS pension in the UK is inheritable. In the US the whole of a deceased spouse's pension can be inherited, although the surviving spouse is entitled only to the higher of his or her own or the deceased spouse's pension, not both. The US system allows a woman to claim half her husband's pension if she has none of her own, but none of the Canadian, Japanese or British earnings-related systems has this additional provision for dependent spouses. This no doubt reflects the fact that the Canadian system includes the universal element paid to all irrespective of work history, while in the UK there is a dependant's addition to the basic state pension worth about 60 per cent of the full amount, and in Japan dependent spouses are entitled to their own basic pension from age 65.

Inheritance of pension rights in Japan is particularly complex. The widow will continue to receive her own basic benefits plus 75 per cent of the earnings-related benefits that her husband was receiving. If she has her own earnings-related benefits then she chooses the higher of her pension or 75 per cent of her husband's. Since 1995 she has also had the option of receiving half of the combined total of her own and her husband's pension rights.

In the three 'pure' social insurance systems of France, Germany and Italy, benefits are strictly work-related and one finds no benefits for dependent spouses as such, although in France a pensioner with a wife who has never worked will receive a (very) small fixed addition to his basic pension worth about 5 per cent of the usual level of the basic pension. Moreover the earnings-related pension can in part be inherited by widows in Italy, France and Germany. In Germany for example 60 per cent of the pension can be inherited by a widow (or widower).

Two issues therefore stand out in this brief discussion of the treatment of spouses. The first is that in fully earnings-related social-insurance-type systems, not only is it the case that only those who have been in the labour market earn pensions in their own right, but married couples do not always receive any additional benefits at all. The position of married women pensioners in such countries is likely to be one of rather less financial independence than in countries such as New Zealand and the Netherlands where the benefit system is not work-related. In this sense the state systems in Germany, France and Italy almost mimic private pension provision in determining couples' entitlements. Not only do such schemes rule out explicit redistribution from rich to poor (other than by various *ad hoc* floors and ceilings), but they also involve less in the way of redistribution from men to women. Since one reform strategy to deal with rising pension costs has been to get public systems increasingly to mimic private contribution-based systems in calculating benefit entitlements (as in the Dini reform in Italy, and in Sweden – see Disney (1999)), this is an important consequence of such reforms.

Second, in those countries that do provide extra pensions for couples, the relativity between the single person's and the married couple's pension tends to be similar across countries, with a single person's pension close to 60–70 per cent of that for the couple. It is worth noting however that through the combination of a trend to more labour force participation among women and of policy reforms reflecting increased sensitivity to 'gender issues', the gap between men and women is decreasing in most countries. Therefore the assumption on which some systems are based of the standard family being a couple in which only the man has earned a full pension is becoming less tenable.

1.2.3 Indexation

An important feature of any pension system is the way in which benefits are indexed. This has two aspects: first, how earnings are revalued at retirement in order to calculate the initial pension level; and second, how rapidly benefits increase once they are in payment.

To understand the importance of this distinction, consider an earnings-related scheme in which the eventual pension depends on average earnings over the working life. If real earnings grow over time, then the value of earnings at the start of the working life will be very low unless revalued in the pension calculation. In fact in all the countries considered here previous earnings are effectively revalued in line with a measure of earnings growth.[5] But that does not mean that, once in payment, pensions need to rise in line with earnings growth. SERPS – the state earnings-related pension – in the UK is a good example of this. The initial payment is calculated by reference to previous earnings revalued to the year of retirement using an earnings index. But, once in payment, the pension is raised each year only in line with prices. So while, other things being equal, each generation of pensioners might get a higher pension than the previous generation, they would then see the value of the annual payment decline through their retirement relative to general living standards.

The way in which pensions are indexed also has a rather fundamental effect on the sustainability of any pension system. If pensions only rise in line with prices, then the economy can readily handle a substantial growth in the pensioner population because the cost of providing any one pension drops substantially over time as a proportion of national income, offsetting the need to pay more pensions as the population ages. The UK is probably the best example of a country in which a move to price indexation of pensions has been instrumental in relieving the pressure of adverse demographic change on

Table 1.3   Indexation of Public Benefits

	Earnings-related component		Flat-rate component
	Pre-retirement	Post-retirement	Post-retirement
Australia	n.a.	n.a.	Wages
Canada	Wages	Prices	Prices
France	Prices	Prices	n.a.
Germany	*Net* wages	*Net* wages	n.a.
Italy: pre-1992	Wages	Wages	n.a.
post-1992	Prices + 1%	Prices	n.a.
Japan	*Net* wages	*Net* wages	Prices
Netherlands	n.a.	n.a.	Wages[a]
New Zealand	n.a.	n.a.	Prices[b]
UK	Wages	Prices	Prices
US	Wages	Prices	n.a.

Notes:
[a] The Dutch have legislation that allows the pension to rise more slowly than wages if the ratio of non-participants to participants in the labour force exceeds 82.6 per cent.
[b] In New Zealand the net rate for a married couple is set to move in a band between 65 and 72.5 per cent of net average (male and female) earnings. While it remains in this band it rises with prices; if this leads to it falling outside an adjustment is made.

the financing of the pension system. A simplified summary of the various indexation procedures in our countries, plus Japan, is contained in Table 1.3.

On the whole in recent years changes to indexation procedures have tended to reduce generosity. An interesting development has been to link indexation explicitly to some notion of sustainability revolving round the growth of GDP per head. Both Germany and Japan now index their earnings-related pension to a measure of after-tax earnings growth rather than to gross wages. The thinking behind this is that as the population ages, taxes on the working population will have to rise. Then net wages will rise more slowly than gross wages, otherwise a pension system indexed to the growth in pre-tax wages would continually increase the pension burden. Indeed in Italy (the Dini reform) and Sweden indexation and revaluation of pension benefits are now linked explicitly to measures of the long-run growth potential of GDP (Disney, 1999). Similar 'feedback mechanisms' occur in the Netherlands and New Zealand. In the former case there is wage indexation unless the labour force participation rate falls below a certain level; in the latter country price indexation is constrained so that the main benefit rate cannot fall below 65 per cent of average earnings.

1.2.4   Pension Ages and Retirement Behaviour

Table 1.4 summarises both the normal pension age built into the public pension system in each country and the proportions of men in the 55–59 age-group and in the 60–64 age-group who are in work. In all these countries (bar Japan) there has been a dramatic fall in the proportion of older men who are working, irrespective of whether or not the official pension age has been rising or falling. We return to the evidence on impacts of changing pension ages shortly, but in the interim note that falling participation can have dramatic implications for the sustainability of the pension system.

These averages do however conceal other country-specific factors. For example in Italy a public pension could be obtained at a much earlier age through an additional 'years of service' criterion, which was especially generous to public sector workers. In the Netherlands, and to a lesser extent in the UK and the US, provision of disability benefits has served as an early route into retirement. There is also direct evidence that changes in official pension ages affect retirement behaviour. In Germany legislation introduced in the early 1970s, which permitted individuals with a long service history to retire early and which also introduced early retirement for reasons of unemployment or disability, was followed by a decade in which the average age of retirement dropped by five years. In the converse direction, raising the official pension age from 60 to 62 between 1991 and 1996 in New Zealand

Table 1.4   Normal Pension Ages and Male Employment Rates

	Normal pension age (years)[a]		Male employment rates (%)	
	Men	Women	Ages 55–59	Ages 60–64
Australia	65	61[b]	73	47
Canada	65	65	70	43
France	60	60	69	17
Germany	65 (60/63)	60[c]	81	35
Italy[d]	60	55	65	30
Japan	65 (60)	65 (60)	94	76
Netherlands	65	65	57	19
New Zealand[e]	63	63	80	50
UK	65	60[f]	73	50
US[g]	65 (62)	65 (62)	77	53

Notes:
[a]Figures in parentheses show 'early retirement' ages.
[b]To rise to 65 by 2013.
[c]To rise to 65 by 2004.
[d]These figures for Italy refer to 1992. The normal pension age has since risen to 65 for men and 60 for women in 2000. Also note that in Italy pensions can be taken much earlier than shown, especially in the public sector, subject to a (low) minimum number of years of contributions.
[e]Pension age in New Zealand is currently in the process of being raised from 60 to 65.
[f]To rise to 65 by 2020.
[g]Pension age in the US is rising from 65 to 67 by 2027.

was associated with increases in male employment of 18.6 per cent for those aged 60, 20.3 per cent for those aged 61 and 14.8 per cent for 62-year-olds, and even small increases for 63- and 64-year-olds (see Chapter 8). These issues are discussed in greater detail in the specific country chapters and also, for a slightly different sample of countries, in the comprehensive study edited by Gruber and Wise (1999).

1.3   SUSTAINABILITY AND REFORM

There are two quite separate issues involved with the sustainability of pension systems. One is to do with the ageing of the population. The simplest and most widely available measure of this is the dependency ratio, here measured as the number of people aged 65+ divided by the number aged 15–64. Elderly dependency ratios in 1960, 1990 and then in 10-year intervals to 2030 are shown in Table 1.5.

The table clearly shows that our countries have already experienced significant ageing since 1960 and will experience very substantial ageing until at least 2030. In relation to end-point the worst affected will be Germany and Italy – this compounds their existing problem of overly generous pension systems. However as far as *changes* between 1990 and 2030 are concerned it is Japan that faces the worst situation. Its elderly dependency ratio, which started off by far the lowest in 1960 (and was second lowest in the whole OECD after Turkey in that year), is set to rise by more than two-and-a-half times between 1990 and 2030. By that date Australia and New Zealand will have the youngest populations but will still have experienced substantial ageing. A mitigating factor for Japan, as shown in Table 1.4, is that the activity rate of older men has held up much better there than in other countries.

Table 1.5   Elderly Dependency Ratios (population aged 65+ as a % of working-age population)

	1960	1990	2000	2010	2020	2030
Australia	13.9	16.0	16.7	18.6	25.1	33.0
Canada	13.0	16.7	18.2	20.4	28.4	39.1
France	18.8	20.8	23.6	24.6	32.3	39.1
Germany	16.0	21.7	23.8	30.3	35.4	49.2
Italy	13.3	21.6	26.5	31.2	37.5	48.3
Japan	9.5	17.1	24.3	33.0	43.0	44.5
Netherlands	14.7	19.1	20.8	24.2	33.9	45.1
New Zealand	n.a.	16.7	17.1	18.9	24.6	30.5
UK	17.9	24.0	24.4	25.8	31.2	38.7
US	15.4	19.1	19.0	20.4	27.6	36.8
OECD	14.9	19.3	20.9	23.5	29.8	37.7

Source: OECD, 1996.

It is a point worth mentioning that these sorts of projections into the future are notoriously unreliable. The errors seem to have consistently been in one direction – under-prediction of the number of elderly as a result of a failure to predict, or at least to incorporate in projections, improvements in longevity (see Lee and Skinner (1999) and Disney (2000a) for illustrations).

These dependency ratios are however the background to the pertinent issue here, which is the sustainability, from a financial point of view, of pension systems. Pension spending projections, again here drawn from an OECD publication rather than the individual country studies so as to utilise consistent assumptions, are presented in Table 1.6. As with current spending, the countries essentially divide into two groups. France, Germany, Italy and

Japan are heading towards public pensions taking up between 14 and 20 per cent of GDP by 2040. When one considers that *total* public spending in the US for example is currently only just over 30 per cent of GDP and even the European average is between 40 and 50 per cent of GDP, one gets an impression of the potential size of this pension burden. It is probably not sustainable and indeed serious reform efforts are afoot in these countries.

Table 1.6   Projected Pension Spending (% of GDP)

	1995	2000	2010	2020	2030	2040	2050
Australia	2.6	2.3	2.3	2.9	3.8	4.3	4.5
Canada	5.2	5.0	5.3	6.9	9.0	9.1	8.7
France	10.6	9.8	9.7	11.6	13.5	14.3	14.4
Germany	11.1	11.5	11.8	12.3	16.5	18.4	17.5
Italy	13.3	12.6	13.2	15.3	20.3	21.4	20.3
Japan	6.6	7.5	9.6	12.4	13.4	14.9	16.5
Netherlands	6.0	5.7	6.1	8.4	11.2	12.1	11.4
New Zealand	5.9	4.8	5.2	6.7	8.3	9.4	9.8
UK	4.5	4.5	5.2	5.1	5.5	5.0	4.1
US	4.1	4.2	4.5	5.2	6.6	7.1	7.0

Source: OECD, 1996, Table 3.

A second group of countries do not see their future pension burdens exceeding 10 per cent of GDP. In Australia pension spending is not even predicted to move above 5 per cent of GDP, and in the UK it is expected to peak at just 5.5 per cent of GDP. In the US, New Zealand and Canada the peak is expected to be somewhere between 7 and 10 per cent of GDP.

Demographic ageing is not however the only cause of pension systems running into the problem of unsustainability. Combine generous earnings-related unfunded pension schemes with rapidly ageing populations and one is heading for trouble. Low levels of price-indexed benefits, on the other hand, are readily affordable even in the context of a worsening dependency ratio, as has been illustrated in the UK since 1981. So differences in future costs and sustainability have less to do with the relatively modest differences in ageing across countries than with the rather large differences in the structure and generosity of pension systems.

The process of retrenchment and reform in many countries is described in the following chapters. Some major changes are summarised in Table 1.7. Some idea of the general types of reform that have occurred is illustrated in the table, which shows changes in pension ages, in indexation procedures and in pension calculations that have been introduced in recent years. The range

Table 1.7 Major Recent Changes to Public Pension Benefits

	Changes to pension age	Changes to indexation	Changes to benefit calculation
Australia	Phased rise in pension age for women from 60 to 65 by 2013.	Indexation to wages formalised in 1998–99.	Ongoing tinkering with details of the means test.
Canada	None planned.	Already price-indexed.	Introduction of a clawback on basic pension; series of minor changes to financing and benefits of second tier.
France*	Minimum contribution duration rising from 37½ to 40 years, reducing chance of retiring at 60.	Price indexation since 1987.	Wage base for pension calculation rising from best 10 years to best 25 years. Change to way lifetime earnings revalued in pension calculation.
Germany	Women's pension age rising from 60 to 65 by 2004. Actuarial reductions being introduced for retirement before 65.	Indexation to net wages rather than gross wages from 1992.	1999 changes to rules governing service life will cut men's replacement rate by 10%, women's by 15%.
Italy	Complex reforms raising pension ages and minimum number of years of contributions (see Chapter 6).	Move from wage to price indexation after 1992.	Move from traditional defined benefit public scheme to 'virtual' defined contribution, effectively based on each year's salary.

Table 1.7 continued

Japan	Age for first receipt of basic pension rising from 60 to 65 between 2001 and 2013.	Move from gross wage to net wage indexation.	1985 Act put a ceiling on pensions of 68% of average lifetime earnings.
Netherlands	None planned.	Failure to index consistently in the 1980s. Since 1992 benefits can rise more slowly than wages if triggered by low labour force participation.	No major changes to flat pension.
New Zealand	In process of rising from 60 to 65, to reach 65 in 2001.	Indexation to prices but not to fall below 65% of average earnings for a couple – in place since 1993.	Surcharge introduced but now being withdrawn.
UK	Women's pension age to rise from 60 to 65 between 2010 and 2020.	Basic pension only indexed to prices since 1981, greater of prices and earnings before that.	SERPS based on average earnings not best 20 years, to replace 20% of earnings not 25%. Generosity to widows cut.
US	Rising from 65 to 66 in 2009 and to 67 by 2027.	Price indexation.	—

Note: *General scheme.

of similarities is remarkable. In eight of the 10 countries there is some planned increase in pension age or in the minimum number of years of contributions required to earn a full pension, at least for women. By the end of the 1990s only the Australian pension will be indexed to gross wages although at least seven of the remaining nine countries had employed gross wage indexation in the previous two decades. In all those countries running an earnings-related scheme, adjustments have been made that will have the effect of reducing the eventual replacement rate, with popular changes including widening of the earnings base on which the eventual pension is calculated.

1.3.1   Japan: Tentative Reform with Rapid Ageing

Although we leave details on other countries to the other chapters, we supplement these findings with a brief description of the Japanese experience. As Table 1.5 suggested, ageing is more rapid in Japan than in virtually any other country, following a decrease in fertility rates from more than four births per family in 1949 to 2.1 in 1957 and just 1.5 in 1994. As a result the size of the population as a whole is expected to start decreasing from about 2010, and the age dependency ratio is increasing rapidly. There has been a growing realisation that this population ageing alongside a relatively generous pension system makes for unsound finances.

A relatively modest set of reforms was announced in 1994, though even these modest reforms had to wait, as in Italy, for the collapse of the long-term political dominance of one group and a coalition of new parties in power. The reforms involved gradually raising the effective pension age for the first-tier pension from 60 to 65, replacing indexation to gross wages with indexation to net wages and promoting later retirement by effectively subsidising workers to stay on in jobs until age 65.[6]

These reforms are by no means enough to stave off big rises in contribution rates. The payroll pension tax was 16.5 per cent in 1995 and 19.5 per cent in 2000. It is set to rise by jumps of 2.5 percentage points every five years until it reaches a rate of 29.5 per cent in 2020. Note that in part this rate is so high because pension contributions are not levied on the bonuses that nearly all employees receive twice a year and which make up a substantial part of their total remuneration. This is clearly a problem for the financial integrity of the system.

The reforms so far announced have been modest relative to the future financing costs of the system, particularly given the rapid ageing that Japan faces. Current reform options being considered, at least outside of government, include further reductions in pension levels, perhaps further increases in normal pension ages and encouragement for later retirement.[7] As in other countries, possibly the most effective reform would be to go one step further in reducing the generosity of benefit indexation by moving from net wages to prices as the basis for pension increases. But no such change is immediately on the cards.

1.3.2 Intergenerational Redistribution

Pay-as-you-go (PAYG, or unfunded) state pension schemes have evolved in such a way that earlier generations have done much better from such schemes than have later generations, far better even than would have been predicted by a mechanical application of the famous 'Aaron–Samuelson condition' to such programmes.[8] For example, as later chapters show, the process of reform in Italy has quite explicitly protected current generations at the expense of future generations, while in the UK those retiring in the late 1990s are receiving SERPS at its full generosity and a basic pension of 15 per cent of male average earnings whereas those retiring in 2030 will receive SERPS of less than half that value and a basic pension of nearer 7 per cent of average earnings. In Japan, Germany and the US, reforms of public programmes will hit those retiring in future years. But in all these countries contribution rates will not be lower for these later generations. Indeed they will be higher since they have to pay the relatively generous pensions of previous generations of workers.

Figure 1.1 combines estimates for a number of countries of rates of return to successive generations on pension contributions (benefit–cost ratios for Japan). Since these schemes are unfunded, the technique involved in such calculations is to project, according to current contribution rates, the total amount of contributions paid on average by a member of a particular generation over his or her lifetime and then to utilise the pension benefit rules pertinent to each generation in order to estimate the stream of pension benefits to death. The 'rate of return' is then an internal rate of return (IRR) calculation, although present value and benefit–cost ratio calculations are other illustrations of the same method. A striking pattern emerges, of high returns initially (far exceeding the growth of productivity) followed by sharp declines.

Why have rates of return in pension systems evolved in this manner? In schemes of pure transfers across generations (i.e. not social-insurance-based) the first generation would always do well since they never paid contributions into the scheme. However, even in contribution-based social insurance programmes, earlier generations typically did not have to have a full contribution history in order to obtain pension benefits – early accruals were typically accelerated. This evidence is of course consistent with a pure

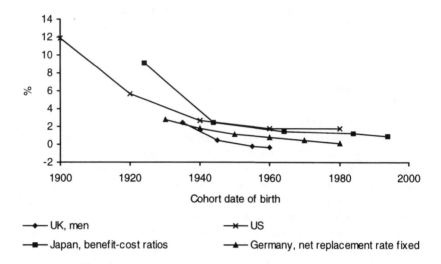

Sources: UK – Disney and Whitehouse, 1993. US – Leimer, 1994. Japan – Takayama, 1992.
Germany – see Chapter 5.

Figure 1.1   Rates of Return to Public Pension Schemes: Selected Countries

intergenerational redistribution motive – particularly as the generation that
typically benefited had lived through two major conflicts and the Great
Depression of the late 1920s and early 1930s. However subsequent
generations seem to have benefited as well, albeit with a steady attrition of
rates of return over time. This may be compatible with other models of
behaviour: for example a public choice model of bargaining between
generations (as sketched out in Disney (1996, Chapter 9)) or a model in which
generations are 'bribed' to retire on relatively attractive terms in order to
increase job opportunities for subsequent generations (Mulligan, 2000). Of
course demographic ageing reduces the scope for such intergenerational
games. Overall however the PAYG 'pension promise' of 'jam tomorrow' has
led to a major conflict between financial sustainability and political pre-
commitment – a conflict which underpins many of the reform strategies
discussed in subsequent chapters of this book.

1.4   THE PRIVATE SECTOR

Public pension provision is only a part of the pension story. In some countries
it is nearly the whole of it, in others less than half. In countries such as
Australia, Canada, the Netherlands, the UK and the US, where publicly

provided pensions have not been generous, the private sector has generally played an important role in pension provision. Conversely where the public sector has traditionally provided very generous pensions the private sector has had little part to play, as in France, Germany, Italy and Japan. Generous public provision seems to 'crowd out' private provision (Disney, 2000b).

New Zealand is however unusual in all this. Private provision has fallen in recent years following a series of reforms to the legislative and tax framework, described in Chapter 8. This contrasts with much of the rest of the world, where the importance of private pensions is growing, partly in response to worries over the long-term costs of unfunded public schemes, partly in the hope of achieving high rates of return on contributions and partly on the assumption that a large funded pension sector will be good for the economy.[9]

It is not our purpose here to discuss in detail the pros and cons of funded as opposed to PAYG financed provision as a whole. Rather we look at the systems of private provision in our countries. We begin by considering employer-provided provision – typically defined benefit plans – known in UK parlance as occupational pensions. These remain the most important form of private provision in most countries. We then look at individual retirement accounts – typically defined contribution plans – which are known as personal pensions in the UK and are increasingly important in a number of countries.

1.4.1 Occupational Pensions

Coverage
Table 1.8 describes some key features of the occupational pension regimes in each of our countries plus Japan. Column 1 shows the size of pension funds, expressed as a percentage of GDP, in the mid-1990s and in an earlier decade, using comparable data collected by the OECD. Columns 2 and 3 show respectively the percentage of pensioners in receipt of private pension income and the percentage of active workers covered by an occupational pension scheme, in the mid-1990s.

The table shows clearly the demarcation between countries with little or no private sector and those with substantial private sector assets. In countries with substantial private pension assets – notably the Anglo-Saxon countries other than New Zealand, plus the Netherlands – pension assets as a share of GDP grew rapidly over the decade to the mid- to late-1990s, as a result of the boom in world equity markets and the maturation of such schemes (increases in contribution inflows). Germany is one exception, in that although there is relatively high coverage by occupational pension schemes, most of the schemes are based on a 'book reserve' system, which means that liabilities just appear as a commitment on the balance sheet of firms. The separate trust fund status of pension assets common in the Anglo-Saxon countries is not reflected in German practice. The other divergent country is New Zealand, which has seen a decline in the value of pension fund assets, largely as a result of radical changes in tax treatment of private pensions in the last decade.

Table 1.8 also provides some summary measures of benefit coverage and scheme membership, largely taken from the country studies represented here. In some countries – notably Australia, Japan and the Netherlands – private coverage is near universal among workers, but this high coverage is not reflected in pensioner incomes in two of these countries – Australia and Japan

Table 1.8   Occupational Pension Coverage, Selected Statistics

	(1) Pension funds (% of GDP)		(2) % of pensioners receiving private benefits	(3) % of working population covered
	1988	1996		
Australia	21	32	c. 20% men, 7% women[a]	87%
Canada	26	43	54% men, 31% women	47% men, 42% women
France	<3	6	Negligible	Negligible
Germany[b]	3	6	21% men, 9% women	42%[c]
Italy	<1	3	Negligible	Negligible
Japan	38	42	10%[a,c]	c. 90%[d]
Netherlands	46	87	76% men, 23% women	c. 90%
New Zealand[e]	(c.25)	(14)	21% men, 10% women	17%
UK	62	75	66% men, 32% women	48%
US	36	58	48% men, 26% women	44%

Notes:
[a]In Australia (and to a lesser extent Japan) pension plans provide largely lump-sum benefits.
[b]See text for discussion of 'book reserves'.
[c]Source: Davis, 1995.
[d]Source: Takayama (1992) for 1991.
[e]Data derived from text.

Sources: Column 1 – OECD (1998) except for New Zealand (see Chapter 8). Columns 2 and 3 – country chapters unless otherwise stated.

– since pension benefits can be taken in lump sums. In Australia there are tax treatment reasons for this pattern; in Japan historically payments to retirees took the form of a severance lump sum rather than an annuity. Canada, the UK and the US, where private plan coverage is by no means universal, are all countries where a substantial fraction of retirees obtain at least some income from private pension sources.

In general a lower proportion of pensioners receive an occupational pension than the proportion of workers who are members. Not all pensioners are ex-workers but, equally important, in some countries occupational pension schemes are not mature – more members of later generations are scheme members. In Australia the vast difference arises partly because of the relatively recent introduction of compulsory membership and partly because accrued pension rights may be taken as a lump sum rather than as a pension, so people are not recorded as receiving any pension from their scheme. The same is true in Japan, where a large proportion of schemes still provide significant lump-sum benefits.

Elsewhere pension benefits in these countries tend be taken as pensions – flows of income in retirement. Defined benefit arrangements, usually based on a measure of final salary and number of years worked, are commonest. In Canada, the UK and the Netherlands 90 per cent or more of scheme members belong to defined benefit schemes. The figure is rather less in New Zealand and the US. Indeed in the US there has been a substantial shift towards defined contribution schemes in the past 20 years, a shift that is now beginning in the UK.

Benefit incidence
To a large extent the characteristics of occupational pension schemes reflect the history and development of private pensions, which tended to grow up first in the public sector, especially among civil servants and the armed forces, and then be negotiated between unions and larger companies, often taking the civil service scheme as a bench-mark.

Table 1.9 uses country-specific data to compare the probability of private pension receipt among the recently retired according to gender and marital status. In all cases married women are much less likely than any other group to be in receipt but, interestingly, single but never married women are more likely to receive a pension than are single but never married men. Married men have the highest likelihood of receipt in most countries. The commonality of these patterns is striking and is of course a reflection of the work-related basis for receipt and lower levels of labour market attachment among women. On the other hand it is among women that coverage is still growing as work patterns change.

Table 1.9   Occupational Pension Receipt: Percentages Receiving Pension, by Gender and Marital Status (%)

	Male	Female	Total
Canada			
Single (never married)	34.2	48.9	42.1
Single (other)	54.1	34.8	38.1
Married or cohabiting	56.3	25.3	42.1
All	54.1	30.8	40.8
Netherlands			
Single (never married)	61.7	67.7	63.6
Single (other)	83.8	60.6	66.8
Married or cohabiting	75.5	12.6	46.7
All	76.4	23.0	50.2
UK			
Single (never married)	54.6	56.2	55.2
Single (other)	56.4	44.8	49.1
Married or cohabiting	69.5	25.8	48.0
All	66.3	32.0	48.7
US			
Single (never married)	33.5	39.7	36.9
Single (other)	41.9	31.0	34.0
Married or cohabiting	49.5	20.4	36.2
All	47.5	25.5	35.5

Table 1.9 tells us how common pension receipt is among the retired in these countries but not how generous it is. Assessing its generosity in the same way as for public systems, by reference to what some illustrative people would receive, is of little or no use because the occupational systems are diverse and the effects of slightly differing work histories on pension entitlement can be dramatic. Instead Table 1.10 presents figures, again calculated from the national micro-data sources, that show what proportion of pensioners' incomes derives from private pensions for four countries.[10]

It is striking that in none of these countries do occupational pensions provide half of total income for pensioners. Indeed only in the Netherlands does the share reach a third. Again there is a common pattern, with couples getting the largest share and single (including divorced, widowed and never married) women the smallest. As demonstrated in several chapters, receipt of private pensions is more important for younger pensioners than for older ones, suggesting that these proportions will change over time.

Table 1.10   Share of Occupational Pensions in Total Family Incomes (%)

	Couples	Single men	Single women
Canada*	26.9	23.7	20.4
Netherlands	37.3	35.7	22.9
UK	26.5	20.1	14.1
US	21.4	21.9	16.7

Note: *Includes income from individual accounts (RRSPs).

Developments in occupational pensions

Many occupational pension schemes were originally set up to recruit higher-quality workers and to encourage the best workers to stay in the same company for many years. Provision of a pension scheme has often been associated with the 'back-loading' of pay, so that salary rises in real terms over the lifetime through regular pay increments and promotions. In a final-salary-based pension scheme therefore there is every encouragement for workers to stay in the same job until retirement. Typically in all the countries here with significant private pension provision, until the 1970s there was no indexation of benefits between leaving a job and retirement, so that the eventual real value of benefits earned in a job that a worker might have left in middle age could be very low indeed, especially in times of high inflation.[11] Indeed most countries did not even require automatic post-retirement indexation of private pension benefits to inflation. Finally it should be noted that many schemes have operated some form of vesting rule, by which workers can only accrue pension rights after a certain number of years' minimum service. Indeed, until they were outlawed as discriminatory, pension schemes in the UK and other European countries could operate both differential vesting rules and limited scheme membership rights (for example debarring part-time workers) as an explicit means of focusing their scheme benefits on long-serving 'core' members of the organisation.

As the labour market has changed since the 1970s, with a greater emphasis on a 'flexible' work-force and with less emphasis on 'lifetime' full-time jobs, so the 'indenture' model (Ippolito, 1997) of pay linked to long-term contracts may have less relevance to employees and employers alike. Traditional final salary occupational pension schemes lock workers into implicit contracts where remuneration is largely deferred until later in life. This is unsatisfactory to those who wish to undertake job or career changes, and particularly to younger workers who want current remuneration to reflect their current 'market worth' more fully. For employers, traditional pension schemes are associated with substantial severance costs for older workers whose relative productivity may be declining. Increasingly therefore labour market participants have wished to change to other remuneration 'packages' – in particular to pension schemes that permit greater flexibility in terms of level of contributions and in preserving pension rights in response to job mobility. It has been in those countries where practice and legislation have changed to offset some of these problems that final salary schemes have prospered. Where this has not happened coverage of such schemes has dropped. The UK and the Netherlands are good examples of the former process, New Zealand and the US of the latter.

In the Netherlands for example most occupational pension schemes are of the defined benefit form, with three-quarters of them defining benefits on the basis of final pay. Typically the object is to supplement the basic flat state pension to 70 per cent of final pay for those who have worked for 40 years. Although the Dutch have not introduced full legal protection against inflation pre- and post-retirement, most funds do index pension payments and deferred pensions at least in line with prices. There are no vesting rules so pensions start accumulating immediately, and recent legislation has ensured that job mobility, within the sector-based pension schemes at least, has less effect on future pension entitlements as new employers assume the pension liability of the previous employer's pension fund. This is a major improvement on past practice.

In the UK too the final salary scheme has proved relatively durable in the face of major labour market changes. Traditionally schemes offered pensions based on one-sixtieth or one-eightieth of final salary for each year of service. In the 1960s such schemes were largely the domain of full-time, unionised, male workers in large companies and in the public sector. However the work-force is now more female, part-time, non-unionised, in small companies and in the private sector. Yet the coverage of occupational pensions has not diminished a great deal, in spite of an important legislative change in 1988 that prevented companies from making membership of their scheme a condition of employment.

New legislation has required indexation of pensions in payment in line with price increases up to 5 per cent a year. In practice most schemes did index benefits in times of low inflation, though only about one in nine private sector schemes actually guaranteed it. Public sector schemes have traditionally offered full indexation, though generally with the initial pension being based on eightieths of final salary rather than the sixtieths common in the private sector. A series of legislative changes also now ensure indexation of preserved (deferred) pension rights of job-leavers up to a maximum of 5 per cent a year. So as long as inflation does not *average* more than 5 per cent a year between leaving a job and drawing the pension, its real value at least should be preserved.

A further reason for the survival of the defined benefit occupational pension scheme in the UK is its integration into the scheme of state pension provision through the mechanism of 'contracting out' of the state earnings-related pension system (SERPS). SERPS was not introduced until 1978, by which time occupational schemes were well developed. With its introduction there were fears that SERPS would spell the end of occupational pension provision, but instead it entrenched defined benefit private schemes by allowing such schemes to contract out of SERPS. This involved both employer and employee paying lower National Insurance contributions and the employee giving up future rights to SERPS. In return the occupational scheme had to promise to provide at least a guaranteed minimum pension (GMP).

Only in Japan is there a similar arrangement allowing people to contract out of the state pension system, though it occurs on a much smaller scale. There are three types of occupational pension plan in Japan. For some years there have been traditional unfunded retirement bonuses. There are also tax-qualified pension plans similar to occupational schemes, as in the UK and US. They cover 30 per cent of the private sector work-force and nearly always pay benefits as lump sums. These cannot contract out of the state scheme, but employees' pension funds (EPFs), introduced in 1966, do allow this. EPFs are on a smaller scale than in the UK, covering just over a quarter of the work-force. Even for EPFs, employers' social security contributions are not completely rebated, and contracting out has not provided the fillip to private pension provision in Japan that has been the case in the UK.

Moreover Japanese private pensions remain largely of the defined benefit (DB) type. In the UK it was the extension of the right to contract out to a wider range of pension schemes in 1988 that gave private pensions a new lease of life. While DB schemes remain much the most popular form of occupational provision in the UK, an increasing proportion of employers in the UK are turning to defined contribution (DC) schemes, which are now eligible for contracted-out status. These impose fewer uncertainties on employers in that the employees just take a share of the invested fund at retirement. There are no promises or guarantees over pension levels. On the other hand such schemes are potentially more attractive to employees who are mobile and who are not following 'traditional' career patterns. They have been especially popular in such areas as retailing and the media. Virtually all new pension schemes set up in the UK since the late 1980s have been of the DC variety, though it remains the case that only about a tenth of occupational pension scheme members are in DC plans (Disney, 1995). In part this is because any move towards group DC plans has been swamped by the popularity of personal pensions.

In contrast in the US, traditional final salary schemes have failed to adapt, or at least have not been forced to adapt. Neither deferred benefits nor pensions in payment are automatically indexed to inflation, and there are still significant vesting rules. The decline in DB plans in the US has been quite dramatic. Between 1980 and 1995 the proportion of full-time employees in medium and large private companies participating in a DB plan dropped from 84 per cent to 52 per cent. There has however been a switch to DC schemes. In particular the switch has been to schemes that are known, in deference to the section of the Internal Revenue code that allowed them similar tax treatment to DB schemes, as 401(k) plans. This section of the tax code was added in 1978, and by 1995 54 per cent of full-time workers in medium and large companies were in 401(k) plans, with the number of participants increasing fivefold between 1983 and 1993 alone. In effect, 401(k) plans are employer-sponsored DC plans with tax relief on contributions and investment growth and penalties on early withdrawal.

The most striking case has however been New Zealand. Private pensions are rather less prevalent in New Zealand than one might imagine, given the flat state pension in that country. Only around 11 per cent of people over the age of 65 receive any income from occupational schemes, and fewer are expected to have one in the future. Yet membership of occupational schemes has been declining, and within the occupational scheme sector there has been a shift towards defined contribution schemes. Between 1990 and 1997 membership of private sector employer schemes dropped from 21 per cent of all employees to 17 per cent (25 per cent to 19 per cent including members of the Government Superannuation Fund, which closed to new members in 1992) while pension fund assets actually dropped by 8 per cent in real terms. An important reason for this shift lies in changes to taxation rules which broadly switched pension tax treatment from an expenditure tax basis to an income tax basis. In addition however most schemes in New Zealand still have very long vesting periods. Even within DC schemes, in 1992 only half fully vested their members after 10 years of employment, though this had risen to 80 per cent by 1996. By 1996 only 30 per cent of DB scheme members would be fully vested after 10 years, and in 46 per cent of schemes it would take scheme members 20 years or longer to become fully vested.

This is an extreme example of the potential lack of relevance of occupational schemes for the actual pension needs of individuals, especially as labour markets become more fluid and mobile. In the US the main response to this has been a very swift growth in the numbers of DC schemes. In the Netherlands legislation ensured immediate vesting and full indexation, while in the UK there has been some move to DC schemes and a sustained legislative effort to protect early leavers. In New Zealand no such efforts have been made. Instead legislation has militated against the growth of the private sector despite the lack of any public earnings-related scheme.

Private pensions and retirement behaviour
As with public disability benefits, occupational pensions have often been used as vehicles for early retirement. In the Netherlands for example schemes will often pay for early retirement, guaranteeing employees a benefit of 70–80 per cent of previous earnings up to age 65. In the past the costs of early retirement were often financed on a PAYG rather than on a funded basis, and pension providers are now having to face the extra costs thereby imposed by reducing benefit levels or by increasing minimum eligibility ages. In particular public sector workers in a variety of countries have often benefited from special provisions permitting retirement after a limited number of years of service (as in Italy) or at a lower minimum retirement age than the general population (as in the UK). Pension schemes for public sector workers are rarely fully funded in practice, in any event.

Where occupational pension schemes *are* fully funded, the concept of 'early retirement' seems problematic; people can choose when to retire on the basis of the annuity pay-out that can be provided given the fund that they have accumulated. But, unlike in defined contribution plans, in defined benefit pension plans the concept of 'early' retirement has some meaning because benefit entitlements need not be tightly linked to contributions; there can be redistribution both across generations of retirees and within generations. For example early retirees are often given disproportionately attractive terms, implicitly at the expense of continued contributors, and disproportionately adverse terms are given to early leavers where deferred benefits are not fully protected against inflation. In addition the structure of schemes can certainly lead companies to be less willing than otherwise to take on older workers, and some have even argued that it encourages the sacking of incumbents. On the other hand the fact that such schemes can effectively be used to ease the pain of redundancies indicates that they may perform an additional role in the welfare state other than simply the provision of retirement pensions.

The impact of occupational pensions on early retirement in the UK is illustrated in Figure 1.2. It shows employment survival curves for men with and without an occupational pension. Those without occupational pensions, who tend to be lower paid and lower skilled, leave the labour force more rapidly in their 40s and early 50s. But after around age 55, the exit rate for those in occupational pension schemes accelerates. More detailed analysis of the effects on retirement behaviour of incentives built into private defined benefit pension schemes has been carried out in the US in several studies by Lumsdaine, Stock and Wise (1990 for example) and by Stock and Wise (1990). They make use of the fact that many pension plans in the US have offered specific incentives to encourage workers to retire at particular ages, and they have found substantial effects on retirement arising from these incentives. The structure of private pension plans and the use to which they are put by companies clearly can have a very great effect on retirement behaviour. Just as people make use of generous government-sponsored early retirement programmes, so they react to the design of private systems.

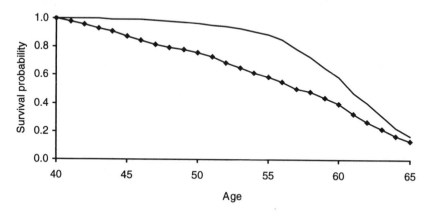

Source: Blundell and Johnson, 1998.

Figure 1.2   Survival Functions for Men (probability of remaining in employment) in the UK, 1994

1.4.2   Individual (Personal) Pensions

Thus far we have concentrated on occupational pension provision. Historically it has been much the most important form of private pension provision in countries across the world, outside perhaps Latin America. However in those countries that have traditionally relied on a strong occupational sector and where membership is not universal, personal or individual pensions are becoming increasingly important. This is certainly the case in the UK, the US and Canada. Except in Canada, they are relatively recent innovations and so have relatively little impact on the incomes of current retired people. The exception has been arrangements for the self-employed, but they are not considered in great detail here. To this list also should be added the centralised superannuation arrangements that were introduced in Australia and extended in 1992, which were basically a form of nationally negotiated deferred pay award. These are described in greater detail in Chapter 2.

Registered Retirement Savings Plans

Registered Retirement Savings Plans (RRSPs) have been available in Canada since 1957 and were specifically introduced to ensure that everyone, including those whose employer did not run an occupational scheme, could benefit from the tax-favoured treatment that they attracted. As with occupational schemes in Canada (RPPs), contributions are tax-exempt, investment income is not taxed but withdrawals are subject to tax. An annuity has to be taken by age 71. The maximum tax-exempt contribution limit has been periodically increased and in 1999 stood at 18 per cent of earnings to a maximum of Can$13 500. Total assets are somewhat more than a third of all the assets held in occupational pensions (RPPs and RRSPs).

It is quite possible to be a member of both an RPP and an RRSP subject to a limit on total contributions, and indeed many are members of both. So the numbers of contributors to RRSPs are large and are not confined just to those without occupational provision. Indeed among those with above-average earnings, over 90 per cent made some contribution over the three-year period 1991–93. On the other hand contribution rates among the low-paid are much lower: only 20 per cent of those with incomes below Can$10 000 (about a quarter of average earnings) contributed over that same three-year period. Given their lower resources this is no surprise, but it is also worth mentioning that the extensive means-tested element of the Canadian state system is likely to reduce substantially the incentive to make contributions.

Individual Retirement Accounts

Tax-favoured Individual Retirement Accounts (IRAs) were introduced in the US in 1974 by the Employee Retirement Income Security Act (ERISA), again with the specific intention of providing workers who did not have employer-sponsored pensions with access to tax-deferred retirement savings. Contributions are tax-deductible up to an annual limit, accrual of interest is tax-free and there are penalties for early withdrawal.

The annual limit on contributions is a rather meagre US$2 000 per person, though as with RRSPs IRAs are available to those who also have an occupational pension. In any year about three-quarters of contributors make the maximum contribution, though Gale and Scholz (1994) showed that only 30 per cent of IRA contributors contribute at the limit for each of three consecutive years. Since 1986 among those with a company pension only lower-income individuals have been able to claim tax relief on contributions into IRAs. Withdrawals have to be made from age 70½ at the latest, either through the purchase of an annuity or in the form of simple cash withdrawals. Withdrawals before age 59½ are discouraged with a 10 per cent penalty. But the fine dividing line between pension provision and other forms of saving has been well exemplified in 1998 by the fact that penalty-free withdrawals are now permitted for first-time home purchases as well as for some higher education expenses. What effect this has on the use of IRAs and the level of contributions to them it will be interesting to see.

Approved personal pensions

Approved personal pensions (APPs) were introduced in the UK in 1988 as a result of 1985 legislation, giving individuals the option of contracting out of the State Earnings-Related Pension Scheme, not just into a standard defined benefit occupational pension scheme but alternatively into an individual retirement saving account. Instead of actually paying lower National Insurance (payroll tax) contributions, as happens with a member of a contracted-out DB scheme, an APP scheme member pays the full rate of contributions but then a proportion of them are redirected to the pension scheme by the government as a contribution 'rebate'. Compulsory occupational pension scheme membership was also abolished, so individuals could choose not to join (or even to leave) their scheme and purchase an APP.

One of the great differences between IRAs in the US and APPs in the UK is the age distribution of contributors. On the whole contributors in the US have been in their 50s and early 60s. In the UK APPs attract contributions largely from those in their 20s and 30s. This very much reflects the different histories of the two systems, and in particular the way in which APPs in the UK can be used to contract out of SERPS. In the absence of these factors the American experience is very much what one might have expected – all the evidence suggests that it is when people reach middle age that they begin to start substantial voluntary saving for retirement.

However in the UK, since the same level of rebate was initially offered for everyone – 5.8 per cent of salary plus, initially, a 2 per cent incentive bonus – the straightforward effect of compound interest meant that the rebate was effectively worth much more to younger people. In addition the fact that reforms to SERPS were simultaneously being phased in meant that the value of SERPS to younger people was much less than its value to older people. This rebate, especially when combined with the additional 2 per cent incentive payment, provided an enormous incentive for people in their 20s and at least up to their mid-30s to contract out. This they did in their millions, costing the government substantial sums in lost revenue that it would never recoup in lower pension payments from SERPS.[12] Since 1995 however these APP rebates are age-related, with younger workers receiving a lower rebate.

A number of other policy issues have been thrown up by the experience of APP provision. Not least among them is the question of how private provision should be regulated. The crux of the issue was the selling of APPs to people who were already in occupational pension schemes. This generally meant the loss of the employer contribution as well as the usual costs of leaving a final salary scheme early. Several hundreds of thousands of APPs were sold to this group who, in terms of prospective benefits, would probably have been better off remaining in their occupational pension scheme. The industry, at the insistence of the government, is now going through a long and expensive review of mis-selling cases, and compensation is slowly being made available to those who were mis-sold the products. A second issue is administrative costs and, in particular, front-loaded charges in APPs. In 1999 new proposals for a 'stakeholder pension' were canvassed, designed to deal with the problem of perceived high charges for APPs. Whether a further contracting-out 'route' reduces the scope for mis-selling is however more doubtful; the issue is discussed at greater length in Chapter 9.

1.5   PENSIONERS' INCOMES

The final judgement on the efficacy of a specific pension system requires concrete knowledge about the level and distribution of incomes that it implies for pensioners. To form definitive conclusions is difficult because it requires household micro-data in each country in order to construct an equivalent measure of income in each case and to derive comparable summary statistics. The problems encountered in such an exercise include different definitions of what constitutes a pensioner, alternative definitions of income, trouble assigning incomes to people within households (does the income belong to the pensioner or the adult child living with him or her?), differences in whether incomes are recorded net or gross of tax, differences in the sampling strategy for the data, and a whole host of other practices unique to one country or another.

In addition it is necessary to decide on the unit of analysis – the individual, the nuclear family or the household – as well as on how to compare the incomes of families or households of different sizes and on whether to measure income gross or net of tax. What should one do about issues such as the value of goods and services in kind that are provided by the state and about housing costs, in particular the differences between those still renting and those who live in a property that they own outright?

Finally there are problems of presentation and comparison. How do we compare a pensioner in the US with US$20 000 and one in France with FF100 000?[13]

There is no single correct way to approach these questions. But a few basics are clearly necessary: first, access to comparable household datasets in each country; second, experts in using and understanding the data for each country; and third, a common framework applied consistently across countries. A key object of this book was for the experts from each country to use their own micro-data to answer these questions on a comparable and consistent basis. In these three things this book is probably unique. Only for Japan were we unable to provide a comprehensive description of pensioner incomes at this micro-level.

The key results in the successive chapters are based on the following definitions and criteria:

- The unit of analysis is the 'family' – that is an individual, any spouse and any dependent children. So where a pensioner for example lives in a household with another person who is not his or her spouse or dependent child then we only take account of the pensioner's income and not that of others in the household. We show the number of pensioners living in multi-unit households in each country for which data are available and some results on a household income basis to show the effects of this, but since the main aim is to show the effects of pension systems on incomes it seems right to concentrate just on the incomes of pensioners themselves.
- A pensioner is anyone aged 60–64 who is retired and anyone at all aged 65+. That means including, in some countries, some older people still in work, but it is not obvious that a better definition is available. In the case of couples the definition as a pensioner couple depends on the status of the man.
- Income is total cash income (earnings plus pensions plus social security incomes plus income from investment) net of direct taxes. No account is taken of housing costs or of 'imputed income' from owner-occupation. We illustrate the potential importance of this by comparing homeownership rates. Also no account is taken of the value of free services such as healthcare or cheap transport.
- Finally we do not compare cash amounts across countries. It would not be especially interesting to know that American pensioners are richer than British pensioners. Given that GDP per capita in the US is greatly in excess of that in the UK, it would be astonishing if anything else were the case. What is interesting to know is how well off pensioners are in each country relative to the population as a whole, and how their incomes are composed.

1.5.1 The Household versus the Family

Table 1.11 provides evidence on the proportions of pensioners living in households with other people. For each country it shows the proportions of couples, single men and single women in two groups – all pensioners and those over 75.

The reasons for the variability across countries are of course complex, but the relative lack of generosity of the Australian benefit system is likely to play a role there, while the housing market in Italy encourages young adults to stay in the family home for a longer period. It is also noticeable that home sharing

Table 1.11   Percentage of Pensioners Living in Households with People Other than Their Spouse (%)

	Couples		Single men		Single women	
	All	75+	All	75+	All	75+
Australia	18	9	34	37	26	24
Canada	16	9	13	14	16	11
Germany	18	7	13	17	13	17
Italy	33	17	27	25	24	18
Netherlands	14	6	18	16	14	13
UK	12	6	17	15	19	18
US	10	7	24	22	27	23

Table 1.12   Living Arrangements of the Elderly in Japan and the US (%)

	Age 65+		Age 75+	
	Japan	US	Japan	US
Men				
With spouse	37	75	32	67
Alone	5	16	6	22
With relatives	57	7	62	9
Women				
With spouse	18	40	8	24
Alone	15	41	15	51
With relatives	67	17	77	22

Source: Yashiro, 1997.

tends to be less common among older pensioners, presumably because young adults have left the family home. A striking additional comparison can be seen in Table 1.12, which compares household formation in Japan and the US: 77 per cent of older female pensioners in Japan live with people other than their spouse compared with just 22 per cent in the US; half of elderly women in the US live alone compared with fewer than one in six in Japan.

These differences have to be kept in mind when comparing the own incomes of pensioners across countries, especially where comparisons are made on a household basis as well as on the standard income unit basis.

1.5.2   Incomes of Pensioners relative to Non-pensioners

Table 1.13 pulls together data from the individual country studies and shows the average incomes of pensioners relative to the rest of the population. It divides the pensioner population by gender, marital status and age-group and comprises all sorts of income – not simply public (state) provision. The figures show the average income of each group as a proportion of the average income of the whole non-pensioner population. To compare the living standards of family units of different sizes, we work with equivalised (or equivalent) incomes, a standard procedure in work on income distributions. The main set of figures use an equivalence scale that assumes that a couple requires 1.7 times the income of a single person and that any child requires half the income of an adult. This is one standard scale used by the OECD.

The choice of scale is clearly important in making comparisons, so we have also included figures based on alternative assumptions in which a couple requires 1.5 times the income of a single person and any child requires 30 per cent of the income of an adult. The figures in parentheses in Table 1.13 use this alternative scale. The main effect is that, because this scale assumes that less money is required for extra adults and for children, the relative incomes of *single* pensioners appear significantly lower. The effect on the relative incomes of couples varies by country.[14]

Two things are immediately striking. First, on average pensioners are not much worse off than non-pensioners. Second, there is a remarkable degree of similarity among all the countries, irrespective of the structure of the public pension system, the degree of private provision and so on. For pensioner couples incomes range from 80 to 103 per cent of those of non-pensioners, other than in Australia, which appears as something of an outlier. The result serves to illustrate the lack of information content in comparisons that are based entirely on the main state pension scheme and ignore additional means-tested benefits on the one hand and receipt of private pensions on the other.

Table 1.13   Incomes of Pensioners as a Percentage of the Incomes of All Non-pensioners (%)

	Age-group				
	60–64	65–69	70–74	75+	All 60+
Australia					
Couples	62 (64)	68 (69)	71 (73)	68 (69)	68 (69)
Single men	54 (49)	70 (63)	73 (66)	67 (61)	67 (60)
Single women	65 (59)	65 (59)	65 (59)	60 (54)	63 (56)
Canada					
Couples	74 (85)	86 (99)	89 (103)	85 (97)	85 (97)
Single men	79 (69)	110 (96)	102 (89)	98 (86)	99 (86)
Single women	69 (60)	93 (81)	85 (74)	81 (71)	83 (72)
France					
Couples	107 (105)	106 (103)	104 (102)	97 (95)	103 (100)
Single men	101 (87)	108 (93)	115 (99)	111 (95)	106 (91)
Single women	109 (94)	95 (82)	93 (80)	86 (74)	92 (80)
Germany					
Couples	90 (74)	98 (80)	89 (73)	88 (72)	92 (75)
Single men	85 (69)	108 (88)	108 (88)	99 (81)	102 (83)
Single women	81 (67)	84 (69)	84 (69)	74 (60)	80 (66)
Italy					
Couples	95	91	97	78	89
Single men	132	126	102	96	111
Single women	96	92	86	84	89
Netherlands					
Couples	86 (83)	88 (84)	83 (80)	79 (76)	84 (81)
Single men	106 (90)	115 (98)	108 (92)	100 (85)	106 (90)
Single women	90 (77)	91 (78)	89 (76)	85 (73)	88 (75)
UK					
Couples	80 (79)	89 (88)	77 (76)	72 (71)	80 (78)
Single men	74 (65)	89 (78)	78 (68)	76 (66)	79 (69)
Single women	83 (72)	75 (65)	68 (59)	65 (57)	69 (60)
US					
Couples	81 (83)	95 (97)	86 (87)	75 (76)	85 (86)
Single men	68 (61)	92 (82)	88 (79)	78 (70)	82 (74)
Single women	49 (44)	67 (60)	61 (55)	56 (50)	58 (53)

Note: Here and elsewhere figures for France, Germany and the Netherlands are for pensioners in households where there are no non-pensioners. In these countries it is not possible to assign incomes to particular people in multi-unit households. In other countries figures are for all pensioners. Pensioners are, as defined in the text, all aged 65+ and all retired aged 60–64. Main figures use an equivalence scale of (1, 0.7, 0.5) for single people, additional adults and additional children respectively; figures in parentheses use (1, 0.5, 0.3).

There is more variation in the (relative equivalent) incomes of single pensioners. The generally favourable position of single men even relative to couples is surprising, especially given that single (never married) men tend to be poorer than married men and less likely to have private pension provision. Part of the answer to this lies in the employment-related nature of many pension systems. In countries such as France and Italy there is virtually no additional payment of state pension to a married man than to a single one so, other things being equal, a single man would expect a higher equivalent income than a married one whose wife had not accumulated any pension rights of her own. In France, Germany and the Netherlands this result may, to some extent, be an artefact of the data, which do not allow the inclusion of (generally poorer single) pensioners who live in households with others. Certainly the very low incomes of single women recorded in the US reflect the opposite. There appear to be substantial numbers of single female pensioners in the US who live in households with others and who have little or no income of their own, which may reflect the fact that those not entitled to the main contributory state pension (OASDI) face a *household* means test. So the numbers for the US will substantially underestimate the incomes actually available to poorer single pensioners.

By age it is no surprise to see younger pensioners being better off than their older counterparts. This is largely a cohort effect – younger generations are richer than their predecessors. It is noticeably less marked in Australia, where reliance on means-tested benefits is high at all ages, and in countries such as Canada and France that have relatively mature pension systems, whether state or private. Looking at couples, the effect is more pronounced in the UK than anywhere else. This reflects the continued maturation of both SERPS and occupational schemes, which results in substantially higher payments to the most recently retired. The long-term indexation of all elements of income to prices at best also plays a part here.

On the whole incomes vary by age more for single women than for the other groups. In large part this reflects the changing composition of single women at different ages. At younger ages a large proportion of them are single but never married. As we saw in Section 1.4.1 on occupational pension receipt, these women have patterns of pension receipt very similar to those of men. At older ages widows predominate among single women.

1.5.3   The Distribution of Pensioner Income

Table 1.14 illustrates the distribution of incomes among pensioners in the various countries. It compares the incomes of pensioners at the 90th percentile

Table 1.14 Inequality among Pensioners: Ratios of the 90th to the 10th Percentiles of Pensioner Incomes

	Age-group				
	60–64	65–69	70–74	75+	All 60+
Australia					
Couples	2.5 (3.7)	2.8 (3.7)	2.2 (3.1)	2.5 (2.9)	2.5 (3.4)
Single men	1.8 (2.5)	2.6 (2.9)	1.8 (3.6)	2.9 (2.7)	2.4 (2.9)
Single women	2.6 (4.4)	2.0 (3.4)	2.0 (3.1)	1.7 (2.3)	1.9 (3.1)
Canada					
Couples	4.9 (4.2)	2.8 (2.8)	2.8 (2.9)	2.6 (2.6)	2.8 (2.9)
Single men	4.7 (4.7)	3.2 (3.0)	2.8 (2.7)	2.5 (2.7)	3.0 (3.0)
Single women	3.9 (3.8)	2.7 (2.7)	2.3 (2.6)	2.1 (2.4)	2.4 (2.6)
France					
Couples	3.3	3.6	3.7	3.5	3.5
Single men	2.9	4.1	3.8	4.2	4.0
Single women	4.3	3.6	3.2	3.1	3.4
Germany					
Couples	3.0	3.5	3.3	3.5	3.3
Single men	3.6	3.4	3.4	4.6	4.0
Single women	3.2	2.9	3.0	2.7	2.9
Italy					
Couples	4.1 (4.6)	3.6 (4.5)	3.2 (3.9)	2.5 (3.2)	3.6 (4.3)
Single men	4.6 (6.8)	3.9 (5.1)	4.0 (5.4)	3.7 (5.7)	4.1 (5.6)
Single women	4.0 (5.9)	3.4 (4.9)	3.1 (4.1)	3.0 (4.2)	3.4 (5.1)
Netherlands					
Couples	2.7	2.9	2.6	2.6	2.7
Single men	3.0	2.8	2.9	2.7	2.9
Single women	2.3	2.4	2.2	2.2	2.2
UK					
Couples	3.6 (3.6)	3.6 (3.6)	3.0 (2.9)	3.0 (3.1)	3.3 (3.3)
Single men	3.5 (3.5)	3.5 (3.4)	2.7 (2.7)	2.9 (3.0)	3.1 (3.0)
Single women	3.2 (2.9)	2.9 (3.0)	2.7 (2.7)	2.8 (2.8)	2.8 (2.8)
US					
Couples	7.1 (5.9)	5.3 (4.9)	4.6 (4.3)	5.7 (4.3)	5.1 (4.8)
Single men	9.4 (7.4)	6.5 (5.9)	5.0 (4.6)	4.9 (4.7)	5.5 (5.2)
Single women	>100 (8.5)	5.7 (5.0)	4.5 (4.4)	4.5 (4.4)	5.0 (4.8)

Note: Household relativities are given in parentheses.

(nine-tenths of the way up the distribution) with those of pensioners at the 10th percentile (just one-tenth of the way up). This is of course just one of very many ways of looking at inequality, but it is simply understood and readily calculated. In interpreting the figures in the table remember that the differences are large in this context. For the 90/10 ratio to rise from two to three in any country would require for example the incomes of richer pensioners to rise by 50 per cent with no rise at all in the incomes of poorer pensioners.

What explains this international pattern of inequality? The figures for the US show dramatically high levels of inequality. In part this just mirrors the greater income inequality in the US more generally. The poorest 10 per cent of the youngest women pensioners in the US have virtually no income of their own – hence the figure of >100 in the bottom left-hand corner of the table. The figures in parentheses, which show the 90/10 ratio of household incomes, are much more within the normal range.

Conversely the reasons for equality in Australia are clear enough. With a very high proportion of the population receiving means-tested benefits and relatively low levels of receipt of private pension income there is little scope for a great deal of income inequality. That is *not* to say that there is little inequality in wealth or in living standards, given the use of pension lump sums and the distribution of property ownership.

Perhaps surprising at first sight is the rather high level of inequality encountered within the pensioner populations in Italy and France – countries with very extensive systems of state pension provision and with relatively equal wage and earnings distributions, at least by comparison with those in the UK and the US.[15] But of course equality is neither the intention nor the outcome of the earnings-related social insurance systems in place in these countries. They are not intended to be redistributive and, by and large, they are not. All those who were previously high earners end up with high pensions; all low earners end up with low pensions. The social safety nets in such countries tend to be relatively undeveloped and not terribly generous.

So, oddly in some eyes, countries such as the UK and the Netherlands that rely to a much greater extent on private provision actually end up with a more equal distribution of pensioner incomes than do Italy and France. This is all the more remarkable in the case of the UK, which has a very unequal income distribution across the population as a whole. It results directly from the existence of a flat-rate state pension and, in the UK, an extensive set of social assistance benefits. Inequality is substantially lower in the Netherlands than in the UK, largely as a result of the greater generosity of its flat-rate pension. The rather low inequality in Canada can also be put down largely to the effectively flat-rate and relatively generous nature of its social security system.

The patterns of inequality by age are also rather instructive. Different degrees of inequality at different ages can indicate one or more of a number of things. If the older groups are more unequal than the younger ones it could indicate that they were more unequal when they reached retirement; or it could mean that they have become more unequal as they have aged – for example because those with higher incomes to start with enjoyed better indexation than those who started with lower incomes.[16] Many of the ensuing country studies draw out the relative importance of these reasons, and in particular consider the somewhat specific factors lying behind the income inequality of 60- to 64-year-olds.

1.5.4 Income Composition

The individual country studies give a good deal of information on the sources of income – in particular the share that comes from private as opposed to public sources – for each of the countries under review. The pattern in the bottom quintile is the same everywhere: nearly all the income comes from the state. That is as true in countries such as the UK and the Netherlands as it is in Germany and France. Nowhere does the private sector provide a substantial part of the incomes of poor pensioners.

By the time we get to the middle quintile two groups of countries are beginning to emerge. In Australia, Germany, France and Italy the state remains the only important source of income. In Canada especially, but also in the US, the UK and the Netherlands, private pensions are beginning to be important. Even so it is only in Canada that the combined income from private pensions and investments even comes close to that from the state.

It is only in the top quintile that private incomes really come into their own. Interestingly, given the way we have defined pensioners, earnings form an important part of the incomes of the richest groups, especially in the US. This comes in part from younger wives earning and in part from continued participation in employment past 65. The high proportions derived from earnings can also be misleading since they can be increased substantially by a few very high earners. Even so the state still provides a majority of income, even to this rather rich group, in France, Germany and Italy and appears relatively unimportant only in Australia and Canada.

Since there is no chapter on Japan, Table 1.15, drawn from Yashiro (1997), shows the major income sources of the elderly in Japan, the US and the UK.[17] It suggests a considerable dependence on earned income among the older population in Japan, but also a rapidly changing situation, with the income source defined as 'support from children' declining in importance between 1981 and 1990 and the importance of earned income also having fallen over

Table 1.15   Sources of Income of the Elderly in Japan, the US and the UK (%)

	Japan		US	UK
	1981	1990	1990	1990
Earned income	31	24	11	6
Public pension	35	54	55	69
Private pension	4	2	14	18
Investment income	7	6	13	3
Support from children	16	6	1	–
Other	7	8	7	5

Note: Numbers here are *not* comparable with numbers in other tables.

Source: Yashiro, 1997.

that period. This implies that the income sources, and probably income levels, of Japanese pensioners are changing rather rapidly, possibly converging on a more western pattern than hitherto. The tiny share of income attributed to private pensions results from the fact that most private pension arrangements in Japan make lump-sum payments.

1.5.5   Pensioner Income Distributions relative to Average Earnings

Our final income comparison, in Table 1.16, provides for some of the countries an indication of the incomes of pensioners at various points of the pensioner income distribution, relative to a measure of average earnings. For consistency an earnings measure taken directly from the micro-datasets is used as the point of comparison – namely net male median earnings. The figures in the table show the decile points, for couples and single people separately, as a proportion of this measure of average earnings. So for example 10 per cent of couple pensioners in the UK have an income of 49 per cent or less of net male median earnings and 60 per cent of single pensioners in the UK have an income of less than 51 per cent of net male median earnings.

In all the countries shown the richest couples have incomes well above average earnings; in Germany and Italy the richest 10 per cent of pensioner couples have incomes of about twice average earnings or more. But in the Netherlands and the UK even the richest 10 per cent of single pensioners do not have incomes that reach median male earnings.

Table 1.16   Pensioner Incomes at Percentile Points as a Percentage of Net Male Median Earnings: Couples and Single People Separately (%)

%	Australia		Canada*		Germany		Italy		Netherlands		UK	
point	C	S	C	S	C	S	C	S	C	S	C	S
10			49	30	68	40	51	31	63	37	49	29
20	61	36	70	40	80	47	62	35	71	42	57	33
30			78	43	90	53	70	41	76	45	64	38
40	64	38	84	46	99	58	79	47	82	48	71	42
50			94	50	108	64	89	54	88	52	78	46
60	73	43	106	53	121	71	100	61	96	57	86	51
70			120	58	138	81	115	71	109	64	99	58
80	93	54	137	68	166	98	136	85	131	77	118	70
90			167	84	219	129	181	108	165	97	152	89
			252	139								

Notes:
C = couples; S = single people.
*Figures for Canada are decile means rather than decile points. Hence the extra figures.

There appear to be more similarities at the bottom of the distributions than at the top. In the UK, Italy, Canada and Australia the poorest couple pensioners have incomes somewhere around half net male median earnings, with single pensioners at about 30 per cent of this bench-mark.

1.6   CONCLUSIONS

The differences and similarities across the different pension systems considered here are striking. The greatest differences arise from the structures of pension systems themselves. There is little common ground between the German and Australian pension systems for instance, and the German system is but one example among the many fully fledged social insurance pension schemes common in continental Europe. The Australian system in contrast is an extreme example of the 'state provides the basic minimum, private sector does the rest' school of pensions practised in one form or another in the Netherlands and New Zealand, with the UK, the US, Canada and Japan at various points between the two models.

Given this diversity of starting-points the similarity in the reforms that have been, or are being, enacted is all the more remarkable. Raising pension ages, lowering the generosity of indexation procedures and where relevant reducing the generosity of earnings-related systems have been implemented by most countries. Despite the commonality of an ageing population and consequent increased spending, the differences in urgency are as important as the commonality of experience. Those countries with generous earnings-related schemes face much greater difficulties than the others and they face these difficulties not because their populations are ageing faster but rather because the scale of the pension promises they have made is more than can be redeemed.

In the private sector there are also common trends. With the exception of New Zealand private coverage is rising in all those countries where it is not crowded out by state provision. In the Netherlands and Australia this increased coverage has involved virtually 100 per cent coverage of workers by occupational schemes. In both countries the collective bargaining system played an important role. The Australian experience has involved widespread movement to a defined contribution set-up – a trend seen on a smaller scale in the US and the UK. In these two countries and Canada wider levels of private coverage have also been achieved through the introduction of tax-favoured individual pension arrangements. None of these countries though has achieved the levels of coverage seen in Australia and the Netherlands.

The impact of these various types of system on pensioner incomes and their distribution was the final subject of this introduction. A surprising finding is that the average levels of pensioner income were not greatly divergent among the countries. The main exception – Australia – is not surprising given that it has a system of means-tested benefits and lump-sum pay-outs from pension funds. Conversely there are significant differences in the distribution of income among pensioners and the composition of that income. Perhaps surprisingly those countries with extensive social insurance systems – France, Germany and Italy – have relatively high levels of pensioner inequality. This is because the social security system is so closely tied to wages. High earners all end up with high benefits and low earners with low benefits. In addition the systems of means-tested minimum benefits in these countries are perhaps less well developed than those in countries such as the UK where they have long played an integral role in the benefit system. As a result pensioners in continental European countries are spread right throughout the overall income distribution, while elsewhere they cluster in the middle to lower reaches, though not generally right at the bottom. Again Australia is unusual in the very high proportion of its pensioners who are in the lower half of the overall income distribution.

So what are the key messages of all this? The first seems to be that a good average standard of living among pensioners can be achieved by pension systems that do not rely on huge state expenditures. The private sector can play an important role. On the other hand systems that rely on a more minimal state system and a private sector, which even in the Netherlands gives far from complete coverage of the pensioner population, tend to end up with fewer pensioners with incomes at or above average earnings levels.

Second, future problems over spending levels are more a function of the design of pension systems than they are of population ageing *per se* (Disney, 1996). In many cases reforms were left until very late because the political will needed for change was simply lacking. Even where reform has been legislated it is often *future* generations of pensioners who will bear the brunt of the changes, exacerbating the tendency of social insurance systems to reward earlier generations at the expense of later ones.

Third, the private sector needs a conducive legislative framework in which to survive. Tax legislation in New Zealand has had severe consequences for private pensions, while the structure of private provision in the US has shifted dramatically away from defined benefit schemes because of their failure to adapt to changing market circumstances. The development of comprehensive coverage in Australia and the Netherlands suggests that strong and centralised wage-bargaining systems facilitate employment-based private pension provision. In contrast the UK experience with personal pensions emphasises the importance of getting incentives and regulatory frameworks right, and that overgenerous incentives can induce massive 'opting out' of state provision but with very little budgetary 'reward' for the government.

Fourth, and very importantly, one should be clear and explicit about the purpose of a country's pension system. Is it to provide a minimum living standard for pensioners or is it to ensure that all pensioners get good levels of earnings replacement in retirement?

Finally, nevertheless there are lessons to be learnt from the country-specific studies, which bear on future issues of reform and system design:

- The New Zealand (and to a lesser extent the UK) experience of constant reforms and counter-reforms serves to emphasise the importance of stability and political consensus. For example in New Zealand the reaction to the proposal to means-test the pension for current pensioners emphasises the importance of protecting legitimate expectations among those who have no opportunity to alter their circumstances.
- In many countries the failure to plan for the long run has been a striking feature of pension policy-making. This is not just true of France, Germany and Italy. SERPS was introduced in the UK as recently as 1978 with no long-term expenditure estimates, and Japan also embarked on an enormous extension of the generosity of its state scheme in the 1970s.
- The payment of private 'pensions' as lump sums in both Japan and Australia makes policy-making extremely difficult, especially in the context of the Australian means-tested system. Again one needs to think

about the purposes of pension provision and of state support through taxation or compulsion. The provision of a decent *income* in retirement and removing the weight of provision from the government are two aims not served by lump-sum provision in the private sector. The same issue applies to a lesser extent in the UK's favourable tax treatment of the occupational pension lump sum.

- The promotion of early retirement, often as a means of 'freeing up jobs' for younger people, as was practised explicitly in France and implicitly in many other countries including the Netherlands and the UK, can be a very costly business which can itself undermine the integrity of the pension system.

- On a positive note however pension systems throughout the OECD have in their different ways brought greatly improved incomes and security to the growing numbers of pensioners. In nearly all countries the debate about pensions is now central to government thinking and the issues are better understood than ever before. With sensible reforms sooner rather than later, viable pension systems that provide effective support for the elderly can be maintained.

NOTES

1. Although there is no country chapter for Japan, we have obtained some comparative data for that country which are utilised in this overview.

2. Throughout the introduction, and most chapters, the term 'pension' is utilised to comprise both public (state) and private provision. In US parlance, provision of pensions by the state is termed 'social security', although in other countries, such as the UK, 'social security' is often used to refer to the whole gamut of state income transfer programmes, including unemployment and sickness insurance.

3. For comparable studies of pensioner income distributions, see Atkinson, Rainwater and Smeeding (1995), Antolin, Dang and Oxley (1999), Burniaux et al. (1998), Disney, Mira d'Ercole and Scherer (1998), Hauser (1998) and Whitehouse (2000). For studies of future sustainability see Roseveare et al. (1996), Chand and Jaeger (1996) and Hviding and Mérette (1998) amongst others.

4. As with other comparative tables the figures shown should be taken as illustrative. While all efforts have been made to ensure that the figures have been calculated on a similar basis there are inevitably differences resulting especially from data limitations.

5. This revaluation procedure is not always adopted in private 'defined benefit' pension schemes. Note also that where accrued pension rights are revalued in line with economy-wide average earnings growth, this growth rate will not in general be the same as the individual's own lifetime earnings profile. Moreover there may be ceilings and floors to eligible earnings which are indexed in a quite different manner – for example to price inflation; see Disney and Whitehouse (1991) for an illustration from the UK.

6. Japan is unusual in that most firms have a mandatory retirement age of 60. However many workers stay on in a job with a much reduced wage after 60. Potential benefit receipt was often more than could be earned in this situation so there was a big disincentive to staying on. The new system actually pays a subsidy to people to work at low wages after age 60 so as to avoid having to pay them full benefit levels.

7. See Takayama (1996).

8. The seminal papers of Aaron (1966) and Samuelson (1958) argued that PAYG schemes could provide a rate of return equal to the growth of the real wage bill (approximately the growth of the size of the labour force plus productivity growth per head). With a 'baby boom' in many developed countries after 1945, followed by a decline in fertility, one might expect a slow secular decline in rate of return on these grounds alone.

9. High-profile support for these arguments was provided by the World Bank (1994), which provides a well-articulated case for greater private provision and better-targeted public provision. Perhaps it comes as no surprise to observers of that organisation that it also sponsored one of the most combative critiques of that very position (Orszag and Stiglitz, 1999).

10. Again we include only Canada, the Netherlands, the UK and the US. The predominance of lump sums in Australia and Japan makes figures on the receipt of incomes from occupational pensions almost meaningless. France, Germany and Italy are excluded as being uninteresting from the point of view of private provision, and data sources in New Zealand are inadequate to provide similar information. More details concerning income shares are given in later chapters.

11. For illustrations for the UK see Disney and Whitehouse (1996) and for the US see Bodie, Marcus and Merton (1988).

12. See Disney and Whitehouse (1992a and 1992b) for a detailed documentation and explanation of this phenomenon.

13. Four chapters give conversion factors – Canada, France, Germany and Italy. For the remaining countries, £1 was worth Aus$2.70 (Australia), Dfl. 3.69 (the Netherlands), NZ$3.52 (New Zealand) and US$1.41 (the US) in November 2000. Note however that the US dollar has appreciated relative to the pound since 1997–98 whereas the European currencies have depreciated.

14. Most country-specific chapters have used (1, 0.7, 0.5) as the main equivalence scale and (1, 0.5, 0.3) as an alternative, as in Table 1.13. In the chapters on Australia and Italy only (1, 0.7, 0.5) has been used, and Chapter 8 on New Zealand has used weights of 1 for the first adult, 0.65 for additional adults and factors for children.

15. See for example Atkinson (1996), Atkinson, Rainwater and Smeeding (1995) and Giles et al. (1998).

16. Johnson, Stears and Webb (1998) observe this happening among occupational pensioners in the UK.

17. Note that these figures are not comparable with others quoted here. They just give some idea of how the composition of income in Japan compares with those in the US and the UK.

REFERENCES

Aaron, H. (1966), 'The social insurance paradox', *Canadian Journal of Economics*, **32** (August), 371–4.

Antolin, P., T.-T. Dang and H. Oxley (1999), 'Poverty dynamics in four OECD countries', Organisation for Economic Co-operation and Development, Economics Department, Working Paper no. 212.

Atkinson, A.B. (1996), 'Income distribution in Europe and the United States', *Oxford Review of Economic Policy*, **12** (1), 15–28.

Atkinson, A.B., L. Rainwater and T.M. Smeeding (1995), *Income Distribution in OECD Countries*, Social Policy Studies no. 18, Paris: Organisation for Economic Co-operation and Development.

Blundell, R. and P. Johnson (1998), 'Pensions and labor market participation in the United Kingdom', *American Economic Review, Papers and Proceedings*, **88** (May), 168–72.

Bodie, Z., A.J. Marcus and R.C. Merton (1988), 'Defined benefit versus defined contribution plans: what are the real trade-offs', in Z. Bodie (ed.), *Pensions in the US Economy*, Chicago: University of Chicago Press for National Bureau of Economic Research.

Burniaux, J.-M., T.-T. Dang, D. Fore, M. Förster, M. Mira d'Ercole and H. Oxley (1998), 'Income distribution and poverty in selected countries', Organisation for Economic Co-operation and Development, Economics Department, Working Paper no. 189.

Chand, S. and A. Jaeger (1996), *Aging Populations and Public Pension Schemes*, Occasional Paper no. 147, Washington DC: Fiscal Affairs Department, International Monetary Fund.

Davis, E.P. (1995), *Pension Funds: Retirement Income Security and Capital Markets*, Oxford: Clarendon Press.

Disney, R. (1995), 'Occupational pension schemes: prospects and reforms in the UK', *Fiscal Studies*, **16** (3), 19–39.

Disney, R. (1996), *Can We Afford to Grow Older?*, Cambridge, Mass.: MIT Press.

Disney, R. (1999), 'Notional accounts as a pension reform strategy: an evaluation', World Bank, Social Protection, Human Development Network, Discussion Paper no. 9928.

Disney, R. (2000a), 'Crises in public pension programmes in OECD: what are the reform alternatives?', *Economic Journal, Features*, **110** (February), F1–F23.

Disney, R. (2000b), 'Declining public pensions in an era of demographic ageing: will private provision fill the gap?', *European Economic Review*, **44** (May), 957–73.

Disney, R. and E. Whitehouse (1991), 'How should pensions in the UK be indexed?', *Fiscal Studies*, **12** (3), 47–61.

Disney, R. and E. Whitehouse (1992a), *The Personal Pensions Stampede*, London: Institute for Fiscal Studies.

Disney, R. and E. Whitehouse (1992b), 'Personal pensions and the review of the contracting-out terms', *Fiscal Studies*, **13** (1), 38–53.

Disney, R. and E. Whitehouse (1993), 'Will younger cohorts obtain a worse deal from the UK state pension scheme?', in M. Casson and J. Creedy (eds), *Industrial Concentration and Economic Inequality*, Aldershot, UK and Brookfield, US: Edward Elgar.

Disney, R. and E. Whitehouse (1996), 'What are occupational pension plan entitlements worth in Britain?', *Economica*, **63** (May), 213–38.

Disney, R., M. Mira d'Ercole and P. Scherer (1998), 'Resources during retirement', Organisation for Economic Co-operation and Development, Ageing Working Paper no. 4.3.

Gale, W. and J.K. Scholz (1994), 'IRAs and household saving', *American Economic Review*, **84** (December), 1233–60.

Giles, C., A. Gosling, F. Laisney and T. Geib (1998), *The Distribution of Income and Wages in the UK and West Germany, 1984–1992*, London: Institute for Fiscal Studies.

Gruber, J. and D. Wise (eds) (1999), *Social Security and Retirement around the World*, Chicago: Chicago University Press for National Bureau of Economic Research.

Hauser, R. (1998), 'Adequacy and poverty among the retired', Organisation for Economic Co-operation and Development, Ageing Working Paper no. 3.2.

Hviding, K. and M. Mérette (1998), 'Macroeconomic effects of pension reforms in the context of ageing populations', Organisation for Economic Co-operation and Development, Economics Department, Working Paper no. 201.

Ippolito, R. (1997), *Pension Plans and Employee Performance*, Chicago: Chicago University Press.

Johnson, P., G. Stears and S. Webb (1998), 'The dynamics of incomes and occupational pensions after retirement', *Fiscal Studies*, **19** (2), 197–215.

Lee, R. and J. Skinner (1999), 'Will aging baby boomers bust the federal budget?', *Journal of Economic Perspectives*, **13** (Winter), 117–40.

Leimer, D.R. (1994), 'Cohort-specific measures of lifetime net social security transfers', Social Security Administration, Office of Research and Statistics, Working Paper no. 59.

Lumsdaine, R., J. Stock and D. Wise (1990), 'Efficient windows and labor force reduction', *Journal of Public Economics*, **43**, 131–59.

Mulligan, C. (2000), 'Induced retirement, social security and the pyramid mirage', National Bureau of Economic Research, Working Paper no. W7679.

OECD (1996), *Policy Implications of Ageing: A Critical Policy Challenge*, Social Policy Studies no. 20, Paris: Organisation for Economic Co-operation and Development.

OECD (1998), *Maintaining Prosperity in an Ageing Society*, Paris: Organisation for Economic Co-operation and Development.

Orszag, P. and J. Stiglitz (1999), 'Rethinking pension reform: ten myths about social security systems', presented at conference 'New Ideas about Old Age Security', World Bank, Washington, September.

Roseveare, D., W. Leibfritz, D. Fore and E. Wurzel (1996), 'Ageing populations, pension systems and government budgets: simulations for 20 OECD countries', Organisation for Economic Co-operation and Development, Economics Department, Working Paper no. 168.

Samuelson, P. (1958), 'An exact consumption-loan model of interest, with or without the social contrivance of money', *Journal of Political Economy*, **66** (December), 467–82.

Stock, J. and D. Wise (1990), 'Pensions, the option value of work and retirement', *Econometrica*, **58** (5), 1151–80.

Takayama, N. (1992), *The Greying of Japan: An Economic Perspective on Public Pensions*, Tokyo: Kinpkuniya and Oxford University Press.

Takayama, N. (1996), *Possible Effects of Ageing on the Equilibrium of the Public Pension System in Japan*, Reprint Series no. 170, Institute of Economic Research, Hitotsubashi University.

Whitehouse, E. (2000), *Cross-country Comparisons of Pensioner Incomes*, London: Axia Economics.

World Bank (1994), *Averting the Old Age Crisis*, Oxford: Oxford University Press for World Bank.

Yashiro, N. (1997), 'The economic position of the elderly in Japan', in M. Hurd and N. Yashiro (eds), *The Economic Effects of Aging in the United States and Japan*, Chicago: University of Chicago Press.

2. Pension Provision in Australia

Anthony King, Hans Bækgaard and Ann Harding*

2.1 INTRODUCTION

The Australian retirement income system, with its particular combination of a flat-rate means-tested age pension and occupational superannuation, is unique among the systems of OECD countries. It thus provides an interesting and useful example for any international comparative study of pension systems, and such a study provided the motivation for this work.

This chapter provides a comprehensive picture of the Australian retirement income system and of the incomes of the aged. After a brief overview of the Australian retirement income system (Section 2.2), it provides an account of the role of government cash benefits – principally the age pension – and includes a description of policy developments, entitlements and coverage (Section 2.3). A similar account of privately provided retirement incomes is then given, with a focus on the important recent developments in superannuation policy (Section 2.4). Aspects of the sustainability of the Australian system (Section 2.5) and of labour force patterns (Section 2.6) are presented before an examination of the income distribution of the aged population (Section 2.7).[1]

*The authors gratefully acknowledge the support for the research and useful comments and suggestions from Paul Johnson and others at the Institute for Fiscal Studies, the funders of the project (mainly the Institute of Chartered Accountants in Australia) and participants at the March 1998 International Pensions Conference at the Institute for Fiscal Studies.

2.2 AN OVERVIEW OF THE AUSTRALIAN RETIREMENT INCOME SYSTEM

The Australian retirement income system has two main components – a flat-rate means-tested age pension funded from general revenue, and private occupational superannuation. The age pension has been in place since 1909, has been a relatively constant element of Australia's social security system and is received by over 80 per cent of the population above the qualifying age (including equivalent veterans' pensions), with about two-thirds receiving the maximum rate. Government pensions, and principally the age pension, are the main source of income for the vast majority of those over the qualifying age. Expenditure on the age pension in 1996–97 amounted to \$13.2 billion[2] (Department of Social Security, 1997), or 2.6 per cent of GDP. Including other payments to the aged, the figure is a little over 3 per cent of GDP.

The age pension is a typical element of the Australian social security system, which follows the social assistance model. It comprises a range of flat-rate means-tested payments funded from general revenue, with no major payments of the social insurance type. The role of social assistance payments in Australia is quite different from the role they play in a number of other OECD countries; they are the mainstream form of government income support rather than a residual complement to a social insurance system (Jackson and Bozic, 1997). The maximum rate of age pension for a single person is set at 25 per cent of male gross average weekly earnings.

The introduction of the age pension in 1909 followed consideration of other options, including a social insurance model with compulsory contributions which was rejected because of concerns about administrative costs and the plight of those with no history of contributions (Unikowski, 1989). Social insurance schemes were subsequently included in the National Insurance Bill (1928) and the National Pension and Health Insurance Bill (1938), and recommended in the 1976 'Hancock Report' (National Superannuation Committee of Inquiry, 1976) in response to the falling living standards of the aged, increasing numbers of older people and the level of pension outlays (Foster, 1988, p. 6). However none of the proposals was implemented, although the 1938 proposal did get as far as the enacting of enabling legislation. There was opposition from vested interests in the life offices and concerns about the burdens on employers. The option of a social insurance scheme was most recently revisited in the mid-1980s by the Social Security Review, which concluded that the opportunity for introducing such a scheme in Australia had passed (Foster, 1988, p. 182). Instead the nature of retirement income policy was set out in the 1989 statement by the then Minister for Social Security entitled *Better Incomes: Retirement Income Policy into the Next Century*: '… a flexible and sustainable retirement income policy which delivers fair and adequate incomes needs to build on the twin pillars of the age pension system and private saving such as superannuation' (Howe, 1989, p. iv).

The superannuation pillar had been strengthened somewhat in 1986 with the introduction of Productivity Award Superannuation, whereby industrial awards required employers to pay an amount equal to 3 per cent of earnings into employees' superannuation. Until that time occupational superannuation, with its concessional tax treatment, had been the preserve of a minority of workers – predominantly full-time white-collar men and public sector employees. The new tier of superannuation greatly expanded coverage, though at low contribution rates. The real strengthening of the superannuation pillar occurred with the introduction of the Superannuation Guarantee in 1992.

The Superannuation Guarantee compels employers to make superannuation contributions into individual accounts for their employees. The initial contribution rate was 3 per cent of earnings; the rate was 6 per cent in 1997–98 and will rise to 9 per cent by 2002–03. The Superannuation Guarantee has been the major policy initiative in Australian retirement incomes since the introduction of the age pension. While its impact will obviously take some time to work through, it is projected to have a major impact on national savings, on future budget outlays and on retirement incomes (with an after-tax replacement rate of about 60 per cent). Importantly, while unfunded or only partly funded schemes make up a large proportion of Australian superannuation, retirement incomes stemming from Superannuation Guarantee contributions are fully funded, with clear benefits for the future sustainability of the system.

The two pillars of Australian retirement income policy are nowadays more commonly described as three. On the one side there is publicly provided income through the age pension. On the other side there is privately provided income through occupational superannuation, with two elements – voluntary superannuation and mandated superannuation under the Superannuation Guarantee. The voluntary superannuation covers a variety of arrangements, ranging from the purely voluntary so-called DIY ('do-it-yourself') schemes for the self-employed to the notionally voluntary schemes that provide part of the conditions of much employment. Both voluntary and mandated superannuation attracts substantial tax concessions, which amounted to an estimated $8.7 billion in 1996–97 (Department of the Treasury, 1997), or 1.7 per cent of GDP. This indicates the considerable budgetary support provided to the superannuation side of retirement incomes, in addition to the outlays on cash benefits. While retirement incomes are dominated by the age pension, superannuation is projected to progressively cut into this dominance. It is however a long-term policy and the major effects cannot be expected for 30 years or so.

While the accounts that follow focus on the age pension and superannuation, reference is also made to some other elements of retirement incomes and income support for the retired. These include other private savings, particularly in the forms of homeownership and own businesses, and the non-cash benefits available to the retired, particularly healthcare. With the concerns about future pension costs having been largely addressed by the Superannuation Guarantee, attention has shifted to the future budget demands from healthcare and aged care for an ageing population and there are now moves to increase private provision in these areas too.

The federal system of government in Australia warrants a final word in this brief overview. Income support is the responsibility of the Commonwealth government, which applies a uniform system of social security across Australian states and territories. Broad superannuation policy and regulation are also a responsibility of the Commonwealth government. The states and territories do however play major roles in providing health and other services.

2.3   PUBLIC PROVISION OF RETIREMENT INCOMES

The key social security payment for the retired and aged population is the age pension, which is available on a means-tested basis to men of at least 65 years of age and to women of at least 61 and is the principal source of income for most older retired people. The age of eligibility for the age pension has been explicitly blurred somewhat by the introduction in 1994 of the mature age allowance, which is a similar payment for those aged at least 60 but under pension age, who are deemed to be disadvantaged in the labour market. The disability support pension, which has the same entitlements as the age pension, also plays an important role for the retired population below pension age. A significant number of older people are also entitled to veterans' pensions in respect of their war service. These veterans' pensions are similar to the age pension, though the eligibility age is five years lower. The discussion that follows however is confined to a description of the age pension and associated supplementary payments.

2.3.1   A Brief History of the Age Pension

The Australian age pension was introduced in 1909 (as the old-age pension) in response to the destitution among the aged. It was a means-tested payment for people aged 65 or over, with the eligibility age for women reduced to 60 in 1910. An account of its place in the history of Australian social security policy can be found in Kewley (1980). Unikowski (1989) has drawn from the history to demonstrate how many of the issues in current debate about the age pension have been there from the outset – for example issues about the level of entitlement and about incentive effects.

As already noted the age pension has been repeatedly and intensively reviewed and compared with social insurance alternatives, though it has proved to be not only the oldest but also arguably the most constant element of the Australian social security system. Despite many changes the essentials of the age pension remain as they were when it was introduced over 90 years ago, the basic policy objective being to 'ensure that people who have reached retirement age, and their partners, have adequate levels of income' (Department of Social Security, 1997, p. 43).

2.3.2   Eligibility for the Age Pension

Eligibility for the age pension is governed by residency and age criteria. Except for refugees, eligibility depends on having been an Australian resident for a total of 10 years. The age criterion had stood at a threshold of 65 for men and 60 for women until July 1995. The threshold for women is however being increased to equalise the age thresholds for men and women. Equality will be attained in 2013, and by 1998 the eligibility age for women had risen to 61.

A further equality issue in the treatment of men and women concerns the situation of couples where only one member has reached the qualifying age for the age pension. In the case of a couple where only the male had reached the qualifying age for the age pension, until 1995 the female partner automatically qualified for a wife pension with identical provisions to the age pension. There was however no corresponding payment for the male partner of a female age pensioner. Since 1995 the wife pension has been in the process of being phased out and a partner needs to qualify for a payment in their own right on the basis of, for example, their limited recent work-force experience or their caring responsibilities for a disabled person.

Besides legislating for an increase in women's qualifying age for the age pension, a recent initiative has been to offer an incentive for people to defer taking up their eligibility for the age pension. The Deferred Pension Bonus Scheme was announced in the 1996–97 Budget and implemented in 1998–99; it provides an annual tax-free bonus entitlement of 9.4 per cent of the basic pension entitlement for each full year of employment (of at least 960 hours a year) beyond age pension qualifying age. The measure, designed to be revenue-neutral, was announced as a means of encouraging older people's continued productive participation in the paid work-force and of increasing their retirement savings (Costello and Newman, 1997).

2.3.3 Level of Payment and Indexation

The maximum rates of the age pension at the end of 1997 are shown in Table 2.1. These refer only to the basic pension and exclude the supplementary payments described in Section 2.3.5. Actual entitlements are subject to the means-testing arrangements set out in Section 2.3.4. The rates shown in Table 2.1 contain an implicit equivalence scale of 1.67 for a couple, when a single person is assigned a value of 1.0.

Table 2.1   Maximum Weekly Base Rates of the Age Pension, December 1997 ($ p.w.)

	Maximum base rate of age pension
Single person	173.90
Couple (combined)	290.10

Source: Department of Social Security.

Since 1975, legislation has seen the age pension automatically indexed to changes in the consumer price index (CPI), although a popular political target for the single rate of pension has been 25 per cent of male average weekly earnings. Up until 1998–99 this target was achieved by *ad hoc* pension increases to supplement the indexation increases. From 1998–99 the target has been formalised with legislation to maintain the single rate of pension at least at this level. The measure of average weekly earnings used is male total average weekly earnings – $693.80 in August 1997 (ABS, 1997a, Table 1), when the single rate of pension amounted to 25.1 per cent of this figure. This legislated link between average earnings and the age pension is a major departure from the general system of automatic indexation of pensions and benefits in line with changes in the CPI. The ramifications for both the level of the age pension and relativities within the social security system remain to be seen (though they will clearly depend on real changes in male total average weekly earnings).

Movements in the rate of the age pension over the period since 1970 can be compared with movements in the CPI and average weekly earnings in Figure 2.1. The divergence between the paths for the age pension and the CPI over the period reflects an increase in the real value of the pension of almost 70 per cent over the period. Much of this real increase occurred in the early part of the period and followed a number of studies that highlighted the preponderance of the aged among the poor (Henderson, Harcourt and Harper,

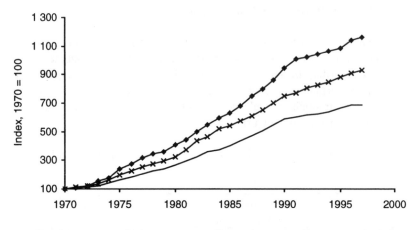

──◆── Pension rate ──✕── Male average w eekly earnings ─────── Consumer price index

Sources: Department of Social Security; Australian Bureau of Statistics, *Average Weekly Earnings: States and Australia*, Cat. no. 6302.0; Australian Bureau of Statistics, *Consumer Price Index*, Cat. no. 6401.0.

Figure 2.1   Indices of the Single Rate of the Age Pension, Consumer Prices and Male Average Weekly Earnings

1970; Commission of Inquiry into Poverty, 1975). Those pension increases raised the level to around 25 per cent of male average weekly earnings by 1975, where it has since hovered.

The 25 per cent relativity between the age pension and male average weekly earnings requires some qualification due to the different tax treatments of income from the pension and of earnings. The income tax system includes a pensioner rebate which, in combination with the general tax-free threshold, is designed to ensure that someone with no income other than the maximum rate of pension will pay no tax. The age pension is in effect tax-free, and in after-tax terms the single rate of pension was about 33 per cent of male disposable average weekly earnings under 1997–98 income tax provisions.

2.3.4   Means Testing

The age pension has always been means-tested, though the nature of the means testing has been subject to considerable variation. For the first 50 years of its life the age pension was subject to a separate income test and 'property limit', with the two then combined in 1960 in the 'merged means test'. There was considerable liberalisation of means testing in the 1970s, which saw means testing removed for people over 70 years old and abolition of the property limit, with asset income streams included instead in the income test. The liberalisation was however short-lived, in line with the greater emphasis on targeting in the Australian social security system from the early 1980s (Mitchell, Harding and Gruen, 1994). By 1983 means testing of people over 70 was being phased back in, and in 1985 an assets test was reintroduced.

Entitlement to the age pension is now governed by separate income and assets tests. The test that gives the lower pension level is the one that applies. In the case of couples the tests are applied to joint incomes and assets. The basic terms of the income test disregard income of $50 a week if single ($88 a week for a couple) and apply a 50 per cent taper rate for withdrawal of entitlement for income above these thresholds, which are indexed. (The figures used here are those that applied in August 1997 to allow comparison with average weekly earnings.) These provisions mean that a part-pension is payable up to quite a high level of other income, as shown in Table 2.2.

Table 2.2   Weekly Income Level at which the Base Age Pension Entitlement Cuts Out, August 1997

	Weekly income ($ p.w.)	Income as percentage of average weekly earnings* (%)
Single person	397.80	57
Couple (combined)	668.20	96

Note: *Male total average weekly earnings.

Sources: Department of Social Security; Australian Bureau of Statistics, *Average Weekly Earnings: States and Australia*, Cat. no. 6302.0.

The assets test operates in a corresponding manner, with thresholds and a taper, although in this case lower thresholds are specified for homeowners than for people who do not own their own homes, because owner-occupied housing is not included in the definition of assets under the test. The limits that applied in August 1997 are shown in Table 2.3. Assets over these amounts reduced entitlement by $1.50 a week for every $1 000 above the limit. The table also shows the asset levels at which the age pension entitlement cuts out completely.

A direct comparison of the thresholds and ceilings shown in Table 2.3 with the distribution of assets among the aged cannot be made as there are no available data. An estimate of the distribution of asset holdings in 1993 is however available (Bækgaard, 1998), and this is used in Table 2.4 to place the assets test in context. The sample numbers of couples and single males who did not own their own homes are marginal, and it needs to be remembered that it is an estimated distribution of assets, but these caveats need not detract from the general picture shown by Table 2.4. This is that the assets test affects only those in the top 20 per cent or so of the respective assets distribution and removes all entitlement for less than 10 per cent.

Table 2.3   Asset Limits for Age Pension Entitlement, August 1997 ($)

	Assets threshold for maximum rate	Assets ceiling where entitlement cuts out
Single person		
Homeowner	125 750	243 500
Not homeowner	215 750	333 500
Couple (combined)		
Homeowner	178 500	374 000
Not homeowner	268 500	464 000

Source: Department of Social Security.

Table 2.4   Assets-test Thresholds and Ceilings expressed as Percentiles of the Corresponding Assets Distribution among Income Units with a Reference Person[a] Aged 65–74, 1993

	Assets threshold for maximum rate (percentile of assets distribution)[b]	Assets ceiling where entitlement cuts out (percentile of assets distribution)[b]
Couples		
Homeowners	80	91
Not homeowners	100	100
Single men		
Homeowners	81	88
Not homeowners	100	100
Single women		
Homeowners	87	94
Not homeowners	97	98

Notes:
[a] In a couple the reference person is taken to be the male partner.
[b] The 1st percentile is the lowest 1 per cent of the assets distribution.

Source: Estimated assets distributions as described by Bækgaard (1998).

These descriptions of the income and assets tests that apply to the age pension present only the basic rules. The tests are considerably more complex, with much detail on the treatment of different forms of income, the valuation of assets and so forth. On top of this complexity there has been considerable change in how the means tests are applied, including the introduction of deeming provisions in 1990, whereby a financial asset is deemed to provide a certain income stream irrespective of whether that income stream is received. Developments in this area have been designed partly to encourage pensioners to receive a competitive return on their assets and partly to counter financial mechanisms set up to avoid the means tests. The outcome of the many changes over recent years is a means-testing system of considerable intricacy that proves daunting to many of those who need to deal with it.

2.3.5 Supplementary Payments

A number of supplementary payments can be received on top of a basic pension or allowance from the Departments of Social Security (now Family and Community Services) and of Veterans' Affairs. Across the population the most important of these are payments for dependent children, though they are of far less significance among the retired population. Two supplementary payments that are important for older people are the pharmaceutical allowance and rent assistance.

All pensioners receive a payment designed to offset the cost of prescription medicines. In December 1997 the value of the pharmaceutical allowance was $2.70 a week for a pensioner couple or a single pensioner. Rent assistance is a more valuable payment, though received by only about 15 per cent of age pensioners. It is a supplement for those who pay rent or similar payments for private accommodation and is tied to the level of rent paid. In December 1997 the maximum weekly levels of rent assistance payable were $35.30 for a couple and $37.40 for a single person. These maximum rates were payable when weekly rent reached reasonably modest levels – $105 for couples and $85 for single people. Pensioners living in public rental housing are not entitled to rent assistance, although they receive generally greater assistance through subsidised rents, which are set according to their income (Landt et al., 1995).

2.3.6 Coverage

The then Department of Social Security (1997, pp. 51–2) estimated the coverage of social security pensions among the aged in June 1996 to be 69.4 per cent of the total population above qualifying age. A further 13.2 per cent were receiving a similar payment from the Department of Veterans' Affairs, giving a total pension coverage of 82.6 per cent. The department estimated that, among the 17.4 per cent not receiving a pension, 1.9 per cent of people were not meeting the residency requirements and the remaining 15.5 per cent were people not meeting the income and assets tests.

Overall in June 1997 67 per cent of age pensioners were receiving the maximum rate of pension. Among the 33 per cent who received a reduced rate, fewer than 5 per cent were receiving only a part pension due to operation of the assets test (Centrelink, 1998). An overview of expenditure on pensions for the aged and of pensioner numbers in 1995–96 is presented in Appendix A of King, Bækgaard and Harding (1999).

2.3.7 Non-cash Benefits

Besides the entitlements to cash benefits, retired people also derive benefit from a range of free or subsidised services, particularly in the areas of healthcare and aged care. The values of non-cash benefits have been estimated by the Australian Bureau of Statistics (ABS, 1996a) and their values for selected household types can be compared in Table 2.5. Households whose principal source of income was the age pension are shown to have received notably high levels of indirect benefits in both absolute and relative terms. For age-pension households in 1993–94 the benefits valued by the ABS amounted to an estimated $150 a week, compared with $135 a week for all households, and accounted for almost 40 per cent of their disposable income plus indirect benefits, compared with under 20 per cent for all households.

The main element of indirect benefits for age-pension households is healthcare, reflecting their high use of Medicare, the universal 'free' healthcare system. For this group welfare benefits include items such as age-care services and the subsidised cost of nursing homes, while housing benefits comprise mainly the subsidised rents payable for public rental housing. There are also a number of specific subsidies tied to the receipt of a government pension that apply to services provided by the states and territories and go under the title of state concessions. The provisions vary from one state to another, though generally include, for example, discounts on utility bills, local government rates and motor vehicle registration. The value of state concessions, which is only partly covered in the ABS estimates presented in Table 2.5, can amount to around $10 a week.

Mirroring the shift toward greater private provision of cash retirement incomes, recent policy developments have sought to move in the same direction, albeit more modestly, with non-cash benefits. One recent public debate for example concerned government measures to reduce the subsidies for nursing-home care by applying stricter means testing. The introduction of policy measures designed to encourage greater use of private health insurance and less reliance on the public system is another example of recent initiatives in this area.

Table 2.5 Estimated Weekly Value of Indirect Benefits, by Selected Household Types, 1993–94 ($ p.w.)

	Household with reference person* aged 55–64	Household with reference person* aged 65+	Age pension is principal source of household income	All households
Private income	502	163	30	626
Direct benefits	108	185	211	97
Gross income	610	349	241	723
Direct tax	101	30	3	137
Disposable income	509	318	238	586
Indirect benefits	*100*	*145*	*150*	*135*
Education	14	3	2	52
Health	57	95	89	60
Housing	5	4	6	4
Social security and welfare	24	44	54	19
Disposable income plus indirect benefits	609	464	389	721
Indirect benefits as a percentage of disposable income plus indirect benefits	16.4%	31.3%	38.6%	18.7%

Note: *The Australian Bureau of Statistics defines the reference person as the household member whose characteristics seem most likely to be associated with changes in household expenditure. In the case of a couple household for example, the reference person is the partner with the higher income. See ABS (1996a, p. 76).

Source: ABS, 1996a, Tables 2 and 8.

2.4   PRIVATE PROVISION OF RETIREMENT INCOMES

Private provision of retirement incomes in Australia is largely a matter of occupational superannuation, in which, as we shall see, private pensions play a small but increasing part. Superannuation benefits are predominantly paid out as lump sums. Other forms of private savings, such as homeownership, own businesses and rental property, are also important and attract some form of financial encouragement from the government, though we confine the following account to a description of the superannuation system. In doing so we include as private provision the major superannuation schemes for public sector employees, although they are largely unfunded pay-as-you-go schemes financed from government budgets. Following Bateman and Piggott (1997) they are considered to be private arrangements because of their basis in a private contract between employer and employee.

2.4.1   Recent Policy Developments

The period since the early 1980s has been one of intensive development in the history of Australian superannuation policy, documented by Bateman and Piggott (1997). As outlined earlier, three broad phases can be identified:

- post-war voluntary superannuation;
- award superannuation from 1986;
- the Superannuation Guarantee from 1992.

The first phase saw tax-encouraged occupational superannuation expand its coverage, though with a marked concentration among certain groups of the work-force. An analysis of the mid-1980s by Gunasekera and Powlay (1987) showed 47 per cent of the work-force to be covered by superannuation – including notably high proportions of public sector employees, males, full-time employees and those in higher-income white-collar occupations. Besides the limited coverage, other problems with superannuation arrangements at the time were identified in the areas of preservation, vesting, portability, prudential controls, the largely unfunded public sector schemes and the predominance of lump sums in the payment of superannuation benefits. The payment of lump sums provided the opportunity for 'double-dipping' whereby a retired person, having enjoyed the superannuation tax concessions, could then, by dissipating a lump-sum payment, enjoy the age pension.

It was the issue of coverage however that prompted the next phase. From the 1970s the trade union movement had sought to expand the coverage of occupational superannuation, and in the 1980s a vehicle for doing so emerged in the form of the Accord – the agreement between the trade unions and the

Labor Government. A wage–superannuation trade-off was agreed in 1986 through which half of the 6 per cent wage increase determined by the centralised wage-fixing authority was directed to be paid by employers into individual superannuation accounts. This Productivity Award Superannuation greatly expanded coverage of superannuation, albeit at low contribution rates, although it suffered from administrative difficulties, particularly when attempts were made to increase the rates of contribution.

The government's response was to introduce the Superannuation Guarantee in 1992, compelling employers to make superannuation contributions into individual accounts for their employees. The initial contribution rate was 3 per cent of earnings; the rate was 6 per cent in 1997–98 and will rise to 9 per cent by 2002–03. The scheme applies to all employees other than those earning less than $450 a month, or about 15 per cent of male average weekly earnings. There is also a ceiling on contributions, reached at a level equal to about 2½ times average weekly earnings. The self-employed are not covered, though tax rebates exist to encourage them to provide superannuation for themselves.

The 1992 announcement also foreshadowed a compulsory 3 per cent employee contribution to be introduced later in the implementation of the Superannuation Guarantee. A timetable for the introduction of this employee contribution, which would have brought total compulsory contributions up to 12 per cent, was announced in the 1995–96 Commonwealth Budget, together with a matching 3 per cent contribution from the government for those workers on low incomes. However these proposed extensions to the Superannuation Guarantee died with the 1996 change in government. Despite apparent bipartisan support for at least the 3 per cent employee contribution and repeated arguments that the level of contributions needed to be increased, there was also increasing disquiet about the impact on the current disposable incomes of low-income workers. Implementation of the Superannuation Guarantee will thus see maximum compulsory contributions of 9 per cent by 2002–03.

Along with the Superannuation Guarantee the government established the Retirement Income Modelling Task Force (which became the Retirement Income Modelling Unit) to analyse policy developments in this area. Such analyses have included projections of the impact of the Superannuation Guarantee on national savings, pension outlays and tax expenditures, and the retirement incomes of the future aged. An indicative projection gives an after-tax replacement rate of about 60 per cent for someone receiving average earnings, if they contribute to superannuation for 40 years, retire at age 65 and so on (Gallagher, Rothman and Brown, 1993).

As well as the compulsory contributions, the retirement income reforms have included important changes to address other features of the superannuation system. Prudential controls and the vesting, portability and preservation characteristics of superannuation have been strengthened markedly. The preservation age of 55 years is being gradually increased to 60 years by 2025. There is also a shift away from unfunded defined benefit schemes. Contributions under the Superannuation Guarantee must be placed in an accumulation fund and the major unfunded public sector schemes are gradually shifting to accumulation defined contribution schemes.

2.4.2   Coverage and Funds

The scale of the changes to Australian superannuation since the mid-1980s is illustrated in Table 2.6. Coverage in employer-provided schemes more than doubled over the period and, when coverage by other schemes is included, the total superannuation coverage of employees in 1994 was 87 per cent.

Table 2.6   Coverage of Employees by Employer-provided Superannuation (%)

	Full-time employees	Part-time employees	All employees
Men			
1984	51	12	49
1994	93	44	87
Women			
1984	35	6	25
1994	94	68	83
All			
1984	46	8	40
1994	93	62	85

Sources: ABS, 1985, Table 5; ABS, 1995a, Table 2.

The greatest gains have been experienced by those groups with lowest coverage to start with: in 1984 just 6 per cent of female part-time employees were covered; by 1994 the proportion was 68 per cent. Coverage of female full-time workers rose from 35 per cent to 94 per cent during the same period.

The proportion of workers in a superannuation scheme is one element of the extent of coverage. The other element is the level of this coverage. Broadly contributions to superannuation can be made as employer or personal contributions. Table 2.7 shows that in 1995 almost all superannuation included an employer contribution (arrangements for the self-employed would account for most of the superannuation that did not). Personal contributions are also made by around half those covered by superannuation.

Table 2.7   Type of Superannuation Coverage, 1995: Employees Aged 15–74 with Superannuation (%)

Type of coverage	Men	Women	All
Personal and employer contributions	48.6	36.3	43.2
Personal contributions only	2.8	1.9	2.4
Employer contributions only	48.6	61.8	54.4

Source: ABS, 1996b, Table 12.

Employer contributions include payments under the Superannuation Guarantee but often amount to considerably more than is required. In the public sector schemes employer contributions would typically be 10–15 per cent of earnings (or the equivalent in defined benefit schemes). It should be recognised that contributions under the Superannuation Guarantee do not supplement those employer contributions that were in place already (actuarially determined contributions in the case of defined benefit schemes). The impact of the Superannuation Guarantee on contributions is thus much less than the product of the number of employees and the required contribution rate.

In some schemes personal contributions are often described as compulsory when they are tied to higher contributions being made by the employer. Strictly speaking such personal contributions are voluntary, though they are often made under offers that few would refuse. Among the 50 per cent of workers making personal contributions, these were classed as not compulsory in 66 per cent of cases. Among those classed as compulsory, the personal contributions were higher than the required level in about one in four cases (ABS, 1996b, Table 3). The personal contributions thus genuinely have a high voluntary element. Personal contributions are typically 5–10 per cent of earnings (Table 2.8). Payments by the self-employed into their own superannuation funds are another form of personal contribution and attract specific tax concessions.

Table 2.8   Own Contributions to Superannuation as a Percentage of Earnings, 1995: Employees Aged 45–74 with Superannuation (%)

Contribution as percentage of earnings	Men	Women	All
Less than 5%	38.7	37.3	38.2
From 5% to less than 10%	46.5	46.3	46.4
10% or more	14.8	16.3	15.4

Source: ABS, 1996b, Table 13.

Source: Insurance and Superannuation Commission, 1997, Table 5.

Figure 2.2   Assets and Members of Australian Superannuation Funds, by Benefit Structure, September 1997

The expansion of superannuation coverage is mirrored in the rapid growth of funds in superannuation. In current prices, assets in superannuation funds totalled just over $20 billion in the early 1980s and had risen to around $250 billion by 1996 (Bateman and Piggott, 1997, p. 11). They are projected to increase to over $800 billion by 2010 and to over $1 500 billion by 2020 (Rothman, 1997). An important feature of Australian superannuation funds has been the large share of defined benefit rather than accumulation (defined contribution) schemes, particularly in the public sector. This is changing, but slowly, and the 1997 benefit structure of Australian superannuation is shown in Figure 2.2. Superannuation assets are roughly equally split between accumulation and defined benefit funds, while members are predominantly in accumulation schemes except for those members of public sector schemes. The difference in structures that emerges from looking at assets and at members reflects the shift toward new members being in accumulation funds, in line with the provisions of the Superannuation Guarantee.

2.4.3   Taxation of Superannuation

The existence of substantial tax concessions for superannuation, amounting to $8.7 billion or 1.7 per cent of GDP in 1996–97, was noted earlier in the overview. These concessions are a very important element of superannuation policy, and the extent of voluntary contributions to superannuation largely flows from the tax-favoured status of saving through superannuation. A guide to the tax treatment of superannuation in Australia has been provided by Bateman and Piggott (1997) and the main elements are listed below. Note that Australia is unique among OECD countries in taxing superannuation at all three possible points: in the hands of contributors, funds and beneficiaries.

Contributors
- Employer contributions are tax-deductible up to certain age-related limits: about $10 000 a year for an employee aged under 35, rising to about $65 000 for an employee aged over 50.
- Personal contributions by employees are generally made out of after-tax income.
- Low-wage employees (i.e. those with earnings less than about 85 per cent of male average weekly earnings) can claim a tax rebate of up to $1 000 a year for their personal superannuation contributions.
- Self-employed people and employees without employer support for superannuation are entitled to a tax deduction in respect of contributions up to the age-related limits.

Funds
- Contributions and investment earnings are generally taxed at a rate of 15 per cent. This compares with a corporate tax rate of 36 per cent and a top personal marginal rate of 47 per cent.
- Contributions that have not already received concessional tax treatment, such as most personal contributions made out of after-tax income, are not taxed.
- The actual tax rate that applies to fund earnings depends to an extent on the form of these investment incomes, and Bateman and Piggott (1997) note that the effective tax rate on fund earnings is considerably lower than 15 per cent.
- The income of unfunded schemes is not taxed, though benefits from these schemes are taxed at a higher rate.
- Since 1996 a superannuation contributions surcharge has increased the superannuation contributions tax rate above 15 per cent for people with annual incomes above $70 000 (in 1996–97). The surcharge increases the

rate to a maximum of 30 per cent for those with annual incomes in excess of $85 000 (in 1996–97), or about 2.4 times male average annual earnings.

Beneficiaries
- Taxation of superannuation benefits is particularly complex and depends for example on the type of benefit, the size of benefit, age (whether the preservation age has been reached) and the extent to which the benefit reflects contributions made at different times under different tax regimes.
- Reasonable benefit limits (RBLs) restrict the amount of superannuation benefit that can receive concessional tax treatment. The RBLs in 1996–97 were $435 000 where the benefit was taken entirely as a lump sum and $870 000 where at least half of the benefit was taken as a pension or annuity.

2.4.4   Today's Retirees

The expansion of superannuation since the mid-1980s will take some time to have a marked effect on people's privately provided retirement incomes. The situation of today's retirees thus has much more to do with the partial

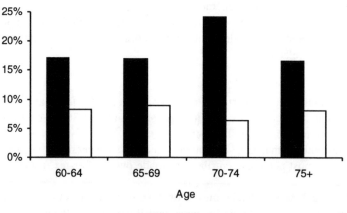

Note: *Retired population defined as in Section 2.7.

Source: ABS 1995–96 Survey of Income and Housing Costs, unit record file.

Figure 2.3   Incidence of Private Pensions among the Retired Population,
1995–96

coverage of superannuation over the post-war years. As Figure 2.3 shows, private pensions were not prevalent among the older population in 1995–96. They were received by less than 10 per cent of women and had a coverage peak of just 24 per cent of 70- to 74-year-old men. This peak may however be a statistical artefact of the small numbers in the sample receiving private pensions. We have also examined corresponding data for 1993–94 and 1994–95 and such a peak was not evident.

When private pensions are received, they are often small (Figure 2.4). Remembering that in 1995–96 the single rate of pension was about $170 a week, 21 per cent of the private pensions received by males in 1995–96 were worth less than $100 a week and 42 per cent were worth less than $200 a week. For females, private pensions are even lower: 40 per cent were below $100 a week and 63 per cent below $200 a week. Figures on the receipt of private pensions however provide a poor indicator of the extent of privately provided retirement incomes in Australia because benefits are predominantly received as lump sums.

The breakdown of benefits paid out by superannuation funds, distinguishing lump-sum and pension payments, is shown in Figure 2.5. Overall in 1997 just over 80 per cent of the value of benefits was paid out as lump sums. This makes the tracking of the contribution of superannuation to retirement

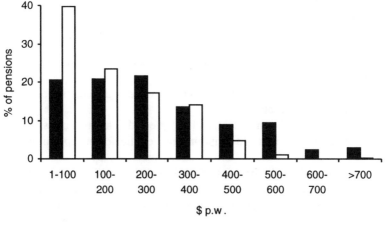

Source: ABS 1995–96 Survey of Income and Housing Costs, unit record file.

Figure 2.4 Value of Private Pensions, 1995–96

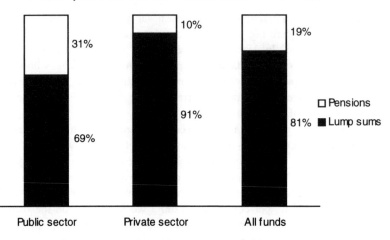

Source: Insurance and Superannuation Commission, 1997, Table 4.

Figure 2.5   Breakdown of Superannuation Benefits Paid, by Type of Benefit, July–September 1997

incomes very difficult, given the possible destinations of lump sums. For example, lump sums may

- be used to purchase an annuity, and then appear in the income distribution data as private pensions;
- be invested in other forms with income streams, and be reflected in reported asset incomes;
- be directed to investments that do not generate an income stream, and be reflected only in assets data;
- be used to reduce housing debt, and be reflected in housing costs; or
- be used to fund current consumption, and be reflected in expenditure data.

Some, but not all, of the benefits of superannuation will thus be included in the income distribution data presented in Section 2.7, and only a small part of what is included can be identified as the fruits of superannuation. However there is something to gain from taking a step back from the income distribution data. A broad picture of the place of privately provided retirement incomes in the situations of today's retirees can be obtained from the Retirement and Retirement Intentions Survey undertaken by the ABS. This survey provides information on superannuation coverage and the main source of income at retirement for two population groups – retirees and those approaching retirement. The specific populations are

- people who retired from full-time work at 45 or over; and
- people aged 45 or more who intend to retire from full-time work.

Obviously each of these populations is quite heterogeneous, particularly with regard to retirement age, and the information on principal source of income is a matter of expectations for the second group. Still, if we appreciate the broad definition of the populations, the potential for actual outcomes to diverge from expectations and the large proportion of intending retirees with 'don't

Table 2.9   Characteristics of Retirees and Intending Retirees[a] Aged 45 Years or More, 1994 (%)

	Men		Women		All	
	Retired	Intend	Retired	Intend	Retired	Intend
Belong(ed) to a retirement scheme	60.9	85.5	40.7	79.7	52.6	83.7
(Expected) age at retirement[b]						
Under 54	22.1	1.4	76.2	8.2	54.4	3.4
55–59	19.6	16.9	11.1	29.1	14.5	20.5
60–64	32.3	22.5	9.6	46.3	18.7	29.5
65–69	22.7	56.7	2.5	15.3	10.7	44.5
70+	3.2	2.5	0.7	1.1	1.7	2.1
(Expected) main source of income at retirement[c]						
Superannuation etc.	15.5	38.6	4.7	22.3	11.1	33.6
Social security pension	29.1	31.9	26.2	33.7	27.9	32.4
Veteran's pension	9.7	0.8	3.0	0.2	7.0	0.6
Other social security	11.3	1.0	5.2	0.7	8.8	0.9
Business, property	2.8	3.9	2.0	3.6	2.4	3.8
Other investment	11.3	11.9	6.0	8.8	9.1	11.0
Savings, asset sales	9.8	3.6	6.2	3.4	8.3	3.6
Part-time work	4.4	5.3	7.4	4.8	5.6	5.2
Other's income	4.3	2.7	38.1	22.1	18.1	8.6
Other	1.8	0.3	1.3	0.3	1.6	0.3

Notes:
[a] See text for definition of retired and intending retiree populations.
[b] Distribution of retirement age for intending retirees excludes the roughly 30 per cent of cases who did not know.
[c] Distribution of main source of income for intending retirees excludes the roughly 15 per cent of cases who did not know.

Source: ABS, 1995b, Tables 2, 3, 9, 10 and 12.

know' answers, the characteristics of these two groups provide a useful impression of retirement incomes today. Given that the first population largely includes people who have retired over the past 20 years and the second population largely includes those who will retire in the coming 20 years, a comparison of the characteristics of the two populations also provides an impression of the changes taking place in retirement incomes.

The characteristics of retired people and intending retirees in 1994 can be compared using Table 2.9. Intending retirees, particularly females, had much higher coverage than their retired counterparts. However the retired group of females contained a very high proportion who had retired before the age of 54, which makes the two female populations covered by Table 2.9 barely comparable. Further comparison is accordingly restricted to men. Privately provided income through superannuation was identified as the main expected source of income at retirement for just over a third of males, government cash benefits for a further third, and other sources, including investment and part-time work, for the remainder. Compared with previous retirees, this group showed a higher reliance on superannuation and a lower reliance on government cash benefits, though the extent of this difference is likely to have been exaggerated by the young retirees in the retired group.

What happens to the 80 per cent of superannuation benefits paid out as lump sums? Table 2.10 shows that most lump sums in the mid-1990s were small, and few were used to purchase an immediate annuity. Besides rolling over lump sums into other funds, Table 2.11 shows that most lump sums were invested elsewhere or used for housing payments. When considering the values of lump sums and private pensions, it should be noted that some superannuation benefits were received partly as a lump sum and partly as a pension or annuity, though payment simply as a lump sum was the most common.

Table 2.10   Value of Superannuation Lump Sums Received in the Previous Two Years by People Aged 45–74 who had Ceased Full-time Work, 1995 (%)

Value of lump sum	Men	Women	All
Under $5 000	19	47	30
$5 000 and under $20 000	19	22	20
$20 000 and under $60 000	23	19	21
$60 000 and under $100 000	16	6	12
$100 000 and under $200 000	15	5	11
$200 000 and over	8	1	5

Note: Shares exclude the 0.9 per cent of 'don't know' responses.

Source: ABS, 1996b, Table 6.

Table 2.11   Actual and Intended Disbursement of Superannuation Lump Sums by People Aged 45–74, 1995 (%)

Disbursement of lump sum	Actual disbursement by those who received a lump sum in the past two years	Intended disbursement by those who expect to receive a lump sum*
Roll over, including deferred annuity	30	32
Purchase an immediate annuity	1	1
Invest money elsewhere	31	35
Pay off home, improvements, new home	13	13
Buy or pay off car, vehicle	5	2
Clear other debts	8	4
Pay for a holiday	2	7
Assist family members	1	1
Other	8	4

Note: *Distribution of intended disbursement excludes the 38 per cent of 'don't know' responses.

Source: ABS, 1996b, Tables 4 and 5.

2.4.5   Some Policy Issues

While retirement incomes policy has been an area of intense activity since the mid-1980s, leading to the implementation of the Superannuation Guarantee, the issue of superannuation continues to generate considerable debate. There is broad consensus over the merits of the basic policy, though much debate has been generated by particular aspects. These include taxation, the interaction between superannuation and the age pension, the circumstances of those with non-standard careers, and complexity.

As already noted superannuation is taxed at three points: in the hands of contributors, funds and beneficiaries. The tax arrangements are however concessionary and amount to substantial tax expenditures. These tax concessions have been widely perceived as regressive, with high income earners receiving higher concessions, and an increase in the tax rate on superannuation contributions from those on higher incomes was introduced in 1996–97. This measure drew considerable protest from those directly affected. One of the main grounds of opposition was the administrative burden imposed on fund administrators, and this, together with the extreme complexity of the taxation of superannuation, is a general concern in this area. The taxation of superannuation benefits is particularly complicated. The introduction in July 2000 of a goods and services tax, with associated personal income tax cuts, has added a further dimension to the superannuation tax issues.

Many commentators have pointed to what looks like a glaring anomaly in Australia's retirement income system – namely the gap between the superannuation preservation age of 55 years and the qualifying age for the age pension (Bateman and Piggott, 1997; Knox, 1996). It is argued that this gap, together with the widespread availability of lump-sum benefits, provides the opportunity for double-dipping and thereby dilution of the impact of compulsory superannuation. The preservation age is being gradually increased to 60 by 2025, though a five-year gap will remain between the preservation age and the qualifying age for the age pension.

The Superannuation Guarantee has not fully addressed the situations of those with 'non-standard' careers, such as people with interrupted labour-force careers or long periods of part-time work. Certainly their superannuation coverage has improved, though they do not look forward to the same benefits as someone who will have worked full-time for 35–40 years. The real concern then is that, although the Superannuation Guarantee should bring some real improvement in their retirement incomes, their relative position among the retired is likely to worsen. Such concerns have included a focus on the situation of women (Economic Planning Advisory Council, 1994), with the treatment of superannuation upon divorce having been a matter of particular attention (Attorney General's Department, 1998). There are similar concerns for those on low earnings, who stand to gain little from the Superannuation Guarantee compared with their entitlements under the age pension. In such cases there are arguments that the money taken in compulsory superannuation contributions would be more usefully directed toward their current consumption or should be allowed to be used to pursue homeownership (Econtech, 1996). A review of aspects of superannuation arrangements has been foreshadowed by the government.

2.5 SUSTAINABILITY

Aspects of the sustainability of the Australian retirement income system were examined by the Economic Planning Advisory Council (EPAC) in 1994 as part of a broad analysis of the impact of an ageing population on social expenditures (Clare and Tulpule, 1994). EPAC drew on projections from the Retirement Income Modelling Task Force, and some relevant results are summarised in Table 2.12. In the absence of the Superannuation Guarantee the projections show overall social security expenditure rising from 6.9 to 9.3 per cent of GDP over the period 1990 to 2051, with payments to the aged (age pension and veterans' pensions) making up an increasing share of this total – from 48 per cent in 1990 to 63 per cent in 2051. Clare and Tulpule (1994) saw concerns about sustainability in these projections but took heart from the projected impact of the Superannuation Guarantee. While having no discernible effect on pension outlays until 2021, the Superannuation Guarantee was then projected to reduce pension outlays increasingly, with this reduction amounting to 1.4 per cent of GDP by 2051.

The projections in Table 2.12 are of course based on a raft of assumptions about individual superannuation 'careers', growth rates, rates of return, savings displacement and population structure (Gallagher, Rothman and Brown, 1993). The figures shown should thus be seen as indicative, and Clare and Tulpule (1994, p. 33) acknowledge that the particular assumptions used in their analysis may overstate the impact of the Superannuation Guarantee.

Furthermore Table 2.12 only covers one side of the budgetary impact of the Superannuation Guarantee. Another side is the tax expenditure arising from the concessional tax treatment of superannuation. Fitzgerald (1993), in a major report on national savings, which again drew on the projections of the Retirement Income Modelling Task Force, suggested that the expansion of superannuation increases the level of tax expenditure by up to 0.2 per cent of GDP. Over the period to 2020, with little impact on pension outlays, the net effect of the Superannuation Guarantee on the government budget is then a

Table 2.12 EPAC Projections of Social Security and Veterans' Pensions Expenditure (% of GDP)

		Without Superannuation Guarantee	With Superannuation Guarantee	Impact of Superannuation Guarantee on
	Total	Age pension and veterans' pensions	Age pension and veterans' pensions	age pension and veterans' pensions
1990	6.9	3.3	3.3	0.0
2001	6.6	3.3	3.3	0.0
2011	7.1	3.8	3.8	0.0
2021	8.1	4.7	4.5	–0.2
2031	9.0	5.6	4.9	–0.7
2041	9.3	5.9	5.0	–0.9
2051	9.3	5.9	4.5	–1.4

Source: Economic Planning Advisory Council, 1994, Tables 3.8, 3.10 and 3.11.

slight decrease in public savings. As pension savings come in, a crossover is projected to occur in around 2025, with increasing public savings thereafter. Using some different assumptions and definitions from those used by the Economic Planning Advisory Council (1994), Fitzgerald (1993, p. 53) estimates the impact of the Superannuation Guarantee to be a reduction in pension outlays by 0.5 per cent of GDP by 2051, with a partly offsetting increase in tax expenditure of about 0.1 per cent, yielding a net positive impact on the budget of 0.4 per cent of GDP in 2051.

The matter of sustainability has also been addressed by the National Commission of Audit, a body established by the incoming government in 1996 to report on a number of key issues, including the impact of demographic change on Commonwealth finances (National Commission of Audit, 1996). The Commission reviewed the EPAC estimates but, beyond suggesting that there was scope for further substitution of private provision for public outlays in retirement incomes, did not dwell on the broad thrust of current policy. Instead it focused on the projected impact of an ageing population on the healthcare and aged care budgets. Although the analysis of the National Commission of Audit has been contested (Mitchell, 1996) its emphasis does reflect an apparent shift in the debate about sustainability. The Superannuation Guarantee appears to have largely addressed the concerns about sustainability, which were an important motivation for its introduction – or at least the issue is out of the spotlight, which is now occupied more by projected healthcare and aged care expenditures (Productivity Commission and Melbourne Institute of Applied Economic and Social Research, 1999).

2.6   LABOUR FORCE ACTIVITY RATES

The November 1997 labour force participation rates of men and women aged 45 or over are shown in Table 2.13. The table distinguishes between single and married women, and the first point to note is that there is little difference between the participation rates for these two groups of women at these ages. The participation rates for men and women fall dramatically as the qualifying age for the age pension is reached – 65 for males and 61 for females. However there is also a substantial fall over the 5–10 years preceding these thresholds, and in this regard the preservation age of 55 years for the payment of superannuation benefits is important. There are also other forms of income support on which retired people can draw prior to reaching age pension age – notably veterans' pensions, disability support pension, mature age allowance and wife's pension.

Table 2.13 Labour Force Participation Rates of Men and Women Aged 45 or Over, November 1997 (%)

	Age-group			
	45–54	55–59	60–64	65+
Men	87.2	72.5	46.6	11.0
Single women	68.9	43.4	18.7	2.0
Married women	69.0	42.2	19.6	4.5

Source: ABS, 1997c, Table 10.

Table 2.14 Percentage[a] of Men and Women Aged 55–69 Receiving Government Pensions and Allowances,[b] 1995–96 (%)

	Age-group		
	55–59	60–64	65–69
Men			
None	76.6	59.0	20.2
Age pension	0.0	0.0	72.6
Veteran's pension	1.8	4.6	3.5
Disability pension, sickness allowance	10.7	22.2	1.0
Other income support[b]	10.7	13.4	2.2
Overseas pension	0.2	1.7	12.5
Women			
None	61.9	28.5	17.0
Age pension	0.0	63.9	69.5
Veteran's pension	1.1	3.8	12.3
Disability pension, sickness allowance	11.9	0.1	0.0
Other income support[b]	25.3	3.8	1.5
Overseas pension	0.2	7.1	10.9

Notes:
[a]Percentages may sum to over 100 through receipt of more than one type of pension or allowance.
[b]Excludes payments made solely in respect of dependent children.

Source: ABS 1995–96 Survey of Income and Housing Costs, unit record file.

The extent of receipt of government pensions and allowances among people aged 55 or over but under the qualifying age for the age pension in 1995–96 is shown in Table 2.14. For men the major category of payments was those tied to disability or sickness, which were received by one in five males in the 60–64 age-group. A small proportion received veterans' payments, while the 'other income support' category for men largely included payments related to unemployment, including mature age allowance for those aged 60 or over. Significant numbers of women under their age pension age of 61 also received disability or sickness payments, although the 'other income support' category was the main source of their pensions and allowances. The composition of payments in this category was more diverse for women than for men, as significant numbers received the wife pension and partner allowance – payments that are being gradually phased out.

Table 2.14 clearly shows that, once the qualifying ages for the age pension were reached, the age pension was the dominant pension or allowance, with about 70 per cent reporting receipt of this payment. However a number of other payments also figure in the table for these age-groups. The receipt of other Australian social security payments can be attributed largely to reporting errors where for example long-term recipients of the disability support pension noticed no change when they reached the age when their payments became classified as the age pension. War widows' pensions accounted for the significant number of women over pension age reporting veterans' pensions. Finally there were a large number of people receiving overseas pensions, although often these were small and received in conjunction with the Australian age pension.

The labour force participation rates shown in Table 2.13 are a point in a distinctive trend, which has seen declining participation rates for males, especially in the 55–59 and 60–64 age-groups, and increasing rates for women, particularly for married women (Figure 2.6). There are many facets to the relationship between these retirement trends and policy development. On the one hand the increasing labour force participation rates of women prompted the increase in their age pension qualifying age, while a general call for a more flexible policy treatment of retirement has seen initiatives such as the Deferred Pension Bonus Scheme. On the other hand there is the gap between the preservation age for superannuation and the qualifying age for the age pension – a gap that will still exist after completion in 2025 of the phased increase in the preservation age from 55 to 60. There are frequent calls for this gap to be eliminated, although, once the diversity of retirement decisions and circumstances is recognised, it becomes clear that the appropriate policy response is not straightforward. Bacon and Gallagher (1996) for example estimated that only 22 per cent of early retirement was voluntary, the remainder being roughly divided between retirement for family reasons, such as to look after someone else, and involuntary retirement, such as retrenchment.

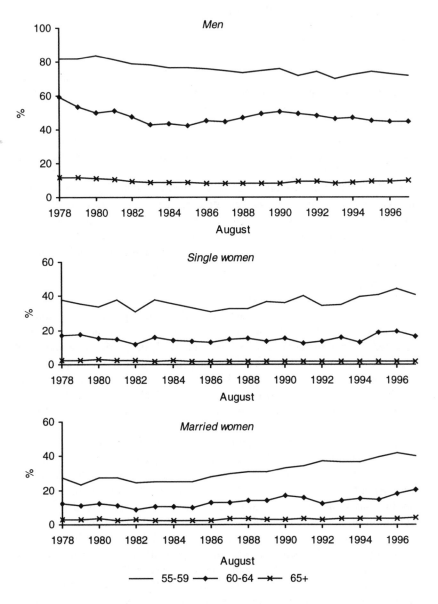

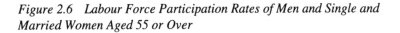

Source: Australian Bureau of Statistics, *Labour Force: Australia*, Cat. no. 6203.0.

Figure 2.6 Labour Force Participation Rates of Men and Single and Married Women Aged 55 or Over

2.7   INCOME DISTRIBUTIONS

2.7.1   Data and Definitions

Data from the unit record file of the ABS 1995–96 Survey of Income and Housing Costs (SIHC) are used here to describe the income distribution of the older cohorts of the Australian population (ABS, 1997b). The SIHC is an annual sample survey that began in 1994–95 and replaced the earlier series of income surveys that were undertaken every four or five years or so. The survey scope excludes those in non-private dwellings, such as nursing homes, so the survey does not present a complete picture of the circumstances of the aged. The institutionalised population accounts for about 2 per cent of 65- to 69-year-olds and about 10 per cent of those aged 75 years or over. While introduction of the SIHC has resulted in more frequent collection of income distribution data, there has been a reduction in sample size. The 1995–96 SIHC sample included 0.1 per cent of the population and, as is indicated in places below, problems with cell sizes can arise in some classifications of the population.

The income data used refer to reported weekly incomes, although the weekly income figures for certain irregular or infrequent income sources, such as income from interest and dividends, are derived by the ABS from the reported annual incomes from these sources. Unless otherwise indicated, after-tax income is used in those tables and figures dealing with total income, while gross income is used where the focus is on income components. After-tax income is gross income less income tax, which is calculated using the value for weekly income tax imputed by the ABS and provided on the unit record file.

The population under examination is termed the 'retired population' and is defined as those aged over the age pension qualifying age – 65 years for men and 60 years for women[3] – or 60 years or over and not employed or self-employed. In the case of couples their inclusion in this population is assessed on the basis of the male partner's characteristics. This is the standard definition of the 'retired' population being used in the IFS comparative study for which this chapter was originally prepared, and the study recognises that it is not a perfect definition. Perhaps most importantly for interpretation of the income distribution data, the population so defined will include a number of female partners in couples who would not normally be considered part of the retired population. It will also exclude any men aged 60–64 who are employed, while including any employed men aged 65 or over.

The SIHC data are examined at the income-unit level, where an income unit can be a couple with or without dependent children, a single person, or a sole parent with dependent children.[4] The presentation does not however separately identify the few among the retired population with dependent children. In those cases, for example, 'single men' and 'single women' include the few sole parents. Dependent children are defined in the SIHC as children living with parents or guardians who are under 15 years old or who are full-time students under 25 years old and are not married and have no children of their own. In some parts of the presentation equivalent income is used and is calculated with a simple equivalence scale of 1.0 for a single person, 0.7 for an additional adult and 0.5 for each dependent child.

An examination of the sensitivity of the results to a household unit of analysis and to the use of a different equivalence scale can be found in Appendices B and C of King, Bækgaard and Harding (1999).

2.7.2 Income Levels

The average total after-tax incomes of income units in the retired population are given in Table 2.15. The mean incomes can be compared with the then base weekly rates of the age pension of around $175 for single people and $290 for couples. After accounting for supplementary payments, such as rent assistance, the incomes of single women were not very much higher than the pension rate, while single men appear to have been about $20–25 a week better off than their female counterparts. The average incomes of couples were about 30 per cent above the base pension rate – a similar margin to that for single men. The broad picture then was of incomes supplementing government pensions, particularly among couples and single men.

Overall there is relatively little variation in mean incomes across the age-groups, reflecting the high degree of reliance on the flat-rate age pension. The average incomes of 60- to 64-year-old couples and single men were however notably low, the figure for single men being only marginally above the pension rate. An explanation of the result for these two groups can be found in the definition of the retired population that is being used. While the older male age-groups include some employed men, and thereby the effect of male earnings, the definition of the retired population explicitly excludes employed men from the 60- to 64-year-old couples and single men. The odd nature of these two population groups needs to be borne in mind when interpreting Table 2.15 and further results in this section.

The average equivalent incomes of the groups in Table 2.15 expressed as proportions of the average equivalent income for the non-retired population ($334 a week in 1995–96) range from a low of 54 per cent for 60- to 64-year-old single men to a high of 73 per cent for 70- to 74-year-old single men. If we exclude the 60- to 64-year-olds, where interpretation is difficult for the

Table 2.15   Mean Total After-tax Incomes of Income Units in the Retired Population and their Equivalent Incomes as a Percentage of Equivalent Income for the Non-retired Population, 1995–96

	Age-group				
	60–64	65–69	70–74	75+	60+
Couples					
After-tax income ($ p.w.)	365*	386	406	384	387
Equivalent income proportion (%)	62	68	71	68	68
Single men					
After-tax income ($ p.w.)	184*	234	243	225	223
Equivalent income proportion (%)	54	70	73	67	67
Single women					
After-tax income ($ p.w.)	218	218	217	199	209
Equivalent income proportion (%)	65	65	65	60	63

Note: *This group includes no employed men.

Source: ABS 1995–96 Survey of Income and Housing Costs, unit record file.

reasons noted above, the income relativities with the rest of the population are broadly similar for couples and single men – at around 70 per cent – but around 65 per cent for single women.

The equal levels of pension entitlement for males and females can be compared with the systematically higher incomes of single men than of single women in the non-retired population (Table 2.16). This table also provides a general picture of the incomes of groups in the non-retired population for comparison with those of the retired population, including distributional measures, which are discussed in the next section. The use of an income unit definition may have an important bearing on the results shown in Table 2.16, particularly those for the younger groups of single people. The main issue here is how young people are treated, and, as noted above, dependent children include only those who live with parents and who are under 15 years old or are 15- to 24-year-old full-time students. The populations of younger single people in Table 2.16 therefore include significant numbers of young people on low incomes who are classed as independent single people but who were in many cases receiving significant parental support.

Among retired couples in 1995–96, men had a slightly greater share of gross income than did their female partners (Table 2.17). The average male share across all retired couples was 56 per cent. Given that the age pension is means-tested on the basis of joint income and assets and equivalent payments are made to each partner, the higher male share of couple income indicates

Table 2.16   After-tax Income Distributions of Groups among the Non-retired Population,* 1995–96 (incomes in $ p.w.)

	Mean	Median	90th percentile	10th percentile	90/10 ratio
Couples, no children, head aged <40	849	847	1 191	420	2.84
Couples, no children, head aged ≥40	700	638	1 180	266	4.44
Couples with children	765	704	1 251	367	3.41
Single parents	391	351	633	210	3.01
Single men aged <40	336	341	587	81	7.25
Single men aged ≥40	383	348	712	115	6.19
Single women aged <40	311	317	515	96	5.36
Single women aged ≥40	303	236	593	132	4.49

Note: *Non-retired population includes single women aged under 60, males aged under 60 or aged 60–64 and employed, and married women if their male partner is defined to be in the non-retired population.

Source: ABS 1995–96 Survey of Income and Housing Costs, unit record file.

Table 2.17   Male Shares of the Gross Income of Retired Couples, 1995–96 (%)

Age of male partner	Male share of gross income of couples*
60–64	53
65–69	57
70–74	58
75+	53
60+	56

Note: *Share of aggregate incomes for the group.

Source: ABS 1995–96 Survey of Income and Housing Costs, unit record file.

that men had a higher share of the private incomes of couples. There was some variation in the male share as age increased, and this can be related to the prevalence of male earnings. The relatively low figure for the 60–64 age-group is likely to reflect the absence by definition of male earnings in this group, while the decline in the ratio for those aged 75 or over reflects the greatly reduced prevalence of male earnings for this age-group.

In looking at the income levels of the retired population, consideration of housing costs can change the picture both within the retired population and between the retired and non-retired populations. We do not attempt to take account of housing costs in this description of the income distribution by looking, say, at after-housing-cost income or by estimating imputed rent. However the pattern of housing tenure among the retired can be compared with that of others in the population (Table 2.18) to give a fairly clear idea of the qualifications that housing costs would make to the picture. In 1995–96 the retired population and the non-retired population aged 40 or over had very similar proportions of homeowners and purchasers (about 76 per cent), though the proportion of outright owners among the retired was very high. Otherwise the retired population was notable for a higher proportion of public renters and a lower proportion of private renters. The two main forms of housing tenure that account for higher-than-average shares among the retired population – outright ownership and public rental – are both associated with relatively low housing costs. Note that Table 2.18 is drawn from survey data that exclude the institutionalised population, and institutional housing provides another important form of tenure for the retired population, particularly for those aged 75 or over.

Further information on the housing circumstances of the retired population has been provided in Appendix D of King, Bækgaard and Harding (1999).

Table 2.18   Housing Tenures of Retired and Non-retired Aged 40 Years or Over, 1995–96 (%)

Housing tenure	Retired population	Non-retired population aged 40 or over
Outright owner	72.9	44.5
Purchaser	3.6	31.3
Public renter	7.2	4.2
Private renter	9.9	16.9
Other	6.5	3.0

Source: ABS 1995–96 Survey of Income and Housing Costs, unit record file.

2.7.3   Distribution of Total Income

Distributional measures for the incomes of the retired population are shown in Table 2.19. Looking first at the median incomes for the different groups, the relative uniformity across age-groups is even more striking than was indicated by the comparison of means in Table 2.15. The median incomes of the single women differed by at most $11 a week in 1995–96 and those of single men above age pension age by just $6 a week. This highlights the strong impact of the flat-rate pension on the income distribution.

The other distributional measures included in Table 2.19 are the 90th and 10th percentile incomes for each group and the ratio of these two incomes. Before looking at the ratios it is reasonable to wonder how all the 10th percentile incomes could be below the basic rate of the age pension. This is attributable at least partly to the operation of the assets test, although it also reflects people who have not yet fulfilled the residency requirements for the age pension. There is also the possibility of under-reporting. The ratios of the

Table 2.19   After-tax Income Distributions of Groups among the Retired Population, by Age-group, 1995–96 (incomes in $ p.w.)

| | Age-group | | | | |
	60–64	65–69	70–74	75+	60+
Couples					
Median	304*	324	319	318	318
90th percentile	582*	632	609	634	608
10th percentile	231*	230	274	250	244
90/10 ratio	2.51*	2.75	2.22	2.53	2.49
Single men					
Median	171*	191	194	190	188
90th percentile	236*	416	291	386	356
10th percentile	135*	160	166	135	151
90/10 ratio	1.75*	2.60	1.75	2.86	2.36
Single women					
Median	184	183	190	179	180
90th percentile	365	313	305	266	301
10th percentile	141	160	153	160	157
90/10 ratio	2.58	1.96	1.99	1.66	1.92

Note: *This group includes no employed males.

Source: ABS 1995–96 Survey of Income and Housing Costs, unit record file.

90th to the 10th percentile incomes range between 1.75 and 2.86, indicating far less dispersion of incomes than in the remainder of the population. Table 2.16 showed ratios ranging between 2.84 and 7.25 for groups in the non-retired population.

The ratios of the 90th to 10th percentile incomes for couples tend to be higher than those for single men which in turn tend to be higher than those for single women. This pattern again suggests the greater receipt of private incomes among couples and among single males. Within each group, examination of the ratios across the age-groups reveals no systematic pattern that can be used to arrive at conclusions about the degree of income dispersion among successive cohorts of the retired. Rather, the notably high ratios for some groups and low ratios for others appear to have more to do with the definition of retirement adopted for this exercise. Thus the high ratios of groups such as 65- to 69-year-old men and 60- to 64-year-old women would be attributable to these groups including small but significant numbers of employed people. They are counted as retired because they are over the age pension ages. On the other hand we return to the point that any employed men are explicitly excluded from the 60–64 age-group of single men, which exhibits a very low ratio of the 90th to 10th percentile incomes. Besides this qualification the percentile measures for single men in the older age-groups need to be treated with some caution due to small sample sizes.

2.7.4 Composition of Incomes

The importance of different income sources for the retired population is shown in Table 2.20, which distinguishes between five types of income: government transfers, primarily the age pension; private pensions; investment income; earnings; and other income. In 1995–96 transfer incomes accounted for about 50 per cent of the incomes of retired couples, just over 55 per cent of the incomes of retired single men (and we should discount the peculiarities of the 60–64 age-group) but for almost 70 per cent of the incomes of retired single women. These figures confirm the earlier indications of the greater importance of private incomes for retired couples and single men than for single women.

Among the private income sources distinguished in Table 2.20, investment income is the major source, followed by private pensions and then earnings. As would be expected the contribution of earnings generally declined with age, while it is difficult to see any age-related pattern in the contributions from private pensions and investment income. Overall, investment income amounted to income shares of 21 per cent for couples, 17 per cent for single men and 15 per cent for single women. The lesser role of private income sources for single women is even more marked in the case of private pensions, which had income shares of 15 per cent for couples, 16 per cent for single men and just 9 per cent for single women. This reflects the patterns of labour force participation and superannuation coverage over the post-war years, when men had higher employment rates and higher superannuation coverage.

With a flat-rate means-tested pension system one would expect government transfers to constitute a declining proportion of total income as total income increased. This was the case in 1995–96, as is shown by Figure 2.7, where the incomes of the retired population have been equivalised and the population divided into quintiles of total equivalent after-tax income. The reducing share of government transfers is at least the case across the 2nd to 5th quintiles, with the 1st quintile posing a problem for interpretation. This quintile would have contained many of those who had low reported pension income for reasons other than income testing, such as assets testing, the residency requirement or under-reporting.

Table 2.20   Composition (Shares) of the Gross Incomes of the Retired Population, by Age-group, 1995–96 (%)

	Age-group				
	60–64	65–69	70–74	75+	60+
Couples					
Transfers	47.3	47.6	50.8	53.4	49.9
Private pension	15.6	13.8	18.8	13.5	15.2
Investment	19.4	16.5	19.9	27.5	20.8
Earnings	14.6	21.4	10.3	5.6	13.3
Other income	3.1	0.7	0.1	0.0	0.7
Single men					
Transfers	78.8	56.5	51.2	53.9	57.4
Private pension	15.0	8.8	16.1	21.0	16.3
Investment	6.2	18.8	13.7	21.6	17.4
Earnings	0.0	15.8	19.0	3.5	8.9
Other income	0.0	0.0	0.0	0.0	0.0
Single women					
Transfers	49.9	62.4	64.7	79.0	68.1
Private pension	11.9	7.6	6.2	9.7	8.9
Investment	9.2	17.2	27.9	10.6	15.1
Earnings	26.6	12.3	0.6	0.0	6.9
Other income	2.4	0.4	0.6	0.7	0.9

Source: ABS 1995–96 Survey of Income and Housing Costs, unit record file.

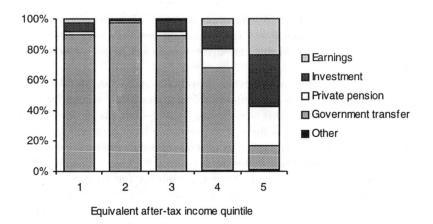

Source: ABS 1995–96 Survey of Income and Housing Costs, unit record file.

Figure 2.7   Composition (Shares) of the Equivalent After-tax Incomes of the Retired Population, by Income Quintile, 1995–96

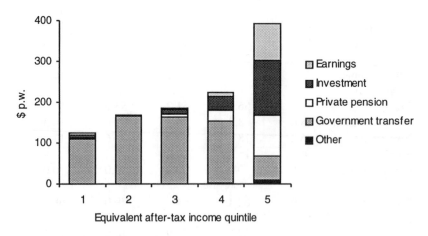

Source: ABS 1995–96 Survey of Income and Housing Costs, unit record file.

Figure 2.8   Composition (Absolutes) of the Equivalent After-tax Incomes of the Retired Population, by Income Quintile, 1995–96

Another perspective on the contributions of different income sources to retirement incomes across the income distribution is obtained by looking at absolute amounts rather than shares. This is done in Figure 2.8, where the concentration of private incomes in the top quintile is very marked. The 5th quintile also stands out as having considerably higher income than the other four quintiles. The average equivalent after-tax income of the top quintile was close to $400 a week, while the incomes of the other four quintiles ranged from about $125 a week to $225 a week. The effect of the flat-rate means-tested age pension is evident in the very similar levels of government transfer income received by the 2nd to 4th quintiles. The distribution of private incomes added the variation to the overall income distribution among the retired population, with these private incomes highly concentrated in the top quintile of the retired population. Correspondingly, means testing resulted in the top quintile receiving considerably lower government transfers.

2.7.5 Retired in the Overall Income Distribution

Finally we look at the position of the retired population in the overall income distribution. This is done in Figure 2.9, which shows the distribution of the retired population across the population-wide distribution of equivalent after-tax income. The figure separately shows the distributions for couples, single men, single women and all retired people. If one of these groups had an income distribution matching that of the whole population, then 10 per cent of

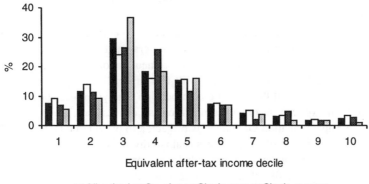

Source: ABS 1995–96 Survey of Income and Housing Costs, unit record file.

Figure 2.9 Percentage of the Retired Population in Each Decile of Equivalent After-tax Income, 1995–96

the members of the group would be found in each decile. This is clearly not the case, with the retired highly concentrated in the 3rd to 5th deciles and having a particularly low representation among the upper deciles. This concentration is evident for all three groups of the retired, though couples are slightly more spread across the income distribution than are single people.

2.8   SUMMARY

The Australian retirement income system is in a state of transition – away from heavy dependence on the flat-rate means-tested age pension and toward a greater reliance on privately provided retirement income through super-annuation. It could be argued that this transition has been under way for a number of years with the gradual growth in superannuation coverage over the post-war years, though it has been greatly accelerated by policy initiatives since the mid-1980s. These culminated in the Superannuation Guarantee, which since 1992 has compelled employers to make superannuation contribu-tions for their employees. The level of required contributions is rising to 9 per cent by 2002–03.

Australia is often identified in international comparative studies as having an unusually heavy reliance on the social assistance model of government transfers. The developments in retirement incomes policy can be seen as a move toward reducing this reliance and increasing the role of social insurance. This social insurance element in the Australian case however is essentially private, though government-regulated and partly mandated by government.

The stick of the Superannuation Guarantee, combined with the carrot of substantial tax concessions, has placed superannuation assets on a rapid growth path. The major impacts on retirement incomes will not be seen however for 20 or 30 years and nor will the impacts on budget outlays. Not until around 2025 will the reductions in pension outlays exceed the offsetting increases in expenditure on superannuation tax concessions. Over the longer term the Superannuation Guarantee is projected to provide budgetary savings of around 1 per cent of GDP. The sustainability of the system is also set to benefit from a shift away from unfunded schemes.

The distribution of incomes among retired Australians is notably flat, reflecting the high degree of dependence on the flat-rate age pension. As the benefits from wider and deeper superannuation coverage start to flow through, a general increase in the incomes of the retired can be expected. This is however likely to be accompanied by increasing dispersion among their incomes in line with the variations in contribution histories. This has led to concerns about the relative position in the future retired population of people with interrupted or 'non-standard' labour force careers, with a particular focus on women. Another continuing concern with the reformed retirement income system lies in the interaction between the age pension and superannuation. The gap between the preservation age for superannuation and the qualifying age for the age pension, and the prevalence of superannuation benefits being paid as lump sums, are seen to risk a dilution of the intended benefits of the reforms.

NOTES

1. The original paper was prepared in March 1998, and rates of payment and other provisions reported in the chapter refer to that period.
2. i.e. thousand million. Throughout this chapter, $ refers to Australian dollars.
3. While women's qualifying age for age pension rose to 60½ years in July 1995, the survey data do not allow us to exactly match that cut-off.
4. The income measures used here include the income of any dependent children, though this is negligible – accounting for just 0.2 per cent of the total income of the retired population income units.

REFERENCES

Attorney General's Department (1998), *Superannuation and Family Law: A Position Paper*, Canberra: Attorney General's Department.

ABS (1985), *Employment Benefits: Australia, August 1984*, Cat. no. 6334.0, Canberra: Australian Bureau of Statistics.

ABS (1995a), *Employment Benefits: Australia, August 1994*, Cat. no. 6334.0.40.00, Canberra: Australian Bureau of Statistics.

ABS (1995b), *Retirement and Retirement Intentions: Australia, November 1994*, Cat. no. 6238.0.40.001, Canberra: Australian Bureau of Statistics.

ABS (1996a), *1993–94 Household Expenditure Survey, Australia: The Effects of Government Benefits and Taxes on Household Income*, Cat. no. 6537.0, Canberra: Australian Bureau of Statistics.

ABS (1996b), *Superannuation: Australia, November 1995*, Cat. no. 6319.0, Canberra: Australian Bureau of Statistics.

ABS (1997a), *Average Weekly Earnings: States and Australia, August 1997*, Cat. no. 6302.0, Canberra: Australian Bureau of Statistics.

ABS (1997b), *1995–96 Survey of Income and Housing Costs, Australia: Confidentialised Unit Record File (CURF) Technical Paper*, Cat. no. 6541.0.15.001, Canberra: Australian Bureau of Statistics.

ABS (1997c), *Labour Force: Australia, November 1997*, Cat. no. 6203.0, Canberra: Australian Bureau of Statistics.

Bacon, B. and P. Gallagher (1996), 'Early retirees: trends and their use of superannuation benefits and social security payments', in Department of Social Security, *Early Retirement Seminar*, Canberra: Australian Government Publishing Service, pp. 41–84.

Bækgaard, H. (1998), 'The distribution of household wealth in Australia: 1986 and 1993', University of Canberra, National Centre for Social and Economic Modelling, Discussion Paper no. 34.

Bateman, H. and J. Piggott (1997), *Private Pensions in OECD Countries: Australia*, Labour Market and Social Policy Occasional Paper no. 23, Paris: Organisation for Economic Co-operation and Development.

Centrelink (1998), *DSS Customers: A Statistical Overview 1997*, Canberra: Centrelink.

Clare, R. and A. Tulpule (1994), *Australia's Ageing Society*, Background Paper no. 37, Canberra: Economic Planning Advisory Council, Australian Government Publishing Service.

Commission of Inquiry into Poverty (1975), *Poverty in Australia: First Main Report*, Canberra: Australian Government Publishing Service.

Costello, the Hon. P. and the Hon. J. Newman (1997), *Savings: Choice and Incentive, Statement by the Honourable Peter Costello MP, Treasurer of the Commonwealth of Australia, and Senator the Honourable Jocelyn Newman, Minister for Social Security, 13 May*, Canberra: Australian Government Publishing Service.

Department of Social Security (1997), *Annual Report 1996–1997*, Canberra: Australian Government Publishing Service.

Department of the Treasury (1997), *Tax Expenditures Statement: 1996–97*, Canberra: Australian Government Publishing Service.

Economic Planning Advisory Council (1994), *Women and Superannuation*, EPAC Background Paper no. 41, Canberra: Australian Government Publishing Service.

Econtech (1996), *Building Superannuation without Demolishing Home Ownership*, Canberra: Real Estate Institute of Australia.

Fitzgerald, V. (1993), *National Saving: A Report to the Treasurer*, Canberra: Australian Government Publishing Service.

Foster, C. (1988), *Towards a National Retirement Incomes Policy*, Social Security Review Issues Paper no. 6, Canberra: Department of Social Security.

Gallagher, P., G. Rothman and C. Brown (1993), 'Saving for retirement: the benefits of superannuation for individuals and the nation', in P. Saunders and S. Shaver (eds), *Theory and Practice in Australian Social Policy: Rethinking the Fundamentals*, Reports and Proceedings no. 112, Sydney: Social Policy Research Centre, University of New South Wales, pp. 171–202.

Gunasekera, M. and J. Powlay (1987), 'Occupational superannuation arrangements in Australia', Department of Social Security, Social Security Review Background/Discussion Paper no. 21.

Henderson, H., A. Harcourt and R. Harper (1970), *People in Poverty: A Melbourne Survey*, Melbourne: Cheshire.

Howe, the Hon. B. (1989), *Better Incomes: Retirement Income Policy into the Next Century, Statement by the Minister for Social Security*, Canberra: Australian Government Publishing Service.

Insurance and Superannuation Commission (1997), *Bulletin, September 1997*, Canberra: ISC.

Jackson, L. and S. Bozic (1997), 'The Australian social security model: revisiting the international debate', *Social Security Journal*, September, 32–55.

Kewley, T. (1980), *Australian Social Security Today: Major Developments from 1900 to 1978*, Sydney: Sydney University Press.

King, A., H. Bækgaard and A. Harding (1999), 'Australian retirement incomes', University of Canberra, National Centre for Social and Economic Modelling, Discussion Paper no. 43.

Knox, D. (1996), 'Contemporary issues in the on-going reform of the Australian retirement income system', *Australian Economic Review*, 2ⁿᵈ quarter, 199–210.

Landt, J., R. Percival, D. Schofield and D. Wilson (1995), 'Income inequality in Australia: the impact of non-cash subsidies for health and housing', University of Canberra, National Centre for Social and Economic Modelling, Discussion Paper no. 5.

Mitchell, D. (1996), 'The costs of ageing: an assessment of the Audit Commission's proposals', paper presented to the seminar 'Beyond the 1996 Budget: Audit Commission and Productivity Commission Blueprints for the Public Sector', Public Sector Research Centre, University of New South Wales, Sydney, 24 September.

Mitchell, D., A. Harding and F. Gruen (1994), 'Targeting welfare', *Economic Record*, **70** (210), 315–40.

National Commission of Audit (1996), *Report to the Commonwealth Government*, Canberra: Australian Government Publishing Service.

National Superannuation Committee of Inquiry (1976), *Occupational Superannuation in Australia: Final Report of the National Superannuation Committee of Inquiry*, Canberra: Australian Government Publishing Service.

Productivity Commission and Melbourne Institute of Applied Economic and Social Research (1999), *Policy Implications of the Ageing of Australia's Population*, Conference Proceedings, Canberra: Ausinfo.

Rothman, G. (1997), 'Aggregate analyses of policies for accessing superannuation accumulations', paper presented to the Fifth Colloquium of Superannuation Researchers, University of Melbourne, 11–12 July.

Unikowski, I. (1989), 'Veterans of labour, veterans of war: Commonwealth payments to the aged, 1909–1987', Department of Social Security, Social Security Review Background/Discussion Paper no. 28.

3. Pension Provision in Canada

Michael Hoffman and Bev Dahlby

3.1 INTRODUCTION

The Canadian retirement income system is often described as consisting of three 'pillars' – the Old Age Security Program, the Canada and Quebec Pension Plans, and Registered Pension Plans and Registered Retirement Savings Plans. The Old Age Security (OAS) Program is a federal programme which is financed out of general revenues and provides a basic flat-rate pension (or demogrant) as well as means-tested benefits for those of at least age 65. The second pillar is the Canada Pension Plan (CPP) and Quebec Pension Plan (QPP) which are compulsory, earnings-related pension schemes which also provide other benefits, such as disability payments. They are financed by a special payroll tax levied on employers, employees and the self-employed. The third pillar consists of Registered Pension Plans (RPPs) and Registered Retirement Savings Plans (RRSPs) which provide advantageous tax treatment to occupational pensions and private retirement savings compared with other forms of savings. In 1996 the OAS and C/QPP programmes each provided \$22 billion[1] in pension benefits, while the RPP/RRSP programmes generated about \$32 billion, or roughly 42 per cent of the total retirement income.[2]

Expenditures on OAS and C/QPP public pensions are about 5.4 per cent of GDP, but they are projected to increase substantially after 2010 when the first wave of the 'baby-boom' generation begins to retire. An opinion poll conducted in October 1994 indicated that less than 30 per cent of respondents under the age of 49 were confident that they would receive OAS and C/QPP benefits. These public concerns about the long-term viability of the public pension system have prompted a number of recent reforms to the Canadian retirement income system. In February 1997 the federal and provincial governments reached an agreement on the reform of the C/QPP which will reduce future benefits and substantially raise contribution rates to ensure the long-run financial viability of these programmes. In this chapter we describe the nature of the Canadian retirement income system and the recent reforms.[3] We also provide statistics on the benefit levels, labour force activity rates and the income distribution among the retired to facilitate comparisons with other countries in this study.

3.2 PUBLIC PENSIONS IN CANADA

Under the terms of the British North America Act of 1867, the provincial governments have exclusive jurisdiction over education, healthcare and social welfare programmes (including public pensions). However the federal government was given the general powers to promote 'peace, order and good government'. This power, along with its superior taxing power, has enabled the federal government to offer conditional grants to the provincial governments to fund federally designed programmes in the areas that are normally under exclusive provincial jurisdiction. Thus the responsibility for public pensions has evolved from one in which the provincial governments had exclusive control to one of joint federal–provincial responsibility with the federal government having the dominant role.

A summary description of the main components of the public pension system – Old Age Security (a federal programme) and the Canada/Quebec Pension Plans (a joint federal–provincial programme) – is shown in Table 3.1. Other income support programmes and benefits for seniors, which are mainly provided by the provincial governments, are described at the end of this section.

3.2.1 Old Age Security

The federal government first became involved in the provision of public pensions with the Old Age Pension Act of 1927 in which it agreed to pay half (and in 1931 three-quarters) of the cost of means-tested pensions administered by the provinces. Dissatisfaction with the means tests and the financial burden placed on the provinces resulted in the Old Age Security Act, whereby the federal government introduced a universal pension of $40 per month to all Canadians over the age of 70 in 1952. Figure 3.1 shows the maximum OAS pension (in 1995 dollars) from 1952 to 1999. Real benefits were increased during the 1950s (usually around election time) to 1967. They tended to decline during the 1960s because benefits were only partially indexed to inflation. Payments were fully indexed to the consumer price index (CPI) in 1973 and real benefit levels have been relatively constant since that time. The

Table 3.1 Public Pensions in Canada

Benefit	Cost (% of GDP)	% of pensioners in receipt[a]		Criteria
C/QPP (*contributory*)				
Retirement	1.82	60–64	46-M 43-F	25% of average yearly maximum pensionable earnings (YMPE) over five previous years times the average ratio of pensionable earnings to YMPE over 85% of the individual's working life.[b]
		65–69	95-M 69-F	
		70+	91-M 51-F	
Survivor	0.41	55+	3-M 18-F	Surviving spouse gets flat rate plus 37.5% of retirement pension of deceased before age 65; increases to 60% at age 65.
Orphan	0.03	—		Flat-rate benefit to orphan of pensioner.[c]
Disability	0.37	55–64	7-M 5-F	Flat rate plus 75% of pension that individual would have been entitled to at age 65.
Child disability	0.03	—		Flat rate per child paid to individual on disability pension.
Death	0.04	—		One-time payment at death to the estate of the deceased.
Total C/QPP	*2.70*			

Table 3.1 continued

OAS (non-contributory)[d]				
OAS pension	2.06	65+	96-M 97-F	Flat-rate benefit at age 65; partial pension to those who have lived in Canada for less than 40 years after the age of 18. Clawback when income exceeds $53 215. Taxable; indexed quarterly to the consumer price index (CPI).
Guaranteed Income Supplement	0.61	65+	32-M 43-F	Flat-rate, means-tested; benefits reduced by $0.50 for each dollar of non-OAS pension income. Non-taxable; indexed quarterly to the CPI.
Spouse's Allowance	0.06	65+	2-M 16-F	Flat-rate, means-tested benefit to spouse of OAS pensioner or to a widow or widower. Benefit reduced by $0.75 for every dollar of non-OAS pension income. Non-taxable; indexed quarterly to the CPI.
Total OAS	2.73			
Total C/QPP & OAS	5.43			

Notes:
[a] Age-range followed by male percentage (M) and female percentage (F).
[b] The individual can eliminate 15 per cent of the years with the lowest earnings and years in which the individual was providing care for children under the age of seven. Individuals can receive the pension starting at age 60 or as late as age 70, with the annual pension being permanently reduced by 6 per cent for each year before 65 that the pension is started and increased by 6 per cent for each year after 65 that the pension is started.
[c] Surviving spouse must be between 45 and 65 with no children or under 45 with dependent children.
[d] 1994 figures for cost and 1993 for age distribution.

Source: Human Resources Development Canada, January–December 1996. Details of the criteria for CPP and OAS benefits can be found at the following website: http://www.hrdc-drhc.gc.ca/isp/common/home.shtml.

95

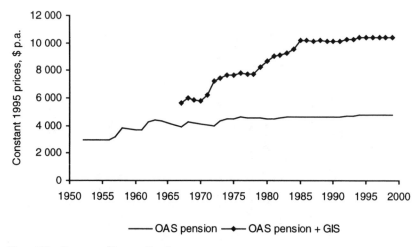

Note: GIS = Guaranteed Income Supplement.

Source: Human Resources Development Canada, various years.

Figure 3.1   Maximum Annual OAS Pension and GIS

age of eligibility was gradually reduced to 65 in 1970. Income from an OAS
pension is taxable under the federal and provincial personal income taxes, and
there is an additional 15 per cent tax or 'benefit clawback' on those with
individual incomes (not family income) in excess of $53 215. The full
pension, which is provided to those who have lived in Canada for at least 40
years after the age of 18, was $420.34 per month in April 2000, and it is
indexed quarterly to the CPI.

The introduction of the OAS clawback in 1989, which shifted the OAS
from a universal to a targeted benefit, was in many ways more symbolic than
real. For example a single senior with $60 000 of income would have his or
her OAS pension reduced by $1 018 but would still receive a net OAS
pension of over $3 700 per year. A couple where each received $50 000 of
income would still be entitled to the full OAS pension. In 1993 the benefit
clawback represented only 3 per cent of total benefits (Statistics Canada,
1996a, p. 110). In the view of many, the 1989 clawback of OAS pensions did
not go far enough in targeting the pension to low-income seniors. In its 1996
Budget the federal government announced that the OAS programme would be
replaced by a new, substantially reformed, Seniors Benefit Program which
would enhance the degree to which the benefits would be targeted to low-
income seniors. However opposition to the proposed changes resulted in the
Seniors Benefit being scrapped.

The second major component of the OAS programme is Guaranteed Income Supplement (GIS) which was introduced in 1967. This is a non-taxable, income-related benefit for OAS recipients. Single individuals with no income other than the OAS pension received $499.55 and a married couple each received $335.71 a month in April 2000. Benefits are indexed to the CPI each quarter and are reduced by 50 cents for each dollar of income, excluding the OAS pension, that the individual or couple receives. Thus the combination of OAS and GIS ensures that a single senior had a minimum monthly income of $919.89 in April 2000, and the GIS benefit is reduced to zero when non-OAS income equals $999.10 per month. Figure 3.1 shows the OAS plus GIS benefit for a single individual since 1967. As a percentage of full-time, full-year male and female earnings, the maximum combined OAS and GIS payment has changed from 18.2 per cent for males and 31.2 per cent for females in 1967 to 25.6 per cent and 35 per cent for males and females respectively in 1995 (see Figure 3.2 for the period 1971–95).

The third component of the OAS programme is Spouse's Allowance (SPA). This programme, which was introduced in 1975, is an income-tested benefit which is paid to the spouse, or to a widow or widower, of an OAS pension recipient. The spouse must be 60–64 years of age and have lived in Canada for at least 10 years after the age of 18. The maximum payment was $745.73 in April 2000, and the benefit is reduced by 75 cents for each dollar

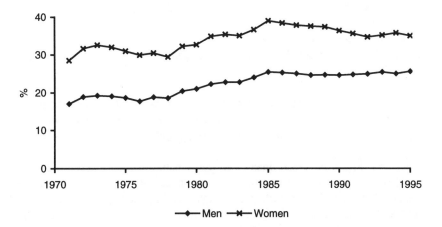

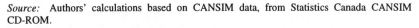

Source: Authors' calculations based on CANSIM data, from Statistics Canada CANSIM CD-ROM.

Figure 3.2 Maximum OAS and GIS as a Percentage of Full-time Average Earnings

of non-OAS income received by the recipient or the couple. Benefits are not taxable and are indexed to the CPI. In 1998 3.7 million individuals received OAS, 1.4 million received GIS and 98 800 received SPA. Of the approximately $22 billion in payments, OAS pensions accounted for almost 77 per cent, GIS was about 21 per cent and SPA was about 2 per cent.

3.2.2   The Canada and Quebec Pension Plans

The Canada Pension Plan (CPP) and Quebec Pension Plan (QPP) are compulsory, earnings-related, public pension schemes established in 1966. The residents of the province of Quebec contribute to the QPP which provides benefits that are similar to those of the CPP. Contributions are completely portable when an individual moves to or from Quebec and the rest of Canada. The federal government administers the CPP and the government of the province of Quebec administers the QPP. However the approval of the federal government and two-thirds of the provincial governments containing at least two-thirds of the population are required for substantive policy changes to the CPP. This effectively gives the government of Ontario, Canada's largest province, a veto over changes to the CPP.

About 90 per cent of the labour force contribute to the plans and about 15 per cent of the population receive C/QPP benefits, which consist of four major programmes – retirement benefits, survivor benefits, disability benefits and death benefits.

Retirement benefits
A contributor is entitled at age 65 to a pension which is based on the following formula:

$$CPP\ pension = 0.25 \times (Average\ YMPE\ over\ the\ previous\ five\ years)$$
$$\times (Average\ ratio\ of\ pensionable\ earnings\ to\ YMPE\ over\ 85\%\ of\ the$$
$$individual's\ working\ life),$$

where YMPE is the yearly maximum pensionable earnings. Since the mid-1980s the YMPE has equalled the average industrial wage. The ratio is set equal to one if a contributor's pensionable earnings in any year exceed the YMPE. A person's working life is defined as the years between the contributor's 18th birthday (or 1 January 1966 if later) and his or her 65th birthday. In computing the average ratio of pensionable earnings to YMPE, an individual may eliminate from the calculation up to 15 per cent of years with the lowest earnings and years in which the individual was providing care for children under the age of seven. An individual who turned 65 in 1999 and who earned the YMPE or higher over his or her entire working life would be entitled to receive 25 per cent of the average YMPE in 1995 through 1999, or $751.67 per month. Subsequent payments are indexed to the CPI each quarter, and all CPP benefits are fully taxable under the federal and provincial personal income taxes.

In 1967 individuals could receive C/QPP benefits at 68. The retirement age was gradually decreased to 65 by 1970. Initially C/QPP benefits received by pensioners under 70 were subject to an earnings test. The earnings test was completely removed from the CPP in 1975, while the QPP earnings test was removed in two stages starting in 1973 and ending in 1977.[4]

Further modifications to the retirement age now allow individuals to elect to receive their pension as early as age 60 or as late as age 70. The annual pension is permanently reduced by 0.5 per cent for each month that it is received before age 65, and it is increased by 0.5 per cent for each month that it is postponed after age 65. The maximum reduction or increase in the CPP pension for early or late retirement is 30 per cent. The average age at which CPP pension benefits begin is 62½. For the fiscal year 1998–99 CPP retirement benefits amounted to $12.4 billion and represented over two-thirds of total CPP expenditures.

Survivor benefits

A pension is paid to the surviving spouse of a CPP contributor if the deceased has been a contributor for some minimum length of time. If the surviving spouse is over 65, the pension is 60 per cent of the deceased contributor's retirement pension. If the surviving spouse is already collecting a C/QPP pension, then there is a ceiling on the maximum pension. The surviving spouse of a deceased contributor who is between the ages of 45 and 65, or under 45 with dependent children, is entitled to a pension that is a fixed rate plus 37.5 per cent of the CPP retirement pension that the deceased would have received. Surviving spouses under 35 who are not disabled or raising a dependent child are not eligible for benefits. An orphan benefit is also paid to the children of a deceased CPP contributor if the child is less than 18 years old or between 18 and 25 and attending an educational institution full-time. In 1998–99 total survivor benefits amounted to $2.77 billion, or 15.2 per cent of total CPP expenditures.

Disability benefits

Individuals who are unable to work because of physical or mental disability are entitled to disability benefits until the age of 65, at which point they receive retirement benefits. The disability benefit is a flat rate plus 75 per cent of the CPP retirement pension that the individual would have been entitled to if he or she had been over 65 at the time of disablement. Additional benefits are also paid if the disabled individual has children under the age of 18 or between 18 and 25 and attending an educational establishment full-time. In 1998–99 disability benefits were $2.82 billion, or 15.5 per cent of total CPP expenditures.

Disability benefits have been one of the fastest-growing components of CPP expenditure. Between 1989 and 1994 the incidence of new disability cases increased from 4.28 to 6.34 per thousand for males and from 2.99 to 5.79 per thousand for females. Part of the reason for the increase in the number of claims is that the administrative guidelines that were issued in 1989 allowed adjudicators determining eligibility for disability benefits to take into account the unemployment rate in the applicant's region, the availability of jobs and the person's skills. The recession of the early 1990s increased the number of applicants who could qualify on the basis of labour market conditions. In addition the Canada Pension Plan Advisory Board has noted that private insurers and the provincial governments increased their efforts to get individuals to apply for CPP disability benefits. For a provincial government, shifting the disabled from provincial social welfare and workers' compensation to the CPP is attractive because it means that the cost of supporting the disabled is borne by all Canadian workers (outside Quebec) and not just the province's own taxpayers.

Death benefits
At the death of the CPP contributor there is a one-time payment of a death benefit to the estate of the deceased. In 1998 the maximum death benefit was reduced from $3 580 to $2 500.

Contributions
A self-employed individual whose pensionable earnings are less than the YMPE makes contributions to the CPP according to the following formula:

$$CPP\ contribution = Contribution\ rate \times (Pensionable\ earnings - YBE),$$

where YBE is the year's basic exemption. Prior to 1998 the YBE was equal to 10 per cent of the YMPE (rounded to the nearest $100). In 1998 and subsequent years the YBE was frozen at $3 500. The contribution rate in 1999 was 7.0 per cent and the YMPE was $37 400. A self-employed individual whose pensionable earnings were greater than or equal to the YMPE paid the maximum contribution of 0.07 × ($37 400 − $3 500) = $2 373 in 1999. An employee pays half of the total CPP contribution and his or her employer pays the other half. The CPP contribution rate is scheduled to increase to 9.9 per cent in 2003. The financing of the C/QPP will be discussed in greater detail in Section 3.4.

3.2.3 Combined OAS and CPP Pension Benefits

The total public pension benefit that a 65-year-old single individual receives is the sum of the OAS demogrant, the means-tested GIS and the earnings-related CPP. Table 3.2 shows the magnitudes of these payments for three hypothetical single individuals retiring in January 1998 who earned one-half, one and two times the average full-time male earnings for their age cohort. It was assumed that these individuals did not have any other source of retirement income, such as an occupational pension. All three individuals received (approximately) $4 886 from the OAS pension in 1998. On the basis of their assumed lifetime earnings, the individuals with one and two times average male cohort earnings received the maximum CPP pension benefit of (approximately) $9 008 in 1998. We have estimated that average male cohort earnings would only have been less than the YMPE in two of the 32 years since 1966 and therefore, given the provision allowing the drop-out of 15 per cent of low-income years, an individual earning this amount would be entitled to a full CPP pension. Since estimated average male cohort earnings were greater than the YMPE in 30 of the 32 years since 1966, an individual earning one-half the average male cohort earnings would have earned on average 82 per cent of the YMPE. The 15 per cent drop-out provision raised this individual's CPP pension from 82 per cent to 87 per cent of the maximum, or

Table 3.2 How Annual Public Pension Income Varies with Lifetime Earnings for an Individual Retiring in 1998

	Average earnings relative to cohort average earnings for males		
	½	1	2
OAS pension	$4 886	$4 886	$4 886
GIS	$1 873	$1 302	$1 302
CPP pension	$7 866	$9 008	$9 008
GST credit (1996 figure)	$304	$304	$304
Total annual income	$14 929	$15 500	$15 500
Annual income as a percentage of:			
Gross male full-time earnings	35.2%	36.6%	36.6%
Average earnings	40.5%	42.0%	42.0%
Annual net income as a percentage of:			
Net male full-time earnings	47.8%	48.6%	48.6%
Net average earnings	54.4%	55.3%	55.3%

Source: Authors' calculations.

$7 866. The receipt of the CPP pension reduced these individuals' GIS entitlement from the maximum of $5 806 to $1 873 for the low-earnings individual and to $1 302 for the other two individuals. Each individual was also entitled to the GST credit which was paid to low-income individuals to compensate them for the effects of introducing the federal value added tax (the Goods and Services Tax). The estimated total pension income of the low-earnings individual is $14 929, or 96 per cent of the public pension income received by the individuals with average or above-average male cohort earnings. The range of public pension income for a single individual is from $10 996 (assuming no CPP but full entitlement to OAS and GIS) to $15 500, or in other words the maximum public pension for a single individual is 1.4 times the minimum pension.

The public pension income for these single individuals is about 41 per cent of average earnings. The personal income tax system contains two measures that reduce the personal income tax burden for seniors. Those who are 65 or older are able to claim a tax credit which is reduced at a rate of 15 per cent for income in excess of $25 921. For low-income seniors this effectively reduces their income taxes by about $1 000. In addition the retired do not pay unemployment insurance premiums or contribute to the C/QPP. As a result the after-tax pension incomes of the hypothetical seniors is about 55 per cent of net average earnings (computed at the 1996 federal and Alberta income tax rates).

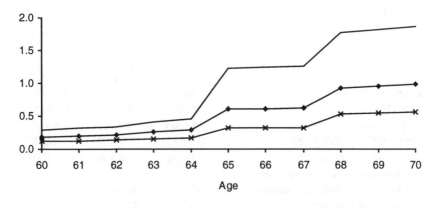

Source: Gruber, 1997, Tables 1, 4 and 5.

Figure 3.3   Pension Replacement Rates for a Married Couple

The replacement rates for married couples have recently been computed by Gruber (1997). Figure 3.3 shows Gruber's calculation of the after-tax replacement rate at various retirement ages for a male (with a wife who is three years younger and has never worked) at the median, 10th percentile and 90th percentile cohort earnings levels and with no other sources of income. For the median earner the replacement rate is about 0.18 at age 60 when he becomes eligible for early CPP benefits. The replacement rate then increases if CPP benefits are delayed, until it jumps to 0.60 when the male reaches 65 and is eligible for OAS pension and his wife is eligible for SPA. There is a further jump to 0.93 at age 68 when his wife turns 65 and also receives the OAS pension. For the 10th percentile earner the replacement rate at age 60 is 0.28 but it jumps to 1.22 at 65 and 1.76 at 68. Thus the combination of the OAS demogrant and the GIS/SPA negative means-tested benefits effectively raises the standard of living of couples with low earnings. For the 90th percentile earner the replacement rate starts at 0.11 at age 60 and reaches 0.56 if he postpones his CPP pension and retires at 70.

3.2.4 Other Benefits for Seniors

In addition to the main public pension programmes, many of the provincial governments provide benefit 'top-ups' for OAS/GIS/SPA recipients. They often provide housing rental subsidies, property tax rebates for seniors and subsidies for prescription drugs. The provincial medicare programmes (which are funded in part through a federal block grant) cover the healthcare costs of seniors as well as of the rest of the population.

3.3 PRIVATE PENSIONS

Private pension schemes in Canada consist of occupational pensions, known as Registered Pension Plans (RPPs), and Registered Retirement Savings Plans (RRSPs). The latter provide individuals who are not members of an RPP (such as the self-employed) with tax advantages on retirement savings which are similar to those extended to the RPPs, and they allow RPP members to 'top up' their retirement pensions with discretionary savings.

3.3.1 Registered Pension Plans

The first occupational pension plan in Canada was established in 1870 for federal civil servants. The 1917 Income War Tax Act allowed the deduction of employer contributions to pension plans, and in 1919 an amendment to the

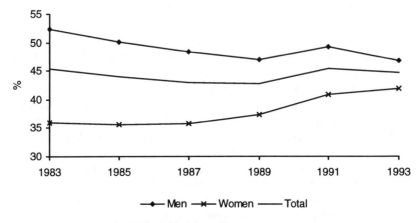

Source: Statistics Canada, 1996a, Table 2-2 (p. 47).

Figure 3.4   Percentage of Paid Workers Covered by an RPP

Act exempted employee contributions to occupational pensions. In 1936 an annual limit of $300 was imposed on the exempt contributions by employees and in 1941 the limit on the deductible employer contribution limit was set at $300. The number of occupational pension plans increased rapidly after World War II, and the combined contribution limit was periodically increased from $1 800 in 1945 to $13 500 in 1999.

In addition to the tax advantages of deductibility of employer contributions and tax exemption for employee contributions, income tax is not imposed on the investment income earned by the pension funds. Private pension income is taxed when it is paid to the pensioner, but the first $1 000 of income from an RPP or an RRSP is exempt from taxation.

Figure 3.4 shows the percentage of paid workers covered by an RPP. In 1983 52.4 per cent of male and 35.9 per cent of female paid workers were members of an RPP. By 1993 the figure for males had declined to 46.8 per cent while that for females had increased to 41.9 per cent. In total 44.6 per cent of paid workers or 35.4 per cent of the labour force were covered by occupational pensions in 1993.

Around 55 per cent of RPPs are defined contribution plans, but these tend to be small, private sector plans. Over 90 per cent of all RPP members have defined benefit plans.

There are significant differences in participation in occupational pensions between the public and private sectors. About 85 per cent of public sector workers are covered by an RPP, whereas only 31 per cent of private sector workers have an RPP (Statistics Canada, 1996a, p. 53). Public sector workers are also more likely to be covered by defined benefit pensions. Whereas 93 per cent of public sector participants receive a pension providing 2 per cent of salary for each year of service or participation, only 21 per cent of private sector participants have as generous a benefit formula as this (Statistics Canada, 1996a, p. 62).

The RPPs have to be funded according to a trust agreement, an insurance company contract or an agreement administered by the federal or provincial governments in order to ensure their solvency. In 1994 total contributions exceeded $20 billion, and over $392 billion in assets was held by trusteed funds, largely in stock and bonds, making them one of the largest sources of investment capital in Canada.

3.3.2 Registered Retirement Savings Plans

RRSPs were created in 1957 to provide all individuals with tax treatment for retirement savings that is similar to that provided to members of RPPs.[5] Initially individuals could get a tax deduction for contributions to an RRSP up to 10 per cent of their income to a maximum of $2 500. This contribution limit has periodically been increased and in 1999 it was 18 per cent of earnings to a maximum of $13 500. Since 1991 unused contribution room can be accumulated and carried forward indefinitely. The investment income earned in RRSPs is not taxed, but cash withdrawals are taxed. By age 71 the accumulated fund must be converted into an annuity or a registered retirement income fund (RRIF), and the proceeds from these are taxed (subject to the $1 000 exemption for taxpayers over 65). The RRSP contribution room for a member of an RPP is calculated as the difference between their annual RRSP contribution limit and their Pension Adjustment (PA) which is a measure of the contribution that has been made to their RPP. Thus many members of RPPs are also able to contribute to an RRSP. In 1997 $27.4 billion was contributed to RRSPs and the total value of RRSP funds invested was over $235 billion.

Over the period 1991–93 over 60 per cent of taxpayers made a contribution to an RRSP or an RPP in at least one year and 40 per cent contributed each year. However, as one might expect, those with high earnings are more likely to contribute to an RPP or RRSP than those with low earnings. Over 90 per cent of those with incomes in excess of $40 000 contributed at least once in the three-year period, whereas less than 20 per cent of those with incomes below $10 000 contributed (Statistics Canada, 1996a, Chart 7-1, p. 127). Low-income individuals have neither the means nor the incentive (given the high implicit tax rate that they face under the GIS and other means-tested programmes) to save for their retirement.

3.3.3   The Recipients of Income from RPPs and RRSPs

Table 3.3 shows the percentage of the retired with private pension income by gender and marital status in 1995. Fifty-four per cent of retired males received private pension income compared with 30.8 per cent of females. Interestingly, among single individuals who never married, a higher percentage of females received private pension income than males. Figure 3.5 shows that the percentage of pensioners with private pension income was highest for pensioners who are in their 70s.

Table 3.3   Percentage of the Retired with Private Pension Income, by Gender and Marital Status, 1995 (%)

	Male	Female	All
Single (never married)	34.2	48.9	42.1
Married or common law	56.3	25.3	42.1
Other	54.1	34.8	38.1
All	54.1	30.8	40.8

Source: Authors' calculations.

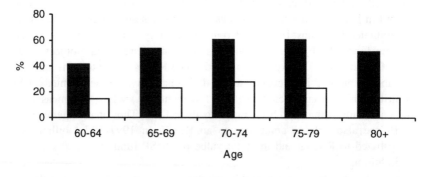

Source: Authors' calculations.

Figure 3.5   Percentage of Pensioners with Private Pension Income, 1995

3.4 SUSTAINABILITY

There is widespread concern in Canada about the sustainability of the public pension system in view of the projected increase in expenditures when the baby-boom generation starts to reach 65 in 2010. Figure 3.6 shows that the percentage of the population over 65 is projected to almost double between 1991 and 2031 when the last of the baby boomers turns 65. The ratio of the economically active population, aged 20–64, to the 65+ age-group will decrease from 5.26 in 1991 to 2.44 in 2031 (Statistics Canada, 1993, Table A3). The increase in the number of seniors, from 3.7 million in the mid-1990s to 8.8 million in 2030, implies that OAS/GIS/SPA expenditures, net of federal income tax and the clawback, will increase from \$21 billion to \$77 billion (Government of Canada, 1996, p. 34).

Whether population ageing will imply a relatively heavy tax burden on taxpayers in the 21st century depends crucially on the assumed rate of economic growth. For example Wolfson and Murphy (1996, Table 2, p. 84) have projected that OAS/GIS/SPA expenditures will increase from 5.5 per cent of aggregate wages in 1994 to 9.5 per cent in 2036 in the absence of real economic growth, but they will *decline* to 3.7 per cent of aggregate wages in 2036 if the economy achieves a 2.0 per cent annual average real growth rate over the next 40 years. When coupled with the fact that the baby-boom

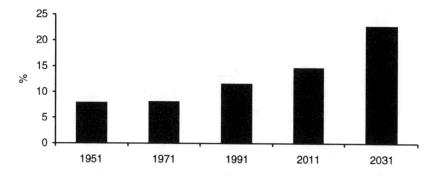

Source: Statistics Canada, 1993, Table A3.

Figure 3.6   Percentage of the Population Aged 65 or Over

generation will be paying income taxes on its RRSP withdrawals and its RPP income, and sales taxes on its consumption expenditures, the authors conclude that 'there is no particular affordability problem with current programs' (Wolfson and Murphy, 1996, p. 95).

While the affordability of OAS/GIS/SPA depends on the future rates of economic growth, it will also depend upon the expenditure burdens that will be imposed by CPP and QPP and by healthcare costs for the elderly.[6]

3.4.1   Reforms to the Canada and Quebec Pension Plans

Figure 3.7 shows past CPP contribution rates and projected future contribution rates following the 1997 reforms to the C/QPP. The figure also shows the historical and projected pay-as-you-go (PAYG) contribution rates. The PAYG contribution rates are the annual total CPP expenditures divided by the total contributory earnings base. The projected PAYG rates reflect the changes to the CPP benefits that were implemented in the 1997 reform and which will be discussed in greater detail below. From 1966 to 1986 the contribution rate was set at 3.6 per cent. Until 1983 the contribution rate exceeded the PAYG rate, and the surplus of revenue over expenditure was used to establish the CPP reserve fund which was invested in provincial government bonds.[7] After 1983 the PAYG rate exceeded the contribution rate,

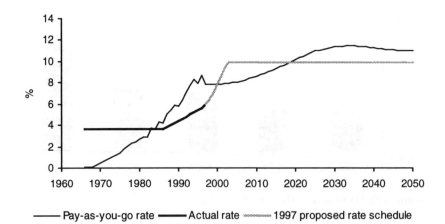

Source: Office of the Superintendent of Financial Institutions, 1997, Table 1 (p. 17) and Table 5 (p. 21).

Figure 3.7   CPP Contribution Rates: Past, Present and Future

in spite of the 0.2 percentage point increases in the contribution rate that occurred after 1986. The CPP reserve fund continued to grow until 1992 because the investment income from the fund exceeded the gap between expenditures and contributions. Since 1993 CPP expenditures have exceeded contributions plus the fund's investment income, and therefore the fund has declined. In 1997 the CPP reserve fund was equal to $40 billion, or about two years' worth of expenditures. In the Fifteenth Actuarial Report of December 1993 (Office of the Superintendent of Financial Institutions, 1995) it was projected that, even with the projected annual 0.2 percentage point increase in the contribution rate, the reserve fund would be exhausted by 2015 and the contribution rate would have to increase to at least 14.2 per cent by 2030.

In an attempt to restore public confidence in the Canada and Quebec Pension Plans and to reduce contribution rates in the 21st century, the federal government and eight of the 10 provinces agreed on a series of reforms to the Canada and Quebec Pension Plans. Table 3.4 contains a summary of the

Table 3.4   Changes to the CPP in 1997

Change	Impact
Financing and investment changes	
Acceleration of contribution rate increases	The contribution rate in 2030 is reduced from 14.2% to 9.9%
Higher rate of return to be earned on a diversified market portfolio for CPP Investment Board	Reduces the long-term contribution rate by 1.5 percentage points
Freezing the YBE	Reduces the long-term contribution rate by 1.5 percentage points
Benefit changes	
More stringent entitlement rules for disability benefits	Reduces the PAYG contribution rate by 0.44 percentage points in 2030
Pensions based on YMPE over the previous five years	Reduces the PAYG contribution rate by 0.44 percentage points in 2030
Limits on combined survivor/retirement and disability/retirement pensions	Reduces the PAYG contribution rate by 0.15 percentage points in 2030
Limits on death benefits	Reduces the PAYG contribution rate by 0.14 percentage points in 2030

Source: Office of the Superintendent of Financial Institutions, 1997.

changes to the CPP and their impacts. Changes to the financing and investment policies of the CPP are expected to account for about three-quarters of the four percentage point reduction in the previously projected contribution rate in 2030. Benefit reductions are responsible for a one percentage point reduction in the contribution rate in 2030. These reforms are described below.

Financing and investment changes
It was agreed to increase the contribution rate from 5.85 per cent to 6.0 per cent in 1997, to 6.4 per cent in 1998, 7.0 per cent in 1999, 7.8 per cent in 2000, 8.6 per cent in 2001, 9.4 per cent in 2002 and 9.9 per cent in 2003, where it is projected to remain for the rest of the 21st century.[8] The contribution rate exceeded the PAYG rate by 2000, and the ratio of the reserve fund to expenditures will increase until it peaks at 4.87 in 2021 and will remain above 4.4 until 2075 (Office of the Superintendent of Financial Institutions, 1997, Tables 1 and 2). This larger fund will be invested in a diversified portfolio of securities, including stocks, so that it can achieve a higher real rate of return (projected to be 3.8 per cent) than was previously attained by investing in provincial government bonds (2.5 per cent). Another measure that will increase contributions is the freezing of the YBE at $3 500 instead of setting it at 10 per cent of the YMPE.

Benefit changes
The rules for the provision of disability benefits are to be tightened. Eligibility for disability benefits will require a longer period of recent work attachment, the qualification rules will emphasise medical disability instead of socio-economic factors, and the conversion of a disability pension to a retirement pension will be based on the increase in prices, instead of the increase in average earnings, since the time of disability. Another important benefit change is that the retirement pension will be based on the average YMPE over the last five years instead of the last three. If the YMPE increases by 4.5 per cent a year due to inflation and productivity growth (as is assumed by the Chief Actuary), then the shift from three-year averaging to five-year averaging is equivalent to cutting the benefit rate from 25 per cent to 24 per cent of the YMPE over the last three years. The other benefit changes include limits on combined survivor/retirement and disability/retirement pensions and limits on death benefits (which are to be reduced from $3 580 to $2 500 and frozen at that level). In summary the 1997 reforms relied on a rapid increase in the contribution rate over a seven-year period, combined with some benefit reductions, to keep the contribution rate after 2015 below 10 per cent.

3.5   ACTIVITY RATES

Public pensions can create an incentive for early retirement if they increase a worker's pension wealth and if an additional year's earnings result in a clawback of pension benefits. The pension wealth created by PAYG financing of the C/QPP and the clawback of benefits under the GIS programme may have induced some workers to take early retirement.[9] In 1961 85.9 per cent of men aged 55–64 and 50.4 per cent of men aged 65–69 participated in the labour force. By 1981 the participation rates for these groups were 75.1 per cent and 21.9 per cent, and by 1993 the rates were 60.9

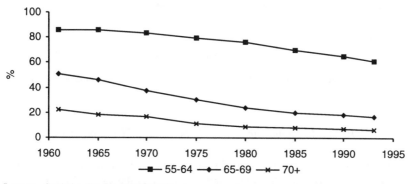

Source: Statistics Canada, CANSIM files.

Figure 3.8   Male Labour Force Participation Rates

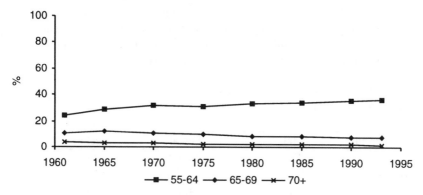

Source: Statistics Canada, CANSIM files.

Figure 3.9   Female Labour Force Participation Rates

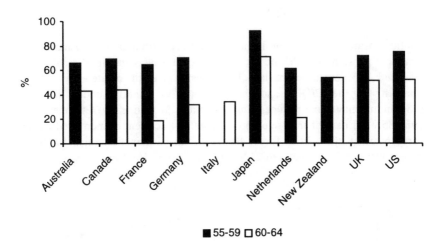

■ 55-59 □ 60-64

Note: The figure for the employment rate for males aged 55–59 is not available for Italy.

Source: Gower, 1997, p. 15.

Figure 3.10   Male Employment Rates in Selected OECD Countries, 1991

per cent and 16.6 per cent.[10] See Figures 3.8 and 3.9 for the trends in labour force participation rates for males and females over the age of 55. Figure 3.10 shows the male employment rates in Canada, Japan and the eight other countries included in this study.

While many believe that the Canadian public pension system has played an important role in the dramatic change in retirement patterns, other factors, such as rising incomes, changing life expectancies, changes in the demand for different occupations, inflation and the amount of wealth accumulated in private pensions, have undoubtedly also been important.

Table 3.5   Percentage of Economically Active Males and Females, by Age-group in 1995 (%)

Age-group	Male	Female	All
60–64	43.1	24.6	33.7
65–69	18.0	7.8	12.6
70–74	9.1	4.0	6.1
75+	4.6	0.8	2.3
All	20.0	8.9	13.9

Source: Statistics Canada, 1996c.

Table 3.5 shows the percentage of men and women over 60 who were economically active in 1995. Less than half of the males and less than a quarter of the females in the 60–64 age-group were economically active despite the fact that OAS pension benefits and full CPP benefits are only available at 65.[11] As previously noted the average age at which CPP pension benefits begin is 62½.

Table 3.6 shows the proportion of males receiving C/QPP and OAS pension benefits in various age-groups. Six per cent of males aged 55–59 receive disability benefits under the C/QPP and 2 per cent receive survivor benefits. In the 60–64 age-group 46 per cent receive the early C/QPP benefits and the percentage receiving disability benefits jumps to 12 per cent. It should be noted that individuals in the 55–64 age-group may also receive provincial social assistance payments if they have low incomes. In the 65–69 age-group about 95 per cent receive both the C/QPP and OAS pensions and 28 per cent receive GIS. In the 80+ age-group the percentage receiving C/QPP drops to 86 per cent while the percentage receiving GIS increases to 44 per cent.

Table 3.6   Proportion of Males Receiving C/QPP and OAS Benefits

Benefit	Age-group					
	55–59	60–64	65–69	70–74	75–79	80+
C/QPP benefits (1996)[a]						
No benefits[b]	0.91	0.44	0.06	0.07	0.08	0.14
Retirement	—	0.46	0.95	0.94	0.93	0.86
Disability	0.06	0.12	—	—	—	—
Survivor	0.02	0.02	0.03	0.04	0.05	0.06
OAS benefits (1993)[c]						
No benefits[d]	1.00	0.98	0.04	0.04	0.02	0.04
OAS pension	—	—	0.96	0.96	0.98	0.96
GIS	—	—	0.28	0.29	0.35	0.44
SPA	—	0.02	—	—	—	—

Notes:
[a] Sum of all components may exceed 1.00 due to the fact that some individuals receive both retirement and survivor benefits or disability and survivor benefits.
[b] Due to insufficient information on the QPP combined benefits by age and gender, the calculation for 'no benefits' is based only on the CPP, assuming the QPP proportions will be the same as the CPP proportions.
[c] Sum of all components may exceed 1.00 due to the fact that GIS recipients must also be OAS pension recipients.
[d] Calculated as 1 minus the proportion receiving OAS pension, since GIS cannot be received without receiving OAS. Nobody aged 55–59 receives benefits. Only SPA is available for 60- to 64-year-olds, so everyone else gets no benefits.

Sources: Human Resources Development Canada, January–December 1996; Régime des rentes du Québec, 1996.

3.6   INCOME DISTRIBUTIONS

The analysis of income distributions presented in this section is based on two Statistics Canada micro-data files which contain data collected by the 1996 Survey of Consumer Finances (SCF) for 1995 incomes. The first data file – 'Individuals, Aged 15 Years and Over, With and Without Income' – contains 66 908 records, representing over 23 million individuals. The second data file – 'Economic Families' – contains 34 296 records, representing over 12 million families. The SCF contains detailed information on income sources along with individual and family characteristics. Each record in these data files is weighted and these weights have been used to produce population estimates.

The SCF represents approximately 98 per cent of the population of Canada due to the exclusion of the following population groups: residents of the Yukon and Northwest Territories; residents of Indian reserves; residents of military barracks; and inmates of institutions, including homes for the aged.

Our analysis is limited to individuals who are pensioners. Since the data do not indicate who is and is not a pensioner, we adopted the following approach. We include all individuals over the age of 65 and all individuals between the ages of 60 and 64 who indicated that they were not in the labour force. When our analysis includes couples, we consider couples to be pensioners when the male satisfies our definition of pensioner. Our definition of pensioners results in the exclusion of an unknown number of individuals who are under 60 and are retired. Although this definition of pensioners is somewhat arbitrarily determined, it does include most individuals who are usually considered to be pensioners as a result of their age.

Total income is defined as income net of all income taxation. This measure of income effectively ignores housing and housing costs. Thus no consideration of an imputed rent is credited to owner-occupiers. When our analysis examines the composition of income, the pre-tax amounts are used. The use of the pre-tax amounts is necessary due to data availability and because of the difficulty of associating taxes with the particular income source from which the taxes are derived.

When the analysis compares incomes of families, we equivalise incomes for family size. We assign the following weights to each member of a family: 1.0 for the first adult in the family; 0.7 for each additional adult; and 0.5 for each child. In some tables, for comparison, we utilise an alternate weighting system of 0.5 for each additional adult and 0.3 for each child.

Our analysis looks at two marital status categories: couples and single people, with the 'single' category being split into single males and single females.

Table 3.7 Average After-tax Pensioner Income, 1995

	Age-group				
	60–64	65–69	70–74	75+	60+
Couples					
Annual ($)	28 644	33 485	34 697	32 837	32 801
Ratio 1	(0.74)	(0.86)	(0.89)	(0.85)	(0.85)
Ratio 2	(0.85)	(0.99)	(1.03)	(0.97)	(0.97)
Single males					
Annual ($)	15 672	21 843	20 267	19 565	19 575
Ratio 1	(0.79)	(1.10)	(1.02)	(0.98)	(0.99)
Ratio 2	(0.69)	(0.96)	(0.89)	(0.86)	(0.86)
Single females					
Annual ($)	13 761	18 504	16 895	16 174	16 499
Ratio 1	(0.69)	(0.93)	(0.85)	(0.81)	(0.83)
Ratio 2	(0.60)	(0.81)	(0.74)	(0.71)	(0.72)

Notes:
Ratio 1 is pensioner income as a proportion of non-pensioner income based on the original equivalence scale (1, 0.7, 0.5).
Ratio 2 is based on the revised equivalence scale (1, 0.5, 0.3).

Source: Statistics Canada, 1996b.

The average pensioner after-tax income is shown in Table 3.7 for our three marital status categories. Pensioners between 60 and 64 years of age are on average poorer than all other pensioners. One explanation of this difference is the fact that members of the 60–64 group do not qualify for OAS. Also this group can choose to receive C/QPP benefits, but their benefits are reduced by 6 per cent a year for every year before the age of 65 that they elect to receive benefits. As a result the state benefits available to the 60–64 group will be considerably less than the benefits available to pensioners aged 65 and over.

For couples and single men the average income remains relatively unchanged once they reach 65. For single women income increases by 34 per cent when they reach the 65–69 age-group but drops by 9 per cent when they reach the 70–74 age-group and again drops slightly when they reach the 75+ age-group. This may be due to younger generations having access to better occupational pension schemes.

The two proportions included in Table 3.7 represent the ratio of the average income for each age-group to the average income of all non-pensioners using the two different family weights when equivalising for family size. Using ratio 1 (based on the weights of 0.7 for other adults and 0.5 for each child) pensioners aged 60–64 earn 70 to 80 per cent of the income of all non-pensioners. The average income of single males is the closest to that of the non-pensioner group, with only single males who are 60–64 having income that is noticeably below the average income for all non-pensioners. What is remarkable is that the average income for couple pensioners aged 65 or over is between 85 and 89 per cent of the average income for all non-pensioners. For single females aged 65 or over, average income is between 81 and 93 per cent of the average non-pensioner income.

Table 3.8 describes the income distribution among different non-pensioner groups. This gives us an indication of how the equivalence scale will influence the position of pensioners relative to the rest of the population. Single parents have a mean income that is relatively close to that of all single males and females. Single people with income in the 10th percentile have incomes that are below the average state benefits received by pensioners. In the 10th percentile single parents have the highest income of all single males and females, but the majority of this income is from state benefits such as welfare support. Younger individuals also tend to have lower incomes.

Table 3.8   Annual After-tax Income Distribution of Non-pensioners, 1995 (incomes in $ p.a.)

	Mean	Median	90th percentile	10th percentile	90/10 ratio
Couples, no children, head aged <40	41 627	38 918	67 744	18 308	3.70
Couples, no children, head aged ≥40	50 915	46 655	84 219	20 470	4.11
Couples with children	49 987	46 053	79 500	23 251	3.42
Single parents	25 603	22 228	44 708	10 928	4.09
Single men aged <40	21 706	19 611	39 809	6 083	6.54
Single men aged ≥40	25 741	22 500	48 047	6 699	7.17
Single women aged <40	18 988	16 891	34 424	5 362	6.42
Single women aged ≥40	24 935	22 874	44 485	7 416	6.00

Source: Statistics Canada, 1996b.

Couples have higher incomes than single individuals. Couples with no children where the head is under 40 have average incomes that are about 20 per cent lower than those where the head is at least 40; couples with children have income comparable to that of couples with no children where the head is at least 40. The couples with children do however earn more than single parents (with the same number of children). In the 10th percentile couples have over double the income of non-couples. While equivalising for family size reduces this difference, couples still have the higher incomes.

The distribution of pensioners' after-tax incomes is shown in Table 3.9. This table indicates that pensioners aged 60–64 tend to be poorer than pensioners aged 65 or over. Again this difference can be attributed to the 60–64 group not receiving OAS and, if they choose to receive C/QPP, the benefits being at a reduced rate. While there is some variation across age-groups by marital status, there is not a clear pattern that indicates that older pensioners are notably poorer. For all three marital status categories the disparity between the 90th and 10th percentiles generally declines as pensioners age. The 90/10 ratio declines for two reasons: the income of those in the 90th percentile generally declines and the income of those in the 10th percentile generally increases, although the changes are not large.

Table 3.9   Annual After-tax Income Distribution of Pensioners, 1995 (incomes in $ p.a.)

	Age-group				
	60–64	65–69	70–74	75+	60+
Couples					
Median	26 198	29 916	28 984	27 941	28 395
90th percentile	49 678	53 223	56 190	51 243	53 022
10th percentile	10 069	19 056	19 760	20 040	18 707
90/10 ratio	4.93	2.79	2.84	2.56	2.83
Single males					
Median	12 224	15 728	16 918	15 665	15 728
90th percentile	30 262	33 390	34 891	29 540	31 016
10th percentile	6 499	10 569	12 459	11 700	10 249
90/10 ratio	4.66	3.16	2.80	2.52	3.03
Single females					
Median	11 476	14 496	14 331	14 095	14 118
90th percentile	25 407	28 840	25 806	24 178	25 667
10th percentile	6 498	10 666	11 141	11 788	10 639
90/10 ratio	3.91	2.70	2.32	2.05	2.41

Source: Statistics Canada, 1996b.

The 10th, 50th and 90th percentiles for the after-tax incomes of the rest of the population are $7 682, $16 698 and $33 506 respectively in 1995, and the 90/10 ratio is 4.36. This suggests that there is less income inequality amongst pensioners than amongst non-pensioners.

It is noteworthy that the largest disparity between the 90th and 10th percentiles for each marital status group occurs in the youngest group. This suggests a dichotomy among the early retired between those retiring with substantial occupational pensions and those leaving work to find themselves dependent on state benefits which are lower before the age of 65. This dichotomy could also be attributed to some in the 60–64 age-group being involuntarily retired and relying on disability benefits and reduced C/QPP

Table 3.10   Composition of Income of All Pensioners, 1995 (%)

	Age-group				
	60–64	65–69	70–74	75+	60+
Couples					
Total earnings	29.2	20.7	10.6	4.7	14.9
Investment income	9.4	10.5	12.6	20.1	13.6
OAS/GIS/SPA	2.8	18.5	24.0	27.2	20.0
C/QPP	13.7	18.4	19.6	18.4	18.0
RPP/RRSP	30.4	26.4	28.3	24.4	26.9
Other government	10.3	3.2	3.2	3.0	4.2
Other income	4.4	2.3	1.8	2.2	2.5
Single males					
Total earnings	30.4	17.5	5.2	2.9	10.7
Investment income	6.7	16.1	12.1	20.9	15.5
OAS/GIS/SPA	1.2	20.9	24.4	27.0	21.4
C/QPP	17.9	18.6	24.9	20.3	20.8
RPP/RRSP	19.7	22.4	28.0	22.8	23.7
Other government	22.5	3.5	4.0	3.8	6.3
Other income	1.6	1.0	1.4	2.2	1.6
Single females					
Total earnings	9.0	6.8	2.2	0.6	3.0
Investment income	7.6	16.2	12.6	17.1	15.0
OAS/GIS/SPA	5.8	28.1	35.3	38.9	32.9
C/QPP	24.8	20.2	22.0	19.9	20.9
RPP/RRSP	27.0	21.7	22.1	17.6	20.4
Other government	20.0	4.3	4.5	4.6	5.9
Other income	5.8	2.7	1.4	1.3	2.0

Source: Statistics Canada, 1996c.

benefits. The incomes of different types of pensioners vary not only by the average amount they receive, but also in the source of that income. The average proportions of income from various sources is shown in Table 3.10 for the three categories of pensioners across various age-groups. Younger pensioners have a higher proportion of their income from earnings. Pensioners in the 60–64 age-group, regardless of gender and marital status, rely heavily on 'other' government benefits (such as social assistance). Once these individuals reach 65 their reliance on 'other' government benefits significantly declines, but they still rely on the government for a major portion of their income as C/QPP and OAS benefits become available.

Couples aged 60–64 rely on the government for much less of their income, and RPP/RRSP and earnings each represent by far the largest components of their income. At 65, couples receive less earnings income, causing the earnings proportion of total income to decline. This decline is offset by a comparable increase in government benefits, particularly OAS. While they still tend to rely less on the government than non-couples, the difference between the two groups is much less for the 65+ age-groups.

For all categories private pension income (through RPPs, RRSPs or annuities) remains relatively stable. Investment income on the other hand increases once pensioners reach 75.

Not only do we see considerable variation in the sources of income for pensioners of different age-groups and marital status, but it is even more pronounced when we examine the income of all pensioners by quintile. Figure 3.11 provides a comparison of before-tax income composition by quintile.

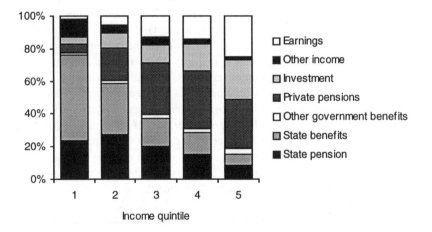

Source: Authors' calculations.

Figure 3.11   Composition of Pensioner Income, by Income Quintile, 1995

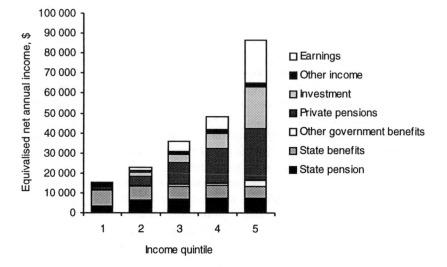

Source: Authors' calculations.

Figure 3.12   Equivalised Before-tax Pensioner Income, by Income Quintile, 1995

Income from government sources represents 19 per cent of the total income received by pensioners in the top quintile, whereas all other pensioners rely on the government for between 31 and 77 per cent of their income. Pensioners in the top quintile receive more income from earnings, investment income and private pensions, while OAS and C/QPP represent only a small portion of their income. For those in the bottom two quintiles OAS and C/QPP are the source of a majority of the income for pensioners, and those in the 3rd and 4th quintiles have less, but still a significant, reliance on OAS and C/QPP. In the 4th quintile there is a shift away from government benefits towards private pension and investment income. Private pension and investment income represents less than 10 per cent of total income for those in the 1st quintile and less than 30 per cent for those in the 2nd quintile.

Figure 3.12 shows the average before-tax income of each quintile. What stands out here is how much better off the top quintile is compared with the rest. The top quintile has an average total income that is 1.8 times that of the 4th quintile and 5.7 times that of the 1st quintile. The key components that cause this difference are private pension income, investment income and earnings. The top quintile has private pension and investment income that is 1.9 times that of the 4th quintile. This difference is even more pronounced when comparing with lower quintiles. OAS income is less for the top quintile, resulting from the lack of GIS benefits. The C/QPP benefits for the top quintile are comparable to those of the 3rd and 4th quintiles and about 14 per cent more than those of the 2nd. Much of this can be attributed to the top quintile having higher pensionable earnings, thus entitling them to larger C/QPP benefits. However, excluding the 1st quintile, there is little variation in total income received from C/QPP and OAS/GIS/SPA. This reinforces the earlier analysis in Section 3.2.

Figure 3.13 shows the proportions of pensioners in each income decile. Only 6.5 per cent of pensioners fall in the poorest decile. This is mainly because this decile tends to consist of the unemployed and lone parents whose government benefits tend to be smaller than those for pensioners, particularly when incomes are equivalised for family size. Over 20 per cent of pensioners fall in each of the next two deciles, and the 2nd, 3rd and 4th deciles contain the majority (54.2 per cent) of pensioners. Almost 80 per cent of pensioners are in the first six deciles, and only 9.1 per cent make it into the richest 20 per cent of the population.

Figure 3.13 also shows the proportions of the different types of pensioners in each income decile. Single females are much less likely to be in the top deciles. We also notice that the distribution of couples most closely follows the distribution of all pensioners. Despite the variation by each type of pensioner, the majority of each type falls between the 2nd and 6th deciles and there is less variation between types in the top deciles.

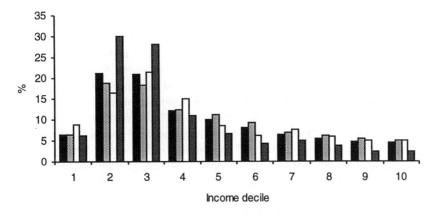

Source: Authors' calculations.

Figure 3.13 Percentage of Pensioners in Each Income Decile, 1995

Table 3.11   Couples' Income Proportions Attributed to the Male and Female of the Couple, 1995 (%)

	Age-group				
	60–64	65–69	70–74	75+	60+
Male					
Earnings	14.2	12.3	6.2	2.6	8.3
Government transfers	20.4	29.4	30.3	29.3	28.3
Other income	36.2	30.0	31.2	31.8	31.7
Total income	70.8	71.6	67.7	63.7	68.3
Female					
Earnings	15.0	8.4	4.4	2.1	6.6
Government transfers	6.3	10.7	16.4	19.3	13.9
Other income	7.9	9.3	11.5	14.9	11.2
Total income	29.2	28.4	32.3	36.3	31.7

Notes:
Figures may not sum to 100 per cent due to rounding.
Government transfers include state pensions (C/QPP), state benefits (OAS/GIS/SPA) and other government transfers such as social assistance and GST credits.
Other income includes RPP/RRSP income as well as investment income.

Source: Statistics Canada, 1996b.

When we examine the total income of couples in Table 3.11, we see that the male is the primary income earner, earning at least 63 per cent of the couple's income on average. Government transfers represent a significant portion of income for all age-groups, and the male share of these is generally double the female share. Other income is considerably higher for the males. This can be explained by the fact that more males have private pensions.

While we ignore the incomes of anyone else in the household (other than a spouse) and concentrate on the incomes of pensioners as units in their own right, income sharing within the household will be important. Table 3.12 shows that around 15 per cent of pensioners live in households containing people other than their spouse. Most commonly this means living with a relative such as a grown-up son or daughter. Interestingly the percentages of single females and couples living with others are similar, while single male pensioners between 60 and 74 are less likely to live with other people. For single females and couples the percentage living with other people declines as the pensioners age.

Table 3.13 replicates the results from Table 3.7 except that we now examine household income rather than benefit unit income. For each status and age-group, average after-tax income is higher. For the 60–64 age-group

Table 3.12   Percentage of Pensioners Living in Multiple-unit Households, 1995 (%)

	Age-group				
	60–64	65–69	70–74	75+	60+
Couples	25.1	19.1	14.1	8.6	16.4
Single males	10.0	16.0	10.9	13.9	13.0
Single females	25.2	22.8	15.7	11.3	16.1

Source: Statistics Canada, 1996b.

Table 3.13   Average After-tax Pensioner Household Income, 1995

	Age-group				
	60–64	65–69	70–74	75+	60+
Couples					
Annual ($)	34 221	37 110	36 623	35 408	36 007
Ratio 1	(0.88)	(0.96)	(0.94)	(0.91)	(0.93)
Ratio 2	(1.01)	(1.10)	(1.08)	(1.05)	(1.07)
Single males					
Annual ($)	18 411	23 947	21 741	26 574	23 477
Ratio 1	(0.93)	(1.21)	(1.09)	(1.34)	(1.18)
Ratio 2	(0.81)	(1.05)	(0.95)	(1.16)	(1.03)
Single females					
Annual ($)	19 904	22 488	20 162	18 227	19 686
Ratio 1	(1.00)	(1.13)	(1.02)	(0.92)	(0.99)
Ratio 2	(0.87)	(0.99)	(0.88)	(0.80)	(0.86)

Notes:
Ratio 1 is pensioner household income as a proportion of non-pensioner household income based on the original equivalence scale (1, 0.7, 0.5).
Ratio 2 is based on the revised equivalence scale (1, 0.5, 0.3).

Source: Statistics Canada, 1996b.

the household income is between 17.5 and 44.6 per cent higher than the benefit unit income. For other age-groups there is less disparity between the household and benefit unit incomes. For single females there is a larger difference between household and benefit unit income than there is for single males and couples, although for single male pensioners aged 75 or over there is a significant difference as household income is over 35 per cent higher than the income of the pensioner alone. The proportions of pensioner to non-

Table 3.14   Household Annual After-tax Income Distribution of Pensioners, 1995 (incomes in $ p.a.)

	Age-group				
	60–64	65–69	70–74	75+	60+
Couples					
Median	27 280	30 272	28 765	28 284	28 872
90th percentile	50 414	53 292	55 275	51 990	52 911
10th percentile	11 952	18 843	19 298	19 724	18 279
90/10 ratio	4.22	2.83	2.86	2.64	2.89
Single males					
Median	14 565	15 569	16 381	15 665	15 691
90th percentile	31 016	31 767	32 837	29 540	30 592
10th percentile	6 550	10 569	12 152	11 146	10 380
90/10 ratio	4.74	3.01	2.70	2.65	2.95
Single females					
Median	13 888	15 235	14 990	14 268	14 568
90th percentile	28 286	28 840	29 168	25 251	27 188
10th percentile	7 361	10 520	11 233	10 672	10 408
90/10 ratio	3.84	2.74	2.60	2.37	2.61

Source: Statistics Canada, 1996b.

pensioner household incomes are slightly higher than the equivalent figures in Table 3.7, suggesting that considering household income rather than benefit unit income makes somewhat more of a difference to pensioners than it does to non-pensioners.

Table 3.14 replicates Table 3.9 but for household income. For the 60–64 age-group we see that the median, 90th and 10th percentile incomes are all slightly higher, and the disparity between the 90th and 10th percentiles is slightly lower for couples and single females. The smallest change is for the single males. For the remaining age-groups there is not much change, although single females in the 70–74 and 75+ age-groups see a slightly larger disparity between the 90th and 10th percentile incomes. The results of Table 3.14 are not necessarily unexpected, given the figures in Table 3.12. Recall that the 60–64 age-group tended to have a larger percentage of pensioners living with other people and the percentages declined as age increased. This would affect household incomes in a manner consistent with Table 3.14.

Table 3.15 reflects the housing status of pensioners and non-pensioners. Over 70 per cent of couple pensioners own their homes outright, less than one-sixth rent and a comparable number have mortgages. Only one-quarter of

Table 3.15   Pensioner and Non-pensioner Benefit Units, by Housing Status, 1995 (%)

	Age-group					Non-pensioners
	60–64	65–69	70–74	75+	60+	
Couples						
Own	70.9	75.3	77.0	75.5	75.1	26.6
Mortgage	15.4	13.0	10.2	8.0	11.3	49.6
Rent	13.6	11.7	12.8	16.5	13.7	23.7
Single males						
Own	33.9	45.0	51.0	51.6	47.2	14.5
Mortgage	9.9	6.9	8.1	2.6	6.1	21.5
Rent	56.2	48.1	40.9	45.8	46.7	64.0
Single females						
Own	40.5	43.6	47.7	41.8	43.4	12.8
Mortgage	10.1	8.3	5.6	5.6	6.5	20.5
Rent	49.4	48.1	46.7	52.6	50.1	66.7

Note: Figures may not sum to 100 per cent due to rounding.

Source: Statistics Canada, 1996b.

non-pensioner couples own their homes and half have a mortgage. Close to half of the single male and female pensioners rent their homes. Of the non-renters, about five times as many own their homes as have a mortgage. Looking at single non-pensioners, an even larger percentage (two-thirds) rent and one-and-a-half times as many of the non-renters have a mortgage as own outright.

Table 3.16 reflects the housing status of pensioners by income quintile. Renting is most common at lower incomes and declines steadily as income increases. Conversely outright ownership increases steadily as income increases. The proportion of pensioners who have a mortgage is relatively unchanged as income changes.

Table 3.17 compares the housing status of pensioners and non-pensioners by income decile. We see that renting tends to decrease and outright ownership increases for pensioners as we move to higher income deciles. A similar trend occurs for non-pensioners. However renting is much more popular for non-pensioners at lower income deciles. At each income decile more non-pensioners tend to have mortgages than own their homes outright and non-pensioners are roughly half as likely as pensioners to own their homes. Pensioners at the lower deciles are much more likely to be owner-occupiers.

This suggests that if we included some measure of imputed income from owner-occupation in our income definitions, fewer pensioners would appear at the bottom of the overall income distribution.

Table 3.16   Pensioner Housing Status, by Income Quintile, 1995 (%)

Pensioner income quintile	Housing status of head of household		
	Rent	Mortgage	Own
1	41.9	8.6	49.6
2	36.4	7.8	55.8
3	23.2	10.4	66.4
4	23.0	9.5	67.5
5	20.7	7.9	71.4

Notes:
Figures may not sum to 100 per cent due to rounding.
Income quintiles are based only on pensioner incomes.

Source: Statistics Canada, 1996b.

Table 3.17   Pensioner and Non-pensioner Housing Status, by Income Decile, 1995 (%)

Income decile of overall distribution	Pensioners			Non-pensioners		
	Rent	Mortgage	Own	Rent	Mortgage	Own
1	43.8	10.8	45.4	64.5	17.3	17.3
2	41.3	7.9	50.8	48.9	25.3	25.8
3	39.6	6.9	53.5	43.2	31.5	25.3
4	30.4	9.6	60.1	38.1	39.6	22.2
5	24.9	11.4	63.8	31.9	41.7	26.4
6	21.0	9.1	69.9	27.6	46.0	26.4
7	24.8	8.1	67.1	26.1	48.8	25.1
8	20.8	11.1	68.1	20.0	52.6	27.4
9	25.2	7.3	67.5	18.2	58.3	23.5
10	16.0	8.5	75.5	15.0	54.3	30.7

Notes:
Figures may not sum to 100 per cent due to rounding.
Income deciles are based on incomes of pensioners and non-pensioners.

Source: Statistics Canada, 1996b.

Table 3.18 Net Income Levels at Each Decile, 1995*

Pensioner income decile	Pensioner couple (proportion of median)	Single pensioner (proportion of median)
1	$14 013 (0.49)	$8 454 (0.30)
2	$19 922 (0.70)	$11 311 (0.40)
3	$21 983 (0.78)	$12 309 (0.43)
4	$23 869 (0.84)	$13 164 (0.46)
5	$26 710 (0.94)	$14 073 (0.50)
6	$30 127 (1.06)	$15 018 (0.53)
7	$33 988 (1.20)	$16 348 (0.58)
8	$38 733 (1.37)	$19 217 (0.68)
9	$47 185 (1.67)	$23 709 (0.84)
10	$71 337 (2.52)	$39 324 (1.39)

Note: *Median male earnings (base for proportions) is $28 325.

Source: Statistics Canada, 1996b.

Finally Table 3.18 provides an idea of how much money is needed for pensioners to get to any point in the pensioner income distribution. Comparisons are made with median male net earnings. For a couple to get into the top decile of the pensioner income distribution they need roughly 2.5 times the average earnings; single pensioners require only 1.4 times average earnings. Single pensioners with the average earnings will be in the 9th decile whereas couples would only be in the 5th decile. At the other end of the income distribution couple pensioners are in the 1st decile if they have half of the average income while single pensioners are in the 1st decile when they have less than one-third of the average income.

3.7   CONCLUSIONS

In this chapter we have described the three pillars of Canada's retirement income system. The OAS/GIS/SPA programmes are primarily income redistribution programmes for the elderly. The C/QPP is primarily an earnings-related public pension scheme. The RPPs and RRSPs approximate expenditure tax treatment for retirement savings. The Canadian public pension programmes, which were introduced in the 1950s and 1960s, have significantly reduced the poverty rate among the elderly, but they may have had adverse effects on savings rates and retirement decisions. The massive intergenerational wealth transfers that are inherent in these programmes have called into question their long-term viability.

The problem of the financial viability of the C/QPP appears to have been resolved with the recently announced increases in the contribution rates between 1997 and 2003, but a political backlash to the higher payroll taxes (and the intergenerational transfers) may still occur. The RPPs and RRSPs are frequently criticised as unwarranted tax expenditures that mainly favour the rich (see Ragan (1996)). All in all it would be premature to say that the Canadian pension system has reached a stable economic or political equilibrium.

One problem with the Canadian version of the three-pillar approach to the public pension system is that reform of each of its components has been considered in isolation, even though the programmes are highly interrelated. For example the OAS reforms (i.e. the Seniors Benefit) that the federal government attempted to undertake were made without reference to the likely changes to the C/QPP, and the changes to the C/QPP did not take account of the discussions of the proposed reforms to OAS. Pension policy in Canada is not well served by this piecemeal approach. We hope that this chapter, by examining all three components of the pension system, will be a first step toward a more comprehensive analysis of pension reform in Canada.

NOTES

1.   i.e. thousand million.
2.   Throughout this chapter, $ refers to Canadian dollars. At the time of writing (4 October 2000), one Canadian dollar is worth US$0.6648 or £0.4558.
3.   Some sections are based on Chapter 14 of Rosen et al. (1999).
4.   Baker and Benjamin (1999) show how the removal of the earnings tests was associated with a relatively large increase in the number of weeks worked, conditional on employment, which took the form of a shift from part-year full-time employment to full-year full-time employment. They note that it appears that individuals who would have otherwise retired decided to continue with their employment once the earnings test was eliminated.

5.   The estimated tax revenue loss, or tax expenditure, from the RPP/RRSP programme for the federal government in 1992 was $13.6 billion (Ragan, 1996, Table 2). For the effect of RRSPs on savings see also Burbidge and Davies (1994).
6.   In 2001 the age and pension income tax credits will be eliminated. The SPA programme will be retained.
7.   The CPP is not a fully funded pension plan. The primary function of the reserve fund is to provide a cushion so that the contribution rate does not have to fluctuate wildly from year to year in the event of economic fluctuations. If the CPP had been designed as a funded pension plan at its inception, it would have required $600 billion in assets in 1995 to finance the projected expenditure. The difference between $600 billion and the actual value of the fund ($40 billion) is referred to as the unfunded liability of the CPP.
8.   The rate for 2000 has remained at 7.0 per cent.
9.   Up until the mid-1980s the CPP may have caused workers to delay their retirement because the phasing-in of benefits meant that postponing retirement increased a worker's pension significantly.
10.   Burbidge (1996, p. 111) and calculations by the authors.
11.   Receipt of OAS and CPP benefits after 65 is not contingent on retirement from work. CPP benefits before 65 are only available for those with low earnings in the year prior to retirement, but there is no earnings limit in subsequent years.

REFERENCES

Baker, M. and D. Benjamin (1999), 'How do retirement tests affect the labour supply of older men?', *Journal of Public Economics*, **71**, 27–51.
Burbidge, J.B. (1996), 'Public pensions in Canada', in J. Richards and W.G. Watson (eds), *When We're 65: Reforming Canada's Retirement Income System*, Toronto: C.D. Howe Institute, pp. 93–128.
Burbidge, J.B. and J.B. Davies (1994), 'Household data on savings behaviour in Canada', in J.M. Poterba (ed.), *International Comparisons of Household Saving*, Chicago: University of Chicago Press for the National Bureau of Economic Research, pp. 11–56.
Government of Canada (1996), *The Seniors Benefit: Securing the Future*, Ottawa: Department of Supply and Services.
Gower, D. (1997), 'Measuring the age of retirement', *Perspectives on Labour and Income*, **9** (2), 11–17.
Gruber, J. (1997), 'Social security and retirement in Canada', National Bureau of Economic Research, Working Paper no. 6308.
Human Resources Development Canada (various years), *Canada Pension Plan, Old Age Security: Statistical Bulletin*, various issues, Ottawa: Human Resources Development Canada.
Office of the Superintendent of Financial Institutions (1995), *Canada Pension Plan: Fifteenth Actuarial Report as at 31 December 1993*, Ottawa: Office of the Superintendent of Financial Institutions.
Office of the Superintendent of Financial Institutions (1997), *Canada Pension Plan: Sixteenth Actuarial Report*, Ottawa: Office of the Superintendent of Financial Institutions.
Ragan, C. (1996), 'A case for abolishing tax-deferred saving plans', in J. Richards and W.G. Watson (eds), *When We're 65: Reforming Canada's Retirement Income System*, Toronto: C.D. Howe Institute, pp. 57–92.
Régime des rentes du Québec (various years), *Le Régime des rentes du Québec: Statistiques*, various issues, Quebec.

Rosen, H., P. Boothe, B. Dahlby and R. Smith (1999), *Pubic Finance in Canada*, Toronto: McGraw-Hill-Ryerson.

Statistics Canada (1993), *Population Ageing and the Elderly: Current Demographic Analysis*, Catalogue 91-533E, Ottawa: Ministry of Industry, Science and Technology.

Statistics Canada (1996a), *Canada's Retirement Income Programs: A Statistical Overview*, Ottawa: Ministry of Industry.

Statistics Canada (1996b), *Survey of Consumer Finances — Economic Families, 1995 Income: 1996 Edition*, one data file (34 296 logical records) and accompanying documentation, Ottawa: Household Surveys Division.

Statistics Canada (1996c), *Survey of Consumer Finances — Individuals, Aged 15 Years and Over, With and Without Income, 1995: 1996 Edition*, one data file (66 908 logical records) and accompanying documentation, Ottawa: Household Surveys Division.

Wolfson, M. and B. Murphy (1996), 'Aging and Canada's public sector: retrospect and prospect', in K.G. Banting and R. Boadway (eds), *Reform of Retirement Income Policy: International and Canadian Perspectives*, Kingston, Ontario: School of Policy Studies, Queen's University, pp. 69–98.

4.   Pension Provision in France

Nadine Legendre and Louis-Paul Pelé[*]

4.1   INTRODUCTION

4.1.1   The Structure of the Pension System

The structure of French social security[1] is complex as a consequence of its incremental development. Most current social security institutions date back to 1945. The main basic scheme created then covered wage-earners in the private sector. It was called the 'general scheme', as its original goal was to cover the whole labour force eventually, but unification has not been achieved so far. Besides the general scheme there are 'special schemes' for workers in the public sector and schemes for the self-employed. Within the public sector, special schemes cover mainly civil servants and workers in state-owned firms. They were set up before the creation of the general scheme and are in general more generous than the main scheme, so public sector workers did not join the general scheme. Pension schemes for the self-employed cover four main groups: craftsmen, self-employed in industry and commerce, the liberal professions and farmers. Some of these schemes have provisions close to those of the general scheme, but others maintain different rules, with lower contribution rates and pensions where the return on professional capital is expected to provide the main source of income after retirement. Table 4.1 summarises the numbers of contributors and pensioners in different schemes.

Like other pension schemes in France, the general scheme is pay-as-you-go (PAYG) financed. Historically some fully funded occupational schemes existed before 1945, but they were ruined by inflation during the 1930s and World War II. The choice of a PAYG system right after the war was

[*]The authors thank Didier Blanchet, Richard Disney, Jean-Michel Hourriez, Paul Johnson and Pierre Ralle for helpful comments on this work.

Table 4.1   Structure of the Pension System in 1995: Contributors and Pensioners

	Contributors (% of labour force)	Pensioners over 65* (%)
General scheme	65.3	52.5
Wage-earners in agriculture	2.9	11.3
Civil servants (including soldiers)	11.0	5.9
Other special schemes	9.8	6.3
Farmers	3.8	14.7
Industry and commerce	2.9	4.8
Craftsmen	2.3	3.0
Liberal professions	1.9	0.9
Ministers of religion	0.1	0.6

Note: *This is the percentage of *pensions* paid to pensioners over 65, but each retiree may receive several pensions. Moreover, as described below, in most schemes retirement is possible before 65.

Source: SESI, 1997a.

motivated by that experience and by the necessity of finding immediate resources to help old people, most of whom had no means of support.

In order to provide retirement pensions beyond this level, complementary schemes were created, first for non-manual and then for all workers.[2] Being affiliated to a complementary scheme became compulsory in 1972 for all private sector wage-earners. There are numerous complementary schemes organised on an occupational basis, but these schemes are federated by two institutions: Association pour le Régime de Retraite Complémentaire (ARRCO) for manual workers' schemes and Association Générale des Institutions de Retraite des Cadres (AGIRC) for non-manual schemes. Like the general scheme, they are PAYG schemes.

Social security institutions are administered by unions and management under the supervision of the state. In practice the influence of the state has been central in the general scheme. In contrast, complementary schemes, while also administered by unions and management, constitute private legal arrangements, so that the government has no right to intervene. Although their budgets are separate from the state budget, social security and the complementary schemes are included in 'public administration' in national accounts, and their deficits enter the 'public deficit' within the criterion of the EU Stability Pact. So, although social security and complementary schemes are not financed out of the general state budget and are not state-run, their pensions are considered as public pensions.[3]

4.1.2 Number of Pensioners

Because of the multiplicity of basic schemes, each retiree may receive several pensions. For this reason the total number of pensions is known but the total number of pensioners can only be estimated. That number was estimated as 11.7 million at the beginning of 1997, of whom 600 000 obtained only survivor benefits.

In 1996 the total population of France was 58.3 million, of whom 12.3 million were children (under 16). To calculate the number of pensioners, we start with the concept of normal retirement age. This differs between schemes. It is 60 in the general scheme as well as for farmers, craftsmen and self-employed in industry and commerce. It is 65 for the liberal professions and ranges from 50 to 60 in special schemes. In special schemes retirement becomes mandatory for most people five years after the normal retirement age. In other schemes there is no mandatory retirement. However benefits are not adjusted upwards if the individual retires after normal retirement age. The main rationale for later retirement is to accumulate more years of contribution (up to a 37½ maximum) in the general scheme.

In 1996 there were around 11.7 million people over 'normal' retirement age (60). Numbers of pensioners and of people over 60 are therefore very similar. In addition there are special schemes where retirement is possible before 60. According to the 1996 Employment Survey the number of people over 55 and inactive was 12.3 million. Almost all economically inactive people over 55 are receiving a pension.

4.1.3 Pension Expenditures

In 1996 retirement pensions amounted to 11.9 per cent of GDP. Old-age means-tested benefits accounted for 0.2 per cent of GDP and other old-age benefits to 0.4 per cent of GDP. Therefore total public benefits for old people amounted to 12.5 per cent of GDP.

Spending on pensions increased rapidly in the years after the creation of social security, when schemes had not yet reached maturity. Over the 1980s and 1990s however spending on pensions continued to increase, albeit at a slower rate (see Figure 4.1). The share of pensions in total public spending also rose over the same period. During this latter period the growth stemmed largely from the increase in life expectancy and from the evolution of earnings and participation of successive cohorts of pensioners: entitlements of later pensioners are higher than those of earlier cohorts, so raising the average pension over time.

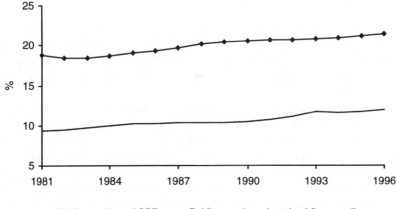

————— Public pensions / GDP —•— Public pensions / total public spending

Note: Total public spending includes spending of the state, of local administrations and of social security.

Sources: SESI, 1997b; INSEE, 1997.

Figure 4.1   Spending on Public Pensions as a Share of GDP and as a Share of Total Public Spending

4.2   PUBLIC SOURCES OF INCOME

As explained previously, retired people often obtain pensions from several schemes. In order to simplify the description the focus is on schemes for wage-earners in the private sector.

4.2.1   Pensions for Wage-earners in the Private Sector

The general scheme
The general scheme is the basic scheme for all wage-earners in the private sector. In this scheme contribution rules and pension calculations are based on the fraction of the wage below the social security ceiling (about 14 000 FF in 1998 in gross monthly amount, close to the average gross wage for a full-time job).

Until 1993 pensions were calculated according to the following formula:

Pension = Average wage (under the ceiling) over the 10 best years
× Rate of pension
× Min { 1, Number of contribution years to the general scheme / 37.5}.

Effectively the pension is a fraction of the average wage over the best years of the working life. But each part of the formula can be considered in more detail.

First, only wages below the social security ceiling are considered in the calculation. This ceiling has always been very close to the average wage, as shown in Figure 4.2. This means, given the actual distribution of wages, that for the majority of workers the relevant wage is below the social security ceiling.

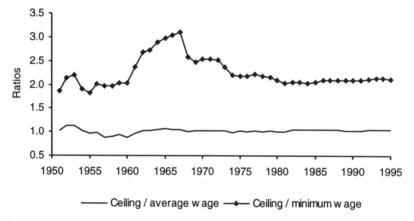

Source: Bayet and Juhlès, 1996.

Figure 4.2 Ratios of Social Security Ceiling to Average Wage and to Minimum Wage (net amounts)

To compute the appropriate average wage, past wages have to be revalued. The rules are rather complex: wages are revalued on a cumulative basis between the year the wage was earned and the year the pension is claimed. Since pensions were indexed to wages before 1987, and subsequently to price inflation, revaluation coefficients for years prior to 1987 incorporate wage growth, with price growth thereafter. Therefore, given that earnings growth generally exceeds inflation, the replacement ratio declined somewhat after 1987.

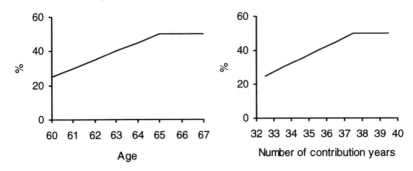

Figure 4.3   Rate of Pension as a Function of Age and as a Function of Contribution Duration

Second, the full rate of pension – 50 per cent of the appropriate revalued wage – is obtained at 65, or from age 60 if the contributor has 37½ years of contribution to all social security schemes. There is a reduction factor such that each year missing at 65 induces a five-point downward adjustment of the rate of pension. Figure 4.3 illustrates the evolution of the pension rate with age and with the number of years of contributions.

The rate of pension is computed both on the basis of age and on the basis of years of contribution, and the higher value is implemented. The possibility of obtaining a full pension with sufficient years of contribution before age 65 was introduced in 1983. In fact most workers fulfil the condition at 60, and thus retire at 60 with a full pension; that is why 60 is now regarded as the normal retirement age.

Since claiming is not possible before 60, for all workers the rate of pension is at least 25 per cent (obtained at 60), regardless of years of contribution. The adjustment for retirement before the full rate is very steep, exceeding an actuarially fair adjustment. Therefore there are strong incentives not to claim before being entitled to a full-rate pension. Indeed less than 10 per cent of pensions are claimed at a reduced rate. But for some categories (people who are disabled or unsuitable for a job) there are exemption rules which give the full rate at 60 without any condition of accumulated contributions.

The third term in the formula implies that the pension from the general scheme is proportional to the number of years (up to 37½) during which the worker paid contributions *to the general scheme*. For example if a worker contributed to the general scheme for 10 years and is entitled to the 50 per cent full rate, his or her pension from the general scheme is equal to the average wage × 50% × (10 / 37.5). If a worker has a complete career in the general scheme (more than 37½ years) and is entitled to the full rate, his or her pension is defined as the average wage × 50%. In this case the third term is equal to 1. Up to 37½ years, the pension is proportional to the affiliation duration in the general scheme.

Of course if the worker contributed to several schemes during his or her working life, he or she may receive several pensions. As suggested above, the general scheme pays a pension that is proportional to the affiliation duration but the worker may also receive pensions from other schemes, the value of which depends on the years of service in the sectoral scheme. In general, pensions in these other schemes will be calculated in a similar manner, revalued to the earnings at which the individual left the scheme. An individual may accrue more than 37½ years in total in contributions to these different schemes, but the total pension is unlikely to exceed that from a single spell in the general scheme (where 37½ years is the maximum) because each scheme's pensions are calculated according to the revalued earnings in that scheme's tenure and not according to the 10 best years in the working life as a whole.

There are different rules that credit people out of work. Basically periods during which workers receive unemployment benefits or pre-retirement benefits are included in the contribution duration, and women are credited two years per child.

As mentioned, the maximum pension from the general scheme is 50 per cent of the average wage over the 10 best years. In 1993 a reform occurred however which phased in new rules:

- The minimum contribution duration entitling people to a full-rate pension is being raised by one-quarter of a year per year, starting in 1994, for cohorts born between 1934 and 1943, so that the minimum criterion eventually reaches 40 years (see Figure 4.4). This change aims to delay retirement, with fewer people fulfilling the condition for a full pension at 60, while not explicitly withdrawing the possibility of retiring at 60 on a full pension for those with sufficient years of service.
- The average wage used to be computed over 10 years. The reform means that one more year is being included in the calculation, starting in 1994, for each new cohort born between 1934 and 1948, ultimately reaching the best 25 years.

Contributions are paid both by employers and by employees, on the wage up to the social security ceiling. Rates in 1998 are 6.55 per cent on the employee and 8.20 per cent on the employer. Employers also pay a 1.6 per cent contribution on the total wage, and in addition specific taxes[4] are levied to finance non-contributory benefits.

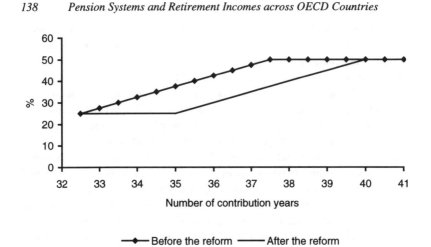

Figure 4.4   Reform of the Contribution Duration Rule

Gross pensions have been revalued in line with inflation since 1987. Between 1984 and 1986 pensions were indexed to wages net of direct social insurance contributions, and before 1984 pensions were revalued in line with the gross wage index. Since, in general, social contribution rates grew faster on wages than on pensions throughout the period, net pensions increased at a faster rate than net wages before 1984. This trend reduced the income gap between retired and active people, so that the standard of living among retired people largely caught up with that of active people. But the changes to indexation rules since 1984 are likely to reopen the gap in the future, although it is still narrowing at the moment because newly retired cohorts have greater pension entitlements than older cohorts. The appropriate method of indexation remains a hotly debated political issue.

Finally spouses of deceased pensioners can get survivor benefits if they are 55 or older, on condition that they were married for at least two years or that a child was born. The basic rule sets the survivor pension at 54 per cent of the deceased spouse's pension. But complex provisions limit the combined amount of pensions in one's own right and from survivor benefits.

Provisions in complementary schemes
In the complementary schemes the pension formula is based on contributions during the working lifetime. Each year, workers pay contributions which are converted into points according to the current 'price' of one point. When a worker claims his or her pension, the pension amount is equal to the product of the accrued total number of points and the unit value of one point, which

has been adjusted over time in line with earnings growth or price inflation. In these schemes conditions for a full pension are the same as those in the general scheme. Nevertheless the reduction in the pension in the case of early retirement is less extreme than in the general scheme and very close to an actuarially fair adjustment. Again workers may of course accumulate points in several different complementary schemes if they switch between sectors.

Contributions to complementary schemes depend on professional status. Manual workers pay contributions to their schemes on their wage up to three times the social security ceiling. Non-manual workers pay contributions below the ceiling to the manual schemes and above the ceiling to the non-manual schemes. For manual schemes the overall contribution rate (employer and employee) is 6 per cent below the social security ceiling, and it is gradually increasing to reach 16 per cent above the ceiling in 2005. For non-manual schemes the contribution rate is 16 per cent. These rates are multiplied by a coefficient (1.25) so that contributions are actually levied at 7.5 per cent instead of 6 per cent and at 20 per cent instead of 16 per cent. The 25 per cent extra contribution does not increase pension entitlements (no extra points are accrued) but is levied to ensure the financial equilibrium of the schemes.[5]

Complementary schemes are undergoing a major reform. The 'price' of one point is increasing faster than wages, so that workers accrue fewer points. The value of one point is indexed at most in line with price inflation, which affects old pensions as well as new ones. In addition survivor benefits are available in complementary schemes. They can be claimed after age 55 and their amount is 60 per cent of the deceased spouse's pension.

The total pension for wage-earners in the private sector

The total pension is therefore made up of a basic pension and one or more complementary pensions. The weights of basic and complementary pensions vary according to the wage level. Table 4.2 shows how the composition of the total pension varies for different groups of retired people in 1993. The share of complementary pensions is significantly higher for non-manual workers with more years of service (and, normally, higher earnings). Note that the category 'other complementary schemes' comprises mainly company-based schemes and that their pensions amount to less than 5 per cent of the total pension.

The importance of complementary schemes can also be assessed using simulated working lives. Consider a worker born into the 1935 cohort. Compute pensions for three male earnings histories, assuming respectively that the worker earned the median wage of his cohort and gender, half the median wage and twice the median wage. Assume also that he achieved a complete career, from age 20 to age 59, and claims his pension at 60 (in

1995), when he is entitled to a full pension. Table 4.3 shows the respective shares of the total pension paid by each scheme, the net[6] replacement rate and the ratio of pension to the average wage as both gross and net amounts.

Table 4.2   Composition of Total Pension for Different Occupations and Career Paths, 1993 (%)

Scheme	Manual	Non-manual (less than 15 years)*	Non-manual (more than 15 years)*	All
General	67.5	53.5	36.3	54.5
Manual complementary	28.4	28.3	19.7	25.0
Non-manual complementary	0.0	17.0	43.7	18.0
Other complementary	4.1	1.2	0.3	2.5

Note: *A worker can change status during his or her working life, most often from manual to non-manual. Contributions to non-manual complementary schemes are rather high, which is why the number of years worked in the non-manual scheme typically matters for the composition of the pension.

Source: SESI, 1997a.

Table 4.3   Amount and Composition of the Weekly Pension of a Private Sector Wage-earner (pensions in FF p.w.)*

	Annual earnings relative to median		
	½	1	2
General scheme pension	664.1	1 291.8	1 306.1
Manual scheme pension	282.1	535.1	537.3
Non-manual scheme pension	0.0	69.7	1 434.0
Total pension	946.2	1 896.6	3 277.4
Net replacement rate (%)	84.2	84.4	72.9
Gross pension (% of current gross male median earnings)	39.2	78.6	136.2
Net pension (% of current net male median earnings)	47.6	95.4	164.8

Note: *This table describes the situation of a pensioner with no dependent spouse. A pensioner whose wife never worked receives a 4 000 FF annual benefit in addition to his basic pension (77 FF per week). Complementary schemes grant no benefit for a dependent spouse. Thus taking into account a non-working wife would imply very small changes in weekly pensions and in ratios.

Source: Authors' calculations.

Whatever the wage level, replacement rates are very high, especially when *net* replacement rates are considered, since social contributions are lower on pensions than on wages.

In the first two situations, with the wage equal to the median wage or half the median wage of men in the 1935 cohort, the basic pension amounts to 70 per cent of the total pension. Wage profiles differ in levels but are similar in evolution: the pension is roughly proportional to the wage level and replacement rates are the same.

In the third case, at twice the median wage, the wage is higher than the social security ceiling. Assume that the worker is in the non-manual sector and pays contributions to the non-manual complementary scheme. Pensions from the general scheme and from the manual complementary scheme are similar to those with the median wage, because with those two wage profiles contributions paid to the basic scheme and to the manual complementary scheme are levied on similar bases, close to the social security ceiling. But the impact of wages above the ceiling differs across types of workers. In the third example, with a wage notably higher than the ceiling, substantial contributions are also paid to the non-manual complementary scheme, the pension of which eventually amounts to more than 40 per cent of the total pension.

4.2.2   Other Schemes

Other schemes primarily cover public sector workers and the self-employed.

Public sector workers, including civil servants, are covered by 'special schemes'. In those schemes the pension amount is defined as a fraction of the last wage, the replacement rate being the product of the number of contributed years (up to 37½) and a specific 'annuity rate' set at 2 per cent. For instance a 30-year career entitles workers to a pension equal to 60 per cent of their last wage. Some provisions credit people with additional years, for some specific occupations or for women according to the number of children. Since contributions are levied on the entire wage (except bonuses), coverage by complementary schemes is limited. Most special schemes receive subsidies from the state. Although their future evolution is preoccupying the government, no major reform has been initiated so far.

Schemes for the self-employed include basic and complementary schemes. Basic schemes were first developed, within social security, with a limited contribution base in comparison with the general scheme. Schemes for craftsmen and the self-employed in industry and commerce were aligned with the general scheme in 1972, and almost all self-employed people are now covered by complementary schemes. Provisions differ widely between complementary schemes, but many of them are undertaking reforms to keep their finances sustainable.

4.2.3   Other Benefits

There are numerous minimum benefits that are available to retired people. Minimum benefits are means-tested, and recipients must fulfil conditions that vary with the type of benefit. But there is a specific old-age minimum benefit ('minimum vieillesse'). This benefit is available to any person over 65 (60 if disabled). Specifically it takes the form of a supplementary allowance that raises annual income to an amount close to 42 000 FF for a single person and 74 000 FF for a couple (in 1997). The number of recipients has been decreasing in the last decades – it halved between 1960 and 1990 and has declined since that date. In 1990 the number was about 1 183 000, but it fell to 822 000 in 1997 – about 7.3 per cent of people aged 60 and over. As shown in Figure 4.5 the structure of the recipient population is striking: old pensioners are much more likely to receive this allowance, and proportions of recipients are higher among old women than among old men. The development of pension schemes, their increase in generosity and rising labour market activity among women account for the rapid decrease in the number of recipients among later cohorts of entrants into retirement. These figures suggest that the number of recipients will continue to fall in the future as more and more people are entitled to a pension over this minimum level, so long of course as the overall generosity of the main state pension scheme remains unchanged.

Table 4.4 describes the historical evolution of the French pension system.

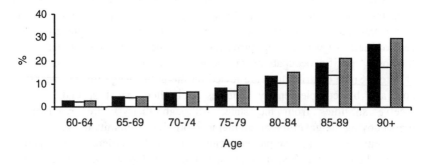

Source: SESI, 1997a.

Figure 4.5   Proportion of Age-group and Gender who Receive the Supplementary Allowance, 1996

Table 4.4   A Summary of the History of French Pensions

1945	Creation of social security general scheme. This scheme eventually covered wage-earners in the private sector. Schemes for public sector workers were created before 1945. Self-employed people created their own schemes later.
1947	Creation of AGIRC (federation of complementary non-manual schemes).
1948	Creation of self-employed schemes (craftsmen, self-employed in industry and commerce, professions).
1952	Creation of farmers' pension scheme.
1961	Creation of ARRCO (federation of complementary manual schemes).
1972	Affiliation to complementary schemes became mandatory for private sector workers.
1983	'Retirement at 60' reform (a full pension can be obtained from age 60 with a condition on the number of contribution years; most workers fulfil this condition at 60; before the reform the full pension could not be obtained before 65, unless exemptions applied).
1993	Reform in the general scheme to be phased in between 1994 and 2008 (decrease in pensions; increase in conditions for a full pension).
1993–96	Reforms in complementary schemes, decreasing replacement rates. If they are maintained until 2040, these reforms enable schemes to keep in balance. Adjustments will be renegotiated in 2005.

4.3   PRIVATE PENSION FUNDS

There are very few funded schemes in France. There are a few company plans, about which there are little data, and there are two (small) funded schemes for civil servants. Because of the extensive coverage and generous benefit levels of current social security schemes, there is not much room left for voluntary affiliation to funded schemes. In recent years supporters of greater funding have stressed the difficulties in financing PAYG social security. But the government does not seem to favour an extension of private funded pensions, which is seen as abandoning its commitment to the public pension system. Instead in 1998 the government initiated a small fraction of prefunding of the public pension schemes (around 2 billion[7] FF). However in

March 2000 the Prime Minister announced a large increase in prefunding, up to 1 000 billion FF in 2020, coming from schemes' surpluses in the next years and from taxes on capital income. Furthermore, while not encouraging the creation of new private pension funds itself, the government has become more disposed to encouraging private savings through company pension plans. However at the time of writing (September 2000) these issues are still under discussion.

4.4   SUSTAINABILITY

The French pension system is forecast to face serious financial problems in this century, due to the dramatic increase in the number of pensioners. Table 4.5 shows that the ratio of the 60+ age-group to the 20–59 age-group is expected to double between 1990 and 2040.

Table 4.5   Demographic Trends between 1990 and 2040

Age-group	1990	2000	2010	2020	2030	2040
20–59 (thousands)	30 094	31 871	32 697	32 029	31 006	30 308
60+ (thousands)	10 764	12 152	14 102	16 989	19 615	21 244
60+/20–59 (ratio)	0.36	0.38	0.43	0.53	0.63	0.70

Source: Dinh, 1994.

However concern over the future of the pension system and its financial balance is recent. Indeed as recently as 1983 retirement age was effectively lowered to 60 for most workers, indicating indifference to the demographic transition. Moreover the divided structure of the pension system makes it difficult to adopt an overall view. However in 1991 a 'White Paper' (Commissariat Général du Plan, 1991) discussed the future of the pension system. In consequence the general scheme was reformed in 1993, as described previously, and some other schemes introduced similar changes. However problems are far from being solved. In 1995 a revised 'White Paper' (Commissariat Général du Plan, 1995) was published, taking into account reforms in different schemes and concluding that further reforms had to be undertaken. In 1999 projections were updated again (Commissariat Général du Plan, 1999). Almost all public schemes were included in the new exercise, and resources and expenditures were projected until 2040. Surprising as it may be by comparison with other countries, it was the first time that demographic trends and fiscal sustainability were examined for such a long period in France. Except for limited reforms in the private sector of the general and complementary schemes, no major change had occurred as a result of the 1991 or 1995 White Papers. Consequently the 1999 projections show significant increases in the deficits in all schemes.

In the 1999 report three economic scenarios were considered, differing in their labour participation projections and long-term unemployment rates (9 per cent, 6 per cent and 3 per cent). Table 4.6 presents the main results for the general and complementary schemes in the intermediate scenario (6 per cent long-term unemployment rate). It shows that the complementary schemes have managed to curb their deficits, thanks to current reforms. These reforms

Table 4.6   Demographic and Economic Projections under Intermediate Scenario[a]

	2000	2010	2020	2030	2040
General scheme					
Demographic ratio (contributors/pensioners)	1.6	1.5	1.2	1.0	0.9
Costs (% of GDP)	3.99	4.44	5.24	6.02	6.45
Required increase in contribution rate[b]	1.3	1.8	5.0	8.3	10.2
Manual complementary scheme					
Demographic ratio (contributors/pensioners)	1.6	1.6	1.1	0.9	0.8
Costs (% of GDP)	1.64	1.66	2.01	2.19	2.13
Required increase in contribution rate[b]	(0.7 surplus)	(1.3 surplus)	0.0	0.7	0.6
Non-manual complementary scheme					
Demographic ratio (contributors/pensioners)	2.3	1.9	1.4	1.1	1.0
Costs (% of GDP)	1.02	1.16	1.29	1.29	1.24
Required increase in contribution rate[b]	1.4	0.5	3.5	3.5	2.4

Notes:
[a]Long-term unemployment rate of 6 per cent.
[b]These figures show the increase in contribution rate, from the value in 1998 (16.35 per cent), that would be required to make up future deficits.

Source: Commissariat Général du Plan, 1999.

Table 4.7   Public Pension Expenditures (% of GDP)

Long-term unemployment rate	1998	2020	2040
3%	12.1	13.5	15.1
6%	12.1	14.1	15.8
9%	12.1	15.0	16.7

Source: Commissariat Général du Plan, 1999.

have been assumed to continue until 2040, which implies that replacement rates would halve between 2000 and 2040. For the general scheme the 1993 reform is insufficient and the deficit remains important.

Since almost all public schemes are included, total pension expenditures can be assessed as a share of GDP. As Table 4.7 shows, the increase is substantial in all economic scenarios.

The main proposal in the 1999 report (Commissariat Général du Plan, 1999) was to raise retirement age. In March 2000 the Prime Minister expressed his support for the reform initiative, and further discussions should take place within schemes between unions and managers. The pension issue has however become very controversial. The projections underlying the proposals were criticised by some for many features: the assumptions on economic growth were regarded as pessimistic, an increase in contributions should be preferred to a delay of retirement age, and so on. However there is little leeway for the direction of future reforms. Employers oppose any increase in contributions, for labour costs are already high in France relative to other OECD countries. On the other hand high rates of unemployment have motivated early retirement policies in the past and it is unlikely that raising the retirement age will be politically acceptable so long as unemployment in France remains high. (In May 2000 the unemployment rate in France remained at over 10 per cent of the work-force.)

4.5   ACTIVITY RATES

In France not only are activity rates extremely low after the age of 60, which is the normal retirement age for most workers, but they are already low before 60, as some special schemes allow retirement before normal retirement age (see Table 4.8).

Early exit from activity has developed over a long period. The policy has been supported by workers, who want to stop work before 65 or 60, by governments, which consider that withdrawing old workers from the labour force can help limit unemployment, and by companies, which can thereby make cut-backs in staff without firing. Whether this choice is socially efficient is problematic, even though it has had the support of all sides of industry. The lowering of normal retirement age to 60 in 1983 did not halt the progress towards even earlier retirement, with unemployment staying at a high rate. Specific schemes were developed to provide benefits to workers becoming inactive before the normal age of retirement. These schemes are called pre-retirement schemes. The structure and the extent of these schemes have changed over time. Some were developed in specific industries, in particular the steel industry. Others cover all workers unconditionally or require an agreement between firms and the government. In addition unemployment insurance provides some specific benefits to old workers.[8] Pre-retirement schemes and unemployment insurance for old workers cover roughly half a million inactive people below 60 (see Figure 4.6).

Another facet that stresses the importance of inactivity at older ages is given by statistics from the general scheme. At the age when they first claim their pension from the general scheme, only a minority of workers are still employed (see Table 4.9).

Table 4.8   Activity Rates, by Gender and Age-group, 1995 (%)

	Age-group		
	55–59	60–64	65+
Men	68.9	16.5	1.9
Women	50.8	14.6	1.2

Source: 1996 Employment Survey.

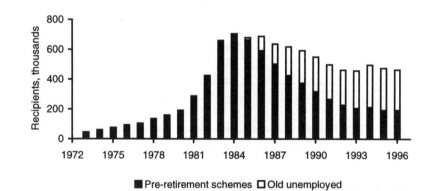

■ Pre-retirement schemes □ Old unemployed

Source: DARES, 1997.

Figure 4.6   Evolution of Pre-retirement Schemes

Table 4.9   Activity Status before Retirement (general scheme, sample of newly retired people, March 1995) (%)

	Men	Women
Employed	39.0	29.4
Unemployed and pre-retired	30.7	19.6
Inactive with other benefits*	14.2	12.0
Other inactive	16.1	39.0

Note: *Among 'other benefits' are inability benefits and benefits from other pension schemes.

Figures 4.7 and 4.8 show the evolution of activity rates among men and among women. One can see that activity rates in the 60–64 age-group had been declining even before 1983 (i.e. before the normal retirement age was lowered to 60), thanks to pre-retirement schemes. Figure 4.7, for men, suggests that after 1983, when retirement was possible at 60 in the general scheme, activity rates also declined in the 55–59 age-group, with the creation of pre-retirement schemes for this age-group. In contrast the general increase in economic activity among women has counteracted early exits from the labour force in the 55–59 age-group. But over age 60 the declining trend has prevailed since the mid-1970s.

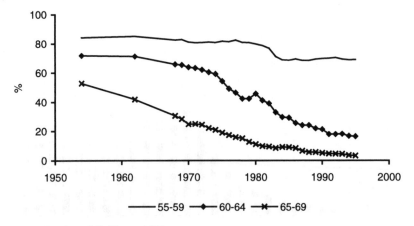

Source: Bordes and Guillemot, 1994.

Figure 4.7   Evolution of Male Activity Rates

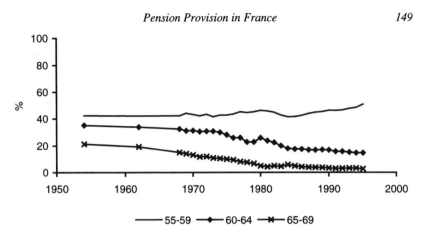

Source: Bordes and Guillemot, 1994.

Figure 4.8 Evolution of Female Activity Rates

4.6 INCOME DISTRIBUTIONS OF PENSIONERS

The data used in this section come from the 1995 Family Budget Survey. A sample of retired including all households whose head is over 60 was extracted from this survey. Households whose heads are between 55 and 60 and not in employment are also included in the sample. These people are essentially inactive, pre-retired or unemployed with little chance of returning to employment. In this sample heads of households can reasonably be considered as retired; however the sample also includes working spouses, and people retired before 55 are excluded.

Income includes numerous benefits, but no correction for housing costs has been applied.[9] Besides, no special treatment has been applied to health expenditures. Pensioners are covered by social security health insurance. They pay mandatory contributions on pensions, through the CSG (generalised social contribution)[10] at 2.8 per cent. Another 1 per cent is levied on complementary pensions. Like economically active people, pensioners can voluntarily contribute to complementary insurance, in particular from mutual insurance companies, in order to get full reimbursement of their medical expenses.

Net income is disposable income, which is gross income net of income tax, property tax and taxes on residence. When income is decomposed, each component is expressed as a gross amount. The main equivalence scale used counts the head as 1, any other adult as 0.7 and any child as 0.5. An alternative is also used which gives an additional adult a 0.5 weight and any child a 0.3 weight. Equivalent income is evaluated from net income.

Table 4.10 shows the average net weekly income among households, by marital status of household and age-group of head. Whatever the status, income is low in the 55–59 age-group. In this group people are no longer economically active but most of them do not yet receive pensions. Their income is made up of benefits (pre-retirement, unemployment insurance and minimum benefits) which are less generous than pensions. After the age of 60 income is decreasing with age among couples and single women. This is the usual result, due to a cohort effect: new pensioners have higher entitlements than old pensioners because of longer contribution histories and higher wages. However the effect does not show up among single men, for whom income increases with age until 75.

Figures in parentheses in Table 4.10 are the ratio of the equivalent average income of each group of households to the average equivalent income of the

Table 4.10   Average Net Weekly Income and Ratios of Equivalent Income of Households, by Marital Status and Age-group of Head (incomes in FF p.w.)

	Age-group					
	55–59	60–64	65–69	70–74	75+	55+
Couples						
Net weekly income	2 613	2 932	2 897	2 854	2 646	2 812
Ratio 1	(0.96)	(1.07)	(1.06)	(1.04)	(0.97)	(1.03)
Ratio 2	(0.93)	(1.05)	(1.03)	(1.02)	(0.95)	(1.00)
Single men						
Net weekly income	1 262	1 631	1 743	1 850	1 777	1 702
Ratio 1	(0.78)	(1.01)	(1.08)	(1.15)	(1.11)	(1.06)
Ratio 2	(0.68)	(0.87)	(0.93)	(0.99)	(0.95)	(0.91)
Single women						
Net weekly income	1 396	1 759	1 531	1 498	1 389	1 485
Ratio 1	(0.87)	(1.09)	(0.95)	(0.93)	(0.86)	(0.92)
Ratio 2	(0.75)	(0.94)	(0.82)	(0.80)	(0.74)	(0.80)

Note: Numbers in parentheses are the ratios of equivalent average income to the average equivalent income of non-pensioners, ratio 1 being computed with the (1, 0.7, 0.5) equivalence scale and ratio 2 with the (1, 0.5, 0.3) equivalence scale.

Source: 1995 Family Budget Survey.

rest of the population, which is exactly 1 608 FF per week.[11] Ratio 1 is computed with the (1, 0.7, 0.5) equivalence scale and ratio 2 with the (1, 0.5, 0.3) scale, which allows measurement of the sensitivity of the results to the choice of equivalence scale. The first set of figures suggest that the equivalent income of retired households is similar to the equivalent income of the rest of the population. This is now a well-known fact in France (Hourriez and Legris, 1995): thanks to generous revaluation of pensions in past decades, the standard of living among retired households has caught up with that of active households.[12] Looking at the second set of figures, the main change is observed for single pensioners. The second scale gives less weight to people who are not heads of households, so it raises the living standards of households including more than one person by comparison with the first scale. Living standards for single men and women are unchanged; therefore the ratios for single pensioners are less favourable than with the first scale. For pensioner couples the situation hardly changes.

Table 4.11   Income Distributions of Different Population Groups (incomes in FF p.w.)

	Mean	Median	90th percentile	10th percentile	90/10 ratio
Couples, no children, head aged <40	2 939	2 724	4 737	1 292	3.67
Couples, no children, head aged ≥40	3 908	3 306	6 467	1 617	4.00
Couples with children	3 994	3 584	6 245	2 035	3.07
Single parents	2 169	1 969	3 481	1 069	3.26
Single men aged <40	1 789	1 564	2 978	481	6.20
Single men aged ≥40	2 382	1 611	3 945	712	5.54
Single women aged <40	1 355	1 273	2 328	281	8.29
Single women aged ≥40	1 899	1 607	3 408	776	4.39
All	3 271	2 969	5 312	923	5.75

Source: 1995 Family Budget Survey.

Table 4.12   Distribution of Pensioner Income, by Marital Status and Age-group (incomes in FF p.w.)

	Age-group					
	55–59	60–64	65–69	70–74	75+	55+
Couples						
Median	2 303	2 456	2 511	2 431	2 283	2 406
90th percentile	4 649	4 566	4 909	4 884	4 447	4 670
10th percentile	1 264	1 371	1 362	1 317	1 255	1 322
90/10 ratio	3.68	3.33	3.60	3.71	3.54	3.53
Single men						
Median	1 153	1 472	1 459	1 371	1 501	1 388
90th percentile	1 949	2 675	3 068	3 249	3 187	3 053
10th percentile	551	922	748	845	759	758
90/10 ratio	3.54	2.90	4.10	3.84	4.20	4.03
Single women						
Median	1 148	1 419	1 374	1 298	1 192	1 283
90th percentile	2 396	2 997	2 703	2 366	2 216	2 467
10th percentile	670	705	757	743	707	721
90/10 ratio	3.57	4.25	3.57	3.19	3.13	3.42

Source: 1995 Family Budget Survey.

Table 4.11 gives statistics concerning the net income among different groups of active people. Couples with or without children have income far above other groups. Conversely single men and women under 40 have very low income and a higher level of inequality.

Income inequality among the retired is lower than in the rest of the population. As Table 4.12 shows, the evolution of inequality with age depends on household composition. Among couples inequality is rather stable, with little change across percentiles. Among men inequality seems to be very low in the 60–64 age-group. Among women inequality decreases with age. This trend can be related to the increase in pension entitlements, which widens the difference between women who had an entire working life and those who never worked. As later cohorts had more years of work, the 90th percentile in particular increases rapidly with younger age-groups in the table.

Table 4.13 focuses on the composition of income. To do so, it separates different sources of income into six categories:

- housing benefits;

- social benefits: unemployment benefits and the means-tested benefit payable between 25 and 65 (known as 'revenue minimum d'insertion' – RMI);
- other benefits, such as disability benefits and child benefits;
- earnings: all income from work;
- pensions: benefits from all pension schemes, survivor benefits, pre-retirement benefits, old-age minimum benefits;
- investment: all income from savings and from professional or personal property.

The income composition varies widely between groups. Benefits and earnings are an important part of income for young age-groups, but among

Table 4.13   Composition of Pensioner Income, by Marital Status and Age-group (%)

	Age-group					
	55–59	60–64	65–69	70–74	75+	55+
Couples						
Housing benefits	0.4	0.2	0.2	0.1	0.2	0.2
Social benefits	12.8	2.9	0.4	0.1	0.1	1.7
Other benefits	7.4	1.4	1.8	1.0	1.2	1.8
Earnings	26.0	26.8	6.9	3.5	0.9	11.0
Pensions	42.9	60.2	80.7	83.5	86.1	74.9
Investment	10.5	8.7	10.1	11.8	11.4	10.4
Single men						
Housing benefits	2.5	0.7	0.4	0.4	0.6	0.7
Social benefits	19.2	1.9	0.0	0.3	0.1	1.8
Other benefits	18.7	1.8	0.6	0.8	0.9	2.3
Earnings	11.1	7.6	3.4	10.4	0.0	4.2
Pensions	43.4	80.9	87.7	77.2	88.3	82.0
Investment	5.0	7.1	7.9	11.0	10.2	9.0
Single women						
Housing benefits	2.8	1.2	1.7	2.1	2.5	2.1
Social benefits	7.5	2.3	0.3	0.0	0.5	0.9
Other benefits	10.7	1.0	0.5	0.7	0.3	0.9
Earnings	15.4	22.0	4.2	1.6	0.4	5.2
Pensions	56.5	62.4	84.3	86.3	85.0	80.6
Investment	7.0	11.0	9.1	9.3	11.3	10.3

Source: 1995 Family Budget Survey.

old age-groups income essentially comprises pensions and investment income. The importance of earnings decreases with age, as expected. It is still high in the 60–64 age-group because some households are not fully retired (especially for couples – the sample includes young working spouses). Earnings in the 60–64 age-group are more important for single women than for single men: women tend to have shorter earnings histories than men; thus they are more likely to have to work until 65 to receive a full-rate pension. Income from investment mostly exceeds 10 per cent of total income. This figure is obtained from declarations by pensioners, but national accounts give a somewhat higher proportion: 20 per cent of total income.

The structure of total income varies across types of household, but it also depends on the income level. Figure 4.9 shows the decomposition of income between all the different sources, by income quintile. The striking feature is that state pensions are the main source across all quintiles, illustrating the generosity of the pension system. Other social benefits sum to a rather low proportion of income, and their importance decreases in the highest quintiles. Conversely the shares of earnings and income from investment increase with the level of income.

Figure 4.10 presents the same decomposition, multiplied by the average equivalent income in each quintile. The income of the 5th quintile is far above that of other quintiles. This is partially due to pensions, which are higher in the top quintile, but earnings and income from investment explain most of the extra income in this quintile.

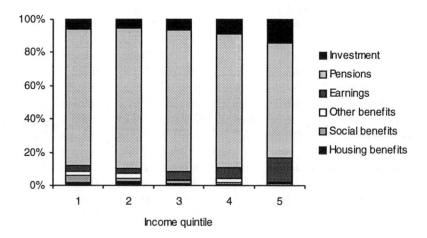

Source: 1995 Family Budget Survey.

Figure 4.9   Composition of Pensioner Income, by Income Quintile

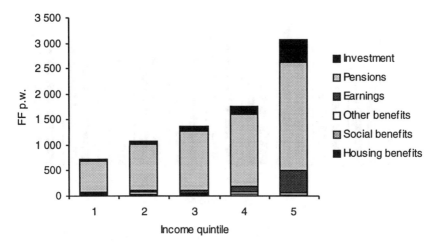

Source: 1995 Family Budget Survey.

Figure 4.10   Equivalised Net Pensioner Income, by Quintile

As suggested previously, the average equivalent income of pensioners is close to the average equivalent income of active people. The position of pensioners in the distribution of equivalent incomes is depicted in Figure 4.11. On the whole, pensioners are under-represented in the 1st decile and slightly over-represented in the next five deciles, but their distribution is almost uniform. Distribution of equivalent income among pensioners is very similar to the distribution in the whole population. This would not be true, of course, if net income were used instead of equivalent income. Considering separately different kinds of households, couples are close to the overall distribution, with proportions slightly lower in the bottom deciles and slightly higher in the top deciles. Indeed couples are the wealthiest pensioners. The distribution for single men deviates from a uniform one and shows two peaks – one in the 3rd decile, the other in the 10th decile. Inequality appears to be more important among single men than among other pensioners. Single women are more likely to be found in the 2nd to 6th deciles, and they are strongly under-represented in the top deciles: women have lower pensions than men because of shorter working lives and they are more likely to get the old-age minimum benefit. However this is not so for later cohorts.

Finally, for completeness, Tables 4.14 and 4.15 illustrate distributions of households by household type and by position in the pensioner income distribution, by housing tenure status. Table 4.14 suggests that pensioners in each category are much more likely to be owners than are non-pensioners.

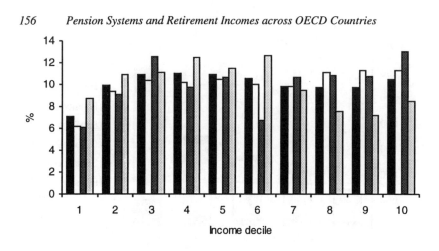

■ All pensioners □ Couples ■ Single men ▨ Single women

Source: 1995 Family Budget Survey.

Figure 4.11   Proportion of Pensioners in Each Income Decile

Table 4.14   Distribution of Households, by Housing Tenure Status (%)

	Pensioners	Non-pensioners
All		
Own outright	61.3	14.3
Mortgage	5.5	34.3
Rent	33.2	51.4
Couples		
Own outright	71.4	15.2
Mortgage	8.2	42.4
Rent	20.4	42.4
Single men		
Own outright	55.2	12.2
Mortgage	2.9	16.6
Rent	41.9	71.2
Single women		
Own outright	49.6	9.6
Mortgage	2.6	17.9
Rent	47.8	72.5

Source: 1995 Family Budget Survey.

Table 4.15   Housing Tenure Status, by Pensioner Income Quintile (%)

Pensioner income quintile	Housing tenure status		
	Rent	Mortgage	Own outright
1	35.4	3.0	61.6
2	42.9	4.2	52.9
3	38.2	5.0	56.8
4	28.7	7.9	63.4
5	20.8	7.2	72.0

Source: 1995 Family Budget Survey.

Table 4.15 shows that, despite a reversal between the 1st and 2nd quintiles, in general higher-income pensioners are more likely to be owner-occupiers than renters.

4.7   CONCLUSIONS

The development of public pension schemes in France has considerably improved living standards among the elderly. The average equivalent income of pensioner households is close to the average equivalent income of active households. In addition public pensions are the main source of income for all pensioners, even the wealthier ones. The number of recipients of minimum old-age benefits is rapidly decreasing, and women increasingly receive substantial pensions in their own right. Moreover over time there has been earlier retirement from economic activity, especially among men.

The sustainability of the pension system is however increasingly being questioned. The dramatic decrease in the support ratio of workers to pensioners raises serious concerns about the future generosity of the public programmes. Some of the schemes have already undergone reforms, but these reforms seem likely to be insufficient to halt the rise in public pension spending as a share of GDP. Moreover some schemes have not so far proved amenable to any reform. After a report in 1999 highlighting these trends, discussions are expected to continue as to the future path of the French pension regime.

NOTES

1.   In France social security includes, in addition to the pension system, health insurance, child benefit and work injury insurance.

2. The use of the terms 'manual' and 'non-manual' here is an approximation to the distinction in France between 'cadres' and 'non-cadres', which results from collective bargaining and varies across sectors.
3. The only scheme explicitly included in the state budget is the civil servants' scheme.
4. The main tax is called the 'generalised social contribution'. This tax is levied on all kinds of income, including capital income.
5. This is a particular way to adjust contributions. In the first years of these schemes, when pension expenditures were low, the coefficients were below 1, meaning that workers paid contributions at a rate lower than the contractual one but got points as though they had paid contributions at the contractual rate.
6. Net amounts refer to wages or pensions from which social contributions have been subtracted. Net wages and pensions are still subject to income tax, but we do not take it into account here.
7. i.e. thousand million.
8. For instance unemployment benefits, which normally decrease over time, are no longer reduced after a given age. The age after which no more reduction applies was initially set at 57½. But it was later gradually raised, up to 59½ in 1997, as conditions for a full-rate pension in the general scheme were strengthened.
9. Information about the housing tenure status of pensioners is given at the end of this section.
10. This contribution is paid on all kinds of income, including capital income.
11. For conversion from French francs, one UK pound is about 10 FF and one US dollar is close to 6 FF. The average equivalent income per week among active people in France (1 608 FF) is very similar to the same income in the UK (£161).
12. The inclusion in income of imputed rents or of medical expenses affects these results to some extent.

REFERENCES

Bayet, A. and M. Juhlès (1996), 'Séries longues sur les salaires (Historical data on wages)', *INSEE-Résultats*, no. 457, série Emploi-revenus, no. 105, Paris: Institut National de la Statistique et des Etudes Economiques.

Bordes, M.-M. and D. Guillemot (1994), 'Marché du travail – séries longues (Historical data on the labour market)', *INSEE-Résultats*, no. 305–306, série Emploi-revenus, no. 62–63, Paris: Institut National de la Statistique et des Etudes Economiques.

Commissariat Général du Plan (1991), *Livre blanc sur les retraites (White Paper on Pensions)*, Paris: La Documentation Française.

Commissariat Général du Plan (1995), *Perspectives à long terme des retraites (Long-term Pension Outlook)*, Paris: La Documentation Française.

Commissariat Général du Plan (1999), *L'Avenir de nos retraites (Pension Outlook)*, Paris: La Documentation Française.

DARES (1997), *La Politique de l'emploi (Employment Policy)*, Paris: La Découverte.

Dinh, Q.C. (1994), 'La population de la France à l'horizon 2050 (Demographic outlook in France until 2050)', *Economie et Statistique*, (274), 7–32.

Hourriez, J.-M. and B. Legris (1995), 'Le niveau de vie relatif des personnes âgées (Relative living standards of the elderly)', *Economie et Statistique*, (283–284), 137–58.

INSEE (1997), 'Comptes et indicateurs économiques: rapport sur les comptes de la nation 1996 (Accounts and economic indicators: report on national accounts,

1996)', *INSEE-Résultats*, no. 547–548–549, série Economie générale, no. 145–146–147, Paris: Institut National de la Statistique et des Etudes Economiques.

SESI (1997a), 'Suivi annuel des retraites, résultats 1995 (Annual report on pensions: 1995 results)', *Synthèses*, no. 9, Paris: Institut National de la Statistique et des Etudes Economiques.

SESI (1997b), 'Les revenus sociaux: 1981–1996 (Social benefits: 1981–1996)', *Synthèses*, no. 14, Paris: Institut National de la Statistique et des Etudes Economiques.

5. Pension Provision in Germany

Axel Börsch-Supan, Anette Reil-Held and Reinhold Schnabel*

5.1 INTRODUCTION

The aim of this chapter is to study the provision of income to the elderly in Germany. Specifically it assesses whether the German social security system provides an adequate retirement income in a sustainable way. As a side product the results of this chapter can be used for studies that need a detailed account of the income of the elderly – for example research on saving behaviour in old age.

At first glance, adequacy of retirement income does not appear to be a problem in Germany. The country has a monolithic provision of income to retirees through the public pension system. The German public pension system (the 'Gesetzliche Rentenversicherung' (GRV) and its equivalents[1]) is ubiquitous because it is mandatory for every worker except the self-employed and those with low earnings. In addition the German social security system is very generous in two respects. First, the system has a high replacement rate such that public pensions represent about 80 per cent of income of households headed by a person aged 65 or over. Second, the system has very generous early retirement provisions including easy ways to claim disability benefits, increasing the number of beneficiaries. Average retirement age is very low in West Germany (about 59) and even lower in East Germany.[2] All this has made public pensions the largest part of the German social budget. In 1996 old-age social security benefits accounted for 12.8 per cent of GDP (see Table 5.1), a share more than 2½ times larger than that in the US.[3]

*Financial support from the Deutsche Forschungsgemeinschaft (Sonderforschungsbereich 504) is gratefully acknowledged. The authors thank Richard Hauser, Paul Johnson and Joachim Winter for their constructive comments.

Table 5.1   Basic Facts about the German Public Pension System, 1996

Public pension spending (% of GDP)	12.8%
	(10.6% GRV only)
Public pension spending (% of public budget)	25.6%
Public budget (% of GDP)	50.1%
Total benefit spending (% of public budget)	72.4%
Number of couple pensioners	7.5 million
Number of single male pensioners	1.4 million
Number of single female pensioners	7.4 million
Number of retired people aged 55 and over	16.5 million
	(14.6 million GRV only)
Dependency ratio (retired/employed people)	57%
Average gross earnings	DM 51 108
Pension fund assets (% of GDP)	c. 4.0%

Note: Not every 'retired' person receives a pension.

Sources: Bundesministerium für Arbeit und Sozialordnung, 1997; Verband Deutscher Rentenversicherungsträger, 1997; authors' calculations.

Sustainability appears to be more of a problem. The prevalence of early retirement comes in addition to an already rather old population and has contributed to a significantly higher ratio of pensioners to workers than in other countries. A hundred German workers paid for 57 pension recipients in 1996, while the figure is only 25 pension recipients in the US. Population ageing will dramatically increase the pressures on the German pension system. The share of persons aged 60 or older in the total population will increase from 21 per cent in 1995 to 36 per cent in 2035, when population ageing will peak (Sommer, 1994). Along with Switzerland and Austria this will be the highest proportion in the world (Bos et al., 1994). The ratio of pensioners to workers will almost double from 57 per cent in 1995 to slightly more than 100 per cent in 2035. As a consequence the German social security contribution rate is expected to increase dramatically and to exceed the rates in other industrialised countries substantially. While in 1998 the contribution rate was about 20 per cent of gross income,[4] even conservative estimates put the contribution rate above 30 per cent of gross income at the peak of population ageing if the generosity of the pension system and labour force participation were to remain as they were in 1998. Key questions for public policy are therefore 'Can the current system survive the challenges of population ageing?' and more importantly 'How can the system adapt if this is not the case? Is an equiproportional cut in benefits a reasonable policy?

Who are the elderly who will be hurt most? Will a benefit cut create significant pockets of poverty?'.

Answers to these questions depend crucially on the role of public pensions in retirement income and the shape of the income distribution among the elderly. Therefore this chapter provides a basis for policy decisions by delivering an account of the level, the sources and the distribution of retirement income in Germany. Section 5.2 contains a general description of the German public pension system, Section 5.3 describes private pensions and other sources of retirement income and Section 5.4 summarises the discussion about the sustainability of the German pay-as-you-go public pension system. The labour market behaviour of older German men and women since 1960 is depicted briefly in Section 5.5. The core of this chapter is Section 5.6, which investigates the distribution and composition of retirement income in Germany. Section 5.7 studies the most important component of wealth, namely housing. Finally Section 5.8 synthesises our findings and concludes.

5.2   KEY FEATURES OF THE GERMAN PENSION SYSTEM

Germany has the oldest formal social security system in the world, introduced in 1889 by Chancellor Bismarck. Table 5.2 gives a summary of the most salient points in the history of the German public pension system. Originally a fully funded disability insurance, it became a mandatory retirement insurance ('Gesetzliche Rentenversicherung' – GRV) which was converted to a pay-as-you-go (PAYG) scheme after its capital stock was severely eroded during the great depression and World War II. In the 1960s and 1970s the German system evolved to one of the most generous pension systems in the world both in terms of its replacement rate and in terms of its early retirement provisions. This is reflected in the budget share of the public pension system (Table 5.3). Germany faces one of the most dramatic population ageing processes in the world, which severely jeopardises the generosity of its social security system. The pension reform that was supposed to be enacted in 1999 planned to phase in significant reductions in the replacement rate, but its main component was revoked after the government changed in 1998.

As opposed to many other countries (for example the UK and the Netherlands) Germany's public pensions are designed to extend the standard of living that was achieved during the working life to the time after retirement. Public pensions are roughly proportional to labour income averaged over the working life and feature little redistribution (much less than in the UK or the US for example). This is why the German pension system is termed 'retirement insurance' rather than 'social security' as in the US, and most workers used to understand their contributions as 'insurance premiums' rather than 'taxes', although this appears to be changing quickly in the face of population ageing.

The retirement insurance system consists of several programmes, each providing benefits which can be accumulated in some cases. The system combines old-age pensions, disability pensions and survivor pensions. East Germany is fully integrated in the West German retirement system, although a few transition rules still apply. Strictly speaking the German retirement insurance is not part of the government budget but a separate entity that is subsidised by the federal government. If there were a surplus, social security contributions could not legally be used to decrease the government deficit, unlike in the US.

Table 5.2   Brief History of the German Public Pension System

1889	Introduction as fully funded system for all blue-collar and some white-collar workers
1911	Extension to all white-collar workers
	Introduction of survivor benefits
1957	Introduction of partial PAYG system
	Indexation to gross wages
1969	Fund depleted: from then on, pure PAYG system
1972	Introduction of flexible retirement age without actuarial adjustments (effective 1973): window of early retirement age 60–65
1992	Shift of retirement window to age 62, equal treatment of men and women, and introduction of semi-actuarial adjustments (effective 2004)
	Indexation to net wages (effective 1992)
1999	Plans to reduce replacement level for new retirees by indexation to life expectancy fail after federal elections

Table 5.3   Shares of Public Pension System (GRV only)

	1960	1970	1980	1990	1995
Public pensions (% of GDP)	6.8	8.1	10.2	9.3	10.6
Public pensions (% of public spending)	20.0	20.7	21.0	20.3	21.2

Source: Bundesministerium für Arbeit und Sozialordnung, 1997, Ch. 7 and 8.

Until 1972 the system only permitted retirement at age 65, except for disability, which however made up for roughly 50 per cent of new retirement entries.[5] The landmark 1972 pension reform introduced the opportunity to retire at different ages during the so-called 'window of retirement' without a direct adjustment of retirement benefits. At the same time the indexation of benefits to the gross wage bill led to an increase in net pensions faster than the increase in net wages and much faster than inflation. In the face of increasing budget problems these two generous provisions were replaced by the second landmark pension reform, in 1992. This enacted a more actuarially fair formula, and indexation was changed to net rather than gross wages. Since the 1992 reform the retirement insurance system has been modified in a continuous flurry of small reform steps. Besides closing several loopholes, partial retirement was introduced. Normal retirement age, already at 65 for men, will gradually be increased to 65 for women too by 2004. Nevertheless it has become increasingly clear that the 1992 pension reform will not master the demographic challenge to come.

This constant change makes it difficult to describe *the* German retirement insurance system. Moreover the recent reforms will only be fully effective after 2004 because most workers are still 'grandfathered' by the pre-1992 legislation. We will focus our description of the German system on (a) the system features between 1972 and 1992, because they describe the behaviour of retirees until about 2000, and (b) the system features after the 1992 reform with all the modifications that have been enacted since, including the 1996 Budget Reconciliation Act and those changes from the 1999 reform that have not been revoked after the change in government.

5.2.1   Coverage and Contributions

The German PAYG public pension system features a very broad mandatory coverage of workers.[6] Only the self-employed (8.9 per cent of the labour force in 1996) and workers with earnings below the official minimum earnings threshold ('Geringfügigkeitsgrenze', 15 per cent of the average monthly gross wage) are not subject to mandatory coverage.[7] Coverage by the public pension system has steadily increased from 77 per cent in 1960 until it reached a plateau around 1980 at almost 90 per cent (see Table 5.4). The increase in the 1960s and 1970s stemmed from the declining share of self-employed and farmers in the labour force. The slight decrease in very recent years was caused by the increase in part-time jobs that are not required to participate in the social safety net.[8]

Table 5.4   Share of Workers Covered by the German Public Pension System (%)

1960	1965	1970	1975	1980	1985	1990	1994
77.0	80.8	83.4	86.0	88.3	88.6	89.4	89.0

Notes:
Share of white-collar workers, blue-collar workers, miners and civil servants in total labour force.
Not included are the self-employed who are voluntary members of the public pension system.

Sources: Statistisches Bundesamt, various years, Table 4.1.1; authors' calculations.

Roughly 75 per cent of the budget of the German public retirement insurance is financed by contributions that are administrated like a payroll tax, levied equally on employees and employers. Total contributions in 1999 were 19.5 per cent of the first DM 8 500 of monthly gross income (upper earnings threshold, 'Beitragsbemessungsgrenze', about 180 per cent of average monthly gross wage).[9] Technically contributions are split evenly between employees and employers, as 9.75 per cent is deducted from employees' gross wages and another 9.75 per cent is paid directly by the employer. While the contribution rate has been fairly stable between 1970 and 1993, the upper earnings threshold has been used as a financing instrument. It is anchored to the average wage and has increased considerably faster than inflation.

The remaining approximately 25 per cent of the social security budget is subsidised by the federal government. This subsidy is also used to fine-tune the PAYG budget constraint which has a minimal reserve of one month's worth of benefits. In 1998 a 1 percentage point increase in value added tax was introduced that is fully earmarked as a subsidy of the public pension system in order to avoid a projected rise in the contribution rate from 20.3 to 21 per cent in 1998. The subsidy was increased in 1999 through an additional 'Eco-tax' – a tax on energy consumption. The indirect contributions through taxation amount to about 8.5 per cent of gross income.

Social security benefits are essentially tax-free.[10] This holds for income taxes as well as for social security contributions. However pensioners have to pay the equivalent of the employee's contribution to the mandatory medical insurance. The other 50 per cent, corresponding to the employer's contribution, is paid by the pension system as a transfer to the health insurance system. In turn pensioners remain covered by health insurance exactly as they were as workers.[11]

5.2.2   Benefit Types

The German public pension system (or, as it is referred to in Germany, retirement insurance system) provides old-age pensions for workers aged 60 and older, disability benefits for workers aged under 60, which are converted to old-age pensions at age 65 at the latest, and survivor benefits for spouses and children. In addition pre-retirement (i.e. retirement before 60) is possible through several mechanisms using the public transfer system, mainly unemployment compensation. We begin by describing old-age pensions.

5.2.3   Eligibility for Benefits and Retirement Age for Old-age Pensions

Eligibility for benefits and the minimum retirement age depend on which type of pension the worker chooses. The German public retirement insurance system distinguishes five types of old-age pensions, displayed in Table 5.5, corresponding to normal retirement and four types of early retirement.

This complex system was introduced by the 1972 social security reform. One of the key provisions was the introduction of 'flexible retirement' after age 63 with full benefits for workers with a long service history. In addition retirement at age 60 with full benefits is possible for women, the unemployed and older disabled workers.[12] 'Older disabled workers' refers to those workers

Table 5.5   Old-age Pensions (1972 legislation, effective for current retirees)

	Pension type	Retirement age	Years of service	Additional conditions	Earnings test[a]
A	Normal	65	5		No
B	Long service life ('flexible')	63	35		Yes
C	Women	60	15	10 of those after age 40	Yes
D	Older disabled	60	35	Loss of at least 50% earnings capability	(Yes)[b]
E	Unemployed	60	15	1.5–6 years of unemployment (has changed several times)	Yes

Notes:
[a] The earnings test does not permit any significant earnings between early retirement and age 65.
[b] See text discussion.

who cannot be appropriately employed for health or labour market reasons and are 60 or older. There are three possibilities for claiming old-age disability benefits. One has to (1) be physically disabled to at least 50 per cent of capacity or (2) pass a strict earnings test or (3) pass a much weaker earnings test. The strict earnings test is passed if the earnings capacity is reduced below the minimum earnings threshold for any *reasonable* occupation (about 15 per cent of average gross wage) ('Erwerbsunfähigkeitsrente' – EU).[13] The weaker earnings test is passed when no vacancies for the worker's *specific* job description are available and the worker has to face an earnings loss of at least 50 per cent when changing to a different job ('Berufsunfähigkeitsrente' – BU). As opposed to the disability insurance for workers under 60 (see below), full benefits are paid in all three cases.

With the 1992 social security reform and its subsequent modifications, the age limits for types B and C of early retirement will gradually be raised to 65. These changes will be fully phased in by 2004. The only distinguishing feature of types B and C of 'early retirement' will then be the possibility of retiring up to five years earlier than age 65 if a sufficient number of service years (currently 35) have been accumulated. As opposed to the pre-1992 regulations, benefits will be adjusted to a retirement age below 65 in the manner described below.

5.2.4 Benefits

Benefits are strictly work-related. The German system does not have benefits for spouses like in the US. Benefits are computed on a lifetime contribution basis and adjusted according to the type of pension and retirement age. They are the product of four elements: (1) the employee's relative contribution position; (2) the years of service life; (3) adjustment factors for pension type and (since the 1992 reform) retirement age; and (4) the average pension. The first three factors make up the 'personal pension base', while the fourth determines the income distribution between workers and pensioners in general.

The employee's relative contribution position is computed by averaging his or her annual relative contribution position over the entire earnings history. In each year, the relative contribution position is expressed as a multiple of the average annual contribution (roughly speaking the relative income position). A first element of redistribution was introduced in 1972 when this multiple could not fall below 75 per cent for contributions before 1972 provided a worker had a service life of at least 35 years. A similar rule was introduced in the 1992 reform: for contributions between 1973 and 1992 multiples below 75 per cent are multiplied by 1.5 up to the maximum of 75 per cent, effectively reducing the redistribution for workers with income positions below 50 per cent.

Years of service life are years of active contributions plus years of contribution on behalf of the employee and years that are counted as service years even when no contributions were made at all. These include, for instance, years of unemployment, years of military service, three years for each child's education for one of the parents[14] and some allowance for advanced education,[15] introducing a second element of redistribution. Official government computations such as the official replacement rate ('Rentenniveau') assume a 45-year contribution history for what is deemed a 'normal earnings history' ('Eckrentner'). In fact the average number of years of contributions is slightly below 40. Unlike the US there is no upper bound on the number of years entering the benefit calculation, nor can workers choose certain years in their earnings history and drop others.

Since 1992 the average pension has been determined by indexation to average *net* labour income. This solved some of the problems that were created by indexation to *gross* wages between 1972 and 1992. Nevertheless wage rather than cost-of-living indexation makes it impossible to finance the retirement burden by productivity gains. The average pension has provided a generous benefit level for middle-income earnings. Table 5.6 shows net and gross replacement rates for three income levels.[16] Note that Germany has little redistribution through the pension system; see Börsch-Supan and Reil-Held (2001). However pensioners with a pension below the poverty line receive social assistance ('Sozialhilfe'; see below) which is included in the figure in parentheses in Table 5.6. The 1999 pension reform was supposed to link the average pension level to both net wages and life expectancy at age 65, which would have led to about a 10 per cent drop in the replacement rate in 2035.[17] This corner-stone of the reform was subsequently revoked; however changes in the rules governing the relevant service life will induce a once-and-for-all reduction in the effective replacement rate of about 10 per cent for male and 15 per cent for female workers (Prognos, 1999).

Before 1992 adjustment of benefits to retirement age was only implicit via the number of years of service.[18] Benefits are proportional to years of service, so a worker with fewer years of service will get lower benefits. With a constant income profile and 40 years of service, each year of earlier retirement decreased pension benefits by 2.5 per cent, and vice versa. The 1992 social security reform will change this but will not be fully implemented until 2004. Age 65 will then act as the 'pivotal age' for benefit computations. For each year of earlier retirement up to five years and so long as the appropriate conditions in Table 5.5 are met, benefits will be reduced by 3.6 per cent (in addition to the effect of fewer service years). The 1992 reform also introduced rewards for *later* retirement in a systematic way. For each year of retirement postponed past the minimum age indicated in Table 5.5,

Table 5.6 Replacement Rates for Old-age Pensions (1972 legislation, single person) (%)

	Income level[a]		
	½	1	2
Net replacement rate	67 (79)[b]	72	75
Gross replacement rate	48	45	40

Notes:
[a]Income level refers to net wage as a multiple of the net wage of an average production worker with 40 years of service.
[b]Figure in parentheses includes social assistance.

Source: Casmir, 1989, pp. 508 and 512.

the pension is increased by 6 per cent in addition to the 'natural' increase arising from the number of service years.

Table 5.7 displays the retirement-age-specific adjustments for a worker who has earnings that remain constant after the age of 60. The table relates the retirement income for retirement at 65 (normalised to 100 per cent) to the retirement income for retirement at earlier or later ages, and compares the implicit adjustments after 1972 with the total adjustments after the 1992 social security reform is fully phased in. For reference the table also displays actuarially fair adjustments at a 3 per cent discount rate.[19]

Table 5.7 Adjustment of Public Pensions, by Retirement Age (%)

Age	Pension as a % of pension obtained if one had retired at 65		
	Pre-1992[a]	Post-1992[b]	Actuarially fair[c]
62	100.0	89.2	80.5
63	100.0	92.8	86.5
64	100.0	96.4	92.9
65	100.0	100.0	100.0
66	107.2	109.0	108.1
67	114.4	118.0	117.2
68	114.4	127.0	127.4
69	114.4	136.0	139.1

Notes:
[a]GRV 1972–92.
[b]GRV after 1992 reform has been fully phased in.
[c]At 3 per cent discount rate, 1 per cent real growth in benefits and survival probabilities based on the 1992–94 life tables.

Source: Börsch-Supan and Schnabel, 1999.

The public retirement system in Germany as enacted in 1972 was particularly distortive. The German social security system tilted the retirement decision heavily towards the earliest retirement age applicable. The 1992 reform has diminished but not abolished this incentive effect.

5.2.5 Related Social Security Programmes

Up to this point we have discussed old-age benefits. The German retirement insurance also pays disability benefits to workers of all ages and survivor benefits to spouses and children.

In order to be eligible for disability benefits a worker must pass one of the two earnings tests mentioned earlier for the old-age disability pension. If the stricter earnings test is passed ('Erwerbsunfähigkeitsrente' – EU), full benefits are paid. If only the weaker earnings test is passed and some earnings capability remains ('Berufsunfähigkeitsrente' – BU), disability pensions before the age of 60 are only two-thirds of the applicable old-age pension. In the 1970s and early 1980s the German authorities interpreted both rules very broadly, in particular the applicability of the first. Moreover the authorities also overruled the earnings test (see below) for earnings during disability retirement. This led to EU-type disability pensions accounting for more than 90 per cent of all disability pensions. Because both rules were used as a device to keep unemployment rates down, their generous interpretation has only recently been reassessed by stricter legislation.

Survivor pensions are 60 per cent of the husband's applicable pension for spouses who are aged 45 and over or if there are children in the household ('große Witwenrente') and 25 per cent otherwise ('kleine Witwenrente'). Survivor benefits are a large component of the public pension budget and of total pension wealth. Certain earnings tests apply if the surviving spouse has her own income – for example her own pension. This is only relevant for a very small share of widows (below 10 per cent). Only recently have male and female survivors been treated symmetrically. The German system does not have a married couple supplement for spouses of beneficiaries. However most wives acquire their own pension by active and passive contribution (mostly years of advanced education and years of child education).

Table 5.8 shows the proportions of beneficiaries by pension type: old-age and disability pensions due to contributions out of own earnings, and survivor pensions. The total number of beneficiaries increased sharply between 1960 and 1995. Among those aged 55 and over, 85 per cent received pensions from the public system in 1995, while this share was only a little above 50 per cent in 1960. Most of those who receive a public pension receive an old-age pension. Disability benefits were rising particularly fast in the early 1980s

Table 5.8   Percentage of People Aged 55 and Over Receiving Public Pension Benefits (%)

	1960	1965	1970	1975	1980	1985	1990	1995
Old-age	20.9	23.4	27.9	34.0	37.6	40.6	47.3	54.8
Disability	9.4	8.5	8.1	8.5	9.6	12.0	8.7	6.0
Survivor	20.2	20.6	21.5	22.6	24.3	25.4	24.7	23.9
Total	50.6	52.4	57.5	65.3	71.4	78.0	80.7	84.7

Notes:
By definition everyone receiving old-age social security is 60 or over.
People receiving disability pensions – share of those aged 55+ estimated from 1992 share.
People receiving survivor benefits – some double counting; very small number of people aged below 55 included.

Source: Verband Deutscher Rentenversicherungsträger, 1997.

until more stringent requirements were put in place. Survivor benefits remained stable.

In addition social assistance ('Sozialhilfe', welfare) and related entitlement programmes such as housing allowances ('Wohngeld') act as a general floor to income in Germany. For example whenever a pension is lower than the level of social assistance, social assistance will top the public pension up to this level. Hence redistribution between the lifetime rich and poor works mainly through the welfare mechanism, while there is very little redistribution through the pension system (Table 5.6). This is in marked contrast to the actuarially unfair design of the pension system, which strongly redistributes income from late to early retirees (Table 5.7). Social assistance is relatively generous in Germany and not just subsistence income. In 1993 a single elderly person received an average of DM 1 188 in monthly social assistance, including an average of DM 493 in housing allowances. This is about 40 per cent of average male earnings, or 57 per cent of average net equivalised household income – see Section 5.6. Nevertheless estimated take-up rates are only between 40 and 50 per cent.

Public health insurance coverage remains essentially unchanged when workers retire. Coverage is generous by international standards such that out-of-pocket health expenditures are low and remain approximately constant through the retirement period.

5.2.6   Pre-Retirement

In addition to benefits through the public pension system, transfer payments (mainly unemployment compensation) enable what is referred to as 'pre-retirement'. As was shown earlier, labour force exit before the age of 60 is common: about 45 per cent of all men call themselves 'retired' at 59. Only about half of them retire because of disability; the other 50 per cent make use of one of the many official and unofficial pre-retirement schemes.

Unemployment compensation has been used as pre-retirement income in an unofficial scheme that induced very early retirement. Before workers could enter the public pension system at 60, they were paid a negotiable combination of unemployment compensation and a supplement or severance pay. At age 60 a pension of type E could start (see Table 5.5). As the rules of pensions of type E and the duration of unemployment benefits changed, so did the 'unofficial' retirement ages. Age 56 was particularly frequent in West Germany because unemployment compensation is paid for up to three years for elderly workers; it is followed by the lower unemployment aid. Earlier retirement could be induced by paying the worker the difference between the last salary and unemployment compensation for three years and the difference between the last salary and unemployment aid for further years – it all depended on the so-called 'social plan' which a firm would negotiate with the workers before restructuring the work-force.

In addition early retirement at 58 was made possible in an official pre-retirement scheme ('Vorruhestandsregelung') in which the employer received a subsidy from unemployment insurance if a younger employee was hired. While the first (and unofficial) pre-retirement scheme was very popular and a convenient way to overcome the strict German labour laws, few employers used the second (official) scheme.

5.2.7   Resulting Retirement Patterns

The regulations of the German pension system are perfectly reflected in the distribution of the ages at which workers receive a public pension for the first time, depicted in Figure 5.1.

There are essentially three ages for entry into the German public pension system: 60, 63 and 65. Very few people enter at other ages. By 1995 60 had become the most popular entry age for male and female workers. For male workers 63 is the next important entry age, while it is 65 for female workers. There is no spike at age 63 for women because they may receive public pensions at 60 unless they have a service life of less than 15 years. This is unlike the pattern among male workers because men receive a public pension at 60 only if they are unemployed or disabled. In turn there are more women receiving a public pension for the first time at 65 because more women than men have short earnings histories. Börsch-Supan and Schnabel (1998) provide a more detailed analysis of the incentive effects of the German public pension system.

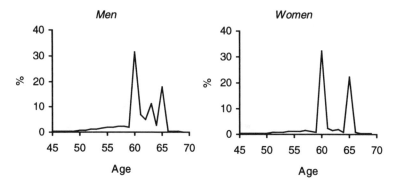

Note: Distribution of age of workers receiving public pension benefits for the first time in 1995, West Germany.

Source: Verband Deutscher Rentenversicherungsträger, 1997.

Figure 5.1   Distribution of Entries into Public Pension System, by Age and Gender

5.3   PRIVATE PENSIONS AND OTHER SOURCES OF RETIREMENT INCOME

German pension income is monolithic, dominated by public pensions, as shown in Figure 5.2. This graph is taken from Börsch-Supan and Schnabel (1999), who used the West German data of the pooled 1993, 1994 and 1995 waves of the German Socio-Economic Panel (GSOEP). Section 5.6 will provide a more detailed account on the basis of a richer dataset in 1993 and will include East Germany. Public pensions account for about 80 per cent of retirement income, while private pensions and other sources of retirement income play a much smaller role than in other countries, particularly the UK and the US.

Although company pensions exist in Germany, their role is subsidiary. Over the period 1993–95 21 per cent of male elderly and less than 9 per cent of female elderly received private pensions. Figure 5.3 shows receivers of private pensions as a share of the number of people at each age. Company pensions were popular in the early 1980s and were used to create internal company funds until the very favourable corporate income tax treatment was abolished. The 'age' pattern in Figure 5.3 therefore displays strong cohort effects in addition to true age effects.

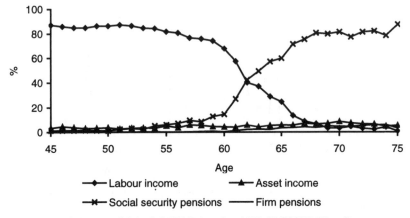

Source: Börsch-Supan and Schnabel (1999), based on 1993–95 GSOEP, West Germany.

Figure 5.2   Source of Household Income, by Age of Householder

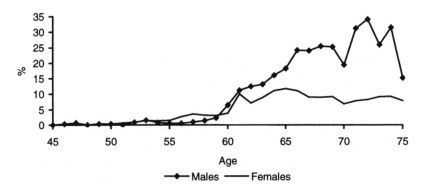

Note: People receiving firm pensions as a share of sample people at given age, 1993–95 average.

Source: Börsch-Supan and Schnabel (1999), based on 1993–95 GSOEP, West Germany.

Figure 5.3   Recipients of Private Pension Income, by Age and Gender

Not only is the incidence of private company pensions low, but the average pension is also low, because it serves only to top up the generous public pension. Thus private pensions make up less than 5 per cent of total retirement income among elderly households (Figure 5.2).

Like pension funds, asset income also plays a much smaller role than in the Anglo-Saxon countries, and it never exceeds 10 per cent on average at any age.[20] A major part of the assets are life insurance policies and asset income from financial assets and real property, mostly real estate.

Other income sources include earnings and intergenerational transfers. The share of earnings of course reflects labour force participation, which is discussed in Section 5.5. Intergenerational transfers, such as regular payments from other family members or one-off payments such as bequests, are small and better covered in the data underlying our analysis in Section 5.6.

5.4   SUSTAINABILITY OF THE CURRENT PENSION SYSTEM

The German PAYG public pension system has only recently matured since its introduction in 1957. High unemployment, together with low old-age labour force participation, is now generating a high dependency burden and an effective contribution rate of more than 28 per cent of gross income (19.5 per cent nominal contributions plus more than 8.5 per cent of gross income through general taxes in 1999). To add to this, the change in the age composition of the German population is slowly but steadily accelerating, as was pointed out in Section 5.1. The demographic old-age dependency ratio is expected to more than double from 21.7 per cent in 1990 to 49.2 per cent in 2030.[21]

The increase in the dependency ratio has immediate consequences for the PAYG social insurance system because fewer workers are available to finance the extra recipients. If the replacement rate and labour force participation were to remain as they were in the early 1990s, the social security contribution rate would exceed 30 per cent of gross income at the peak of population ageing. Based on this, the OECD projects pension expenditures in Germany to increase sharply from 11.1 per cent of GDP in 1995 to 18.4 per cent in 2040 (OECD, 1997) – see Table 5.9. Official estimates of the required contribution rate under the current public pension system were more optimistic and ranged between 26 and 29 per cent, because they assumed considerable adaptation of retirement age, replacement rate and female labour force participation and because they postulated that life expectancy will change only marginally after the year 2000 (Prognos, 1995).

These projections have precipitated a lively discussion and adjustments to the current public pension system. The 1999 pension reform planned to induce a drop in the net replacement rate due to a less generous recognition of non-work service years (see Section 5.2). In addition part of the financing will be shifted from contributions to various sales taxes. The effect of this reform on the projected contribution rate is shown in the last row of Table 5.9.

Table 5.9   Projected Future Costs of Public Pensions: The Key Variables
(%)

	1995	2000	2010	2020	2030	2040
Demographic dependency ratio (65+/15–64)[a]	22.3	23.8	30.3	35.4	49.2	50.6
Ratio of pensioners to workers[b]	57.4	62.4	71.8	83.3	99.9	102.9
Projected share of public pensions in GDP[a]	11.1	11.5	11.8	12.3	16.5	18.4
Projected contribution rate[c] (current labour force participation)	19.3	21.1	24.3	28.2	29.5	30.0
Projected contribution rate[b] (optimistic projection)	19.3	20.0	22.4	24.3	26.3	26.3
Projected contribution rate[d] (after 1999 reform)	19.3	20.0	19.6	21.0	23.7	24.5

Sources:
[a]OECD, 1997.
[b]Prognos, 1995 (p. 12; 'obere Variante').
[c]Börsch-Supan, 1995 (scenario assumes: constant fertility rate; life expectancy increases to age 83 in 2040; annual net immigration of 80 000 people; constant age- and gender-specific labour force participation rates).
[d]Prognos, 1999; Birg and Börsch-Supan, 1999.

Relative to the situation without the 1999 reform, the contribution rate in 2030 will be 2.6 percentage points lower. However this projection is deceiving in so far as it disregards the increase in the share of the pension budget that will be financed by the value added tax and because it relates to a lower level of retirement income than the preceding rows.

Potential avenues to escape threats to the sustainability of the German public pension system are discussed in Börsch-Supan (1998). Short of reducing benefits, the most powerful route is to raise the retirement age, as this increases the number of contributors and at the same time decreases the number of beneficiaries. However in order to compensate fully for the effects of population ageing, the average retirement age has to increase by 9.5 years, to about 69 by 2030.[22] It is unlikely that the labour market is sufficiently flexible to permit this to happen.

Increasing the number of workers without a corresponding decrease in the number of retirees is less effective but still helpful. An increase in female labour force participation will reduce the retirement burden in the short run, although the effect is small for Germany. If female labour force participation were to reach the level of male labour force participation by 2010, the increase in the social security contribution rate would be dampened by only about 6 percentage points. Migration of younger workers is a more powerful mechanism to alleviate the effects of population ageing. In practice one faces two problems. First, the domestic labour market has to be sufficiently flexible to absorb immigrant workers and provide the necessary training. Second, the numbers do not add up: to compensate fully for population ageing in Germany at the given typical age structure of immigrants – immigrants into Germany are, on average, about 10 years younger than the resident population – about 800 000 persons (workers and family) have to migrate annually in net terms into Germany from 2000 through to 2035. These very large numbers are not without a historical precedent but only during a few exceptional years – for example after the opening of the Iron Curtain – and they are unlikely to persist.

Tightening the eligibility for disability benefits – a part of the retirement system that is particularly expensive because benefits occur early in life – is another frequently cited step. About 27 per cent of male workers and 20 per cent of female workers use the pathway of claiming disability in order to retire before 60, most of them between 54 and 59 and most for labour market, not health, reasons.[23] However the effect of tightening the eligibility for disability benefits is smaller than often claimed. Even if all early retirement before 60 were eliminated, the average retirement age would increase by only 2.3 years for male and 1.9 years for female workers.

Thus no single one of these steps can solve the sustainability problems of the German PAYG pension system. Moreover while a combination of the above steps together with a benefit reduction as introduced by the 1999 reform may solve the financial problems, it will inevitably reduce the rate of return implicit in the PAYG system substantially below alternative returns on the capital market and therefore create huge incentives to leave the PAYG system.[24] Figure 5.4 shows the average implicit rate of return under two extreme policy assumptions: maintain the current replacement rate (and thus increase the contribution rate as described above) and maintain the current contribution rate (and thus lower the pension level).

Freezing the contribution rate generates negative rates of return for all cohorts born after 1965 because they will receive a low pension after having contributed fully during what is already half of their working lives. Freezing the replacement rate is more advantageous for the cohorts born between 1930 and 1980, but it does not help cohorts born after 1980 because they will have to pay the rising contribution rates shown in Table 5.9. Thus even with a reduction in benefits targeted to keep social security taxes close to the current 20 per cent, the German PAYG system is likely to face severe sustainability problems if the tax base erodes due to the disadvantageous rate of return.

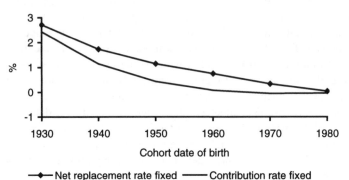

Source: Schnabel, 1998.

Figure 5.4   Rate of Return Implicit in the German PAYG Pension System

5.5   OLD-AGE LABOUR FORCE PARTICIPATION

Germany shares a rapid decrease in old-age labour force participation (Table 5.10) with most other industrialised countries. This decrease accelerated after 1970, at least partly due to the introduction of 'flexible' retirement arrangements in 1972 that did not adjust benefits according to actuarial tables. It is interesting to note that male labour force participation declined from 1970 to 1990 for all ages above 50, and especially for greater ages. In contrast female labour force participation increased for all ages below 60. The

Table 5.10   Male and Female Labour Force Participation Rates in West Germany (%)

Age-group	Female				Male			
	1960	1970	1980	1990	1960	1970	1980	1990
45–49	40.9	48.9	52.2	66.7	96.1	96.8	96.8	96.5
50–54	37.4	44.8	47.1	57.8	94.1	95.1	93.3	93.2
55–59	32.4	37.2	38.7	43.8	89.0	89.2	82.3	81.1
60–64	20.9	22.5	13.0	12.5	72.5	74.7	44.2	35.0
65+	8.2	6.5	3.0	2.0	22.6	19.7	7.4	5.3

Source: Börsch-Supan and Schnabel, 1999.

increases for women aged 50–59 are noteworthy because they contrast with the decline in male labour force participation arising from a high share of disability claims among male workers.

Figure 5.5 looks more closely at current employment status and receipt of public pensions for men and for women in West Germany. Employment status is defined as actual occupation. 'Retired' in this figure refers to people

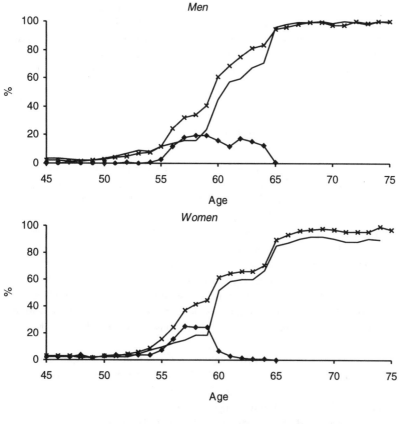

Note: Retired people, pre-retired people and recipients of old-age, disability and civil servant pensions as a share of sample people at given age.

Source: Börsch-Supan and Schnabel (1999), based on 1993–95 GSOEP, West Germany.

Figure 5.5 Labour Force Status and Receipt of Public Pension, by Age and Gender

who call themselves retired, independent of whether they receive some kind of pension. They include disabled people and people who retired before being eligible for public pensions. The graph is based on the pooled 1993, 1994 and 1995 waves of the German Socio-Economic Panel, covering some 12 000 people in West Germany. We do not include East Germany because its retirement pattern is still dominated by transitional effects from unification.

After the age of 55 a substantial number of workers go into early retirement without receiving a public pension (old-age or disability pension). These workers receive some combination of unemployment benefits and severance pay under several pre-retirement schemes. Eventually, by the age of 65, almost all male and most female pre-retirees will receive a public pension. Pre-retirement – i.e. retiring without yet receiving a public pension – is high: it peaks between ages 57 and 59 at 20 per cent for men and 25 per cent for women.

5.6   INCOME DISTRIBUTION

This section looks more closely at the distribution and composition of retirement income and investigates how total retirement income relates to the average income of the working population. Our analysis is based on the 1993 German Income and Expenditure Survey ('Einkommens- und Verbrauchsstichprobe' – EVS), which covers both East and West Germany. The survey is available in scientific-use form. Its design is described in Euler (1982 and 1987) and Statistisches Bundesamt (1997) and roughly corresponds to that of the US Consumer Expenditure Survey. The EVS includes a very detailed account of income by source, consumption by type, saving flows, and asset stocks by portfolio category. A descriptive analysis of these variables for one- and two-person retired households has been carried out by Münnich (1997).

The 1993 survey is a representative cross-section of German households with annual gross incomes below DM 300 000, and it includes some 50 000 households. The large sample size is a distinctive advantage compared with the German Socio-Economic Panel and the Luxemburg Income Study, the databases used by Börsch-Supan and Schnabel (1999) and Hauser, Mörsdorf and Tibitanzl (1997). The latter look at the income distribution of the elderly in an international context.

The data exclude very wealthy households (having annual gross incomes in excess of DM 300 000) and the institutionalised population. The former represent about 2 per cent of households. When we show percentiles, we have corrected for this censoring. Omission of the institutionalised is serious only among the very old. Although less than 4 per cent of all people aged 65 or over in Germany are institutionalised, this percentage increases rapidly with age and is estimated to be about 9.5 per cent of all people aged 80 or over.

The EVS is a stratified quota sample on a voluntary basis. The German Bureau of the Census establishes a target number of households for each stratum defined by household size, income and employment status. To meet these targets, a large number of households are contacted by various mechanisms. The ratio of final acceptances to target size is published and was in excess of 120 per cent in 1983. However this ratio varied between 20 and 150 per cent across strata. Acceptance rates are lowest in the strata of low-income households, one-person households, blue-collar workers and the self-employed. All our results are weighted to match population statistics.

The basic sampling unit of the EVS is the household. In some cases these households are composite – i.e. they contain several nuclei, where we define a family nucleus as a single adult or a couple (married or cohabiting) with their young children. 'Young children' are aged below 16 or below 18 if still in education. Children over 18 or children between 16 and 18 but not in education are considered independent nuclei and adults who could in principle form their own household. Table 5.11 shows the percentage of elderly who live in composite households, by age and marital status. About 18 per cent of couples and about 13 per cent of single people aged 60 or over have other adults in their households. Among the younger elderly (below 70) these people are in most cases adult children still in education and the parent is the head of the household. Most of the very old single people living in composite households have moved in with their children, most probably to receive care, and their children are household heads. The EVS data make it very difficult to assign income to individuals in composite households. We have therefore excluded all composite households from our analysis.[25]

We define 'retired' households as those with at least one person aged 65 or over, independent of labour force status, plus those households with at least

Table 5.11   Percentage of Elderly People Living in Composite Households (%)

	Age-group				
	60–64 & retired	65–69	70–74	75+	60+ & retired
Couples	25.6	20.2	9.7	7.2	17.7
Single men	12.4	10.5	7.4	16.9	12.8
Single women	13.1	10.8	8.2	17.4	12.6

Source: Authors' calculations based on 1993 EVS.

one person who is 60–64 years old and retired (according to self-assessment). We have 6 635 such households in our sample. Of those, 766 are households with a single male and 3 121 are households with a single female (see Table 5.12). If we stratify further by age, sample sizes remain sufficiently large for reliable statistical analysis, with the exception of single-male households, where sample sizes are relatively low.

We use several income concepts. Gross income refers to income before personal taxation and before the employee or pensioner part of social security is deducted. The data also contain gross income by source and household member. These data are very reliable for earnings and public transfers but are less reliable for asset income and private transfers. Hertel (1992) reports that the sum of asset income in the earlier 1988 wave accounted for slightly less than 50 per cent of aggregate asset income, partially due to under-reporting in the sample but mostly because of the censoring of the wealthy in the EVS. Lang (1998) provides an extensive comparison of several aggregate and survey data sources with respect to the major income categories, with similar results. We do not include imputed rent of owner-occupiers as income, but include the profit (or loss) of rented housing.

Net household income refers to gross household income minus taxes and the employee or pensioner part of social security taxes. Because German income taxes are levied on total net income sources in a household, net income by income source or by household member is not a meaningful concept in Germany. When we use it for comparison purposes with other countries, we attribute total household taxes to individuals and/or sources in proportion to gross income. If we present households of different sizes in one table, we have to make household income comparable across different household sizes. We apply the OECD equivalence scale that weights the first adult as 1.0, other adults as 0.7 and children as 0.5.

With these definitions in mind, Table 5.12 shows a high level of equivalised income of the retired (relative to the income of workers), with only little variation across household types and age categories. Overall, equivalised retirement income is 88 per cent of workers' equivalised income, ranging from 102 per cent for single men and 92 per cent for couples to 80 per cent for single women. Note that this ratio is not a replacement rate, as workers and retirees belong to different cohorts with different earnings histories. Given the secular increase in productivity, the actual replacement rate is most likely considerably higher. We conclude that single men are overannuitised in the sense of having a higher income after retirement than before. The difference between male and female single households corresponds to the well-documented differences in lifetime earnings. Because Germany has strictly earnings-related public pension benefits, as pointed out in Section 5.2, the higher earnings levels as well as the longer earnings histories result in significantly higher pensions for men. The high general level of retirement income corresponds to high saving ratios in old age; see Börsch-Supan and Stahl (1991) and Börsch-Supan (1992a). Our results for all retired people over 65 are in line with those of Münnich (1997), although she uses a slightly different definition of 'retired' households. Also she does not differentiate by age and gender.

Table 5.12   Average Annual Net Equivalised Income of the Retired (incomes in DM p.a.)

	Age-group				
	60–64 & retired	65–69	70–74	75+	60+ & retired
Couples					
Mean (absolute)	47 945	52 188	47 394	46 465	48 787
Mean (equivalised)	27 804	30 346	27 862	27 332	28 474
Ratio 1	(0.90)	(0.98)	(0.89)	(0.88)	(0.92)
Ratio 2	(0.74)	(0.80)	(0.73)	(0.72)	(0.75)
Sample size	1 682	1 766	1 246	802	5 496
Single men					
Mean	26 464	33 589	33 714	30 947	31 775
Ratio 1	(0.85)	(1.08)	(1.08)	(0.99)	(1.02)
Ratio 2	(0.69)	(0.88)	(0.88)	(0.81)	(0.83)
Sample size	104	215	199	248	766
Single women					
Mean	25 407	26 220	26 255	22 950	25 014
Ratio 1	(0.81)	(0.84)	(0.84)	(0.74)	(0.80)
Ratio 2	(0.67)	(0.69)	(0.69)	(0.60)	(0.66)
Sample size	516	882	946	777	3 121
All					
Mean					26 450
Ratio 1					(0.88)
Ratio 2					(0.72)
Sample size					9 383

Notes:
'Ratio' refers to the ratio of the mean net equivalised income of the respective group to the mean equivalised income of workers (DM 31 217).
Ratio 1 uses the OECD equivalence scale (1.0, 0.7, 0.5), while ratio 2 uses a steeper scale (1.0, 0.5, 0.3).
See text for definition of 'retired'.

Source: 1993 EVS.

There are several dimensions in which Table 5.12 has to be interpreted with care. The decline of income with old age is more likely a cohort than an age effect, again because of the secular productivity increase. The relatively low income of the very young retirees appears to be a selection effect: this age-group includes early retirees who had, on average, lower lifetime earnings than workers who retired at 65.[26] Labour force participation after 65 is extremely low, as was shown in the previous section. Finally the results are sensitive to the choice of the equivalence scale because more younger than older households have a second adult or children in the household. Weighting these people less increases their equivalised income more than that of smaller households.

Table 5.13 provides a closer look at the distribution of retirement income. For couples and single men income inequality is larger among those aged 70 and over relative to those under 70. For single women however the pattern is reversed. None the less the variation with age is small, and the overall inequality is much smaller than in other countries (Hauser, Mörsdorf and Tibitanzl, 1997).

Table 5.13   Distribution of Net Retirement Income of the Retired

	Age-group				
	60–64 & retired	65–69	70–74	75+	60+ & retired
Couples					
Median	41 539	43 727	38 969	39 597	41 193
90th percentile	81 050	94 001	84 070	82 043	85 841
10th percentile	26 738	26 977	25 579	23 268	26 020
90/10 ratio	3.03	3.48	3.29	3.53	3.30
Single men					
Median	23 260	28 925	29 358	25 976	27 231
90th percentile	43 437	58 646	62 575	59 149	57 131
10th percentile	12 231	17 132	18 472	12 938	14 168
90/10 ratio	3.55	3.42	3.39	4.57	4.03
Single women					
Median	22 134	23 297	23 441	21 326	22 367
90th percentile	43 322	44 206	42 589	36 665	41 020
10th percentile	13 667	15 044	14 363	13 554	14 033
90/10 ratio	3.17	2.94	2.97	2.71	2.92

Note: Incomes in DM p.a., not equivalised.

Source: 1993 EVS.

Table 5.14 Distribution of Net Income in General Population

	Sample size	Mean	Median	90th percentile	10th percentile	90/10 ratio
Couples, no children, head aged <40	2 062	61 198	57 189	105 139	27 960	3.76
Couples, no children, head aged ≥40	4 223	65 963	57 253	118 372	32 887	3.60
Couples with children	12 112	68 113	59 720	113 604	38 182	2.98
Single parents	1 330	36 293	19 283	61 202	19 283	3.17
Single men aged <40	1 483	31 791	28 872	57 229	14 804	3.87
Single men aged ≥40	968	41 712	35 644	78 609	15 642	5.03
Single women aged <40	1 350	29 534	27 621	50 713	13 487	3.76
Single women aged ≥40	1 424	34 451	30 462	60 250	15 319	3.93

Note: Income in DM p.a., not equivalised.

Source: 1993 EVS.

The tight distribution of retirement income reflects the generally tight income distribution in Germany – see Table 5.14. In particular, couples with children have a very condensed income distribution in international comparisons. For this group the ratio between the 10th and 90th percentiles is about one to three. The largest degree of inequality is among men aged 40 and over, where the ratio between the 10th and 90th percentiles is about one to five. The narrow income distribution is also reflected in the closeness of mean and median, although one has to keep in mind that the upper 2-per-cent tail of the income distribution is missing in the EVS data.

None the less Figure 5.6 shows that pensioners are far from a homogeneous group. This graph uses the distribution of net equivalised income in the general population as a yardstick (see Table 5.A2 in the Appendix for the income level at each decile). Except for single men there are fewer retired households in the upper deciles than in the lower ones. Defining low-income households as those with incomes below the lowest decile point,

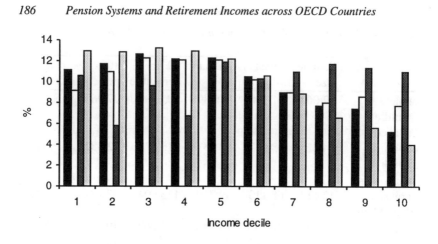

Figure 5.6   Proportion of Retirees in Each Equivalised Population Income Decile

the proportion of low-income single females is particularly high, at about 13 per cent. Correspondingly there are fewer single females in the top income decile than couples and single male elderly.

What are the 'pockets of poverty' among this group of households? About 4.2 per cent of single women in our sample are eligible for social assistance, the German definition of poverty.[27] This figure is not robust however, because the income distribution is concentrated around the poverty line and the definition of the poverty line depends on actual housing expenditures and local guidelines about how much of those are subtracted from gross income. These guidelines cannot be exactly reproduced in our data. A lower bound for the proportion of poor single women is about 3 per cent; an upper bound is 6 per cent including those who qualify for social assistance but do not take it up. The proportion of households receiving social assistance in the general population is about 3.5 per cent, and an additional 3.5 per cent are eligible but do not take up social assistance. Our results are roughly in line with those of Hauser, Mörsdorf and Tibitanzl (1997), who report that 5.2 per cent of single elderly women have incomes below 40 per cent of the average net equivalent income for 1989. We conclude that there is a small pocket of poverty among single elderly females but poverty is not significantly more frequent than in the general population. Münnich (1997) reports that 8 per cent of retired single people in West Germany have a monthly net income below DM 1 200 (which is about 10 per cent higher than the poverty line). The corresponding rate is much higher among East Germans (17 per cent).

We also calculated how these 'pockets of poverty' might change when the level of benefits is reduced. A cut of 10 per cent – roughly the magnitude of the effect of the 1999 pension reform – increases the proportion of single females eligible for social assistance by 60 per cent, from 6 to about 10 per cent.

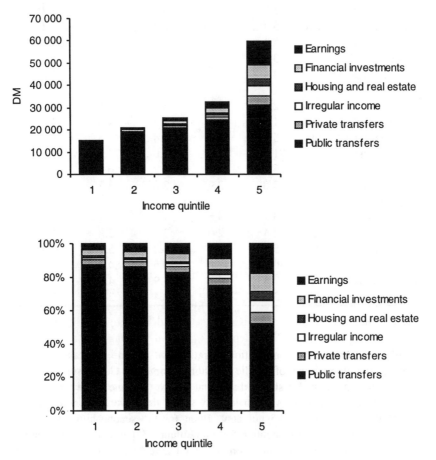

Note: Average share of income component in each quintile, defined by disposable equivalised household income.

Source: 1993 EVS, person-based.

Figure 5.7 Composition of Retirement Income, by Income Decile

Table 5.15   Composition of Retirement Income, by Age and Household Type (%)

	Age-group				
	60–64 & retired	65–69	70–74	75+	60+ & retired
Couples					
Earnings	26.7	15.1	6.4	3.1	14.7
Housing and real estate	1.9	3.6	4.1	3.6	3.2
Financial investments	5.4	7.2	8.3	8.6	7.2
Public transfers	58.1	64.8	71.8	75.5	66.1
Private transfers	3.2	5.0	5.5	5.2	4.6
Irregular income	4.4	4.4	3.8	4.1	4.2
Single men					
Earnings	2.4	7.2	4.9	2.5	4.1
Housing and real estate	1.6	3.1	4.4	3.6	3.6
Financial investments	5.2	8.8	6.4	9.3	8.0
Public transfers	81.5	71.3	77.0	74.3	75.1
Private transfers	5.7	6.7	5.2	6.6	6.1
Irregular income	3.6	2.9	2.2	3.7	3.1
Single women					
Earnings	3.7	3.6	1.9	0.1	2.8
Housing and real estate	2.4	2.0	3.4	2.8	2.3
Financial investments	5.8	5.7	6.8	5.2	6.0
Public transfers	80.9	81.8	80.6	84.9	82.2
Private transfers	3.8	4.2	4.9	4.5	4.5
Irregular income	3.6	2.8	2.4	2.5	2.5

Source: 1993 EVS.

We now turn to the composition of retirement income and take a closer look at the dominance of public pension income in Germany discussed earlier. Indeed Figure 5.7 shows that social security income is the largest part of retirement income. This is particularly so for the lower income quintiles, where its share exceeds 85 per cent. Even for the second-highest income quintile public pensions account for more than 75 per cent of household income. Asset income, mainly from financial investments, is another 6 per cent and firm pensions – almost all of the private transfers – are about 3.5 per cent for the first four income quintiles. The strong correlation between income and the share of earnings is interesting. In the richest quintile earnings are almost 20 per cent of total income of our 'retired' households and public pensions make up only 52 per cent, while regular asset income is about 16 per cent. Irregular transfers cover inheritances and lump-sum payments such as from life insurance policies, and they are significant for the richest quintile.

Table 5.15 extends the analysis of the composition of retirement income to household types, still excluding composite households. Again we see the dominance of public pensions, in particular for elderly women. Across all income quintiles social security income accounts for about 75 per cent of retirement income. This figure is a little lower than those derived from earlier analyses (see Section 5.3), mainly due to better accounting of irregular income sources such as private transfers in the EVS data. The share of private pensions is low – about 5 per cent on average. This is much smaller than the share of asset income (from both real estate and financial investments), which ranges from 8 to 12 per cent.

5.7 HOUSING WEALTH

Interpreting the economic situation of the elderly in Germany by looking at their income only yields a partial view in so far as it makes a big difference whether housing is owned or rented. Rented housing accounts for about a quarter of total consumption, and sometimes, in particular for the poorer elderly, substantially more. Table 5.16 shows that 52 per cent of couples live in owner-occupied housing, with very low cash costs. This substantially improves their economic situation relative to single people, who much more frequently live in rented housing. Only little more than 30 per cent of single women live in owner-occupied housing. On average, owner-occupier households pay about DM 3 200 annually in housing cash costs, including mortgage payments and maintenance, while average annual rent is about DM 6 000. For those who own outright, cash costs are only about DM 1 800 a year (1993 EVS).

However, measured by international standards, homeownership in Germany is very low. This low ownership rate is a general characteristic of the German housing market (see the last column of Table 5.16). For younger couples the ownership rate is about 45 per cent; for younger single people it is about 15 per cent.

Nevertheless there is substantial variation in homeownership across income, with the expected correlation between income and homeownership (see Table 5.17 and Table 5.A4 in the Appendix). This qualifies to some extent the narrow income distribution that we have seen in Table 5.13. Ownership rates are higher for the elderly than for younger people throughout the income distribution. However even in the richest quintile of the elderly, homeownership does not exceed 65 per cent, lower than the overall ownership rate in the UK and the US.

Table 5.16   Housing Status of the Retired (%)

	Age-group					
	60–64 & retired	65–69	70–74	75+	60+ & retired	All others
Couples						
Own outright	28.1	37.8	46.0	46.2	38.4	13.3
Mortgage	19.1	15.6	11.4	6.8	14.2	31.0
Rent	52.8	46.7	42.6	47.0	47.4	55.8
Single men						
Own outright	18.8	32.0	32.9	43.2	35.8	5.7
Mortgage	3.6	7.2	6.6	2.1	4.4	9.7
Rent	77.5	60.9	60.5	54.8	59.8	84.6
Single women						
Own outright	19.5	26.6	30.7	23.6	26.3	6.4
Mortgage	10.4	8.1	3.8	4.6	5.6	8.7
Rent	70.1	65.3	65.6	71.8	68.2	84.8

Source: 1993 EVS.

Table 5.17   Housing Tenure, by Income Decile

Decile of overall distribution	% of pensioners who:			% of non-pensioners who:		
	Rent	Have a mortgage	Own outright	Rent	Have a mortgage	Own outright
1	57.5	4.4	38.1	83.5	7.6	8.9
2	68.9	5.4	25.8	75.8	14.2	10.1
3	69.3	6.1	24.6	72.9	17.1	10.0
4	66.4	6.7	26.9	70.7	18.2	11.1
5	63.0	8.2	28.8	68.2	19.4	12.3
6	60.6	6.4	33.0	68.6	21.7	9.7
7	53.6	10.3	36.2	65.8	23.9	10.3
8	45.9	13.4	40.7	61.0	27.5	11.5
9	39.9	19.0	41.0	57.6	31.3	11.0
10	29.7	26.4	44.0	43.8	44.2	12.0

Note: Income decile by net equivalised income of entire population; see Table 5.A2 in the Appendix.

Source: 1993 EVS.

5.8 CONCLUSIONS

The retirement income system in Germany is monolithic. For the vast majority of elderly households it is dominated by public pensions. This public pension system has been very successful in providing a generous retirement income to all households, resulting in very little income inequality, at least by international standards. On average the ratio of income between the currently retired and the currently working is 88 per cent. This is not a true replacement rate because it compares different populations. Adding productivity increases, the actual replacement rate (retirement income of one person divided by the last pre-retirement income of the same person) is close to 100 per cent. There are even stronger signs of overannuitisation: even without a productivity correction, the average ratio of retirement income to workers' income exceeds 100 per cent for single males. On the other hand there are only small pockets of poverty among the elderly, these being particularly among elderly women. Between 3 and 6 per cent of single elderly women are eligible for social assistance, the German definition of the poverty line. This compares with a share of about 7 per cent of households in the general population that are below the poverty line. However the share of the elderly in poverty may rise if the 1999 reforms are implemented.

Unfortunately this generally happy story is unlikely to extend into the future. The demographic pressures are immense and will double the ratio of pensioners to workers between 2000 and 2040. The contribution rate to the public pension system is already considered an obstacle to international competitiveness and one of the reasons for already high unemployment today. This will be exacerbated in the future. Moreover the labour supply disincentives created by quickly rising social security taxes and the social security regulations in Germany have encouraged early retirement, thus aggravating the imbalance between the number of workers and the number of pensioners in times of population ageing.

The renewed social security debate in Germany, exemplified by the failed 1999 pension reform, has focused on changes in the benefit structure and applicable retirement ages within the current pay-as-you-go system. Major changes, such as a transition from the PAYG system to a partially or fully funded system, are not seriously debated among government officials. While it is possible to maintain the current PAYG system, it will produce very low, even negative, rates of return which will create strong incentives to 'opt out' wherever possible or to decrease labour supply. The erosion of the contribution base and the labour disincentive effects are the strongest challenges for the German public pension system.

APPENDIX

Table 5.A1   Percentage of Pensioners in Each Equivalised Population Income Decile (%)

Income decile	All pensioners	Couples	Single men	Single women
1	11.1	9.1	10.6	13.0
2	11.7	11.0	5.8	12.9
3	12.7	12.3	9.6	13.2
4	12.2	12.1	6.8	13.0
5	12.3	12.1	11.9	12.2
6	10.5	10.2	10.3	10.6
7	9.0	9.0	11.0	8.9
8	7.7	8.0	11.7	6.6
9	7.4	8.6	11.3	5.6
10	5.2	7.7	11.0	4.0

Notes:
This table corresponds to Figure 5.6 in the text.
See Appendix Table 5.A2 for decile points.

Source: 1993 EVS.

Table 5.A2   Income Levels at Each Decile Point

Income decile	Pensioner households		All households	
	Couples, net income	Single people, net income	Equivalised income	Net income
1	24 925 (67.6)	14 662 (39.7)	14 818 (40.2)	31 018 (84.1)
2	29 483 (79.9)	17 343 (47.0)	17 736 (48.1)	37 311 (101.1)
3	33 079 (89.7)	19 458 (52.7)	20 295 (55.0)	42 923 (116.3)
4	36 526 (99.0)	21 486 (58.2)	22 782 (61.8)	48 429 (131.3)
5	39 994 (108.4)	23 526 (63.8)	25 699 (69.7)	54 358 (147.3)
6	44 588 (120.9)	26 228 (71.1)	29 217 (79.2)	61 090 (165.6)
7	50 949 (138.1)	29 970 (81.2)	33 788 (91.6)	70 011 (189.8)
8	61 231 (166.0)	36 018 (97.6)	40 370 (109.4)	83 315 (225.8)
9	80 820 (219.1)	47 541 (128.9)	53 956 (146.3)	107 962 (292.6)

Notes:
Incomes in DM p.a.
Percentages in parentheses refer to the ratio of decile point to male median net earnings (36 893 DM).

Source: 1993 EVS.

Table 5.A3   Composition of Retirement Income, by Income Quintile

	Income quintile				
	1	2	3	4	5
Source (%)					
Earnings	3.3	4.6	6.1	9.1	18.0
Financial investments	3.6	3.7	4.4	6.6	10.4
Housing and real estate	1.3	1.1	1.7	2.6	5.7
Irregular income	1.1	1.3	1.6	2.7	7.0
Private transfers	3.1	2.7	3.3	3.9	6.7
Public transfers	87.6	86.6	82.9	75.2	52.2
Net equivalised income (DM p.a.)	14 496	19 708	23 855	30 372	53 331

Notes:
This table corresponds to Figure 5.7 in the text.
Average share of income component in each quintile, defined by disposable equivalised household income.

Source: 1993 EVS, person-based.

Table 5.A4   Housing Status of the Retired, by Income Quintile (%)

Income quintile	Housing status of head of household		
	Rent	Mortgage	Own outright
1	63.2	5.0	31.8
2	68.0	6.2	25.7
3	63.6	7.4	29.0
4	54.7	9.3	36.0
5	37.2	20.7	42.1

Note: Income quintile by net equivalised income of the retired.

Source: 1993 EVS.

NOTES

1.   For example the retirement system of civil servants.
2.   Mean retirement age in 1995 is the average age of workers receiving a public pension for the first time in 1995.
3.   This includes GRV-equivalents. For GRV only the share is 10.6 per cent of GDP.

4. The nominal contribution rate in 1998 was 20.3 per cent of gross income, shared equally between employers and employees. The effective contribution rate was about 25.4 per cent including contributions paid by general taxes.
5. We use the term 'retirement' to refer to the receipt of a public pension. There is substantial 'pre-retirement' without public pension income; see below.
6. Some professions, most notably civil servants, have their own mandatory retirement system. Although implicit, these systems effectively mimic the general public pension system and are included in it here.
7. About 5.6 per cent of workers lay below this threshold in 1996.
8. Since mid-1999 these low-income jobs are subject to social security taxation.
9. Monthly gross household income in Germany averaged DM 5 500 in 1999, corresponding to a purchasing power of about US$32 000 annually (based on the OECD purchasing power parity of DM 2.06 per US dollar).
10. Technically the return on the PAYG system is taxable. The return is deemed a fixed share of the pension benefits that is below the general income tax exclusion unless the household has substantial non-pension income.
11. This holds *mutatis mutandis* for pensioners who have private health insurance coverage.
12. This *old-age* pension for disabled workers is different from the *general* disability pension for younger workers.
13. See Riphahn (1995) for a detailed description of disability regulations.
14. Three years after the 1992 reform. This number of years has been changed frequently.
15. This allowance used to be very generous but has been dramatically reduced recently.
16. Since 1 January 1992 Germany has a unified public pension system with the same replacement ratios and the same adjustment factors for new pensioners in East and West Germany. For details of the transition in East Germany see Schmähl (1991 and 1992). Same replacement rates do not imply same levels of pensions however, because the replacement rates refer to the relative wage level in either part of the country.
17. More precisely it was planned to link the replacement rate in a less-than-proportional fashion to changes in life expectancy at age 65, lagged by eight years. The drop of 10 per cent is based on government projections that assume very small changes in life expectancy after 2003. See Hain and Müller (1998).
18. Curiously the German system before 1992 provided a large increase in retirement benefits for work at ages 66 and 67. However it was ineffective because the inducements to early retirement by far offset this incentive.
19. See Börsch-Supan (1992b). The actuarially fair adjustments equalise the expected social security wealth for a worker with an earnings history starting at age 20 over all retirement ages from 60 to 70. A higher discount rate yields steeper adjustments.
20. Section 5.6 will take a closer look at the composition of retirement income.
21. OECD (1996), based on World Bank projection by Bos et al. (1994). The OECD dependency ratio relates the number of people aged 65 and over to the number aged between 15 and 64.
22. Börsch-Supan, 1996. See the same source for the following estimates on female labour force participation and migration.
23. Verband Deutscher Rentenversicherungsträger, 1995. In addition to this *general* disability pension for workers aged under 60, an almost equal share of workers claim the *old-age* disability pension between ages 60 and 65.
24. The implicit rate of return in a PAYG system is the discount rate that equalises the present values of the flow of lifetime contributions and the flow of expected pensions; see Schnabel (1998).
25. We plan further research on composite households.
26. This average conceals a bimodal distribution: some workers retire at 65 because their lifetime earnings were too small for a reasonable pension, while high-income workers tend to work longer, potentially for motivational reasons.
27. Eligibility depends on total cash income, household size and a (weak) asset test.

REFERENCES

Birg, H. and A. Börsch-Supan (1999), *Für eine neue Aufgabenteilung zwischen gesetzlicher und privater Altersversorgung (For a New Division of Labour between Public and Private Provision for Old Age)*, Bielefeld and Mannheim: Gesamtverband der deutschen Versicherungswirtschaft.

Börsch-Supan, A. (1992a), 'Saving and consumption patterns of the elderly: the German case', *Journal of Population Economics*, 5 (4), 289–303.

Börsch-Supan, A. (1992b), 'Population aging, social security design, and early retirement', *Journal of Institutional and Theoretical Economics*, 148 (4), 533–57.

Börsch-Supan, A. (1995), 'The impact of population ageing on savings, investment and growth in the OECD area', in OECD, *Future Global Capital Shortages: Real Threat or Pure Fiction?*, Paris: Organisation for Economic Co-operation and Development, pp. 103–41.

Börsch-Supan, A. (1996), 'Demographie, Arbeitsangebot und die Systeme der sozialen Sicherung (Demography, labour supply and social security systems)', in H. Siebert (ed.), *Sozialpolitik auf dem Prüfstand (Social Policy under Scrutiny)*, Tübingen: J.C.B. Mohr (Paul Siebeck), pp. 13–58.

Börsch-Supan, A. (1998), 'Germany: a social security system on the verge of collapse', in H. Siebert (ed.), *Redesigning Social Security*, Tübingen: J.C.B. Mohr (Paul Siebeck), pp. 129–59.

Börsch-Supan, A. and A. Reil-Held (2001), 'How much is transfer and how much is insurance in a pay-as-you-go pension system? The German case', *Scandinavian Journal of Economics*, forthcoming.

Börsch-Supan, A. and R. Schnabel (1998), 'Social security and declining labor force participation in Germany', *American Economic Review*, 88 (2), 173–8.

Börsch-Supan, A. and R. Schnabel (1999), 'Social security and retirement in Germany', in J. Gruber and D. Wise (eds), *Social Security and Retirement around the World*, Chicago and London: University of Chicago Press, pp. 135–80.

Börsch-Supan, A. and K. Stahl (1991), 'Life cycle savings and consumption constraints', *Journal of Population Economics*, 4 (3), 233–55.

Bos, E., M.T. Vu, E. Massiah and R. Bulatao (1994), *World Population Projections, 1994–95*, Baltimore and London: Johns Hopkins University Press for World Bank.

Bundesministerium für Arbeit und Sozialordnung (1997), *Statistisches Taschenbuch (Statistical Pocket-book)*, Bonn: Bundespresseamt.

Casmir, B. (1989), *Staatliche Rentenversicherungssysteme im internationalen Vergleich (International Comparison of Public Pension Systems)*, Frankfurt: Lang.

Euler, M. (1982), 'Einkommens- und Verbrauchsstichprobe 1983 (The German Income and Consumption Survey 1983)', *Wirtschaft und Statistik*, (6), 433–7.

Euler, M. (1987), 'Einkommens- und Verbrauchsstichprobe 1988 (The German Income- and Consumption Survey 1988)', *Wirtschaft und Statistik*, (8), 664–9.

Hain, W. and H.-W. Müller (1998), 'Demographische Komponente, zusätzlicher Bundeszuschuss, Verstetigung des Beitragssatzes und finanzielle Auswirkungen des RRG 1999 (A demographic factor, an additional state subsidy, a steady contribution rate and the financial consequences of the pension reform law 1999)', *Die Rentenversicherung*, (1–2/98), 105–24.

Hauser, R., K. Mörsdorf and F. Tibitanzl (1997), 'Dokumentation empirischer Daten zur Alterssicherung in der Europäischen Union und Nordamerika (Documentation of empirical data about old age provision in the European Union and North America)', University of Frankfurt, mimeo.

Hertel, J. (1992), 'Einnahmen und Ausgaben privater Haushalte im Jahr 1988 (Income and expenditures of private households in 1988)', *Wirtschaft und Statistik*, (9/92).

Lang, O. (1998), *Tax Incentives and Investments during the Life-Cycle: Empirical Analyses of Savings Behavior and Portfolio Decisions of Private Households in Germany*, Baden-Baden: Nomos Verlag.

Münnich, M. (1997), 'Zur wirtschaftlichen Lage von Ein- und Zweipersonen-haushalten (The economic status of one- and two-person pensioner households)', *Wirtschaft und Statistik*, (2/97), 120–35.

OECD (1996), *Ageing in OECD Countries: A Critical Policy Challenge*, Paris: Organisation for Economic Co-operation and Development.

OECD (1997), 'Ageing populations, pension systems and government budgets: simulations for 20 OECD countries', Organisation for Economic Co-operation and Development, Economics Department, Working Paper no. 168.

Prognos AG (1995), *Perspektiven der gesetzlichen Rentenversicherung für Gesamtdeutschland vor dem Hintergrund politischer und ökonomischer Rahmenbedingungen (Perspectives of the Public Pension System in Germany in Light of the Political and Economic Situation)*, DRV-Schriften 4, Frankfurt am Main: Prognos.

Prognos AG (1999), *Versorgungslücken in der Alterssicherung: Privater Vorsorgebedarf für den Schutz im Alter (Gaps in Old Age Security: The Need for Private Old-age Provision)*, 561-5338, Basel: Prognos.

Riphahn, R.T. (1995), 'Disability retirement among German men in the 1980s', Ludwig Maximilians University of Munich, Münchner Wirt-schaftswissenschaftliche Beiträge 95-20.

Schmähl, W. (1991), 'Alterssicherung in der DDR und ihre Umgestaltung im Zuge des deutschen Einigungsprozesses: Einige verteilungspolitische Aspekte (Old age security in the GDR and its redesign during the process of unification: some aspects of redistributional policy)', in G. Kleinhenz (ed.), *Sozialpolitik im vereinten Deutschland (Social Policy in the Unified Germany)*, Berlin: Duncker & Humblot, pp. 49–95.

Schmähl, W. (1992), 'Public pension schemes in transition: Germany's way to cope with the challenge of an ageing population and the German unification', University of Bremen, Centre for Social Policy Research, mimeo.

Schnabel, R. (1998), 'Internal rates of return of the German pay-as-you-go public pension system', University of Mannheim, SFB 504 Discussion Paper no. 98-56.

Sommer, B. (1994), 'Entwicklung der Bevölkerung bis 2040: Ergebnis der achten koordinierten Bevölkerungsvorausberechnung (The development of the population until 2040: results of the eighth population projection)', *Wirtschaft und Statistik*, (7), 497–503.

Statistisches Bundesamt (1997), *Einkommens- und Verbrauchsstichprobe 1993: Aufgabe, Methode und Durchführung (The German Income and Consumption Survey 1993: Task, Methodology and Implementation)*, Fachserie 15, No. 7, Stuttgart: Metzler-Poeschel.

Statistisches Bundesamt (various years), *Fachserie 1: Bevölkerung und Erwerbstätigkeit, Reihe 4.1.1: Stand und Entwicklung der Erwerbstätigkeit*, Stuttgart: Metzler-Poeschel Verlag.

Verband Deutscher Rentenversicherungsträger (1995), *Rentenzugangsstatistik*, Frankfurt am Main: VDR.

Verband Deutscher Rentenversicherungsträger (1997), *Die Rentenversicherung in Zeitreihen (The German Public Pension System in Time Series)*, Frankfurt am Main: VDR.

6.   Pension Provision in Italy

Agar Brugiavini and Elsa Fornero[*]

6.1   OVERVIEW

During the 1990s the Italian pension system has been undergoing a process of radical change. Two major reforms have been enacted – the Amato reform in 1992 and the Dini reform in 1995[1] – while preserving the pay-as-you-go (PAYG) nature of financing the social security programme. For over 40 years the system had remained almost untouched in its original set-up, with legislative innovations aimed mainly at extending and increasing benefit generosity. It would be fair to say that at the beginning of the 1990s in cross-country comparisons the Italian pension system stood out as the typical example of a system on the verge of a crisis.

Three major aspects of this crisis could be identified:

- An extreme generosity of benefit payments. In particular almost every benefit outlay was characterised by relatively high replacement rates and generous pension indexation. The existence of an early retirement option attracting no actuarial penalty further exacerbated this aspect.
- A pervasive and often perverse redistributive feature. This was a consequence of the coexistence of many different schemes following markedly different, *ad hoc* rules. Policy-makers made extensive use of differential treatments across funds to gain political consensus.
- A structural financial unbalance, clearly visible in the persistently high (present and projected) deficits between payroll taxes and expenditures

[*]The authors wish to thank Rocco Aprile, Onorato Castellino, Richard Disney, Pier Marco Ferraresi and Carlo Mazzaferro for useful comments. They are also indebted to participants at the IFS International Pensioners' Incomes Conference (London, 19–20 March 1998) for helpful discussion.

Financial support from the Italian Ministry of University and Research (MURST) and the TMR – Training and Mobility of Researchers – (EU-DGXII) project on 'Savings and Pensions' is gratefully acknowledged.

(see Section 6.3.3). This applied to almost every public fund and emerged from estimates of net pension liabilities and from projected equilibrium contribution rates.

The reforms aimed to tackle these anomalies. The Amato reform mainly targeted financial unsustainability by means of pension cuts, both immediate (i.e. through the abolition of pension indexation to real wages) and long-term (i.e. through the lengthening of the period used for computing pensionable earnings and the gradual abolition of the extremely generous rules for public employees). The Dini reform was more timid in terms of further immediate cuts but changed the institutional design more profoundly, by switching from an earnings-related to a 'contribution-based' pension formula and by introducing actuarial fairness as the basic principle inspiring benefit computation for all workers. Both reforms however largely safeguarded the 'acquired' pension rights of present workers, thus placing the main burden of adjustment onto the younger and future generations.

Finally further benefit cuts – a mild version of a much more radical plan covering the whole welfare system[2] – were introduced in the budget law for 1998, by the Prodi Government. The main feature of these provisions is an acceleration of the abolition of the remaining differences between private and public employees regarding early retirement.

It is of course possible to view these overall developments either in terms of the many things that remain to be done or in the more optimistic terms of the big changes that have been achieved, particularly in the light of the strong social opposition to any benefit reduction. As a result of these changes Italy is certainly now moving towards a less unbalanced, less distorted and more uniform pension system. However an excessively long transition – the new system will be fully phased in only in the very distant future (around 2050) – coupled with very unfavourable demographic dynamics, makes further changes necessary in the near future.

6.2   BASIC FEATURES OF INCOME PROVISION FOR THE ELDERLY

Public pension expenditure in Italy (including old-age benefits, disability and survivor benefits plus income maintenance provisions for the very old) still absorbs a large fraction of the country's GDP. Although overall social protection expenditure remains below the European average (25.9 versus 28.1 per cent of GDP) pension expenditure ranks amongst the highest in the European Union (16 per cent of GDP in 1997) (see EUROSTAT (2000)). It

Table 6.1 *Sources of State Income Available to Pensioners, 1997–98*

Payment (benefits)	Type	Contribution rates (% of gross earnings)	Expenditure (% of GDP)	No. of pensions (× 1 000) [% of population 60+][a]	Eligibility criteria
Old-age, seniority and survivor pensions	Contributory	Public employees: 32.7 Private employees: 32.8 (23.91 + 8.89)[b] Self-employed: 16	12.22	14 621 [113%]	*At present:* earnings-related *In the future:* contributions-related (see Table 6.2)
Disability pensions	Contributory	(Included in the above)	1.61	3 121 [24%]	(Partly) means-tested
Income support ('pensione sociale' and integration to minimum pension)[c]	Non-contributory	—	0.91	2 073 [16%] (of which 691 are 'social pensions')	Means-tested
Other payments (mainly TFR[d])	Contributory	7.41	1.91	—	Accumulated funds available at job termination
Benefits in kind	Non-contributory	0.6	—	—	Means-tested

16.6

Notes: See overleaf.

Notes to Table 6.1:
[a]It must be recalled that the ratio of pensions to the population aged 60+ is rather ambiguous since the numerator includes some double counting (one person receiving more than one pension) while the denominator also includes economically active people.
[b]The first figure refers to the employee, the second to the employer contribution.
[c]'Social pensions' are granted to people aged 65 or over with no other means; 'integration' relates to all contributory pensions (first two rows) below a given floor; their number overlaps therefore with the first two kinds of pensions.
[d]TFR = 'Trattamento di Fine Rapporto'. This is a severance pay fund providing a lump-sum benefit at the time of job termination (see endnote 14).

Sources of Table 6.1: Ministero del Tesoro, 1999; Commissione per l'Analisi delle Compatibilità Macroeconomiche della Spesa Sociale, 1997a; ISTAT, 1999.

follows that pensions represent by far the largest item in social protection expenditure (65.1 per cent versus an EU average of 45.2 per cent).

These figures show the widespread use of public pensions for general welfare provision in Italy, largely at the expense of other social expenditure items (expenditure for families and children, unemployment, housing and social exclusion totalled 5.4 per cent of social expenditure in 1997 versus an EU average of 19.4 per cent).

Table 6.1 shows a summary of the various components of Italian social expenditure for the elderly.

The reliance on public pensions as a 'safety net' also emerges in the frequent use of pre-pensioning schemes, which improperly transfer the burden of industrial restructuring to the pension system by allowing redundant workers to retire early on a full pension.[3] A further example is the widespread use of an unemployment benefit scheme – known as 'cassa integrazione' – in favour of workers approaching retirement age who are in danger of losing their jobs. This scheme (which is under revision) guarantees to workers a large share (normally 80 per cent) of take-home pay while preserving the employment status, thereby allowing them to accumulate seniority while they are laid off.[4] On the other hand options for gradual retirement are practically non-existent, although some 'bridging' provisions are provided for by law.

Reliance on generous public pensions is also the main reason for the very minor, complementary role of private pensions (see Section 6.4).

As for health insurance, all individuals over 65 with household income not greater than 70 million lire (about double the 1995 average income) are entitled to almost free access to doctors, medicines and hospital care. Most elderly people also get considerable discounts both on railways and on local transport, while other provisions (especially nursing homes and home-care facilities) are typically managed by local health authorities and municipalities and thus vary greatly between cities and regions of the country.[5]

Finally the possibility of cumulating pension benefits and income from work is restricted, particularly for early retirees;[6] however the existence of illegal employment not only allows circumvention of this prohibition but may somewhat reduce the role of public pensions as the main source of income for the elderly. Although we cannot provide a reliable estimate of black economy activities for retirees, it is fairly common for a pensioner to engage in labour market activities, mainly in part-time jobs.[7]

6.3   PUBLIC PENSION PROVISION

6.3.1   Recent Developments and the Present Situation

Due to past *ad hoc* legislation and the long transition to the new regime, the Italian pension system is by no means a harmonised programme. Rather it is the result of the combination of different schemes. In terms of covered workers and pensioners the most important schemes are:

- the private sector employees' fund (INPS-FPLD), covering some 11.7 million active workers and 10.4 million pensioners;[8]
- the public sector employees' schemes, with 3.3 million workers and 2.4 million pensioners; and
- the INPS self-employed schemes (6.5 million workers and 3.4 million pensioners).[9]

All schemes are mandatory and provide old-age and disability pensions as well as benefits to survivors. Pension benefits are (and will remain for many years) earnings-related (see Table 6.2). Apart from these common features there are striking differences in payroll tax rates and in benefit calculation across funds. In turn each fund has experienced (with a different timing and to a different extent) a financing deficit hence calling for the government to bail them out through public money.

FPLD is by far the most important fund. It was established in 1919 with a mixed financing method, featuring aspects of both PAYG and funding. The 1939–45 war and post-war inflation however almost nullified reserves – largely invested in long-term Treasury bonds – and by 1952 the scheme had basically turned to pure PAYG. It was later transformed into a mainly redistributive device (as opposed to an insurance mechanism) by successive benefit-increasing innovations, mostly introduced during the 1960s and 1970s. These included: 'seniority pensions' (early retirement), whereby pension benefits could be collected, irrespective of age, after 35 years of work; the adoption of a final salary formula to calculate benefits (see Table 6.2); and automatic indexation of benefits to real wages. Redistribution took place not only across cohorts of workers but also within each cohort, due to the different rules in place for different funds and/or different individuals, thus leading to very different implicit rates of return that workers could expect on their contributions.[10] Although the need to finance these innovations led to a steady increase in payroll tax rates, this has been insufficient to reduce the gap between present (and projected) expenditure and contributions (see Table 6.5 in Section 6.3.3).

Similar and even more generous developments took place for the other schemes; public employees in particular had the possibility of retiring on a full pension after 20 years of service (15 years for married women), while after 1990 the pension entitlements of self-employed workers were equalised to those of private employees in spite of their contribution rates having been (and still being) markedly lower.

Table 6.2   Pension Determination Formulae

	Private employees		Public employees		Self-employed	
Before the Amato reform						
Pension formula	2% of last five years' average salary		2% of last monthly salary		2% of last 10 years' average earnings	
Indexation	All benefits indexed to statutory minimum wage					
Eligibility	F	M	F	M	F	M
age/seniority	55/35	60/35	65/15	65/20	60/35	65/35
Amato reform long-run provisions						
Pension formula	2% of the average of whole-working-life earnings, each amount adjusted for inflation and further revalued by 1% per year					
Indexation	All benefits adjusted for inflation					
Eligibility	F	M	F	M	F	M
age/seniority	60/35	65/35	65/35	65/35	60/35	65/35
Dino reform long-run provisions						
Pension formula	Based on value of contribution payments 'notionally' accumulated, compounded at the GDP growth rate; this is then converted into a lifetime annuity according to actuarial criteria; actuarial coefficients growing with age, irrespective of gender					
Indexation	All benefits adjusted for inflation					
Eligibility	Minimum age 57 (after age 65 no further growth of actuarial adjustment)					

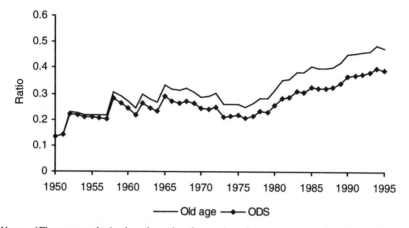

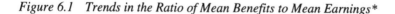

Note: *Figures are obtained as the ratio of mean benefit over mean earnings for each year (average for both males and females). We include old-age benefits and old-age plus disability and survivor benefits (ODS).

Sources: INPS, 1970a, 1970b and 1996; Ministero del Tesoro, 1981; ISTAT, *Annuario Statistico Italiano*, various years.

*Figure 6.1   Trends in the Ratio of Mean Benefits to Mean Earnings**

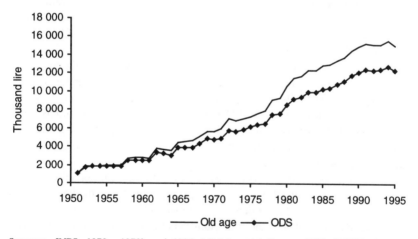

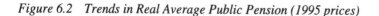

Sources: INPS, 1970a, 1970b and 1996; Ministero del Tesoro, 1981; ISTAT, *Annuario Statistico Italiano*, various years.

Figure 6.2   Trends in Real Average Public Pension (1995 prices)

Table 6.2 summarises for the main schemes the various eligibility criteria and pension formulae.

Figures 6.1 and 6.2 show the effects of the growing generosity of the public pension system in terms of the aggregate replacement rate, i.e. the ratio of mean pension to mean earnings (Figure 6.1), and in terms of the real average pension (Figure 6.2). For both indicators the upward trend is clearly visible and particularly marked from the mid-1970s until the early 1990s.

This is the situation that the Amato and Dini reforms set out to correct in the presence of considerable political constraints of maintaining social consensus. Retrenchment in pension expenditure could be achieved only at the cost of preserving the *status quo* of senior workers[11] through the application of a pro rata method of benefit calculation.

In order to illustrate how the system operates in the early stage of the transitory period we carry out a simulation and present the results in Table 6.3. This is based on the transitional regime operating in 1998, when a retiree would typically have a large share of his or her old-age benefits computed according to the pre-1992 reform (pre-Amato regime) and a small share computed according to the rules of the 1992 reform (Amato transition). The steady-state calculations for the Amato and Dini regimes are instead described in Table 6.4 in Section 6.3.2. Note however that the Amato regime will never reach its steady state, as the Dini regime will be gradually phased in (the new contribution-based formula will entirely apply only for pensions maturing from about 2030). In practice, up to 2030, people will retire with benefits determined according to transitional rules, which imply actual replacement ratios in between those of Table 6.3 and those of Table 6.4 (see Ferraresi and Fornero (2000)).

In Table 6.3 we take the example of a single man retiring at the age of 63 on 1 January 1998, assuming he earned the median (in each year for both his cohort and gender)[12] full-time wage since 1958 (hence working for 40 years) and paid contributions to the FPLD fund. As a variant of the base case (full career, median earner) we consider the same individual with a five-year gap in his working career, occurring between ages 49 and 54, thus leaving the last eight years prior to retirement with a full wage.

We contrast these two bench-mark cases with two further cases where earnings are 25 per cent of median earnings and three times median earnings respectively. We have chosen these extreme variants of the base case in order to explore situations where the minimum benefit and benefit-capping would apply.

In the example we focus on two types of benefits: old-age benefit (pension) providing an annuity from the retirement age and a one-off benefit obtained from the severance pay fund (TFR, 'Trattamento di Fine

Table 6.3 How the Italian Old-age Pension Varies with Lifetime Earnings: Single Men Retiring in 1998, INPS-FPLD Fund Only (incomes in thousands of 1997 lire)

	Annual earnings related to the median					
	¼		1		3	
Number of years without contributions	0	5[a]	0	5[a]	0	5[a]
Yearly gross pension	8 874	8 874	26 878	23 519	72 506	65 071
Yearly net pension	8 567	8 567	21 972	19 948	51 416	47 030
Gross pension (% of current gross average earnings)[b]	23.7	23.7	71.6	62.7	193.2	173.4
Net pension (% of current net average earnings)[b]	32.0	32.0	82.2	76.6	192.3	175.9
Gross replacement ratio (%)	103.0	103.0	78.0	68.2	70.1	62.9
Net replacement ratio (%)	103.1	103.1	90.4	80.3	84.6	77.4
TFR (severance pay fund)	11 539	8 898	46 154	35 593	138 464	106 778
% of TFR on last yearly gross earnings	133.9	103.3	133.9	103.3	133.9	103.3

Notes:
[a]Refers to a five-year gap in working career.
[b]The ratios are obtained with respect to the 1997 average earnings in industry (gross earnings are 37.5 million lire; net earnings are 26.7 million lire).

Source: Authors' calculations based on a sample of workers drawn from the archive of the Istituto Nazionale Previdenza Sociale (INPS) administrative records.

Rapporto').[13] Old-age benefits are computed according to the pro rata method envisaged in the Amato transition, as our retiree has 35 years of contributions under the pre-Amato (before 1993) regime and five years of contributions in the transitional regime. Table 6.3 shows how these entitlements vary with lifetime earnings for both the continuous and the discontinuous career.

Taking first the median-earnings, full-career case, our retiree receives a pension of (approximately) 27 million lire in his first year of retirement, plus a lump sum of 46 million lire. The net benefit is substantially below the gross benefit due to a highly non-linear income tax schedule. The gross replacement ratio is 0.780, hence very close to the theoretical replacement ratio of 80 per cent, while the net replacement rate is much higher. This is because earnings attract both social security contributions (inclusive of the TFR contributions) and income tax. Due to income tax progressivity the latter is typically higher than the tax paid on old-age benefits.

For retirees characterised by low earnings, minimum benefit provision applies which brings the benefit level to a given pre-set level. Hence a low earner has on average a higher replacement rate than a retiree at median earnings.

For a high earner a piecewise linear function operates.[14] This applies lower rates of return to higher brackets of pensionable earnings. Hence the gross replacement rate for the high earner in Table 6.3 is 60–70 per cent.

Turning to the discontinuous-career case, first it should be noticed that the gap in earnings history does not greatly affect the results for the median earner (or for the high earner). This is due to the fact that the gap occurred before the average-salary calculation period, hence pensionable earnings do not change. However the reduction in the number of years of contributions, also used in benefit calculations, generates a slight reduction in old-age benefits. Moreover the low-earnings retiree is not affected by the gap at all, as his computed benefit level is lower than the minimum guaranteed level even with a full working history and is therefore automatically topped up. The gap in contribution history obviously affects the results for the severance pay fund entitlement as a smaller number of contributions are accumulated over the working life.[15]

Overall our results confirm that the current transitional system is extremely generous.

6.3.2   Outlook for the Future

The 1995 reform basically confirmed the importance of the public pension system in delivering economic support for the elderly. This is most evident in the high payroll tax rate envisaged not only for the transitional period but also projected for the distant future. Since 1995 the contribution rate for private sector and public sector employees has been at the level of 33 per cent of gross earnings.[16] On the one hand this contribution rate is inadequate to cover pension expenditures, while on the other hand it is too high for private pensions to play a role in old-age insurance (see Section 6.4).[17]

The future steady state (post-1995 regime, Dini reform) rests on four principles:

1. Most significantly, the contribution-based method of benefit computation. Lifetime payroll taxes will be 'notionally' accumulated and the notional fund will accrue a return equal to the (geometric mean of)

GDP growth rates. At retirement the fund value will be converted into a lifetime annuity in accordance with actuarial criteria (see Table 6.2). The pension benefit level will be a function of (a) the individual wage profile (or earned income for the self-employed) as reflected in the notional fund, (b) the length of working life, (c) retirement age and (d) the growth rate of the economy.

2. Flexibility of retirement age. This is strongly related to the contribution-based benefit method. In fact retirement age and length of working life are now major determinants of the pension level. Therefore a window of retirement ages (between 57 and 65)[18] is available to retirees irrespective of gender. The actuarial factor used in converting the fund into an annuity increases with retirement age, hence the trade-off between retirement age and the level of old-age benefits is built into the system and clearly spelt out to prospective retirees. Minimum benefit levels still apply should the computed benefit fall below that amount.

3. Uniformity of rules. Actuarial fairness will prevail not only across generations, but also across different working groups – a striking change from the present maze of different schemes. In particular, privileged funds – such as the public sector employees' funds, the self-employed funds and the special funds for journalists and bank clerks – will gradually disappear.[19]

4. Financial equilibrium. This is intended through two features of the new system: the first is the equality of the internal rate of return on contributions with the GDP growth rate and the second is a periodical revision of the 'actuarial coefficient' on the basis of updated mortality tables.[20]

Table 6.4 shows a comparison between the Amato and Dini regimes by presenting two summary measures – the replacement rates and the ratio between average pension and average earnings – under various assumptions concerning the growth rate of the economy GDP (g) and the earnings growth rate (y). (Both parameters are assumed to be constant.)

Comparing the two reforms at their steady states, it can be seen that neutrality between the two regimes is achieved for a worker who retires at age 62 and seniority 37. This is when earnings growth exceeds the GDP growth rate by half a percentage point. For higher seniority and retirement ages the Dini regime implies both a higher replacement ratio and a higher ratio of average pension to average earnings, but the decision to retire at younger ages will carry a higher penalty. Taking 1989 as an example, the percentage of people retiring before age 62 was about 95 per cent. This gives an idea of how effective the Dini reform will be in forcing people to choose between a lower pension or a higher retirement age.

Table 6.4   A Comparison between the Amato and Dini Regimes

Age (years)	Seniority (years)	y	g	Replacement ratio (%)		Average pension / average earnings (%)	
				Amato	Dini	Amato	Dini
57	35	2	1.5	58.6	50.1	55.4	47.4
		3	2.5	54.4	50.2	46.7	43.1
60	37	2	1.5	61.3	57.8	57.9	54.6
		3	2.5	57.0	57.8	48.9	49.6
62	37	2	1.5	61.3	61.7	57.9	58.3
		3	2.5	57.0	61.8	48.9	53.0
65	40	2	1.5	65.9	73.7	62.3	69.6
		3	2.5	61.0	73.8	52.3	63.3

Notes:
y = earnings growth rate (assumed constant).
g = growth rate of economy GDP (assumed constant).

Source: Castellino (1995); similar results are reported in Banca d'Italia (1995), Antichi (1997) and Ferraresi and Fornero (2000).

6.3.3   Projections and Sustainability

In spite of the reform efforts to restore financial stability, sustainability of the Italian pension system is still a long way off. Financial equilibrium will be reached only at the end of a very long transitional period, when not only the present pensioners – whose benefits have largely remained untouched – but also future pensioners, whose benefits will be derived in accordance with the pro rata mechanism, will have passed away. 2050 is a realistic date for the new Dini regime to be fully phased in; until then the yearly deficits of the system will have to be covered by public money. The main reason for a persistent deficit is the inability of the transition rules to counterbalance the very unfavourable demographic evolution.

The most recent official estimates[21] of the equilibrium payroll tax rates (which obviously differ from the actual ones) are presented in Table 6.5. After the 1995 reform the statutory contribution rates are 32.7 per cent for private and public employees and about 17 per cent for the self-employed. The increases in the actual payroll tax rates required to bridge the gap are simply not feasible. This means either that further pension cuts will be inevitable or that the difference between expenditure and contributions (over 3 per cent of GDP) will have to be financed through general taxation or

Table 6.5   Equilibrium Payroll Tax Rates (%) and Fund Imbalances (% of GDP)

	2000	2010	2020	2030	2040	2050
Private employees (FPLD)						
Equilibrium tax rates	45.0	47.8	48.4	48.4	42.3	34.5
Deficit	2.03	2.46	2.56	2.56	1.57	0.29
Public employees						
Equilibrium tax rates	48	45–50	45–50	45–50	?	?
Deficit	1.06	1.05	1.10	1.15	?	?
Self-employed						
Equilibrium tax rates	19.9	26.8	31.1	31.4	26.3	22.1
Deficit	0.10	0.37	0.55	0.55	0.30	0.10
Independent farmers						
Equilibrium tax rates	152.3	146.5	177.7	84.3	55.0	38.9
Deficit	0.73	0.54	0.35	0.20	0.10	0.05
Overall deficit	3.92	4.42	4.61	4.46	?	?

Sources: For private employees, self-employed and independent farmers, INPS (1998). Equilibrium tax rates for the self-employed are weighted averages between craftsmen and shopkeepers. Annuity values are supposed to be revised every 10 years according to current life tables. For public employees, authors' calculations and projections on the basis of Monorchio (1994, p. 36).

through an increase in explicit public debt (this last option however is hardly feasible under the Stability Pact of the EU).

In discussing pension policy the Italian government has only recently focused attention on the ratio of pension expenditure to GDP, and the pros and cons of future policy changes are evaluated against a target level of this measure. Projections published by the Treasury[22] show an increase in the pension/GDP ratio under most demographic and economic scenarios until 2030–35, followed by subsequent moderate decreases, largely determined by the phasing-in of the recent reforms. However at the end of the simulation period (in 2045–50 approximately) the expenditure/GDP ratio will still be somewhat higher than the starting figure (13.63 per cent in 1995), regardless of the economic scenario.[23] While economic growth and the recent reforms may help in reducing the expenditure/GDP ratio, these gains will be more than offset by unfavourable demographic trends.

Clearly however the impact of the recent reforms is going to be severe even on current pensioners, now that only price (and not wage) indexation of benefits is envisaged.

6.4   PRIVATE PENSIONS

6.4.1   The Present

Not surprisingly pension funds play a negligible role in the Italian economy. Up to 1992 pension funds were not even regulated; there were over a thousand schemes (some very small) which covered about 7 per cent of the work-force, largely concentrated in the service sector and banking and insurance sector and in northern regions of the country. After a failed attempt by the Amato Government to promote a private pension system as a relevant 'second pillar' of the social security system,[24] the Dini reform took up the issue, apparently with more success.[25]

6.4.2   Likely Future Developments

The present legislation envisages a path to build up a stronger private component of the Italian pension system. It is however a very gradual and narrow path, relying mainly on occupational pension funds rather than on individual accounts, and on the accumulation in the new pension funds of financial flows now accruing to the severance pay fund (TFR). Legislation also encourages additional voluntary contributions from both the employee and the employer, by providing tax incentives. These consist mainly of tax deductibility of contributions up to a threshold level and under the condition that the employee has switched (at least partially for current employees, but completely for new workers) the new TFR flows to a pension fund.[26]

Indeed participation in pension funds will be mainly determined by negotiations between employees and employers. However, since the ultimate decision is left to the individual worker, it will strongly depend on the employee's advantages relative to alternative investment opportunities (coinciding with the *status quo* in the case of the TFR flows). Various parameters[27] influence the implicit net-of-tax return rate and therefore the three choices open to an employee: joining a pension fund, maintaining the TFR in its current form (a credit towards the employer, which the employee cashes in at job termination) and choosing alternative saving instruments (namely group life insurance policies) for any further contribution.

Simulation exercises (Fornero, 1999) show that, in spite of incentives offered by the Dini reform, current legislation does not treat pension funds particularly favourably: joining a pension fund is unambiguously convenient only for workers characterised by high marginal tax rates and, oddly enough, for short participation periods. New provisions approved by Parliament in 1998 are likely to increase this advantage, starting from 2001. In the mean time the government plans a more marked shift from TFR to pension funds.

The implicit rate of return is not however the only relevant parameter in the decision to join a pension fund; heterogeneity in preferences as well as variation in annuitised resources must also be taken into account. Factors weighing against pension funds include the high level of compulsory social security coverage for employees and the capping on lump-sum withdrawals. Also private annuity contracts, although already available, are not particularly popular in households' portfolios. Factors in favour of pension funds include the lively interest stimulated by their introduction as a new financial product and as a new instrument in industrial relations, as well as fear of further cuts in social security.

The complex interaction of these different aspects makes it hard to reach any definite conclusion on the future development of private pension funds. Simulation exercises show that the new inflows will remain comparatively low in the near future. It is thus difficult to envisage scenarios, even when considering relatively high interest rates, in which the ratio of pension funds' assets over GDP will be more than a few percentage points (i.e. over 5 per cent).

6.5 ACTIVITY RATES

Activity rates play a crucial role in determining future developments of a PAYG pension system. While several studies have addressed the impact of demographic trends on the financial distress of the Italian pension programme, very few have pointed to the importance of trends in labour force participation, particularly for the age-group close to retirement age.[28] Activity rates have declined substantially in recent years: a marked decline can be observed in labour force participation for men between 1960 and 1994 (Figure 6.3). As previously mentioned, the statutory retirement age currently varies by gender, type of fund and number of years of contribution. As a result there exists some relevant variability in actual retirement ages. The generosity of the early retirement option has further enhanced this variability by encouraging many workers to leave the labour force at relatively young ages.[29] This is reflected in time-series data: male participation rates have dropped substantially for the 60–64 age-group (from just below 60 per cent in 1960 to approximately 30 per cent in 1994) and a non-negligible decline can be observed for the 50–59 age-group. The drop in activity rates of older women is counteracted by the growth in participation rates of younger cohorts (Figure 6.4), as is the case in many other European countries.

Table 6.6 is based on survey data and gives a finer classification of activity rates by age-groups. In particular it shows that only 65 per cent of men aged

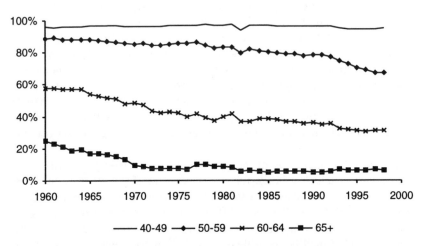

Source: Authors' calculations based on ISTAT (1960–80, 1975–85 and 1986–94).

Figure 6.3   Male Activity Rates

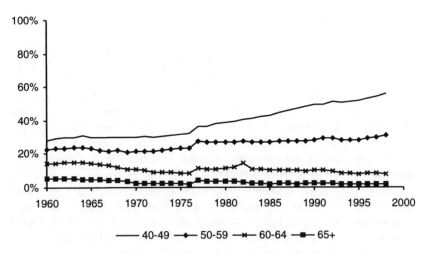

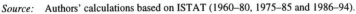

Source: Authors' calculations based on ISTAT (1960–80, 1975–85 and 1986–94).

Figure 6.4   Female Activity Rates

Table 6.6   Percentage of Economically Active Men and Women, by Age-group, 1989–95 (%)

	Age-group		
	55–59	60–64	65–69
Men	64.6	29.5	9.0
Women	18.2	7.0	2.0

Source: Authors' calculations from the Bank of Italy Survey of Household Income and Wealth.

55–59 are still active, while the proportion for women is as low as 18 per cent (this is an average over the years 1989–95). However it should be mentioned that black economy activities are quite common in Italy for early retirees and that this income source does not show up in survey data. Hence we are possibly overestimating the extent to which there exists detachment from the labour force at young ages.

6.6   INCOME OF THE ELDERLY

In order to analyse the distribution of income for the elderly we use a sample of Italian households (drawn from the Bank of Italy Survey of Household Income and Wealth – SHIW) which spans seven years and contains four waves: 1989, 1991, 1993 and 1995. In order to avoid potential biases in the results due to the effects of macro-shocks, we merge the four waves and obtain a large cross-sectional sample.[30] Although the survey is designed to collect data on wealth and financial aspects of Italian households it contains detailed information on different sources of income for each individual in the household. Because of the time-span covered by our sample our data reflect the transitional period between the pre-Amato regime and the Amato regime. The Appendix provides details on characteristics of the sample.

In our investigation the unit of analysis is the household: we distinguish between couples, single men and single women. There are 23 404 households; 74 per cent are couples, 8 per cent single men and 18 per cent single women; a large fraction of single women are in the 75-and-over age-group.

We use a particular definition of pensioner and of pensioner income.

We define a pensioner as a male aged 60 or over or a female aged 55 or over or any individual aged 55 or over if retired. The first criterion is an age criterion based on statutory retirement ages prevailing for private sector employees. The second criterion intends to include all those who are actually retired, starting from an arbitrary retirement age.[31] However it should be noted that on the one hand in the public sector the statutory retirement age is 65 for both men and women and public sector employees represent a non-negligible part of the working population, but on the other hand the early retirement option was much more favourable to public sector employees, particularly women.[32] Our definition implies that we include in the pensioner group some individuals who are working on a full-time basis between the ages of 60 and 65. Furthermore the current Italian legislation allows people to claim some benefits while still working, hence there could be a sizeable fraction of earnings in the pensioner group at all age-groups but this is most likely at younger ages. For couples we assume that the household is a pensioner household if the husband is a pensioner (and attribute all the income of husband and wife to the husband). This has the effect of including also some working wives. Our definition is somewhat arbitrary and it leaves out a substantial group of people from the pensioner category who have retired before the age of 55, particularly women previously working in the public sector who had the chance to claim old-age benefits at a very early age. The advantage of this definition is that we include all individuals (households) who retire as a result of their age and not because of their economic conditions; in fact a large fraction of young pensioners could be a self-selected group (either taking advantage of the early retirement option or receiving disability benefits).[33]

Living with other earners is very common in Italy. Table 6.7 shows that 33 per cent of all couples where the head of the household is a pensioner live in multiple benefit units. We define as multiple benefit units the households where members of the household, other than the nuclear benefit unit, have income. It is important to stress that the size of benefit units does not correspond to the actual household size. While the former is used to illustrate the extent of income sharing within the household the latter will be used to compute equivalence scales in order to account for family structure.

Table 6.7   Percentage of 'Pensioners' Living with Other Benefit Units (unit of analysis is benefit unit) (%)

	Age-group					All pensioners
	55–59	60–64	65–69	70–74	75+	
Couples	47.0	39.7	29.2	22.1	17.0	32.7
Single men	33.3	30.4	27.4	21.1	25.3	26.8
Single women	47.1	28.9	22.7	14.8	17.8	23.9

Sources: SHIW, 1989, 1991, 1993 and 1995.

Table 6.8   Proportion of Pensioners in Each Macro-region

	North	Centre	South
Percentage	39.3%	39.1%	35.9%
Total number of households	8 791	5 029	9 584

Sources: SHIW, 1989, 1991, 1993 and 1995.

In Italy grown-up children often live with their parents even if they are engaged in labour market activities. There are no definite explanations for this co-residence; it is probably due to housing market imperfections but income sharing may also be an important determinant. This explains why the percentage of multiple benefit units is particularly high (47 per cent) for pensioner couples and for single pensioner women in the 55–59 age-group. However it is hard to establish the extent of actual income sharing within the household: in many cases the basic benefit unit provides housing services and other goods and services with no corresponding transfer of income from younger members.

What Table 6.7 does not show is that there are also a non-negligible number of 'extended families'. An extended family is a broader concept than a multiple benefit unit. For example there are families where the head of the household (or the couple) is relatively young and lives with his or her pensioner parents or other older pensioners. In our sample 2 per cent of all benefit unit couples (including non-pensioners) are extended families; this percentage rises to 5 per cent for all benefit unit single women. While we cannot describe all cases of extended families, extended families where the head is a pensioner appear in Table 6.7 as multiple-benefit-unit pensioners.

An important feature of the Italian economy is the regional distribution of resources. Many argue that there exist two separate economies – the rich northern regions and the poor southern regions. Given our interest in income distributions we have also provided information at macro-regional level. For example Table 6.8 shows that pensioners seem to be uniformly distributed across three macro-regions (North, Centre and South), with a slight predominance in northern and central regions, mostly due to the age structure of the population in different regions.

Total income of the benefit unit is defined as after-tax income (net of social security contributions and income taxes), excluding imputation of income from owner-occupied houses, and it is the result of the aggregation of income of the individuals belonging to the basic benefit unit.[34] Although we focus the attention on husband and wife (for couples) and single heads of household, we want to take account of family composition. In order to

Table 6.9   Average Italian Pensioner Income, by Marital Status and Age-group, based on Benefit Units (incomes in thousands of 1994 lire per year)

	Age-group					All pensioners
	55–59	60–64	65–69	70–74	75+	
Couples	38 893	40 357	35 259	31 940	27 313	35 883
Ratio	(0.86)	(0.95)	(0.91)	(0.97)	(0.78)	(0.89)
Single men	24 064	33 684	28 697	23 203	23 505	26 788
Ratio	(0.96)	(1.32)	(1.26)	(1.02)	(0.96)	(1.11)
Single women	28 870	24 636	21 538	18 363	18 302	21 471
Ratio	(0.95)	(0.96)	(0.92)	(0.86)	(0.84)	(0.89)
Number of benefit units	981	2 047	1 921	1 286	1 736	7 971

Note: Ratio is the ratio of average equivalent income of each cell to average equivalent income of the relevant non-pensioner household group.

Sources: SHIW, 1989, 1991, 1993 and 1995.

compare incomes for families of different sizes we compute equivalised income on the basis of a very simple equivalence scale of 1 for a single person, 0.7 for any additional adult and 0.5 for any children.

In Table 6.9 we present sample averages of total income in thousands of 1994 Italian lire per year.[35] We distinguish two main groups – pensioners and non-pensioners – and focus our attention on pensioners. Within the pensioner sample we distinguish different age-groups. In each cell the first row is average income in thousands of 1994 lire, while the second row shows (in parentheses) the ratio of average equivalent income of each cell to average equivalent income of the relevant non-pensioner household group. Hence for example for the group defined as 'couples, all pensioners' we observe a ratio of equivalent incomes equal to 0.89, because equivalent income for pensioner couples is 15 931 thousand lire (mean equivalent income for non-pensioner couples is 17 900 thousand lire).

Pensioners do not fare substantially worse in terms of their equivalised incomes when comparing with the equivalised income of non-pensioners. Single men are even richer than the non-pensioner group. Overall the group aged 60–64 seems to enjoy a high level of income – higher than the 65–69 age-group. A peculiar feature of the table is the rise in income between the 55–59 age-group and the 60–64 age-group and then the regression to the overall mean by ages 65–69. This is due to our definition of pensioners: while we include all males aged 60 or over and all females aged 55 or over (because of the age criterion based on statutory retirement ages), we also include actual pensioners between ages 55 and 60. This implies that we include in the pensioner group some individuals who might still be working on a full-time basis between the ages of 60 and 65. Our results suggest that single men, given their household structure, are overprotected by the social security system when compared with other pensioners and with the non-pensioner group. However single male pensioners are also a small fraction of the sample.

Income distribution within the household is quite stable across age-groups. For pensioner couples the share of income belonging to the husband is approximately 78 per cent of total income of the couple.[36]

As we previously argued multiple benefit units are very common in the Italian economy. This implies that looking at total income of the basic benefit unit may be misleading as income sharing could take place within the household and pensioners could have access to resources provided by other members of the family. Table 6.10 provides the same calculations as presented in Table 6.9 but the unit of analysis is now the household rather than the benefit unit; hence total income includes incomes of all members of the household. Although the equivalence scales used are the same as in Table 6.9 (each additional adult counts for 0.7 units regardless of whether he or she has income), this change in the definition makes a difference to the results.[37] While the basic pattern across groups seems the same as in Table 6.9 (for example single men enjoy incomes higher than those of other groups in the population and higher in equivalised terms than those of the non-pensioner population) average income increases for all groups taken together.[38] In terms of equivalent income this is making pensioner households much better off: for

Table 6.10 Average Italian Pensioner Income, by Marital Status and Age-group, based on Households (incomes in thousands of 1994 lire per year)

| | Age-group | | | | | All |
	55–59	60–64	65–69	70–74	75+	pensioners
Couples	39 595	40 459	35 130	31 972	27 143	35 711
Ratio	(0.88)	(0.95)	(0.90)	(0.85)	(0.76)	(0.88)
Single men	23 685	33 133	28 470	22 637	23 330	26 508
Ratio	(0.96)	(1.34)	(1.26)	(1.04)	(0.96)	(1.12)
Single women	29 154	24 889	21 004	17 995	17 795	21 017
Ratio	(0.98)	(0.97)	(0.91)	(0.84)	(0.82)	(0.88)
Number of households	1 212	2 380	2 088	1 361	1 823	8 864

Note: Ratio is the ratio of average equivalent income of each cell to average equivalent income of the relevant non-pensioner household group.

Sources: SHIW, 1989, 1991, 1993 and 1995.

Table 6.11   Income Distributions of Different Population Groups (incomes in thousands of 1994 lire per year)*

	Mean	Median	90th percentile	10th percentile	90/10 ratio	No. of house-holds
Couples, no children, head aged <40	44 083	41 485	67 437	20 629	3.3	889
Couples, no children, head aged ≥40	40 127	33 395	69 246	17 668	3.9	2 992
Couples with children	39 629	33 751	66 213	18 266	3.6	8 203
Single parents	23 945	22 469	39 031	8 444	4.6	482
Single men aged <40	29 041	25 148	48 384	13 802	3.5	575
Single men aged ≥40	32 399	25 299	52 259	13 286	3.9	445
Single women aged <40	24 573	23 419	37 481	11 526	3.2	361
Single women aged ≥40	22 943	20 988	38 078	7 985	4.8	593
North	35 450	29 317	62 226	13 583	4.6	8 791
Centre	32 933	26 878	58 706	12 329	4.8	5 029
South	29 539	24 126	53 686	10 274	5.2	9 584

Note: *This table is based on the non-pensioner group as defined in the text (women younger than 55, men younger than 60, and people older than 55 who are still economically active). We also provide the income distribution according to three macro-regions; in this case we are using the entire sample of pensioners and non-pensioners.

Sources: SHIW, 1989, 1991, 1993 and 1995.

example couples end up enjoying almost the same standard of living as all non-pensioners. This result is observed in particular for the 60–69 age-group, when one is most likely to find working children living with their parents.

Equivalence scales are obviously relevant for the above result. In order to illustrate the effect of our choice of equivalence scale we present in Table 6.11 some indicators of the income distribution for different population groups by restricting our attention to non-pensioners.

Amongst non-pensioners, couples with no children have the highest median income. Couples are on average richer than single households. Single women and single parents have low levels of the 10th percentile of income, close to the minimum benefit level and below the official poverty line of 1994. These are also the groups with highest inequality in the distribution of income. Hence Tables 6.9 and 6.11 suggest that, particularly for certain groups of the population, pensioners are not the poor ones. This conclusion was also reached by Cannari and Franco (1990) in a study based on the 1987 SHIW sample.

Finally from Table 6.11, for the whole sample, we find no evidence of large regional imbalances, the northern regions being characterised by slightly higher average income and slightly lower inequality.

Table 6.12 looks at the income distribution of pensioners. Couples have the highest median income in the pensioner group: the ratio of the 90th percentile to the 10th percentile indicates that income inequality is not particularly high in this group. Amongst pensioners the highest income inequality occurs for single men.

Table 6.13 looks at the distribution of pensioner income using the household as the unit of analysis rather than the benefit unit. Again the underlying pattern of Table 6.12 is preserved (inequality is higher for single men and for the 60–64 age-group). However Table 6.13 shows that including

Table 6.12   Distribution of Pensioner Incomes, based on Benefit Units (incomes in thousands of 1994 lire)

	Age-group					All
	55–59	60–64	65–69	70–74	75+	pensioners
Couples						
Median	25 338	25 771	23 316	22 954	20 712	23 684
90th percentile	46 345	53 210	48 348	45 898	35 506	48 049
10th percentile	13 102	13 071	13 511	14 293	14 187	13 511
90/10 ratio	3.54	4.07	3.58	3.21	2.50	3.56
Single men						
Median	15 817	20 352	17 327	15 790	14 507	16 219
90th percentile	27 341	43 079	34 385	34 438	29 923	34 876
10th percentile	8 274	9 458	8 904	8 668	8 162	8 516
90/10 ratio	3.30	4.55	3.86	3.97	3.67	4.10
Single women						
Median	16 206	14 739	14 115	13 404	12 409	13 759
90th percentile	30 308	31 129	27 129	24 100	23 280	26 823
10th percentile	8 107	7 783	7 929	7 906	7 686	7 831
90/10 ratio	3.74	4.00	3.42	3.05	3.03	3.42

Sources: SHIW, 1989, 1991, 1993 and 1995.

Table 6.13   Distribution of Pensioner Incomes, based on Households (incomes in thousands of 1994 lire)

	Age-group					All
	55–59	60–64	65–69	70–74	75+	pensioners
Couples						
Median	34 559	33 639	27 467	25 660	22 448	28 785
90th percentile	65 260	72 379	66 943	57 714	47 454	65 360
10th percentile	15 079	15 582	14 966	14 966	14 841	15 070
90/10 ratio	4.33	4.64	4.47	3.86	3.20	4.34
Single men						
Median	20 509	24 496	20 461	17 256	17 735	20 083
90th percentile	44 808	74 393	51 549	48 898	48 470	51 549
10th percentile	11 701	10 962	10 058	9 052	8 403	9 133
90/10 ratio	3.83	6.79	5.12	5.40	5.77	5.64
Single women						
Median	24 008	18 073	16 694	14 737	14 012	15 982
90th percentile	53 569	48 424	40 676	33 518	33 716	41 975
10th percentile	9 659	8 266	8 377	8 182	8 042	8 210
90/10 ratio	5.55	5.86	4.86	4.10	4.19	5.11

Sources: SHIW, 1989, 1991, 1993 and 1995.

other income units not only increases mean and median income substantially but also, surprisingly enough, increases inequality. This is due to the growth in the income of the 90th percentile while the 10th percentile is often unaffected by the inclusion of additional incomes. The difference in results is particularly acute for single women, which suggests that the poorest households are the ones where there is only a basic income unit, most likely a single person, while co-residence is common for middle-income or high-income families.

Differences in sources of income could partly explain the observed income variation and the differential inequality patterns between groups. In Table 6.14 we look at the average proportions of income from various sources. We aggregate income from the subcategories and distinguish between income from the state, investment income and earnings, making use of the aggregate values of income as defined in the survey. We further disaggregate income from the state into types of provision.[39]

The largest income item for pensioners is income from the state, from old-age pensions, means-tested income maintenance programmes and disability insurance. Private pensions are negligible (only seven individuals in the sample reported receiving a private pension). Income from the state accounts for between 65 and 90 per cent of total income.

*Table 6.14 Composition of Pensioner Incomes, by Marital Status and Age-group (%)**

| | Age-group | | | | | All |
	55–59	60–64	65–69	70–74	75+	pensioners
Couples						
Investment income	9.5	9.4	9.1	9.3	8.7	9.2
Earnings	9.6	23.0	6.3	2.8	0.8	10.8
State	80.9	67.6	84.6	87.9	90.5	80.0
of which:						
Income maintenance	0.0	0.0	3.0	3.9	6.5	2.7
Old age	69.6	58.4	74.4	77.0	77.1	69.6
Disability insurance	11.0	8.9	7.1	6.9	6.8	7.7
Single men						
Investment income	12.0	13.7	13.6	11.6	12.0	12.8
Earnings	1.6	18.3	4.1	2.4	1.0	5.8
State	86.4	68.0	82.3	86.0	87.0	81.4
of which:						
Income maintenance	0.0	0.0	1.0	1.6	2.0	1.0
Old age	70.2	59.0	73.2	80.5	80.5	73.2
Disability insurance	16.0	8.6	9.1	3.6	4.5	6.9
Single women						
Investment income	11.6	11.5	10.6	11.6	12.6	11.6
Earnings	17.2	7.9	0.8	0.5	0.4	3.9
State	71.2	80.6	88.6	87.9	87.0	84.5
of which:						
Income maintenance	0.1	1.0	4.2	3.8	5.7	3.8
Old age	66.1	72.3	79.2	80.2	76.0	75.8
Disability insurance	5.0	7.0	4.9	3.7	5.0	4.8
By macro-region	North		Centre		South	
Investment income	12.7		10.1		8.4	
Earnings	6.7		8.3		9.4	
State	80.6		81.6		82.2	
of which:						
Income maintenance	2.0		2.6		3.6	
Old age	73.1		71.4		70.3	
Disability insurance	5.4		7.5		8.1	

Note: *Figures for components of income from the state do not add up to the total of income from the state because of rounding.

Sources: SHIW, 1989, 1991, 1993 and 1995.

The second item is either investment income or earnings according to the age-group. As we have explained, our definition of pensioners includes some people working between the ages of 60 and 65. Investment income (which excludes imputed income from owner-occupied houses) ranges from 13 per cent for single men to 9 per cent for couples. Due to under-reporting of financial assets, figures might understate the actual income from assets; however there is no evidence that under-reporting varies systematically with our age–status groups.

Earnings are a small but non-negligible fraction of income for pensioner couples (even neglecting the 60–64 age-group where earnings represent an important source). This reflects the facts that the wife of a pensioner can be economically active and that the pensioner himself, though retired, can have earnings from part-time activities.

Because the bulk of income for the pensioner group comes from pension benefits, and this is basically constant across age-groups, it is useful to provide further information on the specific sources of income from the state. We distinguish three components:

- basic maintenance income ('pensione sociale', provided by INPS);[40]
- old-age and early retirement pension income plus pension to survivors plus war pensions and other minor cases (all of these are provided by INPS and the two public employees' funds – Treasury Fund and Government Employees Fund);
- disability benefits (in the pre-1995 legislation these are the only means-tested benefits).

Our results show that income maintenance provisions are a larger fraction of income for old single women than for other pensioners; this is an indication that the very poor pensioners might be in this group. Old-age benefits seem a constant income share between groups, while disability benefits are a higher share for couples and single men in the young age-groups.

One important feature of the data is homeownership. In Table 6.15 we show the tenure status of pensioners. The proportion of benefit units that are outright owners is remarkably high, while mortgages are of considerable size only for the non-pensioner group. This is due to housing and financial markets imperfections which strongly discourage the demand for mortgages while encouraging intergenerational informal arrangements. Two typical cases occur: either (1) the owner-occupied house is received as an inheritance or inter vivos gift from previous generations or (2) the young household needs to build up its own assets in order to make a house purchase and parents provide substantial financial support to their children at the time of the purchase.

Table 6.15   Pensioner Benefit Units, by Housing Tenure (%)

	Age-group					All pensioners	All non-pensioners
	55–59	60–64	65–69	70–74	75+		
Couples							
Own outright	63.2	68.3	70.2	69.1	67.9	68.1	48.1
Mortgage	6.7	5.9	3.6	3.4	0.8	4.4	11.6
Rent	30.1	25.8	26.2	27.5	31.3	27.5	40.3
Single men							
Own outright	60.6	65.5	59.3	54.5	54.5	58.5	44.6
Mortgage	3.0	1.4	0.6	1.6	0.5	1.1	6.5
Rent	36.4	33.1	40.1	43.9	45.0	40.4	48.9
Single women							
Own outright	55.2	55.6	52.1	49.2	44.2	50.2	40.2
Mortgage	4.5	1.7	2.3	2.1	0.7	1.9	6.9
Rent	40.3	42.7	45.6	48.7	55.1	47.9	52.9

Sources: SHIW, 1989, 1991, 1993 and 1995.

Table 6.16   Pensioner Housing Status, by Income Quintile (%)

Pensioner income quintile	Housing status of head of household		
	Rent	Mortgage	Own outright
1	34.8	3.6	61.6
2	32.1	2.3	65.6
3	35.9	3.3	60.8
4	38.9	4.2	56.9
5	34.0	3.2	62.8

Sources: SHIW, 1989, 1991, 1993 and 1995.

Table 6.16 looks at the housing status of pensioners by income quintile.[41] Owner-occupation is almost uniformly spread over the income distribution. A slight difference emerges for the bottom and top quintiles (1st, 2nd and 5th), where owner-occupation amongst pensioners is more likely. Households that have a mortgage on their owner-occupied house are a very small fraction throughout.

Table 6.17 shows that the proportion of outright owners is approximately constant over the income distribution, both for pensioners and non-pensioners, and also that the two distributions are not too dissimilar. Hence pensioners do not differ substantially from the rest of the population in their housing tenure choices. The major difference is that while approximately 64 per cent of pensioners are outright owners, only around 48 per cent of non-pensioners own their houses outright. This is due both to an age effect (some pensioners have paid off their mortgages) and to a cohort effect (new generations face a gradually more flexible mortgage market). Interestingly enough the non-pensioners who start up a mortgage are mostly at the top of the income distribution.

The composition of pensioner income is shown for each quintile in Figure 6.5 and the average net income of each quintile is given in Figure 6.6. In both cases we compute quintiles on the basis of equivalent income for the pensioner group only. As argued above, the poorest 20 per cent of the sample of pensioners has almost all its income coming from the state (this also includes a non-negligible fraction from the income maintenance provision). The richest 20 per cent has a much higher equivalised income from investment.

In Figure 6.7 we present the proportion of pensioners in each decile of the population income distribution.[42] It is worth pointing out that the level of equivalent income defining the bottom decile is slightly below the poverty line for 1994. Overall there is a substantial proportion of pensioners in the

Table 6.17   Housing Tenure of Pensioner and Non-pensioner Populations, by Income Decile

Income decile of overall distribution	% of pensioners who:			% of non-pensioners who:		
	Rent	Mortgage	Own	Rent	Mortgage	Own
1	35.4	5.0	59.6	47.6	5.6	46.8
2	29.9	3.4	66.7	44.2	5.5	50.3
3	29.4	3.7	66.9	41.3	8.3	50.4
4	30.9	3.2	65.9	42.4	9.2	48.4
5	32.0	4.9	63.1	43.7	8.9	47.3
6	33.7	5.2	61.2	43.8	9.6	46.7
7	34.2	5.6	60.2	39.7	11.7	48.6
8	31.3	3.9	64.8	38.5	14.7	46.8
9	30.4	2.8	66.8	41.3	13.6	45.1
10	24.7	5.6	69.7	41.9	13.8	44.3

Sources: SHIW, 1989, 1991, 1993 and 1995.

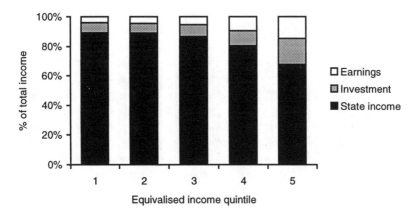

Sources: SHIW, 1989, 1991, 1993 and 1995.

Figure 6.5 Composition of Pensioner Income, by Income Quintile

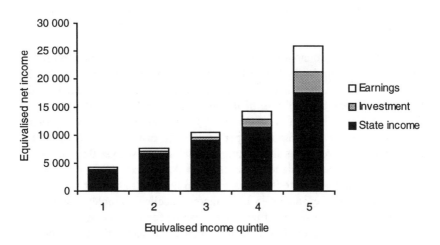

Sources: SHIW, 1989, 1991, 1993 and 1995.

Figure 6.6 Equivalised Pensioner Income Components, by Income Quintile

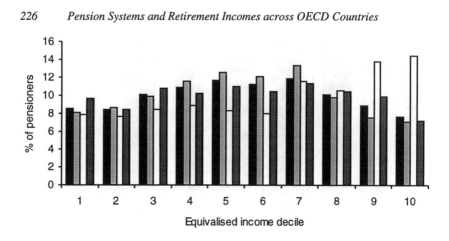

■ All pensioners ▨ Couples ☐ Single men ▨ Single w omen

Note: *For exact percentages see the Appendix.

Sources: SHIW, 1989, 1991, 1993 and 1995.

Figure 6.7   Percentage of Pensioners in Each Income Decile, based on Benefit Unit Income*

first four deciles (around 40 per cent), and this percentage declines to reach 8 per cent in the top decile. When breaking this figure into status and gender groups we see that there is a sizeable percentage of pensioner couples in the first four deciles, but the bulk of the distribution is between the 4th and 7th deciles. A similar pattern is observed for the proportion of single pensioner women, while for men almost 50 per cent of the distribution lies in the top four deciles. However, as the 'entire sample' figure shows, this group has little weight in the population (see also the Appendix). The general result emerging from this picture is that, apart from the small group of single men, the proportion of pensioners in each income decile is roughly constant: if anything a larger proportion of pensioners can be found in the middle income ranges rather than at the lower deciles. Figure 6.8 shows the proportion of pensioners in each income decile when the deciles are based on households rather than benefit units. In this case there is a higher percentage of single women and couples in the lower income deciles than for benefit units. This confirms the findings of Table 6.10: when considering total household income, some single-women-pensioner and couple-pensioner households fall in the lower deciles because they do not have additional sources of income.

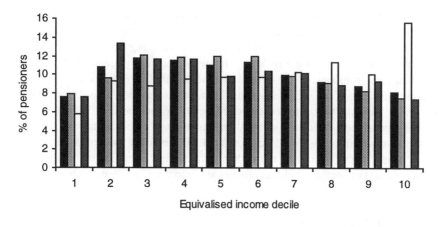

■ All pensioners ▣ Couples □ Single men ▨ Single w omen

Note: *For exact percentages see the Appendix.

Sources: SHIW, 1989, 1991, 1993 and 1995.

*Figure 6.8 Percentage of Pensioners in Each Income Decile, based on Household Income**

Table 6.18 Net Income Levels at Each Decile Point

Pensioner income decile	Pensioner couple		Single pensioner	
	Thousands of 1994 lire	% of overall median income	Thousands of 1994 lire	% of overall median income
1	13 511	50.9	8 106	30.5
2	16 363	61.7	9 247	34.8
3	18 645	70.2	10 846	40.9
4	21 041	79.3	12 566	47.3
5	23 697	89.3	14 302	53.9
6	26 643	100.4	16 254	61.3
7	30 473	114.8	18 790	70.8
8	36 194	136.4	22 509	84.8
9	48 054	181.1	28 520	107.5

Sources: SHIW, 1989, 1991, 1993 and 1995.

Finally we compute how much money is needed for a pensioner to get to any point in the pensioner income distribution by comparing the distribution decile points for each group (pensioner couples and single pensioners) with a measure of average earnings. We compare actual income decile points with actual median income of the overall income distribution (both pensioners and non-pensioners). Table 6.18 suggests that a pensioner couple needs 1.8 times median earnings to get to the top decile of their income distribution, while single pensioners need much less than this average (median income for the overall distribution is 26 525 million lire). However the bottom decile level for couple pensioners is at more than half median earnings, while approximately 40 per cent of single pensioners are below half median earnings.

6.7   CONCLUSIONS

Understandably enough the Italian pension system provides the backbone of elderly income and is crucial in preventing poverty among the elderly.

Much of the system's traditional generosity remains, despite the cut-backs experienced after the 1992 and 1995 reforms. Replacement rates for an employee working continuously for 40 years and earning the median wage of his cohort are, at present, around 80 per cent; in the new regime this will drop slightly, to about 75 per cent for a 65-year-old retiree with 40 years of contribution. The new pension system (reaching the steady state around the year 2050) will be based on actuarial criteria and will avoid many of the drawbacks of a system largely based on political patronage. On the other hand, for individuals with either low earnings or short working histories, computed pension benefits will tend to be low. Nevertheless the system will provide an adequate safety net through income maintenance provisions. The analysis based on survey data confirms that about 80 per cent of pensioner income comes from the state, where about 70 per cent can be attributed to old-age, early retirement or survivor benefits and the remaining 10 per cent comes from income maintenance ('pensione sociale') or disability benefits. These findings are consistent across age-groups and across status–gender groups. However there is not strong evidence that pensioners are poorer than the rest of the population nor that there is strong regional inequality in terms of the pensioner population. Despite this positive finding the financial sustainability of the system is still at risk. The envisaged long transition to the new regime requires extremely high payroll tax rates that might result in non-competitive labour costs. On the other hand raising tax rates or further cutting benefits to induce immediate sustainability may not be politically feasible.

Despite repeated recent reform efforts the Italian pension system is not yet in equilibrium.

APPENDIX

We select the sample by excluding households where some basic information is missing (for example age of the head of the household) or where both benefit units report zero total income. This implies that we are excluding households where some household members, but not the head of the household or the spouse, might have income. A typical example might be where an elderly person is head of the household, despite having no income, and he or she lives with grown-up children who do have income. We use years 1989, 1991, 1993 and 1995. Income for the different years is converted to 1994 lire by means of a general consumer price index ('Indice dei Prezzi al Consumo dell'Intera Collettivita' Nazionale', ISTAT).

Our final sample is as follows:

Overall sample:	23 404 households.
	Note that a couple counts as one observation as we impute the income of the spouse to the head of the household. The number of benefit units is slightly smaller, as explained in the text.
Non-pensioner sample:	14 540 (as defined in the text).
Pensioner sample:	8 864 (as defined in the text).

Deciles are computed for the pensioner sample only and on the basis of equivalent income in the household. However we sort individuals rather than benefit units (households) when calculating the decile points and effectively assign to each adult in the benefit unit the equivalent income of the household. Finally we count the proportion of benefit units (households) falling in each decile for each status group. When we consider household income we use total income in the household including income of other members and then convert this to equivalent income by means of the same equivalence scale (0.7 for each additional adult) used for the benefit unit.

Table 6.A1   Total Composition of the Sample: Couples and Single Households

	Share of the overall sample (%)
Couples	74.0
Single men	7.7
Single women	18.3

Sources: SHIW, 1989, 1991, 1993 and 1995.

Table 6.A2   Pensioner Income, by Composition and Income Quintile, based on Benefit Units

	Quintile				
	1	2	3	4	5
Source (%)					
Investment income	6.0	6.1	8.7	10.3	17.7
Earnings	4.0	4.4	5.3	9.2	14.5
State	90.0	89.5	86.0	80.5	67.8
Average equivalent income (thousands of 1994 lire)	4 264	7 679	10 409	14 154	25 976

Sources: SHIW, 1989, 1991, 1993 and 1995.

Table 6.A3   Income Deciles: Benefit Units

Decile of the overall distribution	% of all pensioners	% of couple pensioners	% of single male pensioners	% of single female pensioners
1	8.7	8.0	7.9	9.7
2	8.5	8.5	7.8	8.4
3	10.2	9.8	8.5	10.9
4	10.9	11.5	8.9	10.3
5	11.8	12.5	8.4	11.1
6	11.2	12.1	8.1	10.5
7	11.9	13.3	11.6	11.4
8	10.2	9.7	10.6	10.6
9	8.9	7.6	13.8	9.9
10	7.7	7.1	14.4	7.2

Sources: SHIW, 1989, 1991, 1993 and 1995.

Table 6.A4 Income Deciles: Households

Decile of the overall distribution	% of all pensioners	% of couple pensioners	% of single male pensioners	% of single female pensioners
1	7.6	7.9	5.8	7.6
2	10.8	9.6	9.4	13.3
3	11.7	12.1	8.7	11.6
4	11.6	11.8	9.6	11.6
5	11.0	11.9	9.7	9.8
6	11.4	11.9	9.7	10.4
7	9.9	9.9	10.2	10.1
8	9.2	9.1	11.3	8.9
9	8.7	8.2	10.0	9.3
10	8.1	7.5	15.6	7.4

Sources: SHIW, 1989, 1991, 1993 and 1995.

NOTES

1. Both reforms are named after the Prime Minister of the day.
2. As envisaged in the final report by the Commissione per l'Analisi delle Compatibilità Macroeconomiche della Spesa Sociale (1997b).
3. This is not identical to the early retirement provisions as it only applies to employees in certain sectors. The use of pre-pensioning was particularly widespread during the 1980s and early 1990s, largely to reduce the costs of unemployment benefits.
4. Various proposals for reform have been advanced, which envisage the gradual abolition of pre-pensioning and a complete revision of the 'cassa integrazione', with the aim of limiting its length and increasing its insurance (as opposed to assistance) character.
5. The present government has undertaken the task of revising the various assistance programmes, plus the National Health Service, with the aim of reducing disparities and malpractices and increasing efficiency, mainly through the introduction of comprehensive and uniform means testing ('riccometro').
6. Workers who benefited from early retirement are only allowed to engage in an independent activity and then they only receive a certain amount of the pension benefit.

7. In order to understand the economic conditions of the elderly in Italy special attention must be paid to the role of the household. Pensioners are often members of extended households, either because the head of the household is a pensioner who has working children living with him or her or because the retiree is no longer the head of the household but lives with his or her children. The existence of these extended households is quite common and it implies potential within-family transfers, which are usually hard to document. There is also evidence of a large increase in charitable and voluntary work by younger pensioners. See ISTAT (1997).

8. INPS ('Istituto Nazionale per la Previdenza Sociale') is the Italian 'National Institute for Social Insurance'. It is the main social security administration fund and manages the largest public pension fund in Italy, the FPLD ('Fondo Pensione Lavoratori Dipendenti') plus a number of minor funds (including those of the self-employed).

9. Data refer to 1998. The total number of pensioners is 16.2 million. Their attribution to the various schemes is difficult because each pensioner may belong to more than one scheme and have more than one pension. The numbers in the text have been obtained by considering a ratio of pensions to pensioners equal to the average. Sources: Ministero del Tesoro, 1999 (*Relazione Generale sulla Situazione Economica del Paese*); ISTAT, 1999.

10. This was generated by various features of the scheme. For example the introduction of benefit-capping and minimum benefit levels implied a redistribution between income groups. The introduction of a minimum benefit had a large impact on redistribution due to the extent of take-up (roughly 46 per cent of pensioners in 1989). On the other hand a final-salary benefit calculation implied, other things being equal, higher implicit returns for steeper earnings profiles. Finally the largest redistributive impact must be imputed to the introduction of seniority pension, which allowed workers to collect their pensions at different ages with no actuarial penalty for early leavers. Early retirees could also benefit from the further advantage of working in self-employment while drawing pension benefits (Castellino, 1995).

11. The 1995 reform envisaged a split-line between junior workers and senior workers at the level of 18 years of contributions. The pro rata method of benefit calculation applies only to junior workers, and even within this group the greater the contributions under the pre-reform regime the higher the share of the pension computed according to the old rules.

12. The cohort of interest was born between 1927 and 1936. The choice of the age band is constrained by the format of the data.

13. The severance pay fund was originally devised as an insurance scheme against involuntary loss of employment but has gradually evolved into a form of deferred compensation, no matter the specific cause of job termination. It is mandatory in those industries and sectors where it is provided and it pays a lump-sum benefit at the time of detachment from the employer. Under TFR regulations, 2/27 (7.41 per cent) of a yearly gross salary must be set aside by the firm; workers are entitled to partial withdrawals from the fund only to finance house purchases or to cover exceptional medical expenses. There is no actual accumulation in a separate fund or trust: the funds are at the firm's disposal and the obligation for firms is to meet TFR benefit payments. This means forced saving for workers as well as availability of low-cost finance for the firm. Until 1982 the fund was generally indexed to nominal earnings, while since 1982 it has been indexed only to the cost of living according to a legislated rule. Indexation is partial ($0.015+0.75\times$CPI). The aggregate size of the fund is estimated as 180–200 thousand billion (i.e. thousand million) lire, i.e. slightly less than 10 per cent of GDP.

14. Similar to the one operating in the US social security system.

15. Normally the severance pay fund lump-sum benefit would be paid at the time of each job separation. Hence our representative worker should have two TFR payments for the two different sub-periods. To keep things simple we assumed that the entire sum is paid at the time of retirement and that the fund keeps cumulating at the same rate in the interim period.

16. The actual contribution rate is 32.7 per cent but workers are credited 33 per cent.

17. For the self-employed however current contribution rates are much lower (see endnote 20), implying lower replacement ratios (about two-thirds) and potentially greater reliance on private pensions.
18. Retiring after the age of 65 will be possible but no further actuarial gain will apply.
19. However the differential treatment of the self-employed with respect to employees will last for some years: the former currently pay a contribution rate equal to 17 per cent (to be gradually raised to 19 per cent in future years), while accruing a 20 per cent contribution rate.
20. However a weakness of the adjustment mechanism is that the update of the coefficient will not be automatic but will be the object of negotiations with the unions.
21. The source of the more updated projections is the Treasury. The other official source of long-term projections – INPS – has not yet published any figures taking the Dini reform into account.
22. See Ministero del Tesoro – Ragioneria Generale dello Stato (1996 and 1998).
23. Brugiavini and Peracchi (1999) add further evidence on the importance that the assumptions on employment growth and productivity growth have for this result. They also show that the introduction of a funded second tier can be implemented at little cost for the generations experiencing the transition from the PAYG to the partially funded system.
24. Despite being the first government to introduce a regulatory framework for pension funds (in 1992), the Amato Government, with a financial crisis on its hands, adopted a very tight fiscal policy for pension funds, effectively discouraging the onset of this new financial product. While policy-makers hoped for a 'launch' of pension funds, because of the tax disincentives no new funds were started at the time and the existing ones suspended new enrolment.
25. Up to September 2000, about 20 occupational pension funds (chemical, engineering, etc.) had been set up and were fully operative. For many others the approval of the supervisory authority was pending.
26. Severance pay funds follow an EET taxation scheme, i.e. contributions and accruing interest are exempt while the capital is separately taxed at the liquidation date at favourable rates. Further contributions to pension funds by employers and employees are deductible up to a limit (the lower of 12 per cent of gross yearly compensation and 10 million lire), on condition that the TFR flows are diverted (completely for new workers).
27. The most important are: marginal tax rates for the work and pension periods respectively; length of pension fund participation; nominal and real interest rates; and real wage growth rates.
28. Livi Bacci (1995a and 1995b) has provided a careful study of future demographic patterns. Recent work by the Italian Statistical Office ('Istituto Nazionale di Statistica' – ISTAT, 1997) and by the Treasury (Ministero del Tesoro – Ragioneria Generale dello Stato, 1996 and 1998) has shown the likely impact on pension liabilities of demographic trends.
29. This point is developed further in Brugiavini (1999). In particular it is shown that for ages between 55 and 60 the marginal cost of working one extra year, both in terms of extra social security contributions and in terms of lost old-age benefits, largely outweighs the marginal advantages. Hence there exists a strong incentive to retire early.
30. For example in 1993 the Italian economy experienced a brief, yet sharp, recession.
31. This is an arbitrary age in the sense that, due to the existence of an early retirement option, workers could retire at a very early age. However 55 is also the statutory retirement age for women in the private sector (hence we are including all retired women of the private sector in the pensioner group) and it is the age at which men are most likely to claim early retirement given that they have to complete 35 years of social security tax payments.
32. Brugiavini (1999) shows that the distribution of retired people by retirement age peaks at 60 for men and 55 for women, but the fraction of people who retire at ages different from the statutory retirement age is sizeable.

33. Hence in our terminology a retired household could be of any age, while a pensioner is necessarily above 60. As discussed in the text people who retire early might engage in black economy activities; this makes it even more compelling not to include them in the pensioner group.

34. Note that each income component is also recorded net of tax. The SHIW provides a definition of income that includes the imputation of income from owner-occupied houses. To obtain income net of income from owner-occupied houses we subtracted the imputed income from the total income of the benefit unit. This gave us a few cases where the benefit unit has zero (or even negative) income; some of these cases are typically self-employed households and we had to drop these from the sample. The same netting-out procedure was also implemented in computing income from capital. However note that investment income is recorded at household level and we cannot distinguish income from capital for the basic benefit unit.

35. One thousand lire in 1994 was worth approximately 50p. We converted nominal values into 1994-lira values by means of a price index ('Indice dei prezzi al Consumo per l'Intera Collettivita'') which we have available for each year and for each region in the survey.

36. We cannot place much emphasis on this income split within the couple because in the SHIW income from capital, though negligible, is all attributed to the husband.

37. Also we are very careful to select the sample on the basis of the same criteria. This is quite important in our dataset as, when subtracting imputation for owner-occupied houses, a number of benefit units ended up having zero income while this does not occur when considering total household income.

38. Equivalent income for all benefit units that are pensioners is 16 338 thousand lire, while for pensioner households it is 16 800 thousand lire. In 1994 lire average income for a pensioner household is 30 086 thousand lire per year.

39. In Table 6.14 we construct pension income as the sum of the various benefit components. Each individual in the survey can receive up to three different types of pension provision. This way benefits can be distinguished by type (disability insurance versus old age, say) and also attributed to specific social security funds. We focus on current state pension figures and exclude the part of the benefit that might be imputed to different financial years. The income grand total obtained by aggregating the various components gave some slight discrepancies with the survey figure (e.g. median total income for older couples is 24 351 thousand lire as opposed to 24 408 thousand lire).

40. This old-age benefit is granted only to those older than 65 with no other incomes. In the table there are cases where (a) income maintenance is obtained by individuals younger than 65 as the income of the spouse (who could be older than the head of the household) is attributed to the head or (b) income maintenance is obtained with non-zero earnings as the spouse could work.

41. Income quintiles are defined in the Appendix. We are calculating the quintiles on the basis of equivalent income of pensioners.

42. Here we use the entire sample and define income deciles on the basis of equivalent income of the entire sample by sorting individuals (adults) rather than benefit units.

REFERENCES

Antichi, M. (1997), 'Quali sono le possibilità di ulteriore razionalizzazione del sistema pensionistico obbligatorio? (What are the possibilities for the final rationalisation of the compulsory pension system?)', Commissione per l'Analisi delle Compatibilità della Spesa Sociale, Allegato 1 al Documento di Base num. 5.

Banca d'Italia (1995), 'La Riforma del Sistema Pensionistico (The reform of the pension system)', *Note del Bollettino Economico*, **25**, 4–19.

Brugiavini, A. (1999), 'Social security and retirement in Italy', in J. Gruber and D. Wise (eds), *Social Security and Retirement around the World*, Chicago: University of Chicago Press.

Brugiavini, A. and F. Peracchi (1999), 'Reforming Italian social security: should we switch from PAYG to funding?', mimeo, University 'Tor Vergata', Rome.

Cannari, L. and D. Franco (1990), 'Sistema Pensionistico e Distribuzione dei redditi (Pension system and the distribution of returns)', Banca d'Italia, Quaderni di discussione.

Castellino, O. (1995), 'Redistribution between and within generations in the Italian social security system', *Ricerche Economiche*, **49** (4), 317–27.

Commissione per l'Analisi delle Compatibilità Macroeconomiche della Spesa Sociale (1997a), Documento di Base num. 1 e Allegato 2 al Documento di Base num. 3.

Commissione per l'Analisi delle Compatibilità Macroeconomiche della Spesa Sociale (1997b), *Final Report*, Rome.

EUROSTAT (2000), *Social Protection Expenditure and Receipts, 1980–1997*, Luxembourg.

Ferraresi, P.M. and E. Fornero (2000), 'Social security transition in Italy: costs, distortions and some possible corrections', Centre for Research on Pensions and Welfare Policies, University of Turin, Working Paper no. 3.

Fornero, E. (1999), *L'Economia dei Fondi Pensione: Potenzialità e Limiti della Previdenza Privata in Italia (The Economics of Funded Pensions: Potentiality and Limits of Private Provision in Italy)*, Bologna: Il Mulino.

INPS (1970a), 'Settant'anni dell'Istituto Nazionale della Previdenza Sociale', Rome.

INPS (1970b), 'Cinquant'anni dell'assicurazione generale obbligatoria per l'invalidità e la vecchiaia', Rome.

INPS (1996), 'FPLD. Indicazioni di carattere statistico', Rome.

INPS (1998), *Modello previsionale 1998*, Rome.

ISTAT (various years), *Annuario Statistico Italiano*, various issues, Rome.

ISTAT (1958–80), 'Annuario del lavoro e dell'emigrazione', Rome.

ISTAT (1975–85), 'Supplemento al Bollettino di Statistica', Rome.

ISTAT (1986–94), 'Rilevazione Nazionale delle Forze di Lavoro', Rome.

ISTAT (1997), 'Gli anziani in Italia', Rome.

ISTAT (1999), *Statistiche sui trattamenti pensionistici, 1998*, Rome.

Legge 08/08/1995 n.335, *Riforma del Sistema Pensionistico Obbligatorio e Complementare*.

Livi Bacci, M. (1995a), 'Evoluzione Demografica e Sistema Pensionistico', *Economia Italiana*, **1** (January–April), 19–40.

Livi Bacci, M. (1995b), 'Popolazione, Trasferimenti e generazioni', in O. Castellino (ed.), *Le Pensioni Difficili. La Previdenza Sociale in Italia tra Crisi e Riforme*, Bologna: Il Mulino, pp. 19–38.

Ministero del Tesoro (various years), *Relazione Generale sulla Situazione Economica del Paese*, vol. 3, various issues, Rome.

Ministero del Tesoro (1981), 'La spesa previdenziale e i suoi effetti sulla finanza pubblica', Rome.

Ministero del Tesoro – Ragioneria Generale dello Stato (1991), *FPLD: una Proiezione al 2025*, Rome.

Ministero del Tesoro – Ragioneria Generale dello Stato (1996), *Tendenze Demografiche e Spesa Pensionistica: alcuni Possibili Scenari*, Rome.

Ministero del Tesoro – Ragioneria Generale dello Stato (1997), *Sanità, Scuola e Pensioni*, Rome.

Ministero del Tesoro – Ragioneria Generale dello Stato (1998), *Demographic Trends and Pension Systems Equilibrium: The Italian Case*, Rome.

Monorchio, A. (1994), *Hearing of the Director of General Account by the IX Parliamentary Commission*, Rome.

7.   Pension Provision in the Netherlands

Klaas de Vos and Arie Kapteyn[*]

7.1   INTRODUCTION

The programmes providing income to the elderly in the Netherlands are characterised by a limited number of salient features. First, there is a distinct cut-off at age 65. Broadly speaking everyone aged 65 or over is entitled to the same basic state pension ('Algemene Ouderdomswet' – AOW). Most other benefits (for example disability, unemployment and welfare) expire when someone turns 65. Second, both above and below 65, in addition to the public entitlement programmes guaranteed by law, many people who stop working are entitled to other, private, pension benefits – for example occupational pensions supplementing the basic state pension for people over 65 and early retirement benefits for people below 65.

Like most other developed countries the Netherlands is faced with an increasing share of elderly in the total population. The share of the population over 65 has grown from 8 per cent in 1950 to 13 per cent in 1995 and is expected to rise to 24 per cent by 2035. If nothing else changes, this will cause a considerable increase in basic state pension expenditures. Faced with this prospect the government has recently come up with policy measures to maintain the sustainability of the general system of old-age pensions.

More immediate concerns are the low participation rate of people below 65 and the costs of the programmes providing income to them, both public programmes, such as disability insurance, and occupational early retirement schemes.

The set-up of this chapter is as follows. We start with a brief description of the structure of the entitlement schemes for the elderly in the Netherlands. We discuss the sustainability of the system in Section 7.4 and present statistics on the labour market behaviour of older people in the Netherlands, both cross-

---

[*]This chapter was written while Kapteyn visited the California Institute of Technology.

sectionally and over time, in Section 7.5. Finally, in Section 7.6, we present figures on the incomes of the elderly in the Netherlands, their distribution and how they compare with the incomes of the younger population.

7.2 PUBLIC SOURCES OF INCOME

In Table 7.1 the various components of state benefits to the elderly are summarised. All in all, about 6.4 per cent of GDP is received by the elderly from the state in the form of pensions and other cash benefits.

Table 7.1   Sources of State Income Available to Pensioners

Payment	Type	Cost (% of GDP)	% of elderly in receipt	Criteria
Basic state pension	Flat-rate Non-contributory	5.2%	99+% of those aged 65+	Above 65, having been resident between 15 and 65
Disability benefit	Earnings-related	0.7%	25% of those aged 60–65	Having lost earnings capacity, under 65
Unemploy-ment benefit	Earnings-related	0.2%	6% of those aged 60–65	Having lost paid employment, under 65
Social assistance	Flat-rate Non-contributory	0.1%	5% of households with retired head aged 60–65	Means-tested
Rent subsidy	Income-related Non-contributory	0.15%	24% of households with head aged 65+ or retired aged 60+	Means-tested

Sources: Figures for basic state pension are based on Statistics Netherlands (1996). Estimates for disability benefits and unemployment benefits are based on CTSV (1996). Social assistance and rent subsidy are based on authors' calculations using the 1993–94 Housing Demand Survey.

7.2.1   Basic State Pension

By far the largest part of state provision to pensioners is the basic state pension. The Basic State Pension Act ('Algemene ouderdomswet' – AOW) was introduced in 1957. Its purpose was to guarantee a sufficient income to virtually everyone aged 65 or over. The basic state pension was preceded by several schemes, such as the so-called Drees Emergency Act[1] ('Noodwet Drees, 1949'), which had a less broad coverage. Since 1980 the level of basic state pension benefits has been linked to the statutory minimum wage. Until 1994 couples with a head over 65 were entitled to a benefit equal to the after-tax minimum wage, and single people over 65 were entitled to a benefit equal to 70 per cent of the (after-tax) minimum wage.

In 1994 the system was changed in such a way that each individual of 65 or over is now entitled to 50 per cent of the minimum wage, with supplements of 20 per cent for single people, 40 per cent for single parents with a

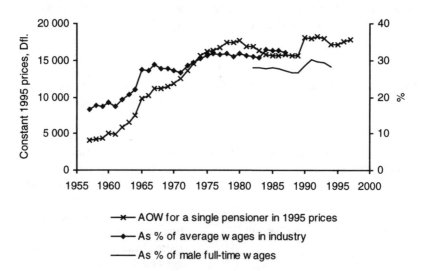

—×— AOW for a single pensioner in 1995 prices

—♦— As % of average w ages in industry

——— As % of male full-time w ages

Note: Pension benefit levels are before taxes but policy decisions are concerned with after-tax pension benefit levels. The jump in before-tax benefit levels in 1990 was mainly a result of the 1990 tax reform. To maintain after-tax pension levels, pensions before taxes had to be increased considerably.

Sources: Pension amounts are from Kluwer (1997). Price indices and average male full-time earnings are from Statistical Yearbooks (Statistics Netherlands, various years). Average wages of adult males (with two children) in industry are from Statistics Netherlands (1989).

Figure 7.1   Level of the Basic State Pension (AOW) in relation to Earnings and Prices

dependent child aged below 18, and up to 50 per cent for people with a partner aged below 65 (in the last case the percentage depends on the income of the partner).

In 1997 the basic state pension benefit level for a single pensioner equalled about 28 per cent of male average full-time earnings. Both in real terms and in comparison with average earnings, the benefit levels increased relatively fast around 1965. Between 1965 and 1980 there was a still considerable increase in real terms, but the increase barely surpassed the increase in earnings. Between 1980 and 1990 the basic state pension actually decreased in real terms. Since then the benefit level has remained fairly stable: see Figure 7.1.

Contributions

The basic state pension is financed purely on a pay-as-you-go basis, largely by a payroll tax on taxable income of people aged below 65. The associated tax rate in 1998 was 16.5 per cent levied on taxable income up to a maximum (of Dfl. 47 184 per annum in 1998 prices). The basic state pension basically provides equal coverage to everyone over 65. An exception is that people who spent part of their working life (aged 15–64) abroad have their benefits reduced by 2 per cent for every year they spent abroad. Eligibility for the basic state pension does not require retirement from the labour force.

Indexation

As mentioned previously, from 1980 the basic state pension was roughly equal to the after-tax minimum wage, which itself was officially linked to a wage index. However in a number of years since 1980 the government chose not to apply one or both of these links. As of 1992, legislation allowed the government to let the benefit levels increase more slowly than wages if the ratio of non-participants in the labour force to participants exceeded 82.6 per cent. On balance according to De Kam and Nypels (1995) the purchasing power of the basic state pension of a couple in 1994 was 93 per cent of that in 1980. Since then the present government has maintained the link between basic state pension benefits, the after-tax minimum wage and the wage index.

7.2.2 Other Public Assistance

A number of programmes exist that enable people to leave the labour force well before their 65th birthday. The main ones are disability insurance, unemployment benefits and various early retirement schemes. Together these schemes have induced the number of people working in the age bracket 60–65 to drop dramatically since the 1960s.

Disability insurance

In 1967 the Disability Insurance Act ('Wet op de Arbeids-ongeschiktheidsverzekering' – WAO) was introduced. Disability insurance covers all employees (except civil servants, who have their own, very similar, arrangements) against loss of earnings due to long-term sickness and disability. Until August 1993 disability insurance guaranteed employees who lost more than 80 per cent of their earnings capacity a benefit of 70 per cent (80 per cent before 1985) of their daily wage up to a maximum and up to age 65. Since then disability benefits start at 70 per cent of previous earnings up to a maximum but fall to a lower level after a certain period (both the length of this period and the percentage depend on age). However most employees have taken out additional insurance to cover the risk of disability insurance benefit falling below 70 per cent of their previous earnings.[2]

In the 1980s disability insurance became a very popular arrangement which employers could use to get rid of elderly, less productive, employees easily.[3] There are severe legal obstacles to laying off employees. Moreover disability benefits were more generous than unemployment benefits: disability benefits would last until the worker reached the age of 65, while unemployment benefits would typically last for only two-and-a-half years – though longer for older workers. Furthermore while on disability benefits, pension rights often accumulated as if the person were still employed – although this would vary by pension fund – whereas an unemployed person would accumulate very few pension rights, if any. As a result of this, both employers and employees had a preference for the disability route out of economic activity. The ensuing rise in the costs of disability insurance has induced the government to limit eligibility for disability insurance by tightening entry conditions and reducing benefit levels. Moreover individuals receiving disability benefits are now subject to a more rigorous screening of their loss of earnings capacity.

Unemployment insurance

As mentioned above, unemployment benefits ('Werkloosheidswet' – WW) are less generous than disability benefits, mainly because they are only paid for a limited period (dependent on the number of years worked before unemployment). However most people aged 60 or above who become unemployed can expect to receive unemployment benefits equal to 70 per cent of their previous earnings up to age 65.[4] Another relevant feature is that unemployed people over 57½ no longer have to register with an employment agency and thus *de facto* can retire from the labour market.

Means-tested benefits

Households without other sources of income (and limited household wealth) are entitled to social assistance ('Algemene bijstandswet/Rijksgroepsregeling Werkloze Werknemers' – ABW/RWW). The level of the benefits is approximately equal to the level of the basic state pension for people over 65. Since these benefits are linked to the minimum wage this implies that for employees earning low wages the replacement rate is about 100 per cent. Hence, in particular for those with low wages who are over 57½ and thus have no obligation to look for a job in order to qualify for benefits, early retirement does not involve a loss of income.

All public benefits for people younger than 65 are only paid as long as the person is not in paid employment.[5] In addition to the benefits supplementing income to the social assistance level, social assistance also provides special assistance to households with low incomes both above and below 65 – for example for the purchase of durable goods such as refrigerators and washing machines.

One other important means-tested benefit is rent subsidy ('Individuele Huursubsidie' – IHS), which subsidises part of the rent of tenants on low incomes if the rent exceeds a minimum amount. About 24 per cent of pensioners receive a rent subsidy; this amounts to 37 per cent of pensioners who rent their accommodation.[6]

Other public assistance to the elderly

In addition to the benefits mentioned above, pensioners are eligible for subsidised health insurance, paid for by a surcharge on the health insurance premiums of the non-elderly. Furthermore a considerable part of health expenditure is covered by statutory social insurance contributions. A large proportion of this is spent on healthcare for the elderly, including most of the costs of home care and of nursing homes. Social assistance finances the stay in homes of the elderly with low incomes and low assets. Like all households, if they have low incomes the elderly may be exempt from paying certain local taxes.

7.3 PRIVATE PENSIONS

In the Netherlands there is no earnings-related state pension. However in addition to the basic state pension a majority of the population over 65 are entitled to a supplementary occupational pension. Meuwissen (1993) estimates that about 80 per cent of households with a head aged 65 or over received some form of additional pension in 1989. Typically occupational pensions supplement the basic state pension to 70 per cent of final pay for people who have worked for 40 years. After tax the replacement rate can be substantially higher.

In general if an employer offers a pension scheme then participation in such a scheme is compulsory. More than 99 per cent of pension schemes are of the defined benefit type,[7] while the remainder (0.6 per cent) are of the defined contribution type. More than 72 per cent of pension benefits are defined on the basis of final pay, the remainder being a mixed bag of various combinations of final pay, fixed amounts and average pay. Combining the effects of the basic state pension and private pension schemes leads to the following before-tax replacement rates for those individuals who have contributed for a sufficient number of years: 34 per cent receive less than 60 per cent of final pay, 27 per cent receive between 60 and 69 per cent, 20 per cent receive between 70 and 79 per cent, and 19 per cent receive at least 80 per cent of final pay. One should keep in mind that after-tax replacement rates will be substantially higher.

Most large firms have their own pension fund. Smaller firms usually participate in sector-wide pension funds. All in all, pension fund reserves in the Netherlands amount to about 130 per cent of GDP.

Private pension arrangements usually require that people leave the job in which they accumulate pension rights at age 65 at the latest. There is no earnings test however and people may consider looking for secondary jobs once they retire.

Table 7.2 shows the percentages of individuals between 65 and 70 who report income from private pensions. Mainly as a result of the low labour force participation rate of women, men are much more likely to be entitled to a private pension than women, especially married women. Overall about half of all individuals between 65 and 70 report an income from a private pension scheme. Those who do not have never worked, or have not worked in

Table 7.2   Percentage of People between 65 and 70 with Income from a Private Pension, by Gender and Household Type (%)

	Men	Women	Total
Single	61.7	67.7	63.6
Divorced / widowed	83.8	60.6	66.8
Married / cohabiting	75.5	12.6	46.7
Total	76.4	23.0	50.2

Source: Based on the 1993–94 Housing Demand Survey.

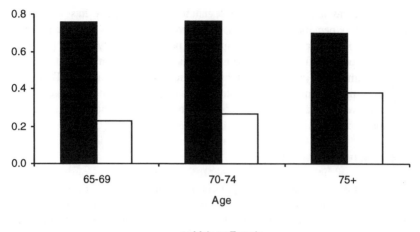

Source: 1993–94 Housing Demand Survey.

Figure 7.2 Proportion of Individuals Over 65 with Income from Private Pension Arrangements, by Age and Gender

pensionable employment – for example because they were self-employed, because they had low earnings or because they had already retired from the labour force before pensions were introduced in their firms. In a limited number of cases people who have built up very small occupational pensions have received a lump-sum amount instead of an annuity.

Figure 7.2 shows the proportion of all those over 65 who receive private pensions. In contrast to Table 7.2 this also includes all people over 70. Again men are considerably more likely to receive income from private pensions than women. The proportion of women receiving a private pension increases with age, as a result of the increasing probability that their spouse dies, leaving the widow with a widow's pension.

When we look at households instead of individuals we find that about 70 per cent of all households with a head aged 65 or over report income from a private pension.[8]

7.3.1 Indexation

Most private pensions are protected against inflation as the pensions are indexed either by a price index or by a wage index. By law the future pensions of early retirees are subject to the same indexation rules as the pensions of current pensioners. Generally there are no vesting rules. One starts accumulating pension rights from the first day of one's employment.

Furthermore, as a result of recent legislation, job mobility has very little effect on one's pension entitlements. Whenever one changes jobs the pension fund of the new employer will assume the pension liability of the previous employer's pension fund. Among other things the effect of this is that pension rights accumulated in different jobs are indexed automatically. This is a marked improvement on the past, when employees who changed jobs frequently would end up with considerably lower benefits than those who did not change jobs.

7.3.2 Early Retirement

Early retirement became increasingly common during the 1980s, when it was viewed as a means of reducing unemployment. In recent years costs of early retirement have increased considerably, and many firms are trying to reduce these costs by reducing the benefits or by increasing the minimum age for eligibility. Typically the early retirement schemes guarantee an employee a benefit equal to 70 or 80 per cent of previous earnings up to the age of 65. In after-tax terms replacement rates are even higher. Furthermore one often continues to accumulate pension rights while early retired, though possibly at a lower rate than if working.

Early retirement may be organised via the pension funds, which also provide the occupational pensions, or via the employer himself. Moreover, in contrast to occupational pensions, early retirement is commonly financed as pay-as-you-go. Early retirement usually requires 10 years of employment with the same employer before the early retirement date, whereas other pension rights are not affected by job changes. Eligibility for early retirement benefits usually requires a complete withdrawal from the labour market.

7.3.3 Taxation

As mentioned above, if the employer offers a pension scheme then participation of all employees is usually mandatory. In fact the tax laws make participation in a pension scheme attractive, since pension contributions are tax-deductible. On the other hand pensions are taxed, but usually at a lower rate, in particular as a result of the fact that the elderly are exempt from most payroll taxes. Deductibility also holds for early retirement contributions and, within certain limits, for contributions to private pension plans.

The favourable tax treatment of pensions is sometimes called into question.[9] In fact the government has already started to reform the present system by limiting the basic state pension contribution rate and by financing the deficit out of general taxation (see Section 7.4). As a result, through their taxes the elderly have started paying part of the state pension burden.

7.4   SUSTAINABILITY

Current government spending on pensions and other benefits received by the elderly in the Netherlands has been estimated to amount to about 6.4 per cent of GDP. More than four-fifths of this goes towards the basic state pension (5.2 per cent of GDP), while the remainder is spent mostly on various benefits for the age-group below 65 (see Table 7.1).

As a result of the expected increase in the population share of the elderly (aged 65 or over) from 13 per cent in 1995 to about 24 per cent in 2035, out-lays on the basic state pension will increase considerably. Depending on as-sumptions about economic growth and labour force participation, these costs are estimated to increase to between 7.5 and 9 per cent of GDP in 2035.[10]

These percentages are already well below the percentages that would have been reached if wage indexation had been maintained consistently throughout the 1980s and early 1990s. Other measures, such as the decrease in the entitlements of couples with a spouse younger than 65 and of single persons (for example siblings) living together, have also contributed toward lowering the costs of the basic state pension.

Still, the expected increase in costs would result in a steep increase in the contribution rate (from 15.4 per cent in 1996 to about 26 per cent in 2035) if the method of financing the expenditures were to remain the same. One reason for this increase in the contribution rate is the fact that the basic state pension is financed by a contribution levied on the lower bracket of the income tax schedule. The fact that the tax brackets are adjusted with prices but the expenditures are adjusted with wages causes an additional increase in the contribution rate if real wages increase.

In order to curb the increase in the contribution rate, parliament has recently passed legislation limiting it to 16.5 per cent and allowing the ensuing deficit to be financed out of general tax revenues. The resulting increase in tax rates can be limited because other government expenditures (in particular interest payments on the national debt) are expected to decrease substantially in the period concerned. Furthermore, given that basic state pension expenditure expressed as a percentage of GDP is expected to peak around 2040 and to decrease thereafter, the government has decided to create a reserve fund out of which the excessive burden in the period from about 2020 to 2060 could be financed. This fund is accumulated on the basis of contributions made by government and from the interest received on past contributions.

Notably the present government does not consider (further) decreases in the entitlements of the elderly to be a viable alternative. The Christian Democratic Party, having participated in government for a continuous period of more than 70 years, was condemned to the opposition benches in 1994 partly as a result of proposing measures to decrease basic state pension benefits. Increasing the pension age has also been rejected. One pragmatic reason is that the labour force participation rate of people approaching 65 is extremely low. This implies that the decrease in basic state pension expenditures resulting from increasing the official retirement age would largely be compensated by increases in expenditures on other public benefits. Of course this is all conditional upon the present pattern of labour force participation. Changing the incentives to work, for example by lowering the generosity of early retirement schemes, will change the picture.

Compared with other countries, the future problems of financing the state pension system in the Netherlands are expected to be somewhat less severe. Occupational pensions, which account for a substantial part of the income of the elderly, are fully funded.

Much greater concerns for the government have been and still are the low labour force participation rate of people under 65 and the benefits going to these non-participants (see Section 7.5). The total amount spent on disability, unemployment and social assistance benefits exceeds that spent on the basic state pension.[11] In particular the number of people receiving disability benefits is much higher than in other countries. Hence successive governments have attempted to decrease the number of people on disability benefits by limiting eligibility and by decreasing the attractiveness of the scheme. Up to now the policy measures appear to have succeeded in stopping the rise in numbers. As yet there has not been a substantial decrease however.

Another area of government concern is the ever-increasing healthcare costs, partly caused by the greying of the population. Although the healthcare system is being reformed almost continually, successive governments have not been able to come up with a successful policy to get the cost increases under control.

7.5   ACTIVITY RATES

Table 7.3 shows that most people are already economically inactive before the official retirement age. In fact fewer than 20 per cent of men and fewer than 5 per cent of women between 60 and 64 participate in the labour force. Even in the 55–59 age-group fewer than 60 per cent of men and fewer than one in four women are working.

Given these activity rates, a relatively low percentage of males aged 60–64 report receiving state benefits (about 41 per cent – see Table 7.4). However 47 per cent of males in this group report receiving an early retirement pension or an old-age pension.

Table 7.3   Percentage of Economically Active Men and Women, by Age-group (%)

	Age-group	
	55–59	60–64
Men	57.2	19.2
Women	22.1	4.8

Source: Statistics Netherlands, Labour Force Survey, 1994.

Table 7.4   Percentage of Men Reporting Receipt of State Benefits or Pensions, by Age-group (%)

Benefit	Age-group		
	55–59	60–64	65–69
None	63.8	58.9	1.4
Basic state pension	0.0	0.3	98.4*
Disability benefits	21.9	26.8	0.0
Unemployment benefits	6.0	3.5	0.0
Social assistance	2.4	2.2	0.2
Rent subsidy	5.4	7.2	10.6
Other or combined benefits	6.9	8.3	1.2

Note: *Includes men reporting private pensions and combined benefits (for example basic state pension and private pension paid as one amount).

Source: Based on the 1993–94 Housing Demand Survey.

Figures 7.3 and 7.4 plot the labour force participation rates of older men and women in different age-groups since 1960. For older men there is a decline in labour force participation in all age-groups. The decline is particularly dramatic for 60- to 64-year-olds. In 1960 about 80 per cent of this age-group were in the labour force, as opposed to only 20 per cent in 1994. For men aged 65 or over, labour force participation declined from about 20 per cent in 1960 to about 3 per cent in 1985. After that year Statistics Netherlands stopped reporting the labour force participation of this age-group.

For women there is a notable increase in the labour force participation rate of the 45–54 age-group (from less than 20 per cent in 1960 to more than 40 per cent in 1994). There is also a slight increase in participation for the 55–59 age-group. The participation rates of the oldest age-groups remained low.

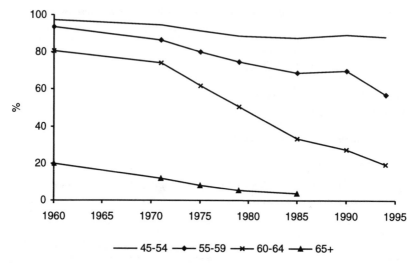

Figure 7.3   Male Activity Rates

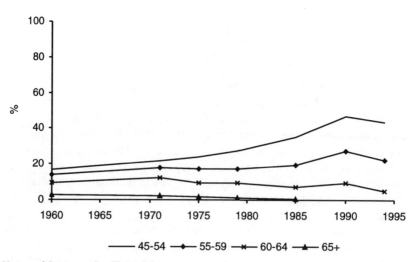

Figure 7.4   Female Activity Rates

It is clear that the changes in the pension system in the period concerned are not the main explanatory factor for the declining labour force participation rates, since the basic state pension only provides an income to people over 65, while the largest decline in labour force participation took place among people younger than 65. Yet the proliferation of occupational pensions in addition to the basic state pension made it less and less likely that people would continue to work after age 65.

In the younger age-groups the relatively generous disability insurance scheme (introduced in 1967) offered an attractive way to retire before the age of 65. In particular in the 1970s and 1980s, when the Netherlands faced periods of rapidly increasing unemployment, the disability route to retirement for older employees became a very popular alternative to general lay-offs. In addition, in the face of continued pressure to decrease labour costs, many firms started to offer even more generous early retirement programmes.

7.6   INCOME DISTRIBUTIONS

The income data presented in this section come from the 1993–94 Housing Demand Survey ('Woningbehoeftenonderzoek' – WBO), which is a survey of around 55 000 households conducted every four years. The data are not collected specifically for the analysis of income distributions, but the available income information and the number of observations make them an interesting source of information on the income distribution. Because the data on household income do not include the incomes of household members other than head and spouse, the WBO data do not allow us to get an exact picture of the income distribution of the total population.

For the purpose of analysing pensioner incomes we have included all single people aged over 65, or over 60 and not working, and all couples with a head aged over 65, or over 60 and not working.

Total income is defined as income net of taxes, both income and payroll. Where income is broken into components, use is made of information on the before-tax amounts. When we compare households of different sizes we use an equivalence scale of 1 for a single person, 0.7 for any additional adult and 0.5 for children aged below 14. To check the sensitivity of the results for the equivalence scale used we also use a (1, 0.5, 0.3) scale. The measure of income ignores housing costs and imputed rent for owner-occupied accommodation.

The average amounts of after-tax annual income for couples and single men and women, broken down by age-group, are shown in Table 7.5. The highest average incomes are found in the 65–69 age-group. Compared with the older age-groups, this generation earned more and had more access to better occupational pensions. The lower incomes of the 60–64 age-group are not caused by lower benefits *per se*, but result from the fact that the figures for 60- to 64-year-olds are based on non-working heads of households only. Since retirement is probably least attractive for those with high earnings, lower incomes are likely to be over-represented among the retired.

Single women have lower average incomes than single men because they are more likely to have a low occupational pension (as a result of a small number of years worked in pensionable employment) or to have a (lower) widow's pension (usually 70 per cent of the full pension).

The figures in parentheses in Table 7.5 show the ratio of the average equivalent income for each group to the average equivalent income for non-pensioners. Using the (1, 0.7, 0.5) scale the average incomes of pensioners are fairly close to those of non-pensioners. For single male pensioners average incomes even exceed those for the rest of the population. Using the (1, 0.5, 0.3) scale single male pensioners still earn 90 per cent of the incomes of non-pensioners on average.

Some information on the distribution of income in different non-pensioner groups is given in Table 7.6. Single men and women below 40 have the

Table 7.5   Average Pensioner Income, by Marital Status and Age-group (incomes in Dfl. p.a.)

	Age-group				
	60–64	65–69	70–74	75+	60+
Couples					
Annual income	36 271	36 948	34 949	33 409	35 483
Ratio 1	(0.86)	(0.88)	(0.83)	(0.79)	(0.84)
Ratio 2	(0.83)	(0.84)	(0.80)	(0.76)	(0.81)
Single men					
Annual income	26 379	28 577	26 851	24 717	26 317
Ratio 1	(1.06)	(1.15)	(1.08)	(1.00)	(1.06)
Ratio 2	(0.90)	(0.98)	(0.92)	(0.85)	(0.90)
Single women					
Annual income	22 391	22 683	22 055	21 194	21 795
Ratio 1	(0.90)	(0.91)	(0.89)	(0.85)	(0.88)
Ratio 2	(0.77)	(0.78)	(0.76)	(0.73)	(0.75)

Note: Numbers in parentheses are the ratios of average equivalent income for each group to the average equivalent income for non-pensioners, ratio 1 being computed with the (1, 0.7, 0.5) equivalence scale and ratio 2 with the (1, 0.5, 0.3) equivalence scale.

Source: 1993–94 Housing Demand Survey.

lowest incomes, with the 10th percentile being lower than the basic state pension. The lower quantiles of these groups largely consist of students living on their own, who – in contrast to unemployed, disabled and retired people – are not entitled to the social assistance minimum of 70 per cent of the minimum wage. The highest incomes are received by couples. There are very few single-parent households with high incomes.

Table 7.7 provides information on the distribution of pensioner incomes. It shows that while the 10th percentiles do not differ much between the various age-groups (essentially because these are all close to the social assistance level), the 90th percentiles show slightly more variation, especially among couples and single men. For couples and single women the biggest 90/10 ratio is for the 65–69 age-group, while for single men the biggest 90/10 ratio is found for the youngest age-group. Inequality among single women is considerably lower than inequality among couples and single men. Comparison with Table 7.6 suggests that inequality among pensioners is somewhat less than that among the rest of the population.

Table 7.6   Income Distributions of Different Non-retired Population Groups (incomes in Dfl. p.a.)

	Mean	Median	90th percentile	10th percentile	90/10 ratio
Couples, no children, head aged <40	58 882	56 530	85 270	30 730	2.77
Couples, no children, head aged ≥40	54 580	47 390	92 700	23 380	3.96
Couples with children	54 846	48 850	86 760	28 920	3.00
Single parents	28 624	25 510	42 080	20 170	2.09
Single men aged <40	26 543	25 220	45 130	9 570	4.72
Single men aged ≥40	33 245	29 610	55 520	15 350	3.62
Single women aged <40	23 109	22 620	37 130	9 380	3.96
Single women aged ≥40	27 972	24 340	46 410	15 120	3.07

Source: 1993–94 Housing Demand Survey.

Table 7.7   Distribution of Pensioner Incomes, by Marital Status and Age-group (incomes in Dfl. p.a.)

	Age-group				
	60–64	65–69	70–74	75+	60+
Couples					
Median	32 460	31 070	29 100	27 610	30 050
90th percentile	57 150	60 590	56 300	54 660	57 260
10th percentile	20 930	21 140	21 580	21 000	21 180
90/10 ratio	2.73	2.87	2.61	2.60	2.70
Single men					
Median	23 670	23 360	23 480	20 140	21 680
90th percentile	42 810	43 120	44 190	40 270	42 800
10th percentile	14 070	15 250	15 380	15 080	14 940
90/10 ratio	3.04	2.83	2.87	2.67	2.86
Single women					
Median	18 610	19 210	19 191	18 490	18 770
90th percentile	33 960	35 550	32 890	32 310	33 190
10th percentile	14 510	15 080	15 280	14 770	14 870
90/10 ratio	2.34	2.36	2.15	2.19	2.23

Source: 1993–94 Housing Demand Survey.

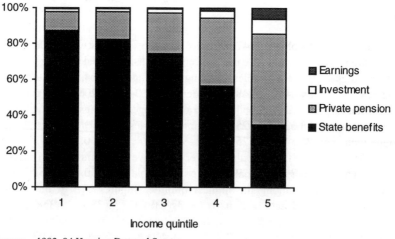

Source: 1993–94 Housing Demand Survey.

Figure 7.5   Composition of Pensioner Income, by Income Quintile

Table 7.8   Composition of Pensioner Income, by Marital Status and Age-group (% of total)*

	Age-group				
	60–64	65–69	70–74	75+	60+
Couples					
State benefits	38.2	55.8	60.3	64.4	54.4
Private pensions	55.1	34.1	31.6	27.7	37.3
Investment income	2.6	3.8	4.9	6.1	4.2
Earnings	4.1	6.3	3.2	1.8	4.1
Single men					
State benefits	44.8	53.4	58.1	62.5	56.0
Private pensions	51.6	33.6	34.1	29.9	35.7
Investment income	3.3	8.3	5.7	6.6	6.2
Earnings	0.2	4.8	2.1	1.1	2.0
Single women					
State benefits	64.1	70.4	71.1	74.7	71.8
Private pensions	29.6	23.7	22.9	20.8	22.9
Investment income	6.0	4.4	4.9	4.0	4.5
Earnings	0.3	1.5	1.1	0.4	0.8

Note: *Approximate composition of net income, making use of (top-coded) information on before-tax income.

Source: 1993–94 Housing Demand Survey.

The average income composition for the retired is shown in Table 7.8. Private pensions (including early retirement pensions) make up more than half of total income for couples and single men aged 60–64, but in the other age-groups and also among single women aged 60–64 state benefits make up by far the largest share of total income on average. Earnings and investment income play a relatively minor part, summing to less than 10 per cent of total income on average.

As a result of the fact that almost everybody over 65 is entitled to the basic state pension, state benefits make up a considerable share (about one-third) of total income even among the highest quintile (Figure 7.5). In the lowest quintile the share of state benefits is almost 90 per cent. Even in the highest quintile the share of earnings and investment income remains limited. Differences in private pensions can be seen to be the main factor contributing toward inequality among pensioners (Figure 7.6).

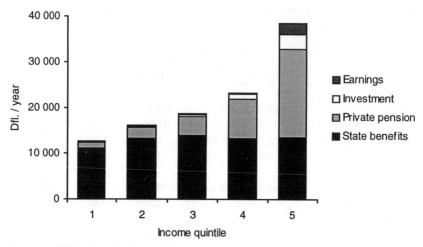

Source: 1993–94 Housing Demand Survey.

Figure 7.6   Equivalised Net Pensioner Income, by Income Quintile

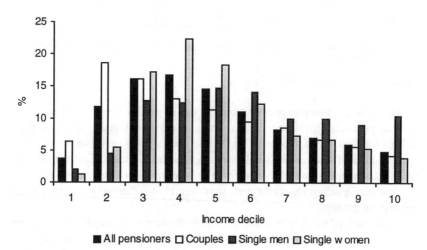

Source: 1993–94 Housing Demand Survey.

Figure 7.7   Percentage of Pensioners in Each Income Decile, Using the (1, 0.7, 0.5) Equivalence Scale

Figure 7.7 shows the proportion of pensioners in each decile of the population (equivalised) income distribution.[12] Fewer than 4 per cent of pensioners fall in the lowest income decile. Almost 60 per cent of pensioners fall in the next four deciles. Almost 11 per cent are in the richest 20 per cent of the population.

The three groups of pensioners by marital status are by no means equally distributed across deciles. Whilst all three groups are under-represented in the lowest decile, almost 20 per cent of retired couples are in the second-lowest decile, while very few single males and females can be found there. Single females are concentrated in the 3rd to 6th deciles (more than 70 per cent of them), while a surprisingly high percentage of single male pensioners are in the highest income deciles. This result depends crucially on the equivalence scale used though. Figure 7.8 gives the distribution of pensioners across deciles using the (1, 0.5, 0.3) scale. Using this equivalence scale all three pensioner types are over-represented in the 2nd to 5th deciles. Among the three groups single males remain the group with the largest representation in the higher deciles.

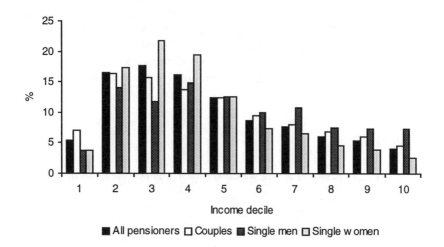

Source: 1993–94 Housing Demand Survey.

Figure 7.8   Percentage of Pensioners in Each Income Decile, Using the (1, 0.5, 0.3) Equivalence Scale

7.7 CONCLUSIONS

In the Netherlands the system of provision for the non-working elderly may be characterised by two main dimensions. First, there is a division by age, between people over 65 and people under 65. Second, both public and private schemes are important. For people over 65 the basic state pension provides an income equal to the social minimum, whilst private pensions play an increasingly important part supplementing the basic state pension. For people under 65 publicly provided disability and unemployment benefits exist alongside early retirement schemes provided by the employer.

To ensure sustainability of the basic state pension in the long run, the government has started to create a reserve fund that should serve to finance the pension payments during the period in which a peak in outlays is foreseen. Moreover, by limiting the social insurance contributions levied on the lower bracket of incomes, an increasing part of basic state pension expenditures will be financed out of general tax revenues. As private (occupational) pensions are fully funded, their financing is not expected to pose problems.

Although the relative position of those receiving only the basic state pension and of other beneficiaries of state benefits has deteriorated somewhat since the early 1980s, the income distribution in the Netherlands may still be characterised by a relatively low level of inequality. Most of the elderly are in the lower part of the (equivalised) income distribution, but non-negligible percentages are in the highest deciles. This holds in particular for single male pensioners.

APPENDIX

Table 7.A1   Pensioner Income, by Composition and Income Quintile

	Quintile				
	1	2	3	4	5
Source (%)					
State benefits	87.5	82.4	74.6	56.9	35.0
Private pension	10.2	15.6	22.4	37.6	50.3
Investment	1.5	1.4	2.4	3.9	8.3
Earnings	0.8	0.5	0.6	1.6	6.4
Average net income (Dfl. p.a.)	12 661	16 043	18 667	23 342	38 551

Source: 1993–94 Housing Demand Survey.

Table 7.A2   Percentage of Pensioners in Each Income Decile, Using the (1, 0.7, 0.5) Equivalence Scale (%)

Income decile	% of all pensioners	% of pensioner couples	% of single male pensioners	% of single female pensioners
1	3.8	6.3	2.0	1.2
2	11.8	18.7	4.5	5.4
3	16.2	16.1	12.8	17.3
4	16.7	13.0	12.4	22.3
5	14.6	11.4	14.8	18.4
6	11.1	9.4	14.2	12.2
7	8.2	8.6	9.9	7.3
8	7.0	6.7	10.0	6.7
9	5.9	5.6	9.0	5.3
10	4.8	4.2	10.4	3.9

Source: 1993–94 Housing Demand Survey.

Table 7.A3   Percentage of Pensioners in Each Income Decile, Using the (1, 0.5, 0.3) Equivalence Scale (%)

Income decile	% of all pensioners	% of pensioner couples	% of single male pensioners	% of single female pensioners
1	5.4	7.0	3.8	3.8
2	16.5	16.4	14.1	17.3
3	17.7	15.7	11.7	21.7
4	16.2	13.7	14.9	19.5
5	12.5	12.4	12.6	12.6
6	8.6	9.4	9.9	7.3
7	7.7	8.0	10.8	6.6
8	6.0	6.9	7.5	4.5
9	5.4	6.1	7.3	4.0
10	4.1	4.5	7.4	2.6

Source: 1993–94 Housing Demand Survey.

NOTES

1. Drees was the Minister of Social Affairs at the time.
2. It should be noted that for single earners who lose more than 80 per cent of their earnings capacity, disability benefits are always at least as high as the relevant social assistance (welfare) level (ABW/RWW), which for a couple is approximately equal to the after-tax minimum wage. In contrast to the entitlement to social assistance, household wealth is not taken into account.
3. See for example Aarts and de Jong (1992).
4. Similar to the case for disability benefits, the unemployment benefit is supplemented by welfare benefits if necessary to reach the social assistance level, without taking household wealth into account. Hence for single earners with low wages the replacement rate can be almost 100 per cent.
5. Benefits may supplement the earnings of people in part-time employment.
6. Figures based on the 1993–94 Housing Demand Survey.
7. The information in this paragraph stems from PN (1987).
8. Meuwissen (1993) finds that approximately 80 per cent of all elderly households draw income from private pensions. The fact that we find about 10 per cent fewer such households may be due to differences in the data used. Possibly households tend not to report pension income if such income is very low, in particular if it is not paid on a monthly basis.
9. A controversial paper by the Secretary-General of the Ministry of Economic Affairs (Van Wijnbergen, 1998), with a proposal to abolish tax deductibility of pension contributions, received considerable press attention.
10. This section uses information from the legal documents (law text and accompanying explanatory memorandum) of the law involved (Tweede Kamer, 1997–98).
11. Notably this is true if expenditures for the non-elderly are included (in contrast to Table 7.1).
12. Because the incomes of members other than head and spouse are not included in household income, household members other than head and spouse aged 18 or over have been ignored in the calculation of equivalised incomes. For exact percentages see Table 7.A2 in the Appendix.

REFERENCES

Aarts, L. and P.R. de Jong (1992), *Economic Aspects of Disability Behaviour*, Amsterdam: North-Holland.

CTSV (1996), *Kroniek van de sociale verzekeringen 1996 (Chronicle of the Social Insurances 1996)*, Zoetermeer: College van Toezicht Sociale Verzekeringen.

De Kam, F. and F. Nypels (1995), *Tijdbom (Time Bomb)*, Amsterdam and Antwerp: Contact.

Kluwer (1997), *Sociale verzekeringswetten (Social Insurance Acts)*, part 4: Algemene Ouderdomswet/Algemene nabestaandenwet (General Old-age Pension Act/General Survivor Pension Act), Deventer: Kluwer.

Meuwissen, P.J.J. (1993), 'AOW-ontvangers en aanvullend (pensioen)inkomen (Persons receiving AOW and supplementary (pension) income)', *Statistisch Magazine*, **13** (1), 11–13.

PN (1987), *Pensioenkaart van Nederland (Pension Map of the Netherlands)*, The Hague: Pensioenkamer.

Statistics Netherlands (1989), *1899–1990 Negentig jaar statistiek in tijdreeksen (90 Years of Statistics in Time Series)*, The Hague: Sdu uitgevers.

Statistics Netherlands (various years), *Statistisch Jaarboek (Statistical Yearbook)*, The Hague: Sdu uitgevers.

Tweede Kamer (1997–98), 'Wijziging van de Wet financiering volksverzekeringen, (Modification of the law on the financing of social insurances)', Tweede Kamer der Staten Generaal (Second Chamber of Parliament), 25699, The Hague: Sdu uitgevers.

Van Wijnbergen, S.J.G. (1998), 'Nederland weer aan het werk (Netherlands back to work)', *Economisch Statistische Berichten*, **82** (4134), 4–8.

8.   Pension Provision in New Zealand

Susan St John

8.1   INTRODUCTION

The New Zealand retirement income system is highly unusual compared with other OECD countries. There are no separate, compulsory saving schemes and no tax incentives for private saving for retirement of any kind. The state provides a flat-rate, taxable, universal pension (New Zealand Superannuation[1]) which is set at a significant level so that for those with few private resources, few additional means-tested income or tied supplements have been necessary, especially for those retirees who own their own home. Eligibility for New Zealand Superannuation is based on meeting the qualifying age (65 by 2001) and simple residency requirements.

Private pension provision in occupational schemes is now the preserve of a relatively small fraction of the working-age population. Saving for retirement is largely considered a matter for individual choice, with some special features of the New Zealand system operating to discourage traditional employer-subsidised schemes. The tax-funded state pension itself can be regarded as the core compulsory arrangement for most workers, who may choose to supplement the state pension with saving in a wide variety of ways, including repaying any mortgage on their own home or investing in their future earning capacity by undertaking education.

New Zealand has not been immune to the debates that have affected other countries, especially the debate over the privatisation of pension provision. The New Zealand system has not yet reached a steady state after a period of extraordinary policy gyrations and experimentation, yet the basic framework has remained intact. However political agreement, which seemed to be embodied in the 1993 Accord on retirement income provision, was then effectively shattered by events following the first mixed member proportional (MMP) election in 1996. It is therefore too early to see the emergence of a new social contract or a restatement of the multi-party Accord. Yet the process has been valuable in clarifying public debate about the purpose of a pension programme and the role of the state in social security – a debate that has often been less vigorous elsewhere.

8.2   A HISTORICAL OVERVIEW[2]

From 1898 New Zealand had an old-age pension for the elderly who passed tests of good moral character and sobriety. Wide welfare state reforms were introduced following the Great Depression, and by the early 1970s all over 65 were entitled to a significant flat-rate universal pension. A tax-free, but income-tested, age benefit of a similar gross amount was also available from the age of 60. At age 65, old-age pensioners could continue to receive this income-tested benefit or elect to take the universal taxable pension. From the early 1970s the New Zealand policy arrangements began to exhibit volatility as summarised in Table 8.1.

Table 8.1   Chronology of Superannuation Policies

1975	New Zealand Superannuation Act 1974 implemented
	• Compulsory contributions from employers and employees
	• Defined contribution pension
	• State-run scheme with contracting-out provisions
1976	New Zealand Superannuation Act 1974 repealed
1977–78	National Superannuation
	• Universal taxable pension
	• 80% of the average ordinary-time wage for a couple
	• At age 60
1985	Surcharge on superannuitant's other income implemented
1988	Rate of surcharge lowered
	Options for state pension reviewed (e.g. social insurance, compulsory saving)
1989	State pension to remain
	• Renamed the Guaranteed Retirement Income (GRI)
	• Funded by a dedicated tax
	• Age to be raised to 65 over 20 years
1988–90	All tax incentives for saving for retirement removed
1991	Budget announcement that GRI would become a welfare benefit from 1992
	• Harsh abatement
	• Joint incomes for married people's income test
	• Age to be raised to 65 over 10 years

Table 8.1 continued

1992	Repeal of Budget legislation
	• State pension renamed National Superannuation
	• Surcharge tightened
	• Lower threshold and rate of surcharge increased to 25%
	• First Todd taskforce examines the case for tax incentives and compulsory provision; recommends voluntary regime, no tax incentives, no compulsion
1993	Multi-party talks
	The three major political parties sign the Accord which establishes:
	• role of the state pension, now called New Zealand Superannuation (NZS)
	• voluntary unsubsidised private provision
	• link provided by the surcharge to reduce the pension for other income
	• indexation via a wage band; couple's rate of net pension to lie between 65% and 72.5% of net average earnings
1995	United Party signs the Accord
1996	More liberal rules for the surcharge announced
	Coalition government reforms
	• Agrees to referendum on compulsory saving
	• Announces that the surcharge will be removed
1997	Periodic Report Group (PRG) begins first review of the policies under the Accord
	White Paper on compulsory saving released on 1 July
	The PRG interim report supports the status quo, with long-term modifications
	Referendum lost in September with a 91.8% no vote
	Final report of the PRG suggests:
	• a new multi-party agreement
	• options for integration of public and private provision are set out for debate
1998	Surcharge removed from April
	Floor in wage band for indexation of NZS reduced from 65% to 60%
	Establishment of Super 2000 Taskforce announced
1999	CPI adjustment only to NZS in April in line with the lowered floor
	Labour/Alliance coalition government replaces the minority National government in November
2000	Indexation changes for NZS reversed and 65% floor restored
	Super 2000 Taskforce abolished
	Labour proposes partial prefunding of state pension

A fully funded, state-run, employment-based contributory scheme was implemented in April 1975 under the New Zealand Superannuation Act 1974. Once it had matured, New Zealand would have had a two-tiered system consisting of the basic state pension supplemented by an inflation-adjusted annuity to be purchased from the balance in a contributor's account at age 65.

Criticism of the scheme emerged quite quickly in the political environment of the 1975 election year. Among many issues there was deep concern at the prospect of state control over a vast pool of investment capital. Women were not happy as they could see that their lower earnings and greater longevity would result in a smaller annuity than for men, leaving them vulnerable to the state's provision of the first tier, which over time might diminish in real value. The scheme proved to be politically unstable and was successfully attacked by the National Opposition who promised a simpler, more generous scheme, particularly attractive to women and which gave the currently retired an immediate boost in income.

Following the election of the National Party, the compulsory scheme was abolished after being in place for only nine months, and employees received back their own and their employer's contributions. The age pension and universal superannuation were replaced in 1977 with a generous tax-funded public pension (National Superannuation) set at 80 per cent of the gross average ordinary-time earnings for a married couple. The pension was an individual[3] taxable entitlement, payable at age 60 if residential requirements were met.[4] While there was no income test, a high top marginal tax rate substantially reduced the net payment for the better-off.[5] Table 8.2 shows that in the mid-1990s the universal pension remained the dominant form of public provision for the elderly.

Over the following years there was a succession of adjustments that reduced the generosity of National Superannuation, including in 1985 the introduction of a controversial surcharge of 25 per cent on a superannuitant's other income over an exempt amount. The top tax rate came down in 1986 from 66 per cent to 48 per cent, and then further in 1988 to 33 per cent. It could be argued therefore that the effect of the surcharge was to restore some tax progressivity for those over 60 with significant amounts of other income. The initial rationale for the surcharge was however purely cost saving. Regardless of the justification, the surcharge was to prove the single most important cause of political instability and public rancour over the next decade.

In the 1980s the Treasury had been determined to reform the tax system by flattening the tax scale and removing all kinds of special tax privileges (see Section 8.3). Between 1987 and 1990 all tax incentives for saving for retirement were abolished, so that saving for retirement in superannuation schemes was treated no differently, for tax purposes, from putting money in

Table 8.2   Sources of State Income Available to Pensioners, 1996–97

Payment	Type	Cost (% of GDP)	% of pensioners in receipt	Criteria
Basic pension NZS or veteran's[a]	Flat rate General tax-based	$5.1 billion (5.4%)	86% (men) 86% (women)[b]	Residency
Disability allowance	Non-contributory	$82 million (0.08%)	14% overall	Income-tested
Accommodation supplement	Non-contributory	$45 million (0.05%)	5% women 3% men	Means-tested income and assets
Special needs / advances and grants	Non-contributory	<$2 million	1.5% overall	Means-tested

Notes:
[a]Most people receive NZS but a small number (1.4 per cent) who qualify have opted for the veteran's pension instead as it has not had an income test.
[b]Some do not pass residency tests. Until 1998 some of those eligible paid the pension back to the state via a surcharge on other income. Some did not claim the pension as their income is too high.

Sources: Department of Social Welfare, 1997; *The Budget Economic and Fiscal Update 1997*, GP Print, Wellington.

the bank. This exercise was not motivated by a focus on overall retirement incomes policies nor by the need to ensure adequacy of provision through combined public and private sources. It was inevitable then that the issue of compulsory saving would be revisited.

During 1988 various options for the state pension, such as compulsory saving and social insurance, were canvassed. In 1989 the Labour Government decided that the existing arrangements were largely suitable, but that the age of eligibility for the state pension, to be called the Guaranteed Retirement Income (GRI), should rise to 65 over the next 20 years. A dedicated tax was to be earmarked to meet the payments expected for the pay-as-you-go (PAYG) state pension.[6] While individuals would be aware of the portion of their tax that was earmarked for pensions, there were no individual accounts and the flat-rate nature of the pension remained.

After an election campaign promising to protect the retired, the National Party came to power in late 1990 with a different agenda. Their pledge to repeal the controversial surcharge, which had acted as a modest income test for the better-off, was abandoned. Instead changes to the GRI were announced that would turn it into a welfare benefit only.[7] At this point it looked as if New Zealand alone among the OECD countries would have no special policies for the provision of retirement income over and above a subsistence, tightly targeted safety net for the poor (St John, 1992).

A period of outrage ensued among the retired. Many only modestly well-off retired people faced a substantially reduced retirement income. After a period of intense lobbying these changes were eventually reversed in an embarrassing U-turn for the government. Arguably that legislation, forced through the House in an all-night sitting after the Budget of 1991, was a critical element in ultimately delivering a new electoral system to New Zealand.[8]

After the backdown in late 1991, the government announced that the state pension (renamed National Superannuation) would remain; however the age of eligibility would continue to be raised quickly, in a series of steps to reach 65 by 2001. It was also announced that a much tighter version of the surcharge would be in place by 1 April 1992. The aborted 1991 changes had heightened awareness of the impact of targeting so that the scramble to find avoidance schemes with the new surcharge continued as before. This in turn contributed to the loss of integrity of the surcharge system and allowed its critics ample ammunition to discredit it.

After the débâcle of the 'mother of all Budgets' in 1991, the government was left with the same sentiments about the need for a reduced state role in retirement income provision, but now turned to private provision to fill the gap. If people could only be forced or persuaded to save for themselves, the government's role could safely diminish. To get advice on how this could be achieved, the government established the Taskforce on Private Provision for Retirement (TPPR). Its first report (TPPR, 1992) considered three broad possible frameworks for New Zealand. The first became known as the enhanced voluntary option, in which a basic state pension was integrated with private provision by means of a surcharge. Private provision was to be encouraged by education and other improvements to the saving environment in a tax-neutral regime. It was this option that found favour, while the other two – the reintroduction of tax incentives and a private compulsory scheme integrated with the state pension – were rejected. Once again, repeating the debates of the 1970s and the late 1980s, the disadvantages of compulsory saving schemes were thoroughly canvassed, and few, if any, advantages for New Zealand emerged in the debate.

In 1993 an Accord between the three major political parties (Labour, National and the Alliance) locked into place New Zealand's unique system of a basic state pension, now to be called New Zealand Superannuation (NZS), and voluntary unsubsidised private saving. The stability provided by the Accord was to be shortlived however, despite the endorsement of the 1997 Periodic Report Group (PRG, 1997a) which reviewed the scheme as required by the Retirement Act 1993. By 1998 the Accord was all but dead (St John, 1999) due to a series of events that shattered the notion that consensus decision-making out of the political arena was possible. Some of these events are detailed later in this chapter. They include: the referendum on compulsory superannuation in 1997; the abolition of the surcharge in 1998; the change to the indexation of NZS in 1999; the reversal of this change in 2000; the setting-up of a new taskforce in 1999; and its abolition in 2000.

8.3   NEW ZEALAND'S RETIREMENT SYSTEM

8.3.1   Public Provision

Much of the income provided by the state for those over pension age stems from New Zealand Superannuation. This is a flat-rate, taxable benefit which has been universal since 1998 when the income test provided by a surcharge payable on other income was abolished. The age of eligibility is rising and will be 65 by 2001. In contrast to other countries with social insurance programmes that pay earnings-related pensions, the New Zealand public pension has always been flat-rate. NZS has three different rates: married couple rate, single rate (60 per cent of the married rate) and a living-alone rate (65 per cent of the married rate). Unlike many other countries, those with no other income pay full tax on their pension, mostly at the rate of 15 per cent. In November 1997 the net rate for a married couple, expressed as a fraction of net after-tax average ordinary-time weekly earnings, was 67 per cent of the combined net average earnings and 60 per cent of male earnings alone.[9]

Unusually the non-contributory basis of NZS has allowed women who are of eligible age to receive the pension on the same basis as men. The surcharge too was an individual-based income test, not a joint one (as in Australia). The individual entitlement basis means that divorce and widowhood do not pose any special administrative problems. The surviving spouse goes from the married rate to the living-alone rate.

Contributions
There is no separate social security tax or contributions basis for NZS. In the 1960s there was a special social security tax, which was never sufficient to fund all social security spending but was seen as a notional contribution by wage-earners. This in turn gave the idea of ownership and right to the

resulting state pension (Ashton and St John, 1988). The social security tax was merged with general income tax in 1969, but the belief that taxes paid have earned the pension has remained among many older people.

In New Zealand general taxation comprises income tax and a comprehensive goods and services tax. From 1988 until 1996 individuals faced a relatively flat personal tax rate structure, with no initial exemption and two statutory rates of 24 per cent and 33 per cent. The bottom rate was modified by the use of a low-income earners' rebate so that the first $9 500 of earned income was effectively taxed at 15 per cent and the second bracket at 28 per cent.

In 1996 and again in 1998 tax cuts were applied to the second long bracket of income, while the threshold for the top rate was raised (Table 8.3). Then in April 2000 the new centre-left government introduced even more prog-ressivity, with a new top tax rate of 39 per cent applying to all income over $60 000. These changes have increased the gap between the effective middle rate and the top tax rate, providing some dilemmas for the tax treatment of superannuation funds, as described later.

Table 8.3   New Zealand Tax Schedule for Personal Income Tax

Bracket	Effective marginal tax rate* (%)		
	1988–96	1/7/98–1/4/00	1/4/00–
$0–$9 500	15	15	15
$9 501–$30 895	28	21	21
$30 896–$38 000	33	21	21
$38 001–$60 000	33	33	33
$60 000+	33	33	39

Note: *Includes the low-income earners' rebate.

From 1985 a surcharge payable on 'other income' was applied to reduce the net amount received by those with significant amounts of other income. At its peak in the early 1990s over 30 per cent of pensioners were subject to the surcharge. Its abolition in 1998 means that today, just as prior to 1985, the pension payment is fully universal. However the top tax rate is now much lower than it was in the early 1980s. Better-off pensioners receive a higher net pension as a fraction of the gross than before.[10]

Indexation and pension levels
In 1978 the gross rate of superannuation for a married couple was 80 per cent of gross average weekly earnings. In after-tax terms the net pension for a couple was then 89 per cent of net average earnings.[11] One of the first

reductions in generosity was to change the 80 per cent relationship from a gross figure to a net figure so that in 1979 the married rate became 80 per cent of net average earnings. From that time the replacement rate has gradually eroded, excluding unusual figures in 1985–86 that reflected adjustments after the wage/price freeze (Krishnan, 1997, p. 159). In 1989 the basis of indexation was changed to the consumer price index (CPI), provided that the net married rate did not fall below 65 per cent of net average earnings (or rise above 72.5 per cent). In 1991 the rate of the state pension was frozen and adjustments were not made again until political agreement was reached over the future of the state pension in 1993.

Under the 1993 Accord the net rate for a married couple is fixed within a band of 65–72.5 per cent of net average earnings. Annual adjustments in this regime are by way of indexation to the CPI until either the floor or the ceiling is triggered. If prices rise more strongly than wages, wage indexation replaces price indexation once the ceiling of 72.5 per cent is reached. Wage indexation also replaces price indexation if wages rise more strongly than prices and the 65 per cent floor is triggered. From 1989 the rate as a percentage of the net average wage slipped continuously. In late 1998 it was announced that the floor would become 60 per cent, so that in April 1999 the relative amount slipped below 65 per cent, as shown in Figure 8.1. The floor was restored following the election of a centre-left government in 2000, at which point the couple's rate was raised to 67.5 per cent of net average weekly earnings.

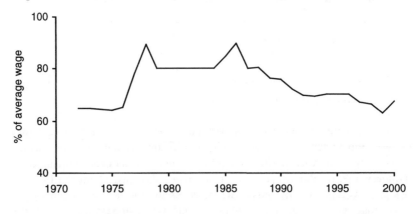

Source: Krishnan, 1997, p. 159.

Figure 8.1   Replacement Rate (net rate for a couple as % of net average earnings for men and women)

Other state assistance received by pensioners

In the year ending June 1997 those aged over 63 received \$5.1 billion[12] gross, or 5.4 per cent of GDP, in NZS[13] and small amounts of other additional means-tested benefits. NZS has been set at a level that has allowed for 'belonging and participation' rather than mere subsistence. For this reason, additional means-tested supplements are little used, as the summary of the various components of cash benefits shown in Table 8.2 indicates. Fewer than 15 per cent of people over pension age receive some income from the state in these forms.

The major supplementary benefit is the accommodation supplement, received by 3 per cent of men and 5 per cent of women. Those who qualify receive a payment based on their actual rent, the maximum set for the region, income and cash assets. Some are also in receipt of rent tenure payments designed to protect them from the move to market rents in housing policy.[14] Homeownership is high among the retired, with only around 14 per cent living in rented accommodation. Only 11 per cent of those on NZS spend more than 25 per cent of disposable income on housing costs, compared with 72 per cent of those on benefits and 32 per cent of all households (PRG, 1997a, p. 36). Around 14 per cent of pensioners receive a disability allowance, due to their own or a dependent child's disability. Very few superannuitants receive other add-on benefits such as the special needs grant. Fewer than 1 per cent claimed a special needs grant for food in the year ended March 1997 (PRG, 1997a, p. 37).

New Zealand provides other non-financial benefits to pensioners. Government spending on the public health system is around 6 per cent of GDP. Medical care is not provided free at the point of use to all New Zealand residents, but a community services card is available to those on low incomes and a high-use card is available for those with chronic illness. NZS recipients do not automatically qualify for the community services card, but their relatively low incomes mean that over two-thirds hold one. This entitles them to higher subsidies for visits to the GP and prescription medicine.[15] Access to the public health system for many formerly widely available services such as cataract operations has diminished markedly, while insurance companies have excluded many by sharp premium rises in recent years. Home-help services are provided in some instances and meals on wheels operate on a user-pays basis. Subsidies for long-term residential care are available on a means-tested basis. There are a range of modest concessions available at the local level, such as for transport, cinema and library, but these are insignificant in the overall picture and far diminished from their role in the 1970s and compared with their current role in countries such as Australia.

8.3.2 Private Provision

On a household basis private sources of income from investments are an important proportion of total pensioner income. As shown later, older households receive 27.5 per cent of their total income from investment and other private sources (Statistics New Zealand, 1997a). But for the reasons outlined below, few retirees have a private pension from an occupational plan, and fewer still can expect to have one in the future. Men are much more likely to have occupational pension income than are women, especially married women. Overall only around 15 per cent of individuals over 65 have income from an occupational pension scheme or a private pension (see Table 8.4).

Among the current work-force, membership of occupational schemes has been declining and new schemes have tended to be defined contribution schemes rather than defined benefit schemes (PRG, 1997a, p. 184). Table 8.5 shows a breakdown of who is contributing to occupational and other personal superannuation schemes. It is clear that men are much more likely to make contributions than women. They are also likely to contribute higher amounts. Table 8.5 does not give information about the nature of the schemes, nor the contribution that may be made by the employer on an employee's behalf. It is safe to assume however that the higher-income contributors are more likely to have matching or greater contributions from employers.

Table 8.4   People Over 65 with Income from Private Sources and Private Pensions, 1995–96

	Men	Women	Total
Numbers >65	143 500	193 000	336 500
% >65 with private income:			
<25% of total yearly income	54.4%	71.7%	
25–49% of total yearly income	20.5%	18.6%	
50–75% of total yearly income	17.6%	7.3%	
>75% of total yearly income	7.4%	2.4%	
% >65 with income from private pensions:			
<25% of total yearly income	7.8%	3.8%	
25–49% of total yearly income	6.4%	4.9%	
50–75% of total yearly income	7.2%	0.9%	
>75% of total yearly income	—	—	
Total % >65 with private pension income	21.4%	9.6%	14.7%

Note: The table excludes those with no regular income and is based on the Household Economic Survey which excludes those living in institutions.

Source: Derived from Statistics New Zealand (1997b).

Table 8.5   Private Superannuation Contributions, by Age and Gender, 1995–96

Age	Total number of people (thousands)	% making contribution
Men		
15–24	207.5	3.7
25–34	205.4	18.2
35–44	237.9	24.0
45–54	180.4	35.8
55–64	127.5	18.8
65+	144.9	0.7*
Total	1 103.6	17.4
Women		
15–24	215.0	3.0
25–34	257.7	10.6
35–44	248.9	11.9
45–54	182.3	18.5
55–64	126.0	8.6
65+	194.4	—
Total	1 224.3	8.8

Note: *Because of sampling error, numbers under 5 000 may not be reliable.

Source: Statistics New Zealand, 1997b.

Taxation[16]

In December 1987 far-reaching reforms to the tax and regulatory treatment of private superannuation schemes were initiated. These reforms made New Zealand the only OECD country not to treat private saving for retirement differently from other forms of saving. Not surprisingly the changes have been regarded as radical, but they did not happen in a vacuum. Rather they were consistent with the broad philosophy of 'the level playing field' approach being applied elsewhere in the tax system and the economy itself. Under these policies any tax preferences, regulations, tariffs, subsidies or controls were regarded as costly distortions, adversely affecting work effort, savings and growth.

Since the early 1980s there has been a widespread perception that New Zealand is a highly taxed country even though the percentage of tax in GDP has been, and still is, only average by OECD standards (Table 8.6). This perception reflects a high reliance on personal income tax although, once

Table 8.6   New Zealand Tax Ratios relative to Other OECD Countries, 1996 (%)

	New Zealand	OECD average*	EU average*
Total tax receipts (% of GDP)	35.8	37.7	42.4
% of total tax receipts			
Personal income tax	43.5	26.8	26.0
Corporate income tax	9.8	8.2	7.5
Social security contribution			
- employee	0.0	7.8	10.1
- employer	0.0	14.5	16.3
Taxes on goods and services	34.5	32.5	31.2
Other taxes	12.2	10.2	8.8
Highest rates of income taxes			
Personal income tax	33.0	47.8	49.7
Corporate income tax	33.0	35.1	36.3

Note: *Unweighted.

Source: OECD, 1999.

allowance is made for employer and employee contributions to social security in other countries, the proportion of tax coming from personal income in New Zealand is not unusually high.[17]

The tax reforms of the 1980s arose because it was apparent that the income tax base had become narrower over time as the result of various tax reliefs. This in turn had resulted in high average and marginal rates. In 1984 the top marginal tax rate for personal income tax was 66 per cent on incomes of over $38 000 – by no means an income at the extreme of the distribution. The other source of tax revenue of significance was the wholesale sales tax which was levied at different rates on a narrow range of goods and which was seen as arbitrary and distortionary.

The attack on the problem was aggressive and the series of reforms to the tax system during the 1980s placed New Zealand at the forefront of change. Among the measures the fringe benefits tax was introduced in 1985 as a base-broadening measure to close loopholes by capturing most of the non-cash income provided by way of company cars, low-interest loans and other business perquisites. On 1 October 1986 the wholesale sales tax was abolished and replaced by a broad-based 10 per cent goods and services tax (GST). This was accompanied by a flattening of the marginal income tax rate schedule and the expansion of targeted tax rebates for those on low incomes.

GST allowed the higher rates of income tax to be lowered, thus reducing incentives to evade and avoid income tax. In contrast to value added taxes in most other countries, GST was also neutral between goods as it was introduced at a single rate with few exemptions. The double taxation of dividends was eliminated when full imputation was introduced in 1988.

The debate over taxing superannuation

The government had signalled its intention to conduct a complete review of the tax treatment of superannuation and life insurance with the 'objective of moving towards a more rational tax regime' in the 1984 Budget. The rationale was that the tax concessions for superannuation (and to a lesser extent life insurance) were costly in terms of forgone tax revenue. This loss was estimated to be around $800 million in 1988–89 which, it was claimed, added about 2.5 percentage points to the average personal tax rate for all taxpayers.

It was also claimed that the benefits of such concessions had been appropriated by high-income earners, usually male, at the expense of taxpayers generally. More fundamentally such concessions were believed to have distorted people's saving and investment decisions, which resulted in inflexibilities in the labour market and created avenues for tax avoidance. Those institutions that had been the recipients of large amounts of funds had an unfair competitive advantage that was inconsistent with the government's goal of financial neutrality.

Professionals in the superannuation industry were generally in agreement that the previous arrangements were ineffective and inequitable, but most wanted the regulations improved, not tax concessions abolished completely. The government however had come to the conclusion that a consistent income tax treatment was the solution. A promised period of consultation with the industry did not eventuate and the decision to abolish all tax concessions, including those applying to existing schemes, was announced in late 1987. Under the new scheme, contributions to savings plans are made out of after-tax income so that contributions may be described as 'taxed'. Income accruing as fund earnings should also be taxed at the appropriate individual marginal tax rate, while withdrawals from the fund are returns of capital and are exempt from tax. The principle is to tax income as it accrues rather than when that income is received or when one secures control over the funds. In the terminology used in the subsequent debate, the traditional expenditure tax treatment involves an exempt/exempt/taxed (EET) regime while the new income tax treatment of savings involves a taxed/taxed/exempt (TTE) regime (Table 8.7).

A complex and uncertain time for private superannuation followed the December 1987 announcement. Arguments that changes to existing schemes

Table 8.7   Different Tax Treatments of Superannuation

	Expenditure tax treatment (prior to December 1987)	Income tax treatment (post-April 1990)
Contributions	Exempt	Taxed
Investment income	Exempt	Taxed
Withdrawals	Taxed	Exempt
	ETT	*TTE*

Note: The expenditure tax treatment was not pure, as often withdrawals could take the form of untaxed lump sums.

involved retrospective legislation fell on deaf ears. The government could point to many other reforms undertaken in the 1980s that entailed a measure of retrospectivity. A transitional regime for previously tax-favoured schemes was supposed to be sufficient to allow smooth adjustment to the new tax environment. This process of consultation and reform took over two years between the announcement of the new regime and its full implementation.

By 1 April 1990 the new tax regime was fully operational, with the Income Tax Amendment Act 1989 and the Superannuation Schemes Act 1989 providing the necessary taxation and supervisory legislation. Schemes became 'registered' by the Government Actuary rather than 'approved' as previously for tax concession purposes.[18]

New Zealand's tax regime for retirement income saving does not distinguish between pension and lump-sum schemes as that is no longer a meaningful distinction. The registration of schemes is not related to tax treatment but is an attempt to provide some degree of supervisory control and protection for members. As there are no concessions there is no restriction on the amount of the employer contribution; nor do restrictions apply as to how scheme benefits must be received, although the trust deed may specify such details.

Private coverage
The PRG (1997a) noted that while many employers are likely to play some role in the provision of retirement planning, 'there has been some question about the extent to which they will continue to offer superannuation itself' (p. 183). Government Actuary figures (Government Actuary, 1999) on membership of occupational schemes show that there has been a reduction in membership since 1990. Membership of private sector employer schemes has dropped from 21 per cent of all employed people to 17 per cent and, while total assets have increased from $9.5 billion to $9.8 billion, after adjusting for inflation real assets have fallen 8 per cent.[19]

Including the Government Superannuation Fund (GSF), which closed to new members in June 1992, total membership of employment-based schemes was 25 per cent of all employed people in 1990, dropping to 19 per cent in 1997. Total assets, inclusive of the GSF, were $11.6 billion in 1990, rising to $13.1 billion in 1997 (PRG, 1997a, p. 183).

The three major likely reasons for the fall-off in membership and assets are: changes to taxation; the imposition of new regulations and requirements; and changes in the nature of the labour market. Changes to the taxation regime have ensured that, far from there being any concessions associated with employer superannuation, there are now tax disadvantages. These, coupled with reporting and disclosure obligations seen as onerous, are changing the traditional view of the role of the employer in providing superannuation schemes directly. The fluidity of the labour market, increased casual employment and self-employment, more part-time work by both men and women, and contract work also call into question the appropriateness of the design of the traditional employment-based schemes with long vesting periods. More flexibility in the labour market has made the defined benefit final salary schemes less relevant. Moreover the PRG noted that among defined contribution schemes, which are increasing in importance, there appears to be a trend towards shorter vesting periods.

> ... defined benefit schemes tend to have longer vesting periods. In 1996, only 30% of members were fully vested after 10 years. In fact, in 46% of defined benefit schemes it took 20 years or longer for members to become fully vested (compared with just 1.3% of defined contribution schemes). There has been no clear trend towards shorter or longer vesting in defined benefit schemes.
>
> (PRG, 1997a, p. 184)

Among other influences on the decline in occupational superannuation schemes may be the requirements of human rights legislation. Benefits for a spouse on the death of a member have been judged to be discriminatory unless equivalent benefits are provided for members without spouses or partners. This applies to members who joined schemes after 1 January 1996.

However, although there has been a move towards defined contribution plans within the sector, overall the trend has been a decline in occupational schemes generally. 'Total remuneration' packages have become more common. In these the employee chooses the nature of the savings instrument and how much to save in it, while the employer's role may be minimal or advisory only. The Office of the Retirement Commissioner is mounting a campaign to encourage employers to take a role in assisting their employees to have security in their retirement, but the precise nature of that assistance will no doubt become quite varied in the future.

8.4   SUSTAINABILITY

The New Zealand population over the age of 65 as a proportion of those aged 15–65 is set to increase over the next 50 years. In 1996 about 12 per cent of the population was aged over 65. By 2031 this proportion is expected to rise to around 22 per cent, levelling off in 2051 at 25 per cent. The elderly population is itself ageing. By 2051 those over 85 will make up 23 per cent of all people over 65, compared with 9 per cent in 1996 (Statistics New Zealand, 1997b, p. 14).

Figure 8.2 shows the gross and net costs of NZS as a percentage of GDP. The rising age of eligibility reduces the percentage until 2001 when the age reaches 65. From then expenditure as a fraction of GDP is expected to rise quite steeply, but not exceed the level of 1990 until after 2020. The difference between gross and net cost also takes account of the surcharge until 1998, when it was abolished. Had the surcharge remained at its relative level of the mid-1990s, it was expected to have reduced the net cost figure of 8.8 per cent of GDP to around 7.8 per cent by 2050.

The first row of Table 8.8 shows the projected cost of the gross NZS payment as a percentage of GDP to 2050. Under various assumptions about the three levers age, indexation and targeting, the next four rows project total expenditure to 2050.[20] The price-indexation-alone option is the one that saves the most money but it has not been seriously considered as it would reduce the state pension to unacceptably low relative levels.

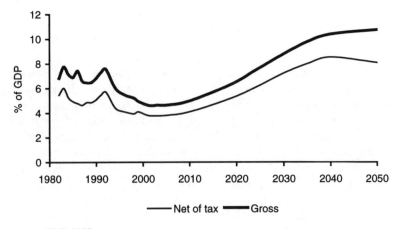

Source: PRG, 1997a.

Figure 8.2   The Projected Net and Gross Cost of NZS

Table 8.8 Future Cost of State Pension, with Reforms (% of GDP)

	2000	2010	2020	2030	2040	2050
No change	4.8	4.8	6.4	8.5	10.1	10.5
Increasing age[a]	4.8	4.8	5.5	6.2	7.9	8.4
Semi-wage[b]	4.8	4.8	6.2	7.6	7.4	8.0
Index prices[c]	4.8	4.3	4.9	5.6	5.8	5.1
Targeting[d]	4.8	4.8	6.1	7.6	8.0	8.6
Scenario 1 Age and targeting	4.8	4.8	5.4	6.7	8.0	8.5
Scenario 2 Semi-wage and targeting	4.8	4.8	5.8	6.5	7.2	7.5

Notes:
[a]The age is raised from 65 to 68, beginning in 2015 and phased in over 12 years.
[b]NZS is adjusted by the average of wages and prices in each year, until a floor for a couple of 55 per cent of net average earnings is triggered. This is expected to be reached in 2050.
[c]Adjustment only by prices.
[d]Reductions achieved by targeting rise from 1 per cent in 2015 to 10 per cent in 2025, thereafter staying at 10 per cent of the gross costs.

Source: Derived from PRG (1997a).

Under current policy settings for the state pension, the PRG (1997a) expected that pressure on the state's budget would require some reduction in expenditure on NZS from 2015. It devised various policy combinations to illustrate that the costs of NZS and total government expenditure could be moderated. Scenario 1 involves an increase in the age of eligibility to 67 by increasing the age by one month for every four months, so in four years the eligibility age reaches 66 and in eight years it reaches 67. It is assumed that raising the age of eligibility would mean a higher rate of labour force participation among those age-groups no longer eligible. The raising of the age is combined with phasing in a targeting regime from 2015 and saves 1 per cent in 2015, rising to 10 per cent by 2025. Under this option, expenditure on NZS is 2.0 per cent of GDP less in 2050 than under the central scenario. Taxes to pay for government expenditure reach 36.5 per cent of GDP by 2050, compared with 38.8 per cent.

Scenario 2 combines targeting by reducing the level of NZS (15 per cent saving in costs by 2030 rather than the 10 per cent of Scenario 1) with changing the indexation formula for NZS. The current formula[21] applies until 2015; then the wage floor is reset at 55 per cent. From this point there is a change to a new indexation arrangement (semi-wage indexation) that adjusts NZS by the average of wage and price movements in each year. NZS is expected to reach the new wage floor (55 per cent) by 2038. Under this option NZS expenses are nearly 3 per cent of GDP lower than the central scenario. Tax revenue reaches 35.9 per cent of GDP by 2050, compared with 38.8 per cent.

However overall figures for government expenditure as a percentage of GDP by 2050, even without adjustment to NZS, are modest in comparison with those in other countries. Factored into these projections was an allowance for the increased expenditure on health for an ageing population, offset by some falls in expenditure on the younger age-group. While adjustment of the age, indexation arrangements and the reintroduction of targeting may be helpful from 2015, it was suggested that these decisions should be made and regularly reviewed in light of factors such as improved longevity and health of older people.

Under the Retirement Income Act 1993, six-yearly reviews of retirement incomes policies are required. The next of these is to be in 2003. The PRG recommended that the issue of reintroducing some targeting be considered well before 2015, not on the grounds of fiscal necessity but in order to promote more intergenerational equity. Universal pensions for wealthy pensioners sit oddly with a welfare state that has become tightly targeted in most respects for the rest of the population (see St John and Rankin (1998)).

For those who were just below the age of eligibility for NZS in the 1996 Census (i.e. 61) about one-third of men and one-half of women were receiving an income-tested benefit of some kind. Women were more likely to be receiving income support as the non-qualifying spouse of an NZS recipient (PRG, 1997a, p. 31). While human rights legislation makes mandatory retirement unlawful, it is clear that, as the age of eligibility for NZS rises, well-paid, full-time employment remains elusive for many. Social change, such as separation, divorce and widowhood, contributes to a picture of many older women facing retirement without adequate private arrangements. An invalid's benefit or a minimal unemployment benefit called the 55+ benefit maintains those who are not in the paid work-force and who need income assistance during their late 50s and early 60s. The tight income test and low level of these benefits suggest that if men and women rely on these benefits for prolonged periods, they are likely to reach the age of entitlement for NZS considerably impoverished. Temporary transitional arrangements for those whose plans were disrupted by the raising of the age of eligibility to 65 over 10 years are due to phase out fully by 2004, and will have affected progressively fewer people over time.

8.5 ACTIVITY RATES

Sustainability depends not only on pension levels and population growth but also on economic activity rates of those under state pension age. Table 8.9 shows that between 1961 and 1986 men over 60 experienced a sharp decline in participation, women aged 50–59 experienced a sharp increase and, except for those aged 60–64, women over 60 had declining rates of participation.[22]

Table 8.10 shows that there was a sudden increase in participation by women aged 60–64 in the mid-1990s. This occurred in both the full-time and the part-time labour force. For men the change has not been so marked. Overall by 1996 rates have returned to 1981 levels for men while they have almost doubled for women.

The marked increase in participation rates between 1991 and 1996 reflects the raising of the age for the state pension, which had become 62 by 1996. Table 8.11 shows that the increase in participation, while most marked for those aged 60–62, was also experienced by all age-groups from 56 to 64.

Table 8.9   Labour Force Participation Rates,* 1961–86 (%)

	Age-group					
	50–54	55–59	60–64	65–69	70–74	75+
Men						
1961	96.6	91.6	69.0	39.1	20.7	7.4
1966	96.8	92.7	71.9	42.1	19.3	6.9
1971	96.3	92.1	69.2	36.1	17.5	5.2
1976	95.9	90.5	57.9	26.7	12.4	4.9
1981	95.2	88.9	46.7	18.1	9.4	3.8
1986	91.6	85.0	39.1	8.8% for 65+		
Women						
1961	27.7	22.1	12.7	6.5	2.8	1.0
1966	31.4	25.4	14.6	7.3	3.1	1.1
1971	35.2	27.5	15.5	7.2	2.7	0.8
1976	40.6	29.0	13.9	5.6	2.1	0.6
1981	44.3	31.6	12.1	3.9	1.5	0.5
1986	52.4	35.4	12.0	1.9% for 65+		

Note: *For those working 20 hours or more, plus the unemployed and those seeking work.

Source: Royal Commission on Social Policy, 1988.

Table 8.10   Labour Force Participation Rates for People Aged 60–64 (%)

	Men	Women
1981	49.9	16.5
1986	41.9	15.7
1991	35.8	16.6
1996	50.2	28.3

Note: Different basis from Table 8.9.

Source: Census.

Table 8.11   Changes in Employment Rates among Older Workers

Age	% of the work-force who are employed, March 1991	% of the work-force who are employed, March 1996	Increase, March 1991 to March 1996 (% points)
Men			
56	75.2	78.3	3.1
57	72.4	76.1	3.7
58	67.7	73.5	5.7
59	63.7	70.6	6.9
60	46.4	65.0	18.6
61	38.1	58.5	20.3
62	33.0	47.6	14.8
63	29.5	37.1	7.5
64	25.7	33.0	7.3
Women			
56	48.1	57.7	9.6
57	42.7	54.4	11.6
58	38.4	49.5	11.0
59	34.1	45.0	10.9
60	23.0	38.5	15.4
61	19.2	33.3	14.1
62	15.1	26.6	11.5
63	12.7	20.8	8.1
64	10.6	17.3	6.7

Notes:
Percentages may not add due to rounding.
Employment is defined as one or more hours of paid employment per week.

Source: PRG, 1997a, p. 28.

8.6 THE DEBATE OVER COMPULSORY SAVING

As described previously, the New Zealand retirement income system is controversial: for example there is no 'second pillar' (World Bank, 1994) of supplementary pensions. The issue of mandatory retirement saving has emerged many times in the debate. In 1975 the New Zealand Superannuation scheme was actually implemented but was quickly overturned (see Table 8.1). The case for such a scheme was re-examined in 1988 and again in 1992 and in each instance rejected.

Concerns about the sustainability of NZS were raised by the New Zealand First Party in the election campaign of 1996. The 1996 coalition agreement between National and New Zealand First promised a referendum on a compulsory saving scheme. The agreement to hold the referendum in September 1997 led to a flurry of activity in early 1997 as the design team was put in place and began the daunting task of designing the Retirement Savings Scheme (RSS) in the space of a few months.

By the time the White Paper on the RSS emerged in early July 1997 (New Zealand Government, 1997), the type of scheme originally proposed by New Zealand First was barely recognisable. Leader of New Zealand First, Winston Peters, had originally wanted increased national savings to 'buy back the family farm' and to make New Zealanders better off in retirement by having access to a pension in addition to NZS. Instead it was clear that the primary intent of the RSS was to save the state money. This entirely different objective led to the design of a one-tier scheme, as a replacement for NZS, not a supplement to it. The regressive nature of the RSS was quickly apparent, and the realisation that the scheme had little potential to make the average retiree better off next century, while enriching the wealthy, took hold quickly (see St John (1999)).[23]

The RSS had the following features:

- The base for contributions was all taxable income, not just employment income as is the case in Australia and Chile.
- The initial contribution rate was 3 per cent, broadly matched by planned tax cuts in 1998, increasing to 8 per cent in the future, with matching tax cuts foreshadowed.
- Most existing employment-based schemes were unlikely to conform to the requirements for an RSS fund and were unlikely to adapt to do so. These requirements included that for the employer contribution to count, it must be fully vested or attributed to the employee at the time of the contribution. In addition the funds were not to be accessed prior to age 65 and at that point must be used to buy an annuity and not taken as a lump sum. In

addition to these restrictive requirements the funds could not be borrowed against and had to be invested in a diversified way.

- Once a target level of saving had been achieved, contributions could cease. The White Paper suggested that, in 1997 terms, the capital sum needed to fund an annuity approximating the value of NZS (33 per cent of the net average wage for a married person) would be about \$120 000. This figure would be revised each year.
- The 85 per cent of women and 60 per cent of men who were not expected to be able to generate sufficient saving in their RSS accounts to meet the capital requirements would be topped up by the state. As annuities would be provided by the private sector, gender equity would be ensured by a special additional capital top-up for all women.[24]
- The RSS annuity included a guaranteed 10-year period of annuity payments, insurance against the collapse of a provider and adjustment for any inflation of up to 3 per cent per annum, with any inflation adjustment above this to be met by the state.

There was to be a long period of transition, during which a taxable NZS would be paid along with the net RSS annuity based on a required capital sum that was gradually to increase to be sufficient to fund a full annuity. By 2038 all payments of NZS would cease for new retirees and the RSS annuity would have replaced the state pension completely. At this point however it is clear that the state would still have a major funding role in the provision of the top-ups.[25] In addition there was an unquantified liability for taxpayers, as the scheme required that the state carry the responsibility for protecting all existing annuities for any inflation beyond 3 per cent.

In all this it was not clear what was the counterfactual. Figure 8.3 is from the White Paper and purports to contrast the costs of the RSS (dashed line) with the costs of the existing scheme (solid line). The RSS line gives the cost to taxpayers of funding all the top-ups and any residual NZS. The impression is that the burden of tax for public payments for retirement would be lower under the RSS from around 2017 and would fall sharply as a proportion of GDP after that. But this was misleading. The 'existing scheme' is the *gross* cost of the *wage-adjusted* NZS, while the RSS 'cost' is based on the cost of funding an annuity that is tax-free and adjusted from point of retirement only by prices. By 2051 these two factors reduce the difference in cost by 4 per cent of GDP (New Zealand Government, 1997, p. 10). It might be further argued that the NZS calculation ignores the surcharge, which was removed under the coalition agreement and should be factored back in for a fair comparison. Finally in considering the real cost to taxpayers the RSS contributions themselves must be added in – the 'transition burden' of moving

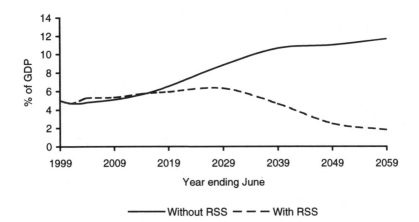

Source: New Zealand Government, 1997.

Figure 8.3 Superannuation Expenditure

from a basically PAYG scheme to a partially funded scheme (given that top-ups will remain) appears to be ignored in these calculations by focusing merely on the residual liability to the public budget.

Apart from sustainability arguments the case for privatisation of the state pension under the RSS was made on grounds that it would encourage individual responsibility and give more certainty, security and freedom from state interference. As people would have contributed their 'own' money to the fund that paid for their basic annuity, it was claimed that the government would be less able to interfere with it. However for a majority of people the size of the capital top-up provided by the state would totally determine the size of their annuity, hardly making them less vulnerable to shifts in policy. In the event of premature death the personal contributions only would become part of the contributor's estate. But had there been no RSS the tax cuts might have been saved anyway. To promote the idea of the RSS being one's 'own money' was hardly a winning card. For these and other reasons the September postal referendum delivered a resounding no vote of 91.8 per cent, with a voter response of 80.3 per cent.

8.7 INCOME DISTRIBUTION[26]

Overall, incomes of households with an age of occupier over 65 come predominately from NZS (56 per cent), with investment and other private

Table 8.12   Sources of Household Income by Age of Occupier, 1997 (% of total income)

Income source	Age	
	65+	>15
Wages and salary	10.4	64.2
Self-employment	1.7	9.8
NZS	56.1	7.8
Social security benefits	4.1	7.3
Investment	15.4	5.7
Other	12.1	5.1

Source: Statistics New Zealand, 1997a.

sources (27.5 per cent) and employment (12 per cent) the two other major sources of income (see Table 8.12). Women are more reliant on NZS than men: for the year to March 1996 72 per cent of women and 54 per cent of men received at least three-quarters of their income from NZS. Just 7 per cent of men and 2 per cent of women received less than a quarter of their income from this source (Statistics New Zealand, 1997b, p. 30).

8.7.1   Housing and Living Arrangements

Census data (1996) show that 47.6 per cent of people aged 65 or over lived in couple-only households, a further 13.7 per cent lived with other family or relatives and 29.8 per cent lived alone. Around 6.2 per cent were in a residential home or hospital. Compared with the rest of the population, older households are much more likely to own their own homes, with 81 per cent owning their house without a mortgage (Statistics New Zealand, 1997a). For the general population only 40 per cent of all households own their home outright, while a further 33 per cent own with a mortgage. Thus it can be inferred that younger households on average have lower standards of living than the older age-group at the same points in the income distribution once housing costs are taken into account.

Table 8.13 shows housing tenure by age and gender, confirming the high rates of homeownership. Those over 80 are less likely to own their own home. There is a greater likelihood that women will be single and live alone, especially if aged over 80. In addition 13 per cent of women over 80 are renting. However, even at the younger age-group (65–79), 10 per cent of men and women are renting. It is to be expected that those who have the highest housing costs are more likely to be experiencing hardship if they are living on the NZS pension alone.

Table 8.13   Housing Tenure, by Age and Gender, for People Aged 65 or Over, 1996 (%)

Housing tenure	Aged 65–79			Aged 80+		
	Male	Female	Total	Male	Female	Total
Owned with mortgage	8.5	7.6	8.0	4.7	5.4	5.2
Owned without mortgage	74.5	72.4	73.4	73.1	67.5	69.5
Owned, mortgage not specified	2.5	3.3	2.9	4.6	4.9	4.8
Provided rent-free	3.4	3.7	3.6	5.2	5.6	5.5
Rented	9.1	10.5	9.8	9.6	13.0	11.8
Not owned, rental status not specified	1.9	2.5	2.3	2.9	3.5	3.3

Source: 1996 Census of Population and Dwellings, quoted in Statistics New Zealand (1997b).

8.7.2   Disposable Incomes

Total disposable income is income net of all direct taxation (excluding local taxes, which are of minor significance in New Zealand and relate to property). Housing and housing costs are ignored so that there is no imputed rent credited to owner-occupiers. Table 8.14 gives a breakdown of personal income by age. Median incomes for all age-groups, male and female, are similar, suggesting that the basic NZS pension is an equalising factor as a predominant source of income for the lowest 50 per cent. Table 8.15 shows the average private income of those with other income. The proportion of older people with other income falls dramatically with age. Women with other income are fewer at all age brackets and they have much less than men with other income.

It is clear from Tables 8.14 and 8.15 that the income distribution for women is more skewed to the lower end than that for men. This reflects the facts that:

- fewer women have an occupational pension, and many of those who do have one have inherited it at a reduced rate, usually 50 per cent, from a deceased husband;
- a smaller proportion of women are still working at any age and women tend to receive a lower wage if they are working;
- women have a lower ability to accumulate savings during the working life.

The average (mean) amounts of before-tax pensioner weekly income in 1996 are shown in Table 8.16 for households aged 65 or over, in contrast to the picture for all households. On average, pensioners are poorer.

As in the UK however, what stands out is how much better off the richest quintile of the old is than the rest, even than the second-richest quintile in terms of other income. The provision of NZS is one factor that means inequality is rather less amongst pensioners than for the rest of the population as a whole. This is illustrated in Table 8.17, which shows the pre-tax unadjusted distribution of household income (Statistics New Zealand, 1997a).

Table 8.14   Total Yearly Personal Income, by Age and Gender, for People Aged 65 or Over, 1996 (%)

	Aged 65–79		Aged 80+		Aged 65+	
	Male	Female	Male	Female	Male	Female
Total personal income:						
Loss or $0–$5 000	2.2	2.8	3.8	4.9	2.5	3.3
$5 001–$10 000	31.8	33.0	28.2	24.0	31.2	30.8
$10 001–$15 000	33.7	42.8	36.7	45.7	34.2	43.5
$15 001–$20 000	11.7	11.2	12.7	13.8	11.9	11.8
$20 001–$25 000	6.6	4.3	6.7	5.1	6.6	4.5
$25 001–$30 000	4.8	2.4	4.6	2.9	4.8	2.6
$30 000+	9.1	3.6	7.3	3.5	8.7	3.5
Median income ($)	12 360	11 658	12 459	12 312	12 378	11 832

Source: 1996 Census of Population and Dwellings, quoted in Statistics New Zealand (1997b, p. 54).

Table 8.15   Average Pensioner Private Income, by Gender and Age-group, 1996

	Age-group			
	60–64	65–69	70–74	75+
Men				
% with private income	67%	29.2%	20.7%	24.2%
Average ($)	25 063	9 345	6 453	11 571
Women				
% with private income	52%	10.5%	13.7%	9.6%
Average ($)	8 814	4 381	5 252	3 833

Sources: Statistics New Zealand, 1997a; Cook, 1997, p. 18.

Table 8.16   Households' Weekly Pre-tax Income, 1996 ($)

Source of income	Households aged 65+	All households
Wages and salaries	52.0	580.7
Self-employment	8.5	90.7
NZS	280.6	69.1
Other welfare benefits	20.9	55.1
Investment	76.7	45.9
Other sources	60.6	46.1
All sources	499.4	887.6

Source: Statistics New Zealand, 1997a.

Table 8.17   Proportion of Those Aged 60 or Over in Each Income Decile

	Mean income ($)	Upper limit ($)	Number in each decile (thous.)	% of people who are retired in each decile	% of people who are males over 60 in each decile	% of people who are females over 60 in each decile
Decile						
1	8 450	13 300	196	28.6	7.9	22.9
2	16 198	18 799	215	41.5	15.4	23.9
3	20 634	22 899	263	30.4	14.7	16.8
4	25 558	28 799	313	19.8	12.1	11.0
5	32 557	36 200	329	11.6	6.2	6.5
6	39 551	44 199	347	8.9	5.2	5.3
7	48 344	53 299	373	4.8	3.1	3.3
8	59 576	67 399	359	2.6	1.9	1.5
9	75 452	87 099	380	2.0	2.2	1.3
10	134 622		386	2.5	3.2	2.6
All	46 155		3 161		6.4	7.9

Source: Statistics New Zealand, 1997a.

The composition of people over 60 who are in each decile shows that far more women than men are in the lowest deciles of income. However the average number of people in the lowest deciles is also low. Thus the figures reflect the predominance in the lowest deciles of single-person households, which will be largely retired. Thus it is a mistake to conclude from these data that retired people are automatically among the poorest in society.

To account for household size, equivalent household disposable income is shown in Table 8.18.[27] The equivalised figures show that households with one or two superannuitants have equivalised incomes of 73 per cent or 80 per cent respectively of the average equivalent income for all family types. It is clear that of those households that have low incomes, superannuitant households are better off than sole parents and beneficiaries. Table 8.19, again using equivalised household income, shows the importance of NZS in reducing inequality and also reinforces the idea that the top quintile is very much better off than the others.

The picture given by the income data is that pensioners' incomes are more equal than those of the rest of the population, but still highly skewed to the

Table 8.18   Equivalent Disposable Income of Households, by Type of Resident, 1995–96 ($)

	Equivalent disposable income
Households with at least one:	
Dependent child or youth	27 080
Superannuitant	21 114
Maori adult	27 215
Pacific Islands adult	23 727
Sole parent	19 489
Beneficiary	18 219
Households comprising:	
One superannuitant	22 781
Two superannuitants	25 115
One or two superannuitants	23 978
Sole parent + child(ren)	17 756
Main income source	
Wage or salary	35 693
Self-employment	45 383
Social welfare benefits	15 512
NZS	19 205
Other	37 652
All households	31 200

Source: Mowbray, 2000.

top end. Housing is an important component of living standards and the omission of housing affects disposable income comparisons. New Zealand does not have an official poverty line, but unofficial estimates indicate that since 1985 the incidence of poverty has been very low. In the late 1990s, as the relativity of NZS to the average wage dropped (see Figure 8.1 in Section 8.3.1), more of the elderly appeared below the 60 per cent median income level (Stephens, Frater and Waldegrave, 2000, p. 29). Around this time concerns were voiced in the community about the re-emergence of poverty among those with no income other than NZS and about high housing costs as a significant social issue. The restoration of the level of NZS in relation to wages in 2000 is yet to be evaluated.

Table 8.19   Mean Incomes of Aged Households, by Quintile of Equivalent Total Household Income, 1995–96 ($)

Quintile	Public provision	Private provision[a]	Total[b]
1	14 619	333	14 689
2	14 937	802	15 807
3	15 077	3 505	19 999
4	13 933	8 736	26 846
5	11 261	24 335	58 134
Total	13 956	7 619	27 227

Notes:
[a]Occupational pensions, investments and dividends.
[b]Includes income from wages and self-employment. Self-employment income is negative for the first two quintiles.

Source: Krishnan, 1997.

8.8   CURRENT ISSUES

8.8.1   Tax and Regulatory Issues

A critical issue at the end of the 1990s is how to reinforce the message that people must save more for their retirement when the conventional methods are actually tax-disadvantaged for many people. There are two major tax issues: one is the need to ensure that each investor pays tax at his or her appropriate tax rate; the other concerns the treatment of imputed income and capital gains.

Under a pure flat tax, making sure that everyone is taxed appropriately is not an issue. Contributions, regardless of who makes them, and fund earnings are taxed at the same flat rate which is the marginal tax rate of all members. In the case of annuities the flat tax rate on fund earnings is priced into the ensuing annuity.

The move further away from flat tax implied by the tax cuts of 1996 and 1998 (see Table 8.3 in Section 8.3.1) and the implementation of a new top rate in 2000 of 39 per cent poses serious problems for both tax equity and tax neutrality. For those who are on a marginal tax rate of 21 per cent, taxing employer contributions to superannuation schemes and fund earnings at 33 per cent is clearly penal. As well, such schemes are taxed on their capital gains and must meet new disclosure rules under the Securities Amendment Act 1996 and the Investor Advisors (Disclosure) Act 1996, both of which came into force on 1 October 1997.

The government established a committee on the Taxation of Life Insurance and Superannuation (TOLIS) to find a solution to the problem. The TOLIS (1997) document indicates the problem is far from easy to resolve. As well as superannuation schemes, life insurance products are also affected. The government considered two possibilities. The favoured one was a tax credit option that involved granting a tax credit to the fund earnings of those members whose tax rate is only 21 per cent. This option dealt with the problem in a theoretically acceptable way but appeared very complex. It was criticised by the industry, which saw the additional costs as another nail in the coffin of employment-based superannuation. The second-best solution was to have a uniform lower tax rate on fund earnings of around 27 per cent. This was also unacceptable to the government on grounds of loss of revenue and avoidance. In 2000 the government proposed tightening the definition of schemes that would qualify for the 33 per cent treatment as it became apparent that superannuation schemes could be used to avoid the top 39 per cent rate. Under legislation before the House in mid-2000, a withdrawals tax of 5 per cent is proposed to discourage short-term saving in superannuation schemes for tax avoidance reasons.

Aside from these tax problems, neutral treatment of all forms of savings has been difficult to achieve in practice. Owner-occupied homes remain tax-favoured as there is no tax on imputed rental and no capital gains tax. Other property too has tax advantages, especially if capital gains can be made. In addition there are anomalies in the tax treatment of capital gains on shares depending on whether an investment is deemed to be passive (such as index funds) or actively traded (such as superannuation funds) (PRG, 1997a, p. 63).

8.8.2 Impact of Recent Reforms

In 2000 the pension system in New Zealand is enduring something of a political hiatus. Between 1993 and 1996 the Accord gave retired people protection against ill-considered changes, and those coming up to retirement could plan with a reasonable degree of certainty. The framework of the Accord was endorsed by the PRG review, which in turn was a requirement of the Retirement Income Act 1993.

The formation of the new coalition government in 1996 had begun to undermine the Accord. While agreement had been reached on the shape of the surcharge for 1997–98, the surcharge itself was abolished from 1998 as part of the coalition agreement. This was the kind of decision that the Accord was to have removed from the disruptive influences of election-year politics. More damaging still to stability in retirement income planning was the deduction in the wage band floor to 60 per cent announced with no warning in September 1998. By 1999 the Accord was fairly judged as over, although the legislation endorsing its provisions remained.

The Labour Government, elected in 1999, reversed the change to the wage band floor, which had caused the married person's pension to fall (see Figure 8.1 in Section 8.3.1). From April 2000 the net pension of a married person was raised, restoring confidence that NZS would be tied to movements in the average wage as before. While the Labour Government also raised the top marginal tax rate from 33 per cent to 39 per cent, there was no suggestion of a return to any kind of income testing such as reinstating the surcharge.

In 2000 talks between the parties on the left are examining the prospect of a dedicated fund for the state pension as a shift from pure PAYG arrangements. However there is no indication that the Accord will be reactivated, and a deep uncertainty pervades the ranks of the retired population. The Retirement Income Act 1993 remains, and with it the appended Accord provisions. The requirement of a further review in 2003 has not been discussed, while the recommendations of the first periodic review in 1997 remain apparently sidelined (PRG, 1997b).

8.8.3 Intergenerational Equity Concerns

Universal pensions have raised concern about equity between generations. As the traditional universal welfare state retreats, working-age taxpayers are paying more directly for healthcare, education and other social provisions than did the currently retired. Almost all other parts of the social benefit system have become tightly targeted, with income and means tests (St John and Rankin, 1998).

As the age has been raised, more people below the age of retirement have accessed a state welfare benefit, such as the invalid's benefit or domestic purposes benefit.[28] The 55+ benefit is a form of the unemployment benefit with less stringent work-seeking requirements. The transitional retirement benefit was introduced at a higher level than the 55+ benefit for those over 60 and less than three years from the age of eligibility who found the age raised on them without sufficient warning. It is due to be phased out by 2004, leaving little support for that group who are unable to work full-time.

If the pension is set at a level that secures an adequate standard of living for those with few other resources, the fiscal pressures of universal provision may require other changes, such as to the age, which may affect people on lower incomes most severely. Universal pensions also raise intragenerational equity issues. New Zealand has been very kind to the wealthiest of current retirees, who have benefited from lower tax rates, no capital gains and no death duties and often have subsidised pension income. While means testing would destroy the character of the New Zealand public pension, there is a strong case in equity for a surcharge-type income test to be reintroduced.

8.9   CONCLUSIONS

The New Zealand pension system is unusual. The scheme is intrinsically simple and has endured many assaults. While it does not conform to the World Bank's model of the three pillars (St John and Willmore, 2000), the two pillars of state pension and unsubsidised private saving appear to be fiscally sustainable, especially if some well-planned adjustments are introduced from 2015.

The lack of a uniform capital gains tax and failure to tax imputed income from owner-occupied housing have meant that tax neutrality has been a chimera. Unresolved problems have also arisen with the intent to tax all saving at the marginal tax rate of the individual. The current 33 per cent applied to the earnings of funds is higher than the tax rate of low-income contributors and lower than the tax rate of high-income contributors.

The removal of tax concessions of all kinds for pensions has added to the trend, by no means confined to New Zealand, away from defined benefit occupational schemes. The onerous nature of reporting requirements and the inability to remove the tax disincentives for many people in formal schemes are also accelerating the move out of occupational and private superannuation plans. The income distribution among the old is already highly skewed, with the possibility that middle incomes will further decline as employer-subsidised pensions become a thing of the past.

A feature of current proposals that may make New Zealand conform more closely to other countries' models is the introduction of partial prefunding of the state pension. The details are yet to emerge on the government's thinking. While no panacea, such a fund might ensure that fiscal surpluses are less likely to be dissipated in tax cuts and thus add to national saving, helping to restore balance in the external accounts. As New Zealand has an underdeveloped share market, which never recovered fully from the 1987 crash, the government's fund may help underpin the ability of local business to raise new capital.

There is now an urgent need to re-establish the political processes that gave certainty and stability during the Accord of 1993–96 (see PRG (1997b)). There have been far too many ill-considered lurches and retreats in pension policy. This however seems to be a matter for political resolution of process, rather than there being any pressing need to change the basic structure of the New Zealand system.

NOTES

1. Superannuation is the term used in New Zealand for retirement income provision. Pensioners are often referred to as superannuitants. Private superannuation may or may not be in the form of a pension.
2. This section draws extensively on St John (1992 and 1999).
3. Each married person received one-half the gross married rate, taxed in their own name.
4. An applicant was to be a legal resident of New Zealand and have lived in New Zealand for a total of 10 years from the age of 20 and five years since the age 50, normally live in New Zealand and be living there when the application is made.
5. In 1982 the tax rate was lifted from 60 per cent to 66 per cent.
6. It was to be about 8 per cent of the current personal income tax base, marked off as a notional tax, not a new one.
7. It was to be income-tested on a couple basis with the same low level of exemption for both a married couple and a single person. The effective marginal tax rate was 92.8 per cent. For those over 70 years old one-half of the benefit would have become a universal, non-income-tested payment, but in essence the only beneficiaries of this change were the wealthiest older retirees who formerly lost all their pension through the surcharge.
8. Mixed member proportional voting replaced first past the post in the 1996 election.
9. In April 1997 the basic weekly rate of pension after tax at the standard rate for a married person was $160.61. A single person received $192.73 sharing accommodation or $208.79 if living alone. People with a non-qualifying spouse received an income-tested rate of $321.22 if first claimed prior to 1991 and of $305.74 if claimed post-1991. Throughout this chapter, $ refers to New Zealand dollars.
10. When the top tax rate was raised to 39 per cent in 2000, the retention by the highest-income pensioners became 61 per cent.
11. Net average earnings is the after-tax, ordinary-time, weekly earnings averaged for male and female wage-earners.

12. i.e. thousand million.
13. Includes a very small amount for veterans' pensions.
14. About 1.3 per cent of all NZS recipients.
15. For example a typical charge for a consultation with a GP might be $25–30 instead of $35–45. Specialist services are excluded from the subsidy.
16. This section draws heavily on St John and Ashton (1993).
17. New Zealand pays for social security through general taxation. While the social security payroll taxes common in other countries may appear different from personal income tax, most of the literature suggests that the burden of both employer and employee contributions falls on the worker.
18. While registration is optional, unless registered, employer contributions are subject to the fringe benefits tax instead of the withholding tax. While in principle these two taxes are equivalent, the fringe benefits tax is the more difficult to comply with. Unregistered schemes are classified as unit trusts and taxed as companies, whereas trustees of registered schemes are taxed under trust taxation as a proxy for scheme members.
19. Between 1990 and 1998 membership of employer-sponsored registered defined benefit schemes fell 25 per cent, while defined contribution scheme membership fell 9.5 per cent (Government Actuary, 1999).
20. The assumptions about growth, participation rates and inflation are outlined in PRG (1997a).
21. The wage band formula prescribes CPI indexation, subject to being within the wage band for the couple rate of NZS, with a floor set at 65 per cent of net average earnings.
22. Labour force participation rates for 1986–96 are not available on the same basis as the figures presented in Table 8.9 for 1961–86.
23. The Council of Trade Unions mounted a vigorous opposition, co-ordinating opposition from many diverse factions (including the Business Round Table) through the Internet.
24. The higher capital sum was to reflect their greater longevity. While this apparently ensured gender equity, as it allowed private insurers to pay the same pension to women as to men, it was viewed by many women more as another instance of having to go 'cap in hand' to the government.
25. It was clear that better-off income-earners who reached the capital-sum goal quickly would be better off, as they would then enjoy the tax cuts. On the other hand low-income earners could contribute for a lifetime and not end up with a higher-than-basic RSS annuity. The impact of funding and pay-outs was highly regressive.
26. The income data presented in this section come from the 1996 Census, from the Household Economic Survey (HES) 1981–97 (Statistics New Zealand, 1997a) and from research work from the Social Policy Agency, Ministry of Social Policy on income distribution (Mowbray, 2000).
27. The 1998 revised Jensen equivalence scale, widely used in New Zealand, is based on two-adults-only = 1.00, one-adult = 0.65 and further scale factors for the presence of children.
28. Benefit for sole parents and certain categories of care-givers.

REFERENCES

Ashton, T. and S. St John (1988), *Superannuation in New Zealand: Averting the Crisis*, Wellington: Institute of Policy Studies.

Cook, L. (1997), 'Retirement in the 21st century: do we have an option?', Statistics New Zealand, Wellington, unpublished paper.

Department of Social Welfare (1997), *Statistics Report 1997 Fiscal Year*, Wellington: Department of Social Welfare.

Government Actuary (1999), *Report of the Government Actuary for the Year Ended June 1999*, Wellington: Government Actuary.

Krishnan, V. (1997), 'The shifting public/private mix of retirement income and declining replacement rates', *Social Policy Journal*, (9), 151–63.

Mowbray, M. (2000), *Incomes Monitoring into the 1990s*, Wellington: Social Policy Agency, Ministry of Social Policy.

New Zealand Government (1997), *You and Your Retirement Savings: The Proposed Compulsory Retirement Savings Scheme*, Wellington: The Treasury.

OECD (1999), *OECD in Figures*, Paris: Organisation for Economic Co-operation and Development.

PRG (1997a), *1997 Retirement Income Report: A Review of the Current Framework – Interim Report*, Wellington: Periodic Report Group.

PRG (1997b), *1997 Retirement Income Report: Building Stability*, Wellington: Periodic Report Group.

Royal Commission on Social Policy (1988), *The April Report*, Wellington: Government Printer.

St John, S. (1992), 'National Superannuation: or how not to make policy', in J. Boston and P. Dalziel (eds), *The Decent Society*, Auckland: Oxford University Press, pp. 126–45.

St John, S. (1999), 'Superannuation in the 1990s: where angels fear to tread?', in P. Dalziel, J. Boston and S. St John (eds), *Redesigning the Welfare State in New Zealand: Problems, Prospects and Policies*, Auckland: Oxford University Press, pp. 278–316.

St John, S. and T. Ashton (1993), *Private Pensions in New Zealand: Can They Avert the Crisis?*, Wellington: Institute of Policy Studies.

St John, S. and K. Rankin (1998), 'Quantifying the welfare mess', Auckland University, Department of Economics, Policy Discussion Paper no. 22.

St John, S. and L. Willmore (2000), 'Two legs are better than three: New Zealand as a model for old age pensions', paper prepared for the International Research Conference on Social Security, Helsinki, 25–27 September.

Statistics New Zealand (1997a), *Household Economic Survey*, Wellington: Statistics New Zealand.

Statistics New Zealand (1997b), *Ageing & Retirement in New Zealand*, Wellington: Statistics New Zealand.

Stephens, R., P. Frater and C. Waldegrave (2000), 'Below the line: an analysis of income poverty in New Zealand, 1984–1998', Victoria University of Wellington, Graduate School of Business and Economic Management, Working Paper no. 2/00.

TOLIS (1997), 'Report to Ministers from the Working Group on the Taxation of Life Insurance and Superannuation Fund Savings (TOLIS)', April, unpublished mimeo.

TPPR (1992), *Private Provision for Retirement: The Options*, Wellington: Taskforce on Private Provision for Retirement.

World Bank (1994), *Averting the Old Age Crisis*, Washington, DC: Oxford University Press.

9.   Pension Provision in the United Kingdom

Carl Emmerson and Paul Johnson*

9.1   INTRODUCTION

The UK pension system balances the private with the public in a distribution of tasks and resources that is unusual among European countries. The state runs a flat-rate, virtually subsistence-level pension system, with a significant tier of means-tested 'benefits in addition to the contributory, but near universal, retirement pension. There is also a supplementary pension, the State Earnings-Related Pension Scheme – universally known as SERPS – but this represents a late addition to the overall scheme of things, and an addition that is remarkable more for its lack of durability than for almost anything else.

Introduced in 1978 – that is, the first rights to it began to be earned in 1978 – SERPS came late enough to incorporate one other unusual feature. This was the facility, built in from the start, for people with a company pension to opt out of SERPS altogether. Mostly providing pensions on a defined benefit/final salary basis and with a history dating back to the last century, occupational schemes in the UK have covered about half of the working population at any one time since the mid-1960s. Altogether privately funded pensions in the UK have assets of around £750 billion,[1] equal to 100 per cent of UK GDP. As a result of their expansion in the 1960s and of various legislative changes that have improved rights for early leavers, more and more people have been retiring with larger and larger amounts of occupational pension income. This is unequally divided, and remains overall less important than the basic pension, but is and will remain central to pension provision in the UK.

*This research was funded by the UK Economic and Social Research Council (ESRC) Centre for the Microeconomic Analysis of Fiscal Policy at the Institute for Fiscal Studies (IFS).

In general pensioners in the UK are defined according to the state pension age – 65 for men and 60 for women – at which the retirement pension (and SERPS) becomes available. There are 3.7 million men aged over 65 and 6.9 million women aged over 60 out of a total population of 58.6 million (including 11.4 million children under the age of 16). There are no official pre-retirement or early retirement benefits, though the majority of men do in fact retire before age 65, and much use is made of incapacity benefits and some means-tested benefits in maintaining people in inactivity during their late 50s and early 60s.

The nature of the UK system – i.e. a largely subsistence-level flat-rate benefit-based scheme – means that state spending on it is relatively low. The retirement pension cost 3.8 per cent of GDP in 1998–99. This provided a pension equal to 15 per cent of average male earnings for a single pensioner or 24 per cent of average earnings for a couple. A further 1 per cent of GDP went on means-tested benefits, which are received by more than one in three of the population over pension age. The cost of SERPS in 1998–99 was 0.4 per cent of GDP.

This low level of benefits has made the UK system perfectly sustainable from a cost point of view. Nevertheless reforms continue apace. The Labour government is to replace SERPS with a new state second pension (S2P) from 2002. This will be significantly more redistributive than SERPS and is in fact intended to become another flat-rate pension on top of the basic pension from about 2007. The range of private schemes available is also being expanded with the introduction, from April 2001, of stakeholder pensions, a new form of defined contribution scheme with stringent controls on the level and structure of charges. This forms part of the government's stated strategy of moving from the situation at the end of the 20th century in which about 60 per cent of pensioners' incomes come from the state with 40 per cent coming from private sources to one in which by 2050 those proportions are reversed.

One problem with the UK pension system is that, while sustainable in terms of cost, the levels of future pension payments are likely to end up being unsustainably low for some people. A second and related consequence of the current system is that it leads to significant inequality among the retired. Those with good private pensions do rather well. Those without do not and may retire on very low incomes. Currently (in 2000) the low level of the basic pension is becoming a hot political issue in a way that it has not been for many years.

In this chapter we start by describing the state system of pension provision, then the private system. We assess the sustainability of the system from a cost point of view and show economic activity rates of those above and just below pension age. Finally we show the levels of pensioner incomes in the UK, their distribution and how they compare with the incomes of non-pensioners.

9.2   PUBLIC SOURCES OF INCOME

In 1999–2000 individuals aged over 60 received £47.6 billion (5.3 per cent of GDP) direct from the state in the form of pensions and other cash benefits.[2] Here we consider each benefit in more detail. A summary of the various components of cash benefits is shown in Table 9.1.

Table 9.1   Sources of State Income Available to Pensioners, 1998–99

Payment	Type	Cost (% of GDP)	% of pensioners in receipt	Criteria
Basic pension	Flat-rate, contributory	3.8	95 (men)* 56 (women)*	NICs for 90% of working life
SERPS	Earnings-related, contributory	0.4	80 (men) 30 (women)	NICs paid, not opted out
Income support	Income-related, non-contributory	0.4	11 (men) 20 (women)	Means-tested
Housing benefit	Income-related, non-contributory	0.5	22	Means-tested
Council tax benefit	Income-related, non-contributory	0.1	30	Means-tested

Notes:
NICs = National Insurance contributions.
*This is the percentage of men or women who receive a full basic pension. For women the figure is made up of 97 per cent of widows who get a full pension on the basis of their husband's contributions and just 39 per cent of non-widows who get a full pension in their own right. Others qualify for smaller proportions.

Sources: Department of Social Security, 1999a and 1999b.

The basic pension, set at little more than subsistence levels, has a long history originating in 1908 with a means-tested benefit available to the over-70s 'of good character'. The 1946 legislation introduced a contributory benefit available to men of 65 years and above and to women of 60 and over, but maintained the subsistence level. For the whole period since 1945 means-tested benefits have played an important role in income maintenance for pensioners, with housing benefit, covering rental costs, being especially important. No meaningful attempt was made to introduce an earnings-related benefit until the Social Security Act of 1975 put SERPS on the statute books, but the rush away from such a system was swift and irreversible. Some of the main events in the 20th century history of UK pension provision are summarised in Table 9.2.

Table 9.2   Changes Made to the UK State Pension System, 1900–2000

1908	A means-tested benefit, at a subsistence level, payable to the over-70s 'of good character'.
1925	Earnings-related contributory pension introduced for the over-65s. This was compulsory for all manual workers and others on low incomes. The over-70s continued to receive the non-contributory, means-tested benefit.
1946	Elements of Beveridge Report of 1942 implemented. Flat-rate system of contributions and also benefits introduced. Basic state pension increased on an *ad hoc* basis although originally intended to be increased in line with prices. (Actually increased faster than earnings between 1950 and the mid-1960s.)
1961	Graduated pensions scheme introduced. Earnings-related contributions and benefits, but benefits earned in nominal terms and not indexed to retirement.
1975	Basic state pension formally indexed to higher of earnings and price inflation.
1978	SERPS introduced, promising 25 per cent of earnings over best 20 years but with ability to 'contract out' into defined benefit occupational schemes. Right of married women to opt out of basic state pension in return for lower level of contributions abolished. Home responsibilities protection introduced.
1980	Basic state pension formally indexed to prices.
1986	SERPS reduced to 20 per cent of earnings over lifetime. Individuals allowed to opt out into defined contribution schemes, including personal pensions.
1995	Equalisation of retirement age for men and women (at 65) from 2020 onwards announced. Further reforms to SERPS formulae reduce its generosity once more.
1999–2000	Commitment made to index income support in line with earnings. Legislation introduced to replace SERPS with state second pension and to introduce stakeholder pensions.

9.2.1   Basic State Pension

By far the major part of state provision for pensioners is the basic state pension. This is a flat-rate benefit payable to those who satisfy certain contributory conditions and have reached the age of 65 (men) or 60 (women). It is set at a relatively low level – about 15 per cent of male average earnings for a single pensioner. Where the wife in a couple does not have a full contributory record, which few do, the couple is entitled to a 'dependant's addition' which brings their combined pension to a level of about 25 per cent of average earnings.[3] The surviving partner can inherit the spouse's pension entitlement, and most widows receive a full pension on this basis.

It is possible for those who do not have an adequate contributory record to qualify for a full pension to receive a proportion of it, subject to this being at least 25 per cent of the full rate.

Contributions

National Insurance contributions (NICs) are paid by individuals and their employers, and are calculated on the basis of a formula dependent on weekly earnings. Contributions are necessary to qualify not only for the basic state pension and SERPS (and for S2P when it is introduced), but also for other benefits such as incapacity benefit and (contributory) jobseeker's allowance. Employer and employee NICs raised £56.4 billion between them in 1999–2000 (HM Treasury, 2000). Expenditure on the basic state pension (£32 billion in 1998–99) takes up easily the largest portion of this income (Department of Social Security, 1999a).

Contributions become payable once earnings exceed a threshold set at £76 a week in 2000–01 (the primary threshold – PT). Rights to benefits are however actually earned once earnings exceed the lower earnings limit (LEL) which in 2000 is £67 a week (about 15 per cent of average male earnings) and which rises annually in line with price inflation. Those with earnings above the PT pay 10 per cent of their earnings between this and the upper earnings limit (UEL). Like the LEL the UEL rises annually in line with inflation and in 2000–01 it is set at £535 a week. The effect of real earnings rises means that the UEL has gradually been eroded relative to average earnings and is now only a little above male average earnings. Employer contributions are set at 12.2 per cent of earnings from the secondary threshold (ST) (£84 per week in 2000–01), which is equivalent to the point at which an individual becomes liable for income tax. Employers of those who are contracted out into a defined benefit occupational pension pay a lower rate of contributions. The most important difference between employer and employee NICs is that there is no upper limit for employer contributions. From April 2001 both employee and employer contributions will start at the same point (£87 per week) as the PT and the ST are equalised. In addition in 2001–02 the UEL will be increased by more than the rate of inflation to £575 per week, and the employers' rate of National Insurance is set to be cut to 11.9 per cent (HM Treasury, 2000).

In principle receipt of the full basic state pension requires NICs to have been made for approximately 90 per cent of a working lifetime. This is currently set at 44 years for men and 39 years for women. However credits are available for time spent out of work as a result of illness, disability or unemployment.

Almost all men have sufficient contributions to qualify for the basic pension. The same is not true for retired women, with only 30 per cent having enough personal contributions to qualify for the full pension. However a further 30 per cent have inherited a full pension from a deceased husband, and a majority of the remainder are currently married to someone who does qualify for the full couple rate (Department of Social Security, 1996). The future for women looks rather different. By 2020 the vast majority will retire with a full pension in their own right. This partly reflects growing rates of economic activity but also the fact that in 1978 the right of married women to opt out of the basic pension, in return for paying a lower rate of NICs, was abolished.[4] Furthermore 1978 also saw the introduction of home responsibilities protection (HRP) which allows time spent out of the labour force looking after children to reduce the number of years of NICs required in order to qualify for a full pension. So in the longer run virtually everyone will receive a full pension in their own right, pretty much irrespective of the number of years of contributions actually made.

Indexation

The basic pension was originally introduced in 1948 and was intended to provide a basic subsistence level of income for those in retirement. The level of the basic pension in both constant prices and relative to average male earnings is shown in Figure 9.1. From its inception until the early 1970s it was increased erratically but by more than enough to keep up with earnings. For a period increases in line with the faster of prices and earnings growth were guaranteed, but since 1981 annual increases have only been in line with price inflation. Hence while in 1982 the basic state pension was worth 19.6 per cent of average male full-time earnings, by 1995 this figure had fallen to 15.2 per cent, and if price indexation continues then the pension is expected to be worth around 6.7 per cent by 2050.[5]

A further effective reduction in the generosity of future basic pension payments was made in legislation passed in 1995, with the introduction of a gradual equalisation of the retirement age in future for men and women. This will be achieved by 2020, when the basic state pension will become payable at 65 for both sexes.[6]

Sources: HM Treasury, 1996; Office for National Statistics website.

Figure 9.1   Value of the Basic State Pension in 1998–99 Prices and as a Percentage of Average Earnings

9.2.2   State Earnings-Related Pension Scheme (SERPS)

While many European countries have a long history of earnings-related benefits, a genuine earnings-related pension scheme was only tacked on to the UK system following the Social Security Act of 1975. This introduced the State Earnings-Related Pension Scheme, referred to by its acronym SERPS.

It did in fact replace something known as the 'graduated pension' which had been introduced as a forerunner to this genuinely earnings-related scheme in the early 1960s. The graduated pension stands as a monument to the cynicism of governments engaged in the provision of pay-as-you-go (PAYG) financed pensions. Introduced to smooth the way from a flat rate to an earnings-related contributory system (under the original Beveridge scheme not only all benefits, but also all contributions, were paid on a flat-rate basis) the rules for the graduated pension contained no provision for indexation. In other words rights to £1 earned in 1970 would be paid as £1 in 1990, with no account taken of the 680 per cent rise in prices in the mean while.

SERPS was introduced by a Labour government – but with cross-party support – in recognition of the increasing divergence in provision between those with and those without an occupational pension. Indeed this motivation is evident in perhaps its main defining characteristic – the facility for individuals to 'contract out' of the scheme if they have an appropriate private sector alternative. Originally this meant access to a defined benefit occupational pension scheme, but from 1988 it has also been possible to contract out into defined contribution schemes, including personal pensions.

By the early 1990s around three-quarters of those eligible to do so had contracted out of SERPS, roughly 50 per cent into occupational schemes and 25 per cent into personal pensions (Dilnot et al., 1994). Opting out into an occupational pension (OP) involves a straightforward reduction in the level of NICs payable. Opting out into a personal pension (PP) involves paying the same level of NICs but having a rebate paid directly into the PP by the government. It is worth noting that the decision to opt out does not preclude an individual from deciding to rejoin at a later date. Overall the degree of opting out is such that second-tier pension provision in the UK is already largely funded and largely privatised.

Originally, on retirement, SERPS was to pay a quarter of average earnings between the LEL and UEL from the *best 20 years* of an individual's lifetime[7] (with each year's earnings increased by the average increase in earnings between that year and state pension age). However the generosity of this scheme was drastically diminished under the provisions of the Social Security Act 1986 which reduced payments to just 20 per cent of average earnings (again between the LEL and the UEL) calculated over the *entire working lifetime*.[8] In addition the Act reduced the amount of SERPS that a surviving spouse could inherit. Under the original scheme a widow would have been able to inherit the whole of her husband's SERPS pension. This was reduced to a half, for those widowed after April 2000, by the 1986 Act.[9]

What stands out from this brief history is how short-lived was the commitment to earnings-related public pensions in the UK. In part this reflects a change in government and in the prevailing ideology. But in large part it reflects the failure of the original architects of the scheme to appreciate fully the future costs of a large new PAYG commitment 50 years hence. Official costings for that distance were not even estimated.[10] The reforms have cut the expected future costs by almost 75 per cent.

From 2002 no further pension rights will be accrued under SERPS as it is replaced by the new state second pension. Whereas SERPS leads to a replacement rate of 20 per cent between the LEL and the UEL, the new S2P is designed to provide a replacement rate of 40 per cent on earnings up to around 40 per cent of the UEL, falling to 10 per cent on earnings above that, with a small band back at 20 per cent just below the UEL. In fact any earnings within the first tranche of earnings will be treated as though they are at the top of that first tranche. This very complex formula is designed to do two things:

1. to substantially retarget the second pension on low earners; and
2. to ensure that, in the short term at least, nobody loses out.

In the longer run the government has announced its intention to make the S2P an entirely flat-rate benefit, with no additional accrual above the 40 per cent replacement band.[11]

More than 50 per cent of individuals over pension age receive some income from SERPS. However the average payment is under £13 per pensioner, mainly because SERPS was only introduced in 1978 and therefore many pensioners, especially older ones, have accrued extremely small entitlements. There is also a difference in the amounts received by men and women. For example 91 per cent of 65- to 69-year-old men receive some SERPS payments, with the average receipt being £15 a week.[12] In comparison only 39 per cent of women in the same age-group receive SERPS, with the average entitlement being just over £8 a week. This result is even more extreme when it is considered that nearly 20 per cent of those women receive SERPS because they have inherited their husband's entitlement.[13]

The state pension that an individual receives will therefore depend first on whether or not sufficient contributions have been made to receive the basic state pension and second on whether the individual made contributions to SERPS. Taking the example of a single man retiring at the age of 65 in 1998 and assuming he had earned the median (in that year for both his age and gender) full-time wage since 1978 and had not chosen to opt out of SERPS, he would expect to receive the basic state pension of £62 a week and SERPS payments of £50 a week. This income is equivalent to 26 per cent of contemporary average male full-time earnings. Examples of how this entitlement would change with differing levels of earnings are shown in Table 9.3.

The first row shows the amount of basic state pension each earner would receive. This does not vary by earnings level but is higher for the couple than for the single person as a result of the dependant's addition payable in respect of spouses who do not have a basic pension in their own right. The next row shows the SERPS pension which rises with lifetime earnings but is the same for the married man and the single man. The next row just adds these two state pension payments together.

Someone who earned half median earnings for a man of that age would only qualify for a SERPS entitlement of under £20 a week. This is because a large proportion of his earnings fall below the LEL, and the LEL in the last year of his employment is subtracted from each year's earnings. Someone whose earnings were continuously at the level of the UEL or above would qualify for a SERPS pension of about £115 per week. The reason why the individual on median earnings in the table has a SERPS entitlement of less

Table 9.3   How the UK State Pension Varies with Lifetime Earnings for an Individual Retiring in 1998 (1997 prices)

	Single person			Person with non-working spouse		
	Annual earnings relative to median					
	½	1	2	½	1	2
Basic weekly pension (£ p.w.)	62.45	62.45	62.45	99.80	99.80	99.80
SERPS weekly pension (£ p.w.)	17.22	49.95	104.88	17.22	49.95	104.88
Gross total weekly pension (£ p.w.)	79.67	112.40	167.33	117.02	149.75	204.68
Gross pension (% of contemporary gross male average earnings)	18.7	26.4	39.4	27.5	35.2	48.2
Gross replacement rate (%)	62.5	44.1	32.8	91.8	58.7	40.1
Net total state pension (£ p.w.)	79.67	110.00	153.94	117.02	149.06	192.24
Net pension (% of contemporary net male average earnings)	24.9	34.4	48.1	36.6	46.6	60.0
Net replacement rate (%)	71.9	50.0	34.7	103.2	65.7	42.4

Notes:
References to average earnings refer to the average full-time earnings amongst men of the same age for each year of the individual's working life. We are assuming that this individual has made enough contributions to qualify for the full basic state pension. Replacement rate is income relevant to the individual's income at age 55 uprated by inflation.

Source: Authors' calculations using data from the New Earnings Survey.

than this amount despite the fact that the UEL is set at around male average full-time earnings is that median earnings for a male in the later years of his working life are slightly less than half the UEL, and hence someone earning twice this amount does not quite accrue a maximum SERPS entitlement.

The next set of information in the table is about the pension as a proportion of gross earnings – first as a proportion of average male earnings and then as a replacement rate for the particular individual. The replacement rate is calculated with reference to the cohort-specific median earnings of someone reaching 65 in 1998, *at the age of 55.* That is, we do not use median earnings among those still in work at age 64. Instead we compare the final pension with median earnings of the cohort when they were aged 55. This avoids the severe problems of selection associated with comparing the pension with the earnings of the minority of individuals who do continue working until 64. Earnings at age 55 are uprated by price inflation to the year of retirement for the comparison to be made. It is immediately clear that the replacement rate for the person on median earnings is higher than the ratio of benefits to overall average earnings. The replacement rate for the person on half median earnings is very high indeed, exceeding 100 per cent when calculated on a net rather than a gross basis for the couple. As one would expect, replacement rates are substantially higher for the couple than for the single person because we have assumed in this case that the wife is not earning.

Reforms made in various Social Security Acts have substantially reduced the pension that individuals can expect to receive in the future. Table 9.4

Table 9.4   How the Reforms to SERPS Affect Individuals on Different Income Levels Retiring in 2045 (1997 prices)

	Earnings relative to median					
	½		1		2	
	Years without contributions					
	0	5	0	5	0	5
Basic state pension (£)	62.45	62.45	62.45	62.45	62.45	62.45
Original SERPS regime (£)	95.26	95.26	160.38	160.38	181.14	181.14
Post-1995 SERPS regime (£)	55.43	49.91	96.26	87.62	106.21	97.58
State second pension regime* (£)	102.95	91.51	102.95	91.51	102.95	91.51
Total state pension (% of median earnings):						
BSP + original SERPS	17.9	17.9	25.4	25.4	27.8	27.8
BSP + post-1995 SERPS	13.4	12.8	18.0	17.1	19.2	18.2
BSP + S2P	18.8	17.5	18.8	17.5	18.8	17.5

Note: *State second pension refers to final flat-rate scheme which is planned to be in place from 2007.

Source: Authors' calculations using data from the Family Expenditure Survey.

shows a comparison of the pay-outs under the original SERPS formula and under the reformed one for an individual who starts work at the age of 20 in 2000 and retires at 65 in 2045. The table also shows the amount of S2P that an individual would get, assuming that the flat rate of S2P, due to be introduced around 2007, were already in place.[14] We have assumed price indexation of the basic state pension, the LEL and the UEL, and all figures are gross of taxation and in 1997 prices. Real earnings growth of 1½ per cent a year has also been assumed. Median earnings are calculated for a full-time male of that age. A comparison is also given for individuals who have a five-year gap in their contribution record. The timing of the five-year gap in contributions with respect to the individual's age will not affect SERPS entitlements significantly, although for the purposes of this analysis we have assumed that the five years are those immediately before retirement.[15] We have assumed that this five-year gap will not reduce the individual's entitlement to the basic state pension, which means that the individual must have credits for contributions made between the ages of 16 and 20.[16]

As Table 9.4 shows, the basic pension is left unchanged by both varying the earnings of the individual and the presence of a five-year gap without contributions. However the SERPS entitlement increases with earnings, especially with the increase from half median to median earnings, since the majority of this additional income falls between the LEL and the UEL and hence accrues additional entitlements. A five-year break in contributions record has no effect under the original formula, but under the post-1995 regime entitlement is reduced, since an individual's earnings are averaged over the entire 49-year (from ages 16 to 65) working life instead of just the best 20 years. Note that the new S2P regime will also penalise those who do not have a full contribution history although, unlike with SERPS, credits will be paid for periods spent caring for a child aged under 5 or for a disabled dependant. This is not as generous as the credits for the basic state pension which are available for those looking after a child of any age and also for periods spent unemployed.

Although these future payments appear large, with someone who continuously earns median male earnings receiving over £160 a week, it should be considered how they relate to the earnings of the rest of the population. As the table shows, this income will be under one-fifth of median male full-time earnings (which by 2045 with earnings growth of 1½ per cent will be around £880 a week). This is for the first year of their retirement, with the pension declining relative to earnings in each subsequent year.[17] Furthermore the flat-rate nature of S2P means that those earning twice median earnings will receive exactly the same state pension as someone on half median earnings.

9.2.3   Means-tested Benefits Received by Pensioners

Means-tested benefits have been and remain an important component of pensioners' incomes. They make up 12 per cent of total pensioner income in the UK at a cost to the exchequer of about 1 per cent of GDP. Around 40 per cent of people over pension age receive some income from the state in these forms.

Income support (IS) (or minimum income guarantee (MIG), as it has been rechristened by the Labour government) is the minimum means-tested benefit and in 2000 is designed to make up the incomes of single pensioners to a minimum of £78.45 a week.[18] This is 16 per cent higher than the basic state pension, and since higher maximum levels of IS exist for older pensioners, the difference is greater for retired people over the age of 74. The government has the stated aim of increasing the level of the MIG in line with earnings (Department of Social Security, 1998).

Some 15 per cent of pensioners receive some IS, three out of four of these being single women and nearly half being aged over 80 (Department of Social Security, 1996). This reflects the fact that the very poorest pensioners are overwhelmingly old single women, mostly widows.

Pensioners may also be able to qualify for another benefit to assist with their rent costs – housing benefit (HB). Those who qualify for HB receive a payment based on their actual rent, and those on IS will receive enough HB to cover the whole of their rent. A little over a fifth of all people over the pension age are in receipt of at least some HB. This figure corresponds to about two-thirds of pensioners living in rented accommodation.[19]

The third means-tested benefit for which UK citizens over the age of retirement may be eligible is council tax benefit (CTB). This is an income-related benefit designed solely to provide assistance in paying the domestic local tax to those with low means. As with HB, all those who receive some IS will be eligible for a full CTB entitlement. Thirty per cent of people over the age of retirement receive at least some CTB, with 34 per cent of those being aged over 80.[20]

The existence of these benefits raises the issue of what the actual minimum income is that a single person or a couple can have in retirement, and how this compares with the income of the working population. The actual minimum is the level of IS, but in this case housing costs will be zero because all rent will be paid. Average rents in the social sector are around £40 a week. In addition an average of about £8 a week will be received in CTB. So the actual minimum income is £78.45 for a single person or £121.95 for a couple, plus rent and council tax. In making comparisons with the working-age population one would want to add these costs on since most people of working age have to pay them. So the minimum income is about £130 for a single pensioner and

£170 for a couple. Since male average earnings are £400 a week or about £300 a week after tax and National Insurance, the *minimum* income for pensioners looks much more healthy, at around 40 per cent of net average earnings for a single pensioner or 56 per cent for a couple.

Means-tested benefits, in particular the MIG, remain an important aspect of the government's pension policy. But, particularly following the 1998 announcement that the level of the MIG will, as resources allow, rise in line with earnings as the basic pension rises with prices, increasing concerns have been expressed over the possible saving incentive problems that will be created. In particular there is concern that it will not be worth while for some lower earners to save in stakeholder pensions, designed specifically to target those on moderate incomes (see Section 9.3.1). Already there is concern on equity grounds that savers are not being rewarded relative to those who have been 'spendthrift' in their working life. While in future S2P will ensure that those with a full working life will at least start their retirement on a level of income above the means-tested floor, this is being phased in over 40 years. As a result the government is currently (in 2000) working on policy to introduce a 'pensioner credit' which would be intended to create some positive return to saving for those close to MIG levels by, perhaps, adding a further means-tested element of benefit tapered away at well below 100 per cent.

9.2.4 Other State Assistance

The UK provides other non-financial benefits to pensioners. Government spending in 1999–2000 on the National Health Service (NHS) was 5.5 per cent of GDP, and although medical care is provided free at the point of use to all UK residents, pensioners tend to receive more (relative to their population proportion) of the benefits from this expenditure.[21] Pensioners, unlike the majority of those of working age, automatically receive free prescriptions and dental treatment. The other main preferential treatment that retired individuals receive in the UK is that they have higher personal income tax allowances – that is, they will pay income tax on a smaller proportion of their income (if any at all).

Local councils in the UK also provide some services to pensioners, although the amount of means testing and the total subsidy vary across the country since many of these services are at each local council's discretion, and hence user charges are often levied. Local councils have to provide a place in a residential home to needy elderly people. This can be means-tested, and an issue that has recently raised a great deal of controversy is that a council can insist on the sale of an individual's assets, including their home, to help pay towards the total cost. Other services provided to the elderly can include items such as weekly visits from a carer to their home and the delivery of hot meals. Local councils also tend to provide pensioners with reduced fares on public transport.

9.3   PRIVATE PENSIONS

Supplementary occupational pensions have been an important part of the UK pension scene for some time. Originating in the public sector, they grew in coverage during the 1950s and 1960s, but since then coverage has hovered around the 50 per cent mark with no sign of further expansion. Indeed the most recent evidence suggests that it is dipping below 50 per cent. Male employees are still more likely to have an occupational pension than women, but the gap between them is closing.

Table 9.5 shows the percentages of individuals in 1995–96 who reached the state pension age in the previous five years who had income from occupational pensions. Men are much more likely to have OP income than are women, especially married women. Overall half of all individuals who reached retirement age in the previous five years have income from an occupational pension scheme. This figure though understates the proportion who have access to such income in their family unit since many married women who have no such income of their own have husbands who do have OP income. In fact two-thirds of benefit units receive income from an OP.

Private sources of income are already an important proportion of total pensioner income in the UK and are set to grow considerably in the future. Pensioners receive income from a variety of private sources: 20 per cent of total pensioner income comes from private pension arrangements, 4 per cent from earnings and 6 per cent from investment income. However this income

Table 9.5   Percentage of People who Reached State Retirement Age in the Previous Five Years with Income from an Occupational Pension, by Gender and Type, 1995 (%)

	Men	Women	Total
Single[a]	54.6	56.2	55.2
Divorced or widowed[b]	56.4	44.8	49.1
Married or cohabiting	69.5	25.8	48.0
Total	66.3	32.0	48.7

Notes:
[a]Single is classified as individuals who have never been married.
[b]Divorced or widowed includes individuals who are separated.

Sources: 1995–96 Family Resources Survey; authors' calculations.

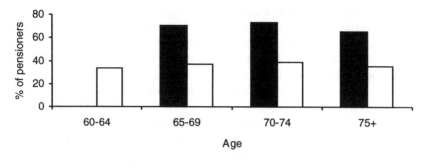

Source: 1995–96 Family Resources Survey.

Figure 9.2   Percentage of Those Over Retirement Age with Income from
Private Pension Arrangements, by Age and Gender, 1995

is far from being evenly distributed, with around a third of pensioner benefit
units receiving less than £5 a week from private sources[22] and hence likely to
be reliant on the income that they receive from the state (these tend to be
single women and older pensioners).

Figure 9.2 shows the proportion of all those over pension age who receive
income from private pension arrangements. Men are much more likely to
have income from this source than women, although there is very little
difference between the cohorts. Moreover, although older pensioners are just
as likely to have some income from an occupational pension scheme, this
income will typically be smaller, due not only to higher earnings for younger
cohorts but also to better indexation of deferred benefits.

The treatment of deferred benefits is a vital element in the typically
defined benefit OP scheme which operates in the UK. Based on years of
service and some measure of final salary, a typical scheme might offer one-
sixtieth of final salary for each year of service. Most schemes pay part of the
pension as a lump sum on retirement (and hence a lower annual pension
thereafter), since there are tax advantages to doing so. It is also common for
occupational pension schemes to deduct the value of the basic state pension
from the earnings on which the pension is assessed. That is, someone earning
£300 a week with x years of service will receive x-sixtieths not of £300 but of
£300 − £67.50, the latter being the value of the basic state pension.

People leaving employment before the normal retirement age are dependent on the scheme's indexation rules for the level of benefit they eventually
receive. A series of legislative changes between 1975 and 1995 have
guaranteed a degree of inflation protection for the benefits of early leavers.

Deferred pensions are now indexed in line with inflation up to 5 per cent a year. Nevertheless the redistribution inherent within the schemes remains strong. Even without price inflation, real earnings growth means that individuals with longer job durations can do much better than early leavers (Disney and Whitehouse, 1996).

Since 1988 membership of an employer's scheme has been voluntary. Employees have a choice between joining their employer's scheme, joining SERPS or joining the other major component of the UK private sector, a personal pension. But if they opt out of the occupational scheme they nearly always lose the value of the employer's contribution to the scheme. It was the several hundred thousand individuals who opted out of an OP and into a PP and thereby lost their employer's contributions who were the ones who suffered from personal pension 'mis-selling' in the first few years after the introduction of PPs. The cost of compensating these individuals is expected to attain the extraordinary figure of £12 billion.

Nevertheless the option to opt out of SERPS into a PP revolutionised private pension provision in the UK. Operating on a defined contribution basis, PPs are particularly widespread amongst younger generations who do relatively badly under SERPS. They will have little impact on pensioner incomes until 2020 or so, but thereafter are likely to form an increasing proportion of people's incomes. In broad terms just under half the employed population are members of OP schemes and up to a fifth have (currently active) PPs.

9.3.1   Stakeholder Pensions

The mis-selling scandal was not the end of the road for the problems of personal pensions. They have also been criticised for having high charges and, in particular, being a bad deal for individuals who do not maintain contributions for the whole length of the contract. Largely as a result of these concerns a new form of private pension – the stakeholder pension – is to be introduced from April 2001. A range of legal structures will be permitted, but the essential feature of these pensions is that they will, like personal pensions, be defined contribution schemes but with a government-set level and structure of charges. In particular charges will have to be levied *only* as a percentage of fund value and cannot exceed 1 per cent of fund value per annum. This is a charging level significantly below the average charge for personal pensions and, perhaps more importantly, a structure of charging that ensures no penalties for those who, for whatever reason, stop or vary their contributions. In addition employers with more than five employees will have to 'make available' a nominated scheme for their employees. Schemes will also have to accept any contribution of £20 or more.

How well this regime will operate in practice has yet to be seen. Despite the very tight charging criteria, it is clear that a number of companies will offer stakeholder pensions. The biggest question that remains concerns the extent to which they will find it profitable to market them to those who do not already have access to a private pension – largely low-income individuals. Evidence shows that those in the government's target group for stakeholder pensions (those earning between £9 000 and £18 500) either already have a private pension or, if they do not, tend to have very low levels of savings and experience fluctuations in earnings and periods of unemployment (Disney, Emmerson and Tanner, 1999).

9.3.2 Taxation

One aspect of government attitude towards the private sector that has been important is the tax treatment of private pensions. These pensions have been taxed under an approximate expenditure tax regime – that is, tax is only levied at one point, in this case once the pension is in payment. So contributions are tax-relieved (at the marginal rate of the contributor), income and capital gains accrued in the fund are tax-relieved and tax is only paid when the pension is in payment. In addition part of the pension (1.5 times final salary in the case of defined benefit schemes; a quarter of the accrued fund in defined contribution schemes) can be taken as a tax-free lump sum. Along with housing this has made pensions among the most tax-privileged forms of saving in the UK. Most saving is done within this tax-privileged sector.

What is the cost of these tax privileges? A simple-minded approach would be to add up the tax forgone on contributions, the accruing fund and the lump sum. A better basis for comparison would look at the opportunity cost in terms of the tax relief accruing to the next-best savings vehicle. It is certainly arguable that a pure expenditure tax is the appropriate comparator, in which case the cost is the cost of allowing a tax-free lump sum. There are no recent official estimates of this, but a cost in the order of £2 billion a year is probably not far off the mark. If in contrast one chooses as a comparator a comprehensive income tax base in which tax is effectively paid twice, the Inland Revenue estimates the cost at £11.4 billion.[23]

Given alternative methods of saving, especially for the financially sophisticated, it is hard to imagine that the UK private pension sector would survive if its tax-privileged status were completely removed. In fact the tax treatment of private pensions has become less generous in recent years. Prior to the July 1997 Budget savings held in private pensions received an even more favourable tax treatment since any dividend income received a tax credit of 20 per cent.[24] This meant that every £1 of dividend income was worth £1.25 to a pension fund. Even after the July 1997 Budget the continued presence of the tax-free lump sum means that private pension saving remains more tax-privileged than savings held in an Individual Savings Account (ISA). This is despite the latter paying a dividend tax credit of 10 per cent until 2004 (Emmerson and Tanner, 2000; Crook and Johnson, 2000) and assumes that the individual is making the contribution to the private pension or the ISA. Employer contributions to private pensions are even more tax-favoured since no National Insurance is levied either when the contribution is made or when the pension is drawn (Emmerson and Tanner, 2000).

9.4   SUSTAINABILITY

As shown by Table 9.1, in 1998–99 state spending on pensions and other benefits received by those over the age of retirement in the UK was 5.2 per cent of GDP. Although the UK population over the age of retirement as a proportion of those aged over 16 is set to increase until around 2040, this increase is expected to be smaller than that in many other OECD countries. In 1999–2000 about 16 per cent of the population are aged over 65, and this figure is expected to climb until around 2030 when it should stabilise at around 23–25 per cent.[25] Any potential funding problems that this increase in the dependency ratio may cause have been solved by legislation passed since 1980 which has substantially reduced the future generosity of state pay-outs.

By far the most important change has been in the indexation rules governing the basic state pension. Indexation only in line with prices since 1980 has reduced spending in 1999–2000 by some £12 billion relative to the level that it would have been had it maintained a link with earnings. While the real cost is set to increase as demographic change occurs, the cost as a proportion of GDP is *not* set to increase. The reason is straightforward enough. With national income rising at, say, 2 per cent a year in real terms, a constant pensioner population would result in a continually decreasing burden of pension financing. In fact the increase in national income will be enough to ensure that the financing burden does not increase. There have though been other very important ways in which future unfunded liabilities have been reduced:

- *The equalisation of the state retirement age.* By 2020 women will not be entitled to a state pension until they have reached 65, the age at which it is payable to men.
- *Alterations to the SERPS formula.* Those individuals accruing SERPS entitlements from April 2000 will receive a pension of 20 per cent of their average earnings calculated over their entire working life. The formula initially used was more generous, offering a quarter of earnings in the best

20 years of earnings. This will lead to a reduction of at least 20 per cent, and in many cases much more, for all those entitled to SERPS.[26] On the other hand projected spending on the new, more redistributive state second pension is projected to be slightly higher than had the new version of SERPS been retained.

- *Reductions in a surviving spouse's SERPS entitlement.* Originally a surviving spouse could inherit all of his or her partner's SERPS pension. This has been changed so that only half can be inherited after October 2002.[27]
- *Individuals opting out of SERPS entitlements.* Higher proportions of younger cohorts have contracted out of SERPS and into alternative occupational or personal pension plans which has reduced future SERPS expenditure. However it should be noted that more has been spent on providing incentives to opt out than will eventually be saved in the future (Budd and Campbell, 1998).

The future costs of state pension payments in the UK are shown in Table 9.6 both in real terms and as a percentage of GDP. Also included are the future dependency ratios and National Insurance contribution rates required to finance this spending. This shows that price indexation of the basic state pension and the other changes discussed will result in future NICs actually being lower than in 2000.

The fact that NIC rates can be held relatively close to 2000 levels implies that future reforms to the state pension scheme are not required on grounds of sustainability. Nevertheless the current system will undoubtedly leave many future pensioners on incomes unacceptably low in relation to the earnings of those in work. However S2P will increase pensions for lower earners, and of course there is an increase in private pension benefits.

Table 9.7 shows how much higher these future costs would have been if the various reforms to SERPS and the basic state pension had not been made. It highlights how expensive the future costs of the original SERPS formula actually were and the importance of price-indexing the basic pension. The table gives the cost of each reform individually. For example indexing the basic state pension in line with earnings from 1999–2000 onwards would cost an additional £58 billion a year in 2050. Restoring the pension back to the 1980 level and indexing with earnings would cost even more. In fact the figures for previous regimes are likely to understate the true costs due to continuous underestimates of longevity (Disney, 1998). It should however be remembered that these reforms have implications for other costs and revenues. For example if state pensions become more generous then fewer pensioners will be able to claim welfare benefits. In addition to this effect is the increase in revenue from NICs that would arise from the earnings indexation of the lower and upper earnings limits, which would follow uprating the basic pension in line with earnings.

The replacement of SERPS with S2P represents the first increase in state pension provision since the introduction of SERPS, with spending in 2030 forecast to be £17.8 billion – some £5.4 billion higher than it would have been under the existing SERPS regime. This is still substantially less than the £47.3 billion implied by the original SERPS scheme.

Table 9.6   Future Costs of Benefits to Pensioners: April 2000 Legislation

	Financial year starting:					
	2000	2010	2020	2030	2040	2050
Ratio of working age to pension age[a]	3.46	3.23	2.76	2.22	2.08	2.10
Ratio without equal retirement ages	3.46	3.23	3.38	2.71	2.42	2.50
Basic state pension[b] (£ billion)	34.4	38.0	41.3	49.4	52.8	51.2
SERPS / S2P[c] (£ billion)	4.9	9.5	12.8	17.8	22.5	30.2
Total state pension cost (£ billion)	39.3	47.5	54.1	67.2	75.3	81.4
Cost[d] (% of GDP)	5.4	5.5	5.4	5.6	5.3	4.9
Required NIC rate[e] (%)	20.2	19.0	18.2	19.2	18.5	17.5

Notes:
All prices are in 1999–2000 levels.
[a]Ratio of the population aged 15 and over and below the state retirement age to the population of at least state retirement age. State retirement age for women is set to increase from 60 by six months each year from 2010 until equalisation at 65 is achieved in 2020.
[b]Includes widows' benefits.
[c]Rebates for S2P are assumed to allow for a top-up for those on low earnings who have opted out of the state scheme. If this is not the case then expenditure on S2P will be slightly lower – for example by £2.7 billion in 2050; see Government Actuary's Department (2000) for more details.
[d]Assuming GDP growth of 2 per cent per year.
[e]Contribution rates assume 1½ per cent real earnings growth per year and exclude the 1.95 per cent rate payable to the National Health Service in 1999–2000. They are based on the contribution regime set out in the March 1999 Budget.

Sources: Government Actuary's Department (1999 and 2000); authors' calculations.

Table 9.7   Future Costs of State Pensions, without Various Reforms
(£ billion, 1999–2000 prices)

	Financial year starting:					
	2000	2010	2020	2030	2040	2050
Basic state pension						
Basic pension cost	34.4	38.0	41.3	49.4	52.8	51.2
Earnings indexation from 1999–2000 onwards	34.9	44.7	56.3	78.3	96.9	108.8
Without equalisation of retirement ages	34.4	38.0	45.9	54.1	55.6	53.7
Earnings indexation of benefits from 1980 onwards	46.8	61.2	74.4	102.8	126.8	139.8
Second-tier pension						
S2P after the 1999 Act	4.9	9.5	12.8	17.8	22.5	30.2
SERPS after the 1995 Act	4.9	8.9	10.9	12.4	12.3	13.3
SERPS with original formula, retirement ages and inheritance rights	4.9	13.8	28.8	47.3	n.a.	n.a.

Note: Earnings growth of 1½ per cent has been assumed.

Sources: Government Actuary's Department, 1999 and 2000; Johnson, Disney and Stears, 1996; authors' calculations.

9.5   ACTIVITY RATES

Sustainability depends not only on pension levels and population growth but also on economic activity rates of those under state pension age. Of particular importance are activity rates among those just under pension age, and these rates dropped dramatically between 1970 and 1997. While it is not possible in the UK to claim a state pension before state pension age, many men and women are economically inactive before they reach this age.

Table 9.8 shows the proportion of men and women in work in the age ranges 55–59, 60–64 and 65–69. Only half of men in the 60–64 age range are in work, despite the official pension age of 65.

Table 9.8   Percentage of Economically Active Men and Women, by Age-group, 1995 (%)

	Age-group		
	55–59	60–64	65–69
Men	77	51	17
Women	58	22	–

Source: Published labour force statistics.

Table 9.9   Percentage of Men Receiving State Benefits or Pensions, by Age-group (%)

Benefit	Age-group		
	55–59	60–64	65–69
None	69.1	56.7	1.4
Basic pension	0.0	0.0	82.0
Sickness benefits	20.1	28.9	30.0
Income support	10.5	13.9	8.2
Housing benefit / council tax benefit	16.5	20.9	21.1
Other state benefits	1.7	2.6	0.3

Note: Recipients may receive more than one benefit.

Sources: 1995–96 Family Resources Survey; authors' calculations.

As previously mentioned it is not possible to claim the basic state pension or any SERPS entitlements before the retirement age is reached. However there is evidence to suggest that invalidity benefit,[28] a contributory state benefit, was being used as an early retirement route by individuals who, either by choice or through inability to find suitable work, retired early (Blundell and Johnson, 1999; Disney and Webb, 1991). Table 9.9 shows the proportion of men who are claiming state welfare benefits or a state pension, split between the three age-groups (the proportions sum to over one since an individual can receive income from more than one source).

Receipt of the basic state pension is only 82 per cent amongst 65- to 69-year-old men because those who were receiving invalidity benefit before the state retirement age were allowed to continue to receive it instead of a basic state pension. Many did so since until its replacement by incapacity benefit it was a non-taxable benefit.

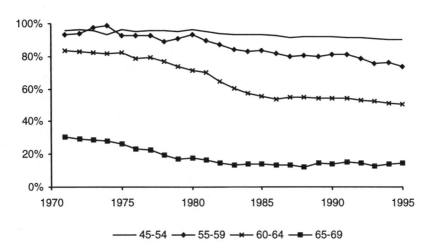

Source: Successive Family Expenditure Surveys.

Figure 9.3 Male Activity Rates

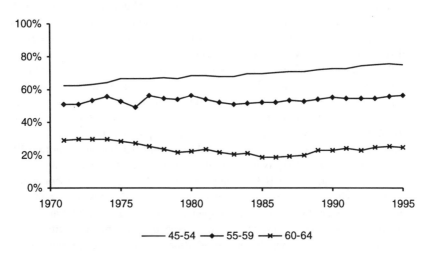

Source: Successive Family Expenditure Surveys.

Figure 9.4 Female Activity Rates

The size of the change in activity rates over time is illustrated by Figures 9.3 and 9.4 which show male and female activity rates over the period 1971–95. For men, especially those in the 60–64 age-group, the drop has been dramatic indeed.

9.6   INCOME DISTRIBUTIONS

The income data presented in this section come from the 1995–96 Family Resources Survey, which is an annual survey of around 27 000 households containing approximately 47 000 individuals. Unless otherwise stated all prices in this section have been uprated to 1997–98 levels. Since this is a household survey it excludes those pensioners residing in nursing accommodation. The data contain detailed information on individual characteristics and incomes from all main sources, and form the basis for the British government's official income distribution series. Collected specifically for the analysis of income distributions, and being nearly four times as big, the dataset has effectively superseded the Family Expenditure Survey as a source of information on the income distribution.

For our purposes here we have included for analysis all those over the state pension age or aged over 60 and not defined as being employed or self-employed. For couples the classification is based on the status of the husband. This has the effect of including some working wives, those over 65 who are working and those aged 60–64 who claim to be unemployed and seeking work. It excludes the retired under the age of 60. Although this sample is to some extent arbitrary it has the advantage of including all those who are usually considered to be pensioners as a result of their age and excludes the self-selected sample who retire very early.

Total income is defined as income net of all direct taxation (including local taxes), but where income is broken into components gross amounts are used because of the difficulty of assigning taxes to particular income sources. Where we need to equivalise in order to compare incomes of families of different sizes we do so using a very simple equivalence scale of 1 for a single person plus 0.7 for any additional adult and 0.5 for any children. We also use an alternative equivalence scale of 1 for a single person plus 0.5 for any additional adult and 0.3 for any children. A measure of income that effectively ignores housing and housing costs is used. This means that no imputed rent is credited to owner-occupiers. It should be noted that around 62 per cent of pensioners in the UK are owner-occupiers compared with 67 per cent of the rest of the population. In addition to this, higher proportions of owner-occupying pensioners compared with other owner-occupiers will have finished paying their mortgages. There is also variation between pensioners, with only 53 per cent of single pensioners compared with 76 per cent of pensioner couples being owner-occupiers.

The average (mean) amounts of net pensioner weekly income are shown in Table 9.10 for couples and both single men and single women, broken down by age-group. Younger pensioners tend to be richer. This is more a cohort

Table 9.10   Average UK Pensioner Income, by Marital Status and Age-group
(incomes in £ p.w., 1995–96 prices)

	Age-group				
	60–64	65–69	70–74	75+	60+
Couples					
Weekly income	242	269	233	219	242
Ratio 1	(0.80)	(0.89)	(0.77)	(0.72)	(0.80)
Ratio 2	(0.79)	(0.88)	(0.76)	(0.71)	(0.78)
Single men					
Weekly income	132	159	140	135	141
Ratio 1	(0.74)	(0.89)	(0.78)	(0.76)	(0.79)
Ratio 2	(0.65)	(0.78)	(0.68)	(0.66)	(0.69)
Single women					
Weekly income	147	134	120	116	123
Ratio 1	(0.83)	(0.75)	(0.68)	(0.65)	(0.69)
Ratio 2	(0.72)	(0.65)	(0.59)	(0.57)	(0.60)

Note: Numbers in parentheses give income as a proportion of average equivalised earnings (rebased to the relevant group) for those not retired, ratio 1 being computed with the $(1, 0.7, 0.5)$ equivalence scale and ratio 2 with the $(1, 0.5, 0.3)$ equivalence scale.

Sources: 1995–96 Family Resources Survey; authors' calculations.

effect than an age effect as younger generations earned more and had greater access to better occupational pension schemes. These results are even stronger once the effects of differential mortality are considered, since (given gender) poorer pensioners tend to die younger (Johnson and Stears, 1998). Single women are on average poorer than men (except for the 60–64 age-group, where women may be entitled to a basic state pension, unlike men). The three main reasons for the lower incomes of women are as follows:

1. Few women have an occupational pension, and many of those who do have one have inherited it at a reduced rate (usually 50 per cent) from a deceased husband.
2. A smaller proportion of women still work at any age, and they tend to receive a lower wage if they do work.
3. Women are less likely to have income from SERPS.

The figures in parentheses in the table show the ratio of the average equivalent income for each group to the average equivalent income for the rest of the population. Ratio 1 uses the $(1, 0.7, 0.5)$ equivalence scale, which gives an average income for the rest of the population of £178 per week.

While this figure appears low it should be remembered that it is a net equivalent figure and using the scale we have used it is equivalent to a couple with two children having well over £400 per week after tax. What is remarkable is that, especially for younger couples, the average incomes of pensioners are remarkably close to those of non-pensioners, being on average something like 80 per cent of those of the rest of the population. Ratio 2 uses the (1, 0.5, 0.3) equivalence scale, which hardly changes the results at all for pensioner couples but does make single pensioners look worse off.

An idea of the distribution of income between different non-pensioner groups is given by Table 9.11. This gives an indication of how the equivalence scale will influence the positioning of pensioners relative to the rest of the population. Single and childless men and women tend to have the lowest incomes, with the 10th percentiles in all these groups having incomes lower than the minimum income received by pensioners from the state. Younger individuals in these categories tend to have even lower incomes. In contrast couples, both with and without children, tend to have higher incomes, with the 10th percentile having higher income than the basic state pension received by a pensioner couple in which both individuals have a full basic state pension entitlement.

Table 9.11   Income Distributions of Different Population Groups (incomes in £ p.w.)

	Mean	Median	90th percentile	10th percentile	90/10 ratio
Couples, no children, head aged <40	431	396	668	198	3.37
Couples, no children, head aged ≥40	375	322	640	144	4.44
Couples with children	410	347	675	179	3.77
Single parents	201	172	308	115	2.66
Single men aged <40	151	132	283	37	7.69
Single men aged ≥40	195	159	355	54	6.58
Single women aged <40	139	124	261	34	7.55
Single women aged ≥40	174	144	303	65	4.65

Note: This table looks solely at the group of individuals whom we have defined as being not retired. This is everyone whose head of household is aged under 60, or is aged under 65 and is in work.

Sources: 1995–96 Family Resources Survey; authors' calculations.

Table 9.12 Distribution of Pensioner Income, by Marital Status and Age-group (incomes in £ p.w.)

	Age-group				
	60–64	65–69	70–74	75+	60+
Couples					
Median	204	214	188	173	194
90th percentile	413	464	375	347	400
10th percentile	114	129	126	117	121
90/10 ratio	3.64	3.59	2.99	3.00	3.31
Single men					
Median	109	122	114	113	114
90th percentile	197	278	211	208	222
10th percentile	57	81	80	72	72
90/10 ratio	3.45	3.45	2.65	2.91	3.10
Single women					
Median	120	111	108	106	109
90th percentile	236	202	186	182	191
10th percentile	74	69	69	65	68
90/10 ratio	3.18	2.91	2.69	2.79	2.79

Sources: 1995–96 Family Resources Survey; authors' calculations.

Factors such as the indexing of the basic state pension to the price level and the increasing amount of income that is received from private pension arrangements have led to a situation where inequality amongst pensioners is rising.[29] An idea of the distribution of pensioner incomes, again net of taxation, is given by Table 9.12. This again shows that for the over-65s older pensioners tend to be poorer and that this result is true not only for those on median incomes but also for those at either end of the income distribution.

The 10th, 50th and 90th percentiles for the incomes of the rest of the population are £63, £149 and £314 respectively. The ratio of the 90th to the 10th percentiles is 5.0, giving some indication that income inequality is rather less amongst pensioners than it is for the rest of the population as a whole. It is noteworthy that the biggest 90/10 differential for each gender/marital status pensioner group is for the youngest age-group. This indicates a dichotomy among the early retired between those retiring with substantial occupational pensions and those leaving work to find themselves dependent on sickness benefits or means-tested income support. It appears to be a dichotomy between the voluntary and involuntary early retired.

Table 9.13   Composition of Pensioner Income, by Marital Status and Age-group (%)

	Age-group				
	60–64	65–69	70–74	75+	60+
Couples					
State pension	4.6	40.6	55.4	57.8	42.2
Means-tested benefits	12.8	3.5	3.3	5.4	5.7
Other benefits	28.8	12.6	5.4	5.7	12.0
Private pension	34.1	26.8	25.0	22.3	26.5
Investment income	7.0	7.2	6.6	6.7	6.9
Earnings	12.7	9.4	4.3	2.1	6.8
Single men					
State pension	0.3	43.4	57.0	56.2	45.7
Means-tested benefits	36.2	10.8	11.5	12.7	15.3
Other benefits	29.9	12.3	4.4	5.2	10.1
Private pension	25.6	21.8	18.9	18.0	20.1
Investment income	6.8	6.1	6.0	6.6	6.4
Earnings	1.1	5.5	2.1	1.2	2.4
Single women					
State pension	42.8	55.8	57.6	58.8	56.2
Means-tested benefits	17.0	14.6	15.6	17.7	16.7
Other benefits	11.5	4.6	4.5	5.6	5.9
Private pension	16.3	16.9	15.5	12.2	14.1
Investment income	5.1	5.3	6.3	5.3	5.5
Earnings	7.3	2.8	0.6	0.3	1.5

Notes:
Percentages may not sum to 100 due to rounding.
'Means-tested benefits' includes income from all means-tested benefits (i.e. income support, council tax benefit and housing benefit), whilst 'other benefits' includes all non-means-tested benefits, such as invalidity or incapacity benefit.

Sources: 1995–96 Family Resources Survey; authors' calculations.

The incomes of different types of pensioners vary not only in the amount received on average but also in the sources of that income. The average proportions of income from various sources are shown in Table 9.13 for each of the three categories of pensioners across the age-groups. Younger pensioners tend to have a higher proportion of their income from earnings, with the exception of single men aged 60 to 64, who are highly likely to remain economically inactive until they reach the state retirement age of 65. Pensioner couples tend to receive a smaller proportion of their income from state benefits than single pensioners of either sex. This is because they are more likely to have income from a private pension. Single pensioner men tend to have a higher proportion of their income from earnings and private pensions than single pensioner women; conversely single women are reliant on the state for a higher proportion of their income.

Not only is there considerable variation in the sources of income for pensioners of different ages and marital statuses, but it is even more pronounced for pensioners of different income levels. Income from a state pension and other benefits still makes up 40 per cent of the total income received by the richest 20 per cent of pensioners. The richest pensioners do however have much larger income from investments, private pensions and earnings. The composition of pensioner incomes is shown for each quintile in Figure 9.5, and the average net incomes of each quintile from the different components are given in Figure 9.6.

Figure 9.5 shows that the state is still an important provider of income for even the richest quintile of pensioners. Again, the poorest 60 per cent of pensioners have only a small proportion of their income coming from private sources, and even those in the fourth quintile receive the majority of their income from the state. Figure 9.6 shows the differences in net income between the quintiles. What stands out is how much better off the richest quintile is than the rest, even than the second-richest quintile. By far the

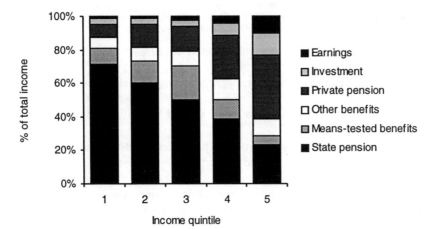

Notes:
'Means-tested benefits' includes income support, council tax benefit and housing benefit, whilst 'other benefits' includes other, non-means-tested benefits such as invalidity or incapacity benefit. For exact percentages see Appendix Table 9.A1.

Sources: 1995–96 Family Resources Survey; authors' calculations.

Figure 9.5 Composition of Pensioner Income, by Income Quintile

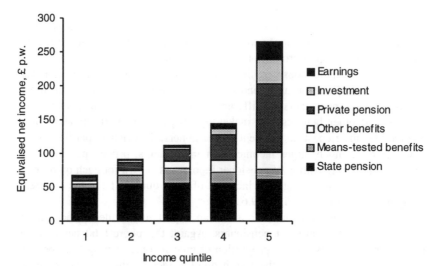

Notes:
Income is net of all direct taxes, including local taxes.
The individual components have been calculated by multiplying the percentage of total income
that they correspond to by the average net equivalised income for each quintile.
For exact amounts see Appendix Table 9.A1.
Note that even in the top quintiles there is significant receipt of means-tested benefits. This
appears surprising but reflects the fact that for some people means-tested benefits, especially
housing benefit, are generous enough to lift them up the distribution.

Sources: 1995–96 Family Resources Survey; authors' calculations.

Figure 9.6   Equivalised Net Pensioner Income, by Income Quintile

major contributor to this is the large amount of private pension income
received by the top group.

Equally important is the position of pensioners relative to the rest of the
population. Figure 9.7 shows the proportion of pensioners in each decile of
the population income distribution. Only 5 per cent of pensioners fall in the
poorest income decile, mainly because this decile tends to consist of the
unemployed and lone parents, whose state benefits tend to be smaller,
especially once their incomes are equivalised. The majority of pensioners (60
per cent) are found in the next four deciles, and they are also over-represented
in the 6th decile. Only 9 per cent of pensioners make it into the richest fifth of
the population.

Figure 9.7 also shows the breakdown of the proportions of different types
of pensioners in each income decile. This shows that single female pensioners
are much less likely to be in the top two deciles than pensioner couples or

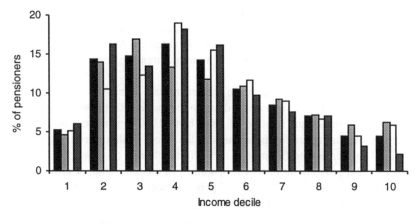

Figure 9.7 Percentage of Pensioners in Each Income Decile

Note: For exact percentages see Appendix Table 9.A2.

Sources: 1995–96 Family Resources Survey; authors' calculations.

single pensioner men. We also observe a higher proportion of pensioner couples in all the top five deciles than of pensioners as a whole. The lack of obvious variation in the bottom decile is likely to be caused not only by the choice of equivalence scale, but more importantly by the treatment of housing costs in this analysis. Those who rent will appear richer than they actually are, especially if they are in receipt of housing benefit. This is likely to be particularly relevant for those in the lower deciles.

Evidently pensioners are a far from homogeneous group. The incomes of the richest are several times those of the poorest, and while the majority are to be found in the lower to middle ranges of the overall income distribution, a significant minority are to be found at the top. The distinguishing characteristic of the better-off is largely that they have high levels of occupational pensions, with a minority having substantial investment income.

Previous work however has demonstrated that this pattern of income receipt has been by no means constant over time (Johnson and Stears, 1995). In the late 1970s pensioners were a much more homogeneous group, with many fewer having substantial incomes from occupational pensions and with state pensions providing a larger proportion of total income. Look further back to the early 1960s and one finds a different pattern again, with very much higher levels of economic activity among those over pension age and a distribution of income that looked more like the current one than the one prevailing towards the end of the 1970s. Instead of pensions shifting people up the income distribution, back then it was earnings. As a result the onset of older age and the inability to earn had a more dramatic effect on overall living standards.

The effects of the UK pension system remain dynamic. The pattern of income receipt will continue to develop, with private pensions becoming increasingly important relative to state benefits. To some extent this will increase inequality among pensioners in that those without private provision will fall further behind (though SERPS will ameliorate this for some). On the other hand a growing number will benefit from more substantial provision. In the longer run the advent of personal pensions will increase the importance of private pension income still further.

9.7   CONCLUSIONS

The UK already has a pension system in which a significant proportion of pensioners' incomes derives from the private sector. As the basic pension continues to wither through price indexation, the government's aim is to increase this proportion still further – to 60 per cent of income by the middle of the 21st century.

Already the system means that higher earners receive a majority of their income from the private sector. This will grow more apparent as the state system becomes more concentrated on lower earners – through increasing levels of means-tested benefits and the replacement of SERPS by the more targeted state second pension. In addition receipt of income from private sources looks set to continue rising even without further reform as the impact of personal pensions begins to be felt in retirement incomes and as reforms to occupational pensions law, particularly the requirements for early leaver benefits, continue to have an effect.

This greater targeting of state benefits has gone hand in hand with a desire to encourage more people to provide for themselves through the private sector. It had been hoped that personal pensions, effectively an option since 1988, would play this role for the half of the work-force without access to an occupational scheme. However they had a disastrous start with mis-selling; continuing high costs, especially for early quitters, persuaded the government that personal pensions could not by themselves play the required role and that a further option – the stakeholder pension – would need to be put in place to provide a cheap and simple alternative with capped charges, particularly for lower earners. The success or otherwise of this policy remains to be seen, though the requirement on employers to make such a scheme available to their employees could be an important element in its success.

Unresolved issues remain. It seems unlikely that the means-tested benefit system can remain, as in 2000–01, with a full pound-for-pound taper on the main benefit. Problems with both fairness and incentives arise. The Chancellor of the Exchequer has already announced further work on this issue. The government has already shown itself concerned about these issues by accompanying the announcement of the intention to raise the minimum income guarantee more quickly with the proposal to introduce the state second pension, the effect of which will be to keep someone with a full earnings history just above the MIG level when they retire (though not throughout their retirement).

The low level of basic state pension is also beginning to attract increased attention. The effect of continued price indexation on levels of the pension was brought home to current pensioners in April 2000 when very low levels of inflation meant that the annual increase in respect of inflation fell below the psychologically important £1 mark (it rose by 75 pence a week).

As yet the UK does not appear to have a distribution of incomes among pensioners that is wildly out of line with that experienced in other countries, in part because of the extensive nature of the UK's means-tested benefit system. It is important in this context not to forget the lessons of the exercise that involved calculating the income of pensioners on income support with their housing costs and local taxes paid. If one compares this with *net* average earnings then the *minimum* that a pensioner should actually be receiving is around 40 per cent of average net earnings. This contrasts with the figure for the basic pension alone of 15 per cent of average gross earnings.

Many of the policy problems that do remain relate to the desire to raise the living standard of the poorest without spending a great deal of extra money on everyone while maintaining incentives to save privately. Possible long-run solutions include a more significant element of compulsory private provision or some upgrading of non-means-tested benefits, possibly through some integration of the basic state pension and the new state second pension.

One thing is clear. Both the state and private systems, and indeed the interaction between them, are horribly complex. The pressure for simplification is likely to be another important element of the UK pension debate for the foreseeable future.

APPENDIX

Table 9.A1   Pensioner Income, by Composition and Income Quintile (%)

Source	Quintile				
	1	2	3	4	5
State pension	71.36	59.89	50.05	38.80	23.37
Means-tested benefits	9.40	13.48	19.90	11.26	5.49
Other benefits	6.44	8.27	8.94	12.30	9.56
Private pension	7.97	13.41	15.05	26.61	38.11
Investment income	3.84	3.57	3.74	6.72	13.24
Earnings	0.97	1.39	2.31	4.31	10.24
Average net income (£ p.w.)	67.29	91.56	112.05	143.51	265.22

Sources: 1995–96 Family Resources Survey; authors' calculations.

Table 9.A2   Percentage of Pensioners in Each Income Decile (%)

Income decile	% of all pensioners	% of pensioner couples	% of single male pensioners	% of single female pensioners
1	5.27	4.59	5.11	6.01
2	14.38	13.94	10.56	16.32
3	14.71	16.90	12.33	13.49
4	16.28	13.32	18.94	18.16
5	14.26	11.77	15.53	16.21
6	10.56	10.92	11.72	9.75
7	8.50	9.24	8.92	7.61
8	7.05	7.23	6.61	7.05
9	4.53	5.87	4.43	3.26
10	4.44	6.22	5.86	2.14

Note: Percentages may not sum precisely due to rounding.

Sources: 1995–96 Family Resources Survey; authors' calculations.

NOTES

1. i.e. thousand million.
2. 1999–2000 out-turn figure for spending on people over working age taken from Department of Social Security (2000a). It excludes spending on invalidity benefits.
3. From April 2000 the basic single pension is £67.50, whilst couples receive an additional £40.40 if only one person qualifies for the basic pension. Couples in which both qualify receive twice the basic state pension, i.e. £135. Figures obtained from the Department of Social Security website.
4. The reduced rate of National Insurance is 3.85 per cent of all earnings. In 1995–96 445 000 women paid this reduced rate, compared with 4.1 million when the option was removed.
5. Assuming real earnings growth of 1½ per cent per year.
6. The retirement age for women is to be increased by six months every year between 2010 and 2020 so that equalisation is achieved by 2020.
7. An individual who consistently earned precisely the LEL would hence acquire no SERPS entitlements and would therefore receive just the basic pension. This is why the relationship between the LEL and the basic pension exists. Similarly, since no contributions are made on earnings above the UEL, no additional pension entitlements are paid for earnings above the UEL.
8. The drop from 25 per cent to 20 per cent of average earnings will occur in 2000, and the calculation of the average from the best 20 years to the entire working life will be phased in between 2000 and 2028.
9. In fact due to some individuals receiving misleading information about this change it has now been delayed until October 2002. In addition those who can demonstrate that they acted on wrong information will be able to inherit the full amount. For more information see Department of Social Security (2000b).
10. Hemming and Kay (1982) produced forecasts that highlighted the extent of future liabilities.
11. For a more detailed discussion of the introduction of stakeholder pensions and the state second pension see for example Agulnik et al. (1999), Disney, Emmerson and Tanner (1999) and Emmerson and Tanner (1999).
12. The high proportion of recipients and the average payments reflect one of the oddities of the original SERPS formula which meant that even those contracted out could end up with a small amount of SERPS.
13. All figures for 1994–95, from Department of Social Security (1994).
14. Agulnik (1999) provides an analysis of the redistributive effect from moving from SERPS to S2P including the impact of higher NICs which are required under S2P.
15. Under the original formula SERPS entitlements would only be reduced if the five-year gap coincided with what would have been one of the individual's best 20 years of service. By using the last five years of employment this will have no effect since earnings tend to decline in the latter working years. Under the new formula any contributions gap will reduce SERPS entitlement, with the actual deduction depending again on what contributions would have been made during those years.
16. For example if the individual was in full-time education. Alternatively credits could be obtained for the period of the five-year gap in contributions for reasons such as caring for an elderly or disabled dependant.

17. When the individual reaches the age of 85 the pension of the 'median earner' will have fallen to under 14 per cent of average earnings.
18. Couples can receive up to £121.95. Higher rates of benefit apply to older pensioners. (Figures taken from Department of Social Security website.)
19. Figure from the 1995–96 Family Resources Survey.
20. Figures from Department of Social Security (1996) and the 1995–96 Family Resources Survey.
21. Figure from HM Treasury (2000). See Emmerson, Frayne and Goodman (2000) for an analysis of the possible effects of an ageing population on NHS expenditure.
22. Figures taken from the 1995–96 Family Resources Survey. Pensioners are classified as the head of benefit unit being aged over 65, or being aged over 60 and not working.
23. Figure from Inland Revenue (1999). Takes account of tax forgone on contribution and investment income, but nets off tax currently received from pensions in payment. See Dilnot and Johnson (1993a and 1993b) for a detailed discussion.
24. Abolishing this raised some £5.4 billion for the Exchequer in 1999–2000 (HM Treasury, 1997).
25. Figures calculated from Government Actuary's Department (1999).
26. Other more technical adjustments have also reduced the future value of SERPS entitlements.
27. See endnote 9 for more details.
28. Invalidity benefit was replaced in April 1995 by incapacity benefit, which although similar involves more stringent testing of whether an individual is able to fulfil *any* work, not just the individual's previous occupation.
29. For a more detailed discussion of pensioner inequality in the UK see Johnson and Stears (1995).

REFERENCES

Agulnik, P. (1999), 'The proposed State Second Pension', *Fiscal Studies*, **20** (4), 409–22.

Agulnik, P., N. Barr, J. Falkingham and J. Rake (1999), *Partnership in Pensions? Responses to the Pensions Green Paper*, CASE Paper no. 24, London: Centre for the Analysis of Social Exclusion, London School of Economics.

Beveridge, W.H. (1942), *Social Insurance and Allied Services*, Cmd 6404, London: HMSO (the Beveridge Report).

Blundell, R.W. and P. Johnson (1999), 'Pensions and retirement in the United Kingdom', in J. Gruber and D. Wise (eds), *Social Security and Retirement around the World*, Chicago: Chicago University Press, pp. 403–37.

Budd, A. and N. Campbell (1998), 'The roles of public and private sectors in the UK pension system', in M. Feldstein (ed.), *Privatizing Social Security*, National Bureau of Economic Research; Chicago: Chicago University Press.

Crook, M. and P. Johnson (2000), *Saving for Retirement: How Taxes and Charges Affect Choice*, FSA Occasional Paper no. 8, London: Financial Services Authority.

Department of Social Security (1994), *Social Security Statistics 1994*, London: Government Statistical Service.

Department of Social Security (1996), *Social Security Statistics 1996*, London: Government Statistical Service.

Department of Social Security (1998), *A New Contract for Welfare: Partnership in Pensions*, Cm. 4179, London: DSS.

Department of Social Security (1999a), *Social Security Statistics 1999*, London: Government Statistical Service.

Department of Social Security (1999b), *Social Security Departmental Report: The Government's Expenditure Plans 1999–2000 to 2000–01*, London: DSS.

Department of Social Security (2000a), *Social Security Departmental Report: The Government's Expenditure Plans 2000–01 to 2001–02*, London: DSS.

Department of Social Security (2000b), 'Pensioners to be protected by new inherited SERPS scheme', Press Release 00/068, 15 March.

Dilnot, A. and P. Johnson (1993a), *The Taxation of Private Pensions*, London: Institute for Fiscal Studies.

Dilnot, A. and P. Johnson (1993b), 'Tax expenditures: the case of occupational pensions', *Fiscal Studies*, **14** (1), 42–56.

Dilnot, A., R. Disney, P. Johnson and E. Whitehouse (1994), *Pensions Policy in the UK: An Economic Analysis*, London: Institute for Fiscal Studies.

Disney, R. (1998), 'Social security reform in the UK: a voluntary privatisation', paper presented to 'Social Security Reform: International Comparisons' conference, Rome, 16–17 March.

Disney, R. and S. Webb (1991), 'Why are there so many long term sick in Britain?', *Economic Journal*, **101** (March), 252–62.

Disney, R. and E. Whitehouse (1996), 'What are occupational pension entitlements worth in Britain?', *Economica*, **63** (May), 213–38.

Disney, R., C. Emmerson and S. Tanner (1999), *Partnership in Pensions: An Assessment*, Commentary no. 78, London: Institute for Fiscal Studies.

Emmerson, C. and S. Tanner (1999), *The Government's Proposals for Stakeholder Pensions*, Briefing Note no. 1, London: Institute for Fiscal Studies.

Emmerson, C. and S. Tanner (2000), 'A note on the tax treatment of private pensions and Individual Savings Accounts', *Fiscal Studies*, **21** (1), 65–74.

Emmerson, C., C. Frayne and A. Goodman (2000), *Pressures in UK Healthcare: Challenges for the NHS*, Commentary no. 81, London: Institute for Fiscal Studies.

Government Actuary's Department (1999), *National Insurance Fund Long Term Financial Estimates July 1999*, Cm. 4406, London: The Stationery Office.

Government Actuary's Department (2000), *National Insurance Fund Long Term Financial Estimates January 2000*, Cm. 4573, London: The Stationery Office.

Hemming, R. and J.A. Kay (1982), 'The costs of the State Earnings Related Pension Scheme', *Economic Journal*, **92** (366), 300–19.

HM Treasury (1996), *Tax Benefit Reference Manual, 1995–96 Edition*, London: HM Treasury.

HM Treasury (1997), *Equipping Britain for Our Long-term Future – Financial Statement and Budget Report, July 1997*, Hc85, London: HM Treasury.

HM Treasury (2000), *Prudent for a Purpose: Working for a Stronger and Fairer Britain – Financial Statement and Budget Report, March 2000*, Hc346, London: HM Treasury.

Inland Revenue (1999), *Inland Revenue Statistics 1999*, London: HMSO.

Johnson, P. and G. Stears (1995), 'Pensioner income inequality', *Fiscal Studies*, **16** (4), 69–93.

Johnson, P. and G. Stears (1998), 'Why are older pensioners poorer?', *Oxford Bulletin of Economics and Statistics*, **60** (3), 271–90.

Johnson, P., R. Disney and G. Stears (1996), *Pensions 2000 and Beyond, Volume 2: Analysis of Trends and Options*, London: Retirement Income Inquiry.

10. Pension Provision in the United States

Alain Jousten[*]

10.1 INTRODUCTION

The US retirement income system relies on two big pillars: on the one hand the public Old-age, Survivors and Disability Insurance (OASDI), also called 'social security', and on the other hand private pension arrangements. The social security system is based on the insurance principle. Social security is not trivial, as it covers approximately 96 per cent of jobs in the US. Coverage has expanded quite rapidly and social security spending as a share of GDP has doubled between 1970 and 2000. Benefit payments in 1996 represented US$305.2 billion,[1] or approximately 4.59 per cent of US GDP. In 1994 91 per cent of elderly households received social security income. In 1996 43.7 million people received monthly benefits. But also at the individual level social security represents a major income source. Calculations from Diamond and Gruber (1999) illustrate that for 16 per cent of households social security represents the only source of income. Furthermore social security represents more than 50 per cent of income for three-fifths of the beneficiaries aged 65 or older. None the less the system is distinctly smaller in size than its counterparts in most continental European countries. In Germany for example the public retirement systems accounted for approximately 13 per cent of GDP in 1995. In Belgium the figure was approximately 10.6 per cent for the same year.

Private pension arrangements vary from occupational pension plans to individual private savings. The overall participation rate of the civilian work-force in occupational retirement plans has not changed a lot over the last 20

[*]The author wishes to thank Richard Disney, Paul Johnson and Jim Poterba for their helpful comments. He is particularly indebted to Ksenia Yudaeva for her exceptional help with the CPS dataset.

years, decreasing slightly from 46 per cent in 1979 to approximately 44 per cent in 1993. Occupational pension plans are of both the defined benefit and the defined contribution type. Over the last few years there has been a noticeable shift from defined benefit to defined contribution schemes, in large part because of the growth of the tax-favoured 401(k) plans in the 1980s.

Individual savings are of two different types: on the one hand traditional savings instruments and on the other the tax-favoured Individual Retirement Accounts (IRAs) as well as the tax-favoured Keogh retirement savings plans for the self-employed. The Employee Benefit Research Institute (EBRI) estimated in 1995 that tax expenditures due to the tax-exempt or tax-favoured status of individual savings plans such as IRAs and Keogh plans was US$9.8 billion in 1993 and was set to grow to US$11.6 billion in 1997. More impressively tax expenditures due to private and public sector occupational pension plans amounted to approximately US$56.3 billion in 1993 and they were projected to grow to approximately US$66 billion in 1997.

From a technical point of view the public social security system does not have to be in strict fiscal balance. Taxes are paid into trust funds, from which benefits are paid out. There are three different trust funds: one for the old-age and survivor system, one for the disability system and one for the health insurance system. In past years positive balances have been built up in an attempt to buffer against future solvency problems of the system. But even with this reserve in the trust funds, the simultaneous effect of three factors will threaten the solvency of the system in the early 21st century. First, there is the combined effect of the drop in fertility rates and the ageing of the 'baby boomers'. Second, the slowdown in the growth of real wages implies a reduction in the growth of the tax base for the financing of social security entitlements. A number of proposals for reforming the system are under discussion. They all contain a mixture of benefit cuts (explicit or through increased taxation of benefits) and increases in contribution levels. None of them has broad political support as nobody wants to take the blame for either cutting benefits or raising payroll taxes.[2]

The structure of this chapter is as follows. In the next section we describe the public retirement income systems, most notably social security. Section 10.3 discusses the main features of private pension arrangements. The financial sustainability of the social security system is illustrated in Section 10.4 using some projections, and economic activity rates around the normal retirement age are presented in Section 10.5. Section 10.6 documents pensioner incomes in the US, their composition and how they compare with the incomes of non-pensioners. Finally Section 10.7 concludes.

10.2   PUBLIC SOURCES OF INCOME

Public income sources for the elderly can broadly be categorised into two groups: those that are organised on an insurance basis and those that are welfare programmes relying on means testing. The main part of the present section is devoted to a description of social security, which is the main public insurance system, but we also give brief descriptions of the public health insurance and assistance programmes as well as of other cash and in-kind means-tested benefits available to the elderly.

10.2.1   History of the Social Security System

The beginning of the present-day social security system dates back to the 1935 Social Security Act. Originally coverage was limited to all workers under the age of 65 in commerce and industry with the exception of railroad personnel. Over the years coverage has substantially expanded, and nowadays the only major group of workers not covered by the system are some state and local government employees. Initially benefits were only available to those aged over 65. In 1956 and 1961 early retirement provisions coupled with reduced benefits for early retirees were introduced, first for women and then for men. The earliest retirement age was fixed at 62. In 1939 dependent and survivor benefits were introduced, with benefits for wives and widows over the age of 65 and children under the age of 18. These provisions were generalised to include husbands and widowers in 1950. Similarly the 1965 and 1983 amendments respectively made divorced women and men become eligible for benefits, conditional on the marriage having lasted for at least 10 years. In 1956 benefit eligibility was extended to elderly disabled workers (aged over 50), and in 1960 it was extended to all disabled workers, independent of age.[3]

Until 1972 benefit adjustments had to pass an Act of Congress. With the 1972 amendment to the Social Security Act, automatic cost-of-living adjustments of benefits tied to the consumer price index (CPI) were introduced, making social security a real annuity contract. Furthermore a delayed retirement credit (DRC) was created which increased benefits for workers who retired after the normal retirement age (NRA), which is 65 for people born before 1938.

The 1977 amendment introduced the present-day benefit structure. Nominal lifetime average earnings were replaced, as the basis for the computation of benefits, by a measure that is adjusted for changes in the cost of living. More precisely the Social Security Administration computes for every worker a summary measure of lifetime average earnings called AIME (average indexed monthly earnings). AIME is an indexed average over the 35 highest-earning covered years of the worker's career. Indexing is done using the changes in the average wage in the economy as a deflator, but not quite correctly. First, it is only done to the year in which the worker turns 60; any additional period of work after age 60 enters the computation in nominal amounts. Second, there is a gap in the indexing between age 60 (when wage indexation stops) and age 62 (when the indexing of benefits starts). These two features would become very important if the US had high and varying inflation.

The 1983 amendment was aimed at addressing the financial problems that the system had begun to face. In an attempt to address projected long-run financial problems, the amendment introduced a gradual increase in the NRA from 65 to 67 for people attaining age 62 between the year 2000 and 2022.[4] The early retirement age was kept unchanged at 62, but as the NRA increased, the reduction factors for early retirement benefits were also increased. For example for a person retiring at age 62 in 2022 the benefit would be 70 per cent of the basic pension amount (PIA), which contrasts with the 80 per cent to which a person in the same situation was entitled prior to the increases in NRA. Individuals attaining 62 in 2000 are the first ones feeling the impact of the 1983 amendment. Their NRA increases by two months to 65 years and 2 months. This increase in the NRA causes an additional reduction of benefits for retirement at age 62 of 5/6 per cent of the PIA. Another major change introduced with the 1983 reform was a gradual increase in the DRC, from the previous 3 per cent a year to 8 per cent a year.[5] Finally the 1983 amendment made part of the social security benefits taxable for certain high-income beneficiaries but left benefits untaxed for all other recipients. The proceeds of these taxes were to be transferred into the different social insurance funds according to a predetermined formula.[6]

10.2.2 Description of the Social Security System

The social security system is financed through a payroll tax levied equally on employers and employees. The tax is applicable on all earnings up to a maximum taxable amount, which is US$76 200 in 2000. The maximum taxable amount is indexed to the changes in the national average wage. The total OASDI payroll tax applicable on earnings up to this maximum is 12.4 per cent, with 10.6 per cent dedicated to the Old-age and Survivors Insurance (OASI) programme and the remainder dedicated to the Disability Insurance (DI) programme.

Both eligibility conditions and benefit formulae vary greatly for the different types of benefit provided under the system. For an Old-age Insurance (OAI) pension a worker has to have a minimum of at least 40 'quarters of coverage', i.e. quarters of work in covered employment. The computation of retirement benefits follows a procedure with several steps. First, AIME is computed as a summary measure of the individual's real lifetime earnings. As already noted the average is computed using the earnings (up to the maximum taxable earnings during that same year) from the 35 highest-earnings years, hence allowing for the possibility that an additional high-earnings year replaces an earlier lower-earnings year. In the next step AIME is converted into the primary insurance amount (PIA) using a non-linear schedule composed of three linear segments. Over a first interval of AIME the conversion into the PIA is done at 90 cents to the dollar; over a second interval the conversion is done at 32 cents to the dollar; the remainder of AIME is converted at 15 cents to the dollar.

The PIA represents the benefits a worker is entitled to if he or she decides to retire at the NRA. Hence, given the non-linear structure of the above schedule, it is easy to see that replacement rates across different income groups may vary substantially. In 1997 for a single worker retiring at 65 the replacement rate varies from approximately 25 per cent for a worker earning close to the taxable earnings maximum to over 60 per cent for a worker with income as low as US$11 000. Table 10.1 illustrates the PIA as well as the gross and net replacement rates for an unmarried man retiring at 65 in 1997 and having worked since his 20th birthday.[7] The replacement rates for the three central scenarios capture the strongly progressive nature of the system. The impact of the incomplete earnings history, with five missing years of earnings at the beginning of the career, is rather limited, both at the NRA and at the early retirement age (the difference in the PIA is approximately 3 per cent in both cases). The impact of adding or dropping five years of earnings

Table 10.1   How US Social Security Benefits Vary with Lifetime Earnings (US$ p.a., 1997 prices)

	Annual earnings relative to median			Incomplete history
	½	1	2	
1. PIA	7 897	12 547	13 932	12 178
2. Gross wage in last year	16 721	33 441	66 882	33 441
3. Gross replacement rate (1./2.)	47.2%	37.5%	20.8%	36.4%
4. Net wage in last year	12 224	22 981	43 104	22 981
5. Net replacement rate (1./4.)	64.6%	54.6%	32.3%	53.0%

Note: Individual retiring in 1997.

Source: Author's calculations.

becomes much larger once we analyse the situation of a person with fewer than 35 years of work. In this case any additional year of work replaces a zero-earnings year in the benefit computation formula, rather than only replacing another positive-earnings year.

Benefits are adjusted on a lifetime basis for both early and delayed retirement. For early retirement they are reduced by 5/9 per cent per month of early retirement for the first 36 months of early retirement and by 5/12 per cent for any additional month beyond 36. For deferral beyond the NRA, a DRC is applicable. For those turning 65 in 1998 the DRC is of 5.5 per cent per year of deferral. The DRC has been growing over time and is set to attain 8 per cent for those born in or after 1943. Even though substantially higher than it has been for previous generations, the DRC is smaller than the actuarial adjustment for early retirement, hence implying a kink point in benefit accruals at the NRA.

Until 2000 all these benefit amounts were subject to an earnings test up to the age of 70, i.e. benefits were reduced if the individual had earnings higher than the maximum allowed amount. For early retirees the earnings limit was US$10 080 for the year 2000 and benefits were reduced by US$1 for every US$2 that the worker's earnings exceeded this limit. For people beyond the NRA the earnings limit was US$17 000 and benefits were reduced by US$1 for every US$3 the individual earned in excess of the specified limit. After 1996 legislation in response to concern about the disincentives implicit in the earnings test, the proposed limits were to be progressively increased in subsequent years at a rate faster than the indexation procedures. However early in 2000 Congress took the more radical step of abolishing this 'earnings test' in subsequent years.

In addition to the worker's old-age benefits the social security programme provides important benefits to some dependants and survivors of covered workers. The spouse of a retired worker is entitled to claim dependant benefits equal to 50 per cent of the worker's PIA. The full amount of spousal benefit is payable if the spouse is older than 65 or of any age if the spouse is caring for a dependent child.[8] Furthermore the total amount of social security benefits a spouse can receive is limited to the larger of this dependent spouse benefit and her own entitlement as a worker. In addition to the spouse young dependants under the age of 18 are also entitled to benefits equal to 50 per cent of the worker's benefit, but the total family benefits cannot exceed a given ceiling which was introduced to make sure that families are not significantly better off after retirement.[9] Surviving widow or widower benefit is equal to 100 per cent of the worker's PIA for a survivor starting to claim at age 65. Benefits claims are possible as early as age 60, but benefits are then actuarially reduced by up to 28.5 per cent relative to the value at age 65. Once again the total benefits a survivor can receive at any time are limited to the maximum of survivor benefits and entitlements based on his or her own earnings record.

Aside from the OASI system, the social security system also contains a substantial DI programme, which provides workers with insurance against the risk of physical incapacity to work. To be eligible, workers have to be younger than 65 and have to have been in covered employment for at least 20 quarters of the 40 calendar quarters preceding the onset of the disability. Benefits are always equal to the PIA, hence being higher than retirement income for people retiring from work before age 65. This feature, combined with the absence of a minimum age for benefit receipt, introduces significant incentives for older workers (especially those aged 50 and upwards) to try to get onto the DI rolls.

10.2.3 Healthcare Programmes

The social security amendments of 1965 also created the Medicare programme, which was initially designed to serve the medical needs of the US population over the age of 65 independently of income. The same amendments also created Medicaid, which is the equivalent of Medicare for people with low incomes and low wealth. Both programmes have undergone numerous changes since their creation.

Medicare was originally set up as a Hospital Insurance (HI) programme and was to become known as Part A of Medicare. The financing of this HI programme is still essentially pay-as-you-go (PAYG), and the payroll tax is 2.9 per cent in 2000 (1.45 per cent paid by the employee, 1.45 per cent paid by the employer). Since 1977 Medicare also provides a voluntary programme of Medical Insurance covering physician services as well as a series of other medical expenses (the so-called 'Part B'). Part B is financed through a monthly premium payable by the participants in the programme as well as by federal general revenue. Part A financing is sufficient until 2001, at which time the projected increase in the cost will drive the system towards financial problems. Indeed the costs of Part A and Part B are expected to increase respectively from 1.63 per cent and 0.92 per cent of GDP in calendar year 1995 to 5.04 per cent and 3.70 per cent in 2070.

In contrast to Medicare, Medicaid is a social assistance programme which is financed through general federal and state tax revenue. Medicaid is aimed at providing basic medical services to the poor. Within the context of the elderly population, these are mainly recipients of the means-tested supplemental security income (SSI), some low-income Medicare beneficiaries, and elderly people who lose their SSI due to income from earnings. For the fiscal year 1995 the Medicaid programme had 4.1 million elderly recipients (approximately one-ninth of the total) who received total payments of US$36.5 billion (approximately 30 per cent of total payments).

10.2.4 Other Means-tested Benefits

Aside from the social security system, described above, which is organised as a social insurance programme, the US also has social assistance (welfare) programmes. In 1972 the state-administered public cash assistance programmes for the aged, the blind and the disabled were replaced by the federal SSI which is administered by the Social Security Administration. The programme sets common standards for eligibility across all states but leaves the individual states with the possibility of supplementing the federal minimum payments for some or all recipients within the state. The SSI programme provides monthly cash benefits for those eligible for benefits on the basis of nationality, income, financial resources, age and disability. Access is essentially limited to US citizens[10] who are aged (over 65), disabled or blind, and have income less than US$5 808 for a single person ($8 712 for a couple) and financial assets limited to US$2 000 for a single person ($3 000 for a couple) in January 1997, when maximum monthly federal SSI benefits for individuals living in their own household were US$484 and US$726 for single people and couples respectively.

Benefits are reduced to reflect other income and in-kind support and maintenance. Total expenditure of the federal and state governments on SSI amounted to US$26.5 billion in 1993, which corresponds to approximately 10 per cent of the spending on social security. In December 1996 6.7 million people received federal SSI payments, state supplementation or both. These payments averaged US$366 per person that same month. Of the total number of recipients there were 1.5 million elderly (approximately 22 per cent) with an average SSI benefit of US$268 during the same month of December.

Another welfare programme of relevance to the elderly is the food stamps programme run by state welfare agencies and local welfare offices. The costs of the programme are financed by the federal government from general revenue. In fiscal year 1996 the total federal food stamp programme cost US$24.4 billion. It served on average more than 25 million people each month, with an average monthly benefit of US$73 per person and more than US$172 per household. To participate in the programme households have to satisfy a resource condition (less than US$2 000 in countable resources, with the figure being US$3 000 for those with a household member over 60 years of age) and income conditions (gross income less than 130 per cent of the federal poverty line; net income after deductions less than 100 per cent of the poverty line).

A third major welfare programme with implications for the poor elderly is housing assistance, which targets needy households.[11] The assistance is provided either in the form of public housing or in the form of rental vouchers or rental certificates usable on the private market. Total spending on housing programmes was US$19.8 billion in 1993. The number of households in public housing units was approximately 1.25 million in 1995, with the elderly making up 34 per cent of this total. The average income of families in public housing units was approximately US$6 500 in 1995. As for rent assistance, a total of 4.7 million families were recipients in fiscal year 1996.

10.3   PRIVATE PENSION PLANS

In addition to the public retirement income sources discussed in the previous section, private retirement income plays an important role in the US. More than three-quarters of pensioner households surveyed in the Current Population Survey (CPS) receive income from private sources: 22 per cent of total pensioner income comes from earnings, private pensions account for 20 per cent and investment income for 17 per cent.

Both occupational and individual pension arrangements exist on a large scale. Apart from investment income, elderly individuals have access to a regular private pension stream, essentially from annuities and occupational pension plans. Targeted retirement saving/income plans either make a lump-sum payment available to the individuals (usually at retirement) or provide regular annuity pay-outs over the retirement period. It is important to notice that, in contrast to social security benefits, regular private pensions are paid in the form of a nominal annuity rather than as a real annuity.

Table 10.2 shows the rate of occupational pension receipt for different demographic categories among the group of individuals who have reached NRA in the last five years. A noteworthy finding is that men are on average much more likely to be the recipient of regular private sources of pension income than wives. This finding understates the access of women to private pension income, mostly through their husbands. When computing the proportion of all pensioners living in a household with positive pension income, 42.3 per cent of the specified population have access to such income. Divorced and widowed women have a rather high rate of pension receipt, at least compared with married women. Notice that at least one-third of this rate is due to the receipt of survivor benefits by widows.

Figure 10.1 illustrates the proportion of those over the early retirement age receiving private pensions. Men are universally more likely to receive private pension benefits than are women. The somewhat lower rate of receipt below the NRA is due to the higher activity rate as well as to the fact that some private pension benefits only start to be paid at the NRA. A similar finding holds for benefit payments before the age of 62: in the age bracket 60–61, only 24.5 per cent of men and 11.1 per cent of women are private pension benefit recipients.

Table 10.2   Occupational Pension Receipt, by Marital Status at State Retirement Age (%)

	Men	Women	Total
Single	33.5	39.7	36.9
Divorced or widowed	41.9	31.0	34.0
Married or cohabiting	49.5	20.4	36.2
Total	47.5	25.5	35.5

Note: Pensions include both private and public sector pensions, survivor benefits and regular income streams from individual IRA arrangements.

Source: Author's tabulations from March 1997 CPS.

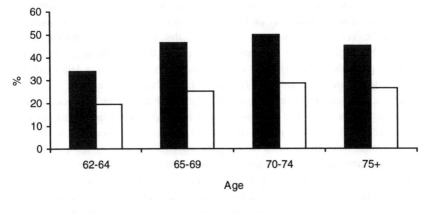

Source: Author's tabulations from March 1997 CPS.

Figure 10.1   Percentage of Individuals over Early Retirement Age with Income from Private Pensions, by Age and Gender

10.3.1   Individual Retirement Income Arrangements

Individual pension arrangements either take the form of traditional investment devices that are subject to the standard tax rules or take the form of tax-favoured IRAs or Keogh plans. Traditional IRAs were established in 1974 by the Employee Retirement Income Security Act (ERISA) with the object of providing workers who did not have employer-sponsored pensions with access to tax-deferred retirement savings. The parameters of the system at the time of ERISA can be summarised as follows: contributions were tax-deductible up to an annual limit, accrual of interest was tax-free and there were penalties for early withdrawal. IRA assets could be invested in almost any kind of financial asset.

IRA eligibility and deduction rules have changed substantially since their beginning. The 1981 Tax Act extended availability to all workers, even those with occupational pension coverage. The annual limit on contributions is US$2 000 plus US$250 for a non-working spouse. In two-worker households the limit is US$2 000 per person, hence a combined US$4 000 for the household. The Tax Reform Act of 1986 restricted the tax deductibility of contributions for those with occupational pensions to only low-income individuals: so for those households with an occupational retirement plan, beyond a given level of adjusted gross income,[12] contributions are not deductible at all, whereas for an intermediate income range[13] they are partially deductible (i.e. some amount less than the maximum contribution of US$2 000) depending on the income level. For those without occupational pension plans deductibility rules did not change. Notice that the 1986 Act did not change eligibility conditions or the tax-free accrual of interest.

Deductible contributions are taxed when withdrawn and non-deductible contributions are not. The interest income is untaxed until the withdrawal of the money, at which time it is subject to income taxation. Minimum withdrawals have to be made starting at the latest at age 70½, either in the form of simple cash withdrawals from the account or through the purchase of an annuity contract. Withdrawals before age 59½ are discouraged with a 10 per cent penalty, unless the individual dies, becomes permanently disabled, faces specific medical insurance or higher-education expenses or is a first-time home-buyer. Further the penalty does not apply if the individual opts for an authorised annuity contract as a means of withdrawing his or her IRA assets.

A new version of the IRA – the so-called 'Roth' IRA – has been created by the 1997 Taxpayer Relief Act. Up to US$2 000 can be contributed to a Roth IRA, with an additional restriction that no more than US$2 000 can be contributed to traditional and Roth IRAs combined. Not all Roth IRA contributions are tax-deductible. Similarly to the traditional IRA, interest accrual is tax-free, and the same penalties are applicable in case of early retirement. Both contributions to and income from these Roth IRAs are tax-free upon withdrawal. Supposing that the tax rate is the same at the time of contributing to the IRA as at the time of withdrawal, this new form of IRA is identical to a traditional IRA in terms of the net present discounted value it generates for the individual. Only in the case of a substantial difference in terms of tax rates between the time when the individual contributes and when he or she withdraws will one or other form be more attractive. But the main motivation behind this new form of IRA is the desire to balance the budget within the next few years. By taxing IRA contributions and earnings earlier than originally scheduled, Congress shifted tax income from the future to the present, hence getting the government closer to its goal of a balanced budget in the very near future.

Keogh plans are the counterpart of IRAs for the self-employed. They function along the same lines as IRAs and generally have higher contribution limits. The number of tax-reporting units claiming Keogh deductions over the period 1975–92 increased slightly from 0.6 million to 0.9 million. The number of taxpayers claiming IRA deductions has on the other hand fluctuated greatly, as illustrated in Figure 10.2. Notice that both the strong

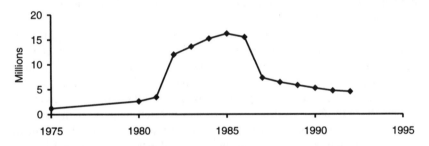

Source: US Department of the Treasury, Internal Revenue Service, various years.

Figure 10.2   Federal Income Tax Returns Claiming IRA Deductions (millions)

Table 10.3   Total Assets in IRAs and Keogh Plans (US$ billion)

	1985	1986	1987	1988	1989	1990	1991	1992
Total assets	228.2	302.4	361.0	419.8	492.1	571.4	680.5	773.1

Source: EBRI, 1995.

growth in the early 1980s and the relatively strong decline after 1986 can easily be linked to changes in the legal framework. But although the number of people claiming IRA deductions decreased substantially in the late 1980s, the assets in IRA and Keogh plans did not respond as dramatically, as can be seen from Table 10.3.

10.3.2   Occupational Pension Arrangements

The first pension plan in the US dates back to 1759. But only in 1875 was the first formal company pension plan established. Since the mid-1940s there has been a significant growth in the numbers of pension plans and of workers covered by such plans. In 1993 57 per cent of civilian workers worked for an employer where a retirement plan was sponsored, corresponding to 67 million people. Of these 67 million, 76 per cent (51 million) actually participated in a retirement plan. Of these 51 million, 86 per cent were vested in the plan, i.e. were participants eligible to receive benefits from the plan.

Participation in occupational pension plans has hovered around 42–46 per cent of the total civilian work-force for 20 years. After a four percentage point decrease between 1979 and 1988, the participation rate climbed back to a level of 44 per cent in 1993. Considering all civilian workers, the female participation rate of 42 per cent in 1993 differs only slightly from that of the male population, which was 45 per cent.

The importance of retirement plans varies substantially across different categories of employers and workers. In the public sector, 90 per cent of employers offer some form of pension plan, and overall participation among public sector employees is running at approximately 75 per cent. In the private sector, large and medium-sized companies (100 employees or more) are much more likely to offer occupational pension plans to their workers than are small businesses. Participation rates are also substantially higher in large and medium-sized companies than in small establishments: in 1994 the participation rate of full-time workers in some form of retirement income plan was 42 per cent for small companies (the same as in 1990), which compares with participation rates for full-time workers in larger companies of 78 per cent in 1993, 80 per cent in 1995 and 79 per cent in 1997. The participation rate of full-time state and local government employees has decreased from 96 per cent to 93 per cent between 1990 and 1992 and then gone up again to 96 per cent in 1994. Over the same period the overall participation rate has stayed approximately constant.

One reason for the success of private occupational pension plans is the favourable tax treatment that they enjoy. A series of tax laws and regulations, starting with the Revenue Act of 1921 and culminating in the Tax Reform Act of 1986, constitute the basis for regulations governing the tax treatment of pension plans. The tax treatment provides incentives both for employers to establish and for employees to participate in plans that satisfy standards set out by the Employee Retirement Income Security Act of 1974. Employer contributions are immediately deductible for the employer and only taxable to the employee at the time of the payment out of the accumulated fund.

Defined benefit (DB) plans covered 50 per cent of all full-time employees in medium and large companies in 1997. DB plans commonly use flat-benefit formulae (giving a flat dollar amount for every year of service), career-average formulae or, especially, final-pay formulae (usually taking into account the last five years of service). Although 65 is the social security NRA, 52 per cent of DB plan participants in medium and large companies can retire early with unreduced benefits, while 96 per cent of plans allow early retirement with or without reduced benefits. However DB plans have become less popular over recent years: from 1980 to 1997 the percentage of full-time employees in medium and large private companies participating in a DB plan dropped substantially from 84 per cent to 50 per cent. Similarly in the case of full-time state and local employees the participation rate dropped from 93 per cent to 87 per cent between 1987 and 1992 and then recovered slightly to 91 per cent in 1997.[14]

The primary explanation for this drop in the participation rate for DB plans is to be seen in the huge success of defined contribution (DC) plans and the reallocation of the occupational pension system towards this particular type of plan. Over the period 1988–97 the participation rate of full-time employees in DC plans went up from 45 per cent to 57 per cent. Employers and employees make defined contributions to the account, but retirement benefits are not predetermined and depend on the performance of the accumulated fund. The rapid growth in participation is due to the strong growth of one particular type of DC plan, namely the 'cash or deferred arrangements' plan. In 1978 section 401(k) was added to the Internal Revenue Code and essentially opened up the possibility for employees of a company sponsoring a so-called '401(k) plan' to defer the taxation of part of their income. The growth in this particular type of retirement income system has been fast even over a relatively short period: in 1997 55 per cent of full-time workers in medium and large companies were in 401(k) plans, up from 43 per cent in 1993.

In 401(k) plans employees are allowed to make tax-deductible contributions, enjoy tax-free accrual of interest and are only taxed upon withdrawal. As is the case for IRAs, 401(k) arrangements have yearly contribution limits and restrictions on withdrawals. Also, 401(k) contributions distinguish themselves from IRA contributions in a number of ways: higher contribution limits, regular payroll deductions (as opposed to potentially erratic individual contributions to IRAs) and a high degree of employer matching of contributions (combined maximum contribution of US$30 000 or

25 per cent of the salary, whichever is smaller). Investment choices in such plans are typically made by the employer and not the employee, borrowing is allowed in some plans and there are differences in withdrawal provisions. For example an employee faces a 10 per cent penalty on leaving a firm if he or she does not roll over the funds into another 401(k) or an IRA or convert them into an annuity. All 401(k) funds enjoy the advantage of tax-free inside build-up, and the fund is only taxed when withdrawn from the account. Withdrawals between the ages of 59½ and 70½ are only taxed as ordinary income, but withdrawals at other ages are penalised.

Table 10.4 illustrates the rapid growth of 401(k) plans over the period 1983–94.

Table 10.4   Participation, Contributions and Assets of 401(k) Plans

	1983	1985	1987	1989	1991	1993	1994
Participants (millions)	4.4	10.3	13.1	17.3	19.1	23.1	25.2
Contributions (US$ billion)	n.a.	24.3	33.2	46.1	51.5	69.3	c.75
Total assets (US$ billion)	n.a.	144	215	357	440	616	675

Source: US Department of Labor, 1997.

Both DB and DC plans have vesting rules determining when a plan participant becomes eligible to receive benefits. DC plans generally have relatively short vesting requirements for employer contributions: for example one-third of employees in medium and large private companies participating in DC savings and thrift plans enjoy immediate vesting of employer contributions, and only 10 per cent have vesting periods longer than five years.[15] DB plans usually have cliff-vesting provisions as well as somewhat longer vesting periods. Cliff-vesting means that the participant only becomes entitled to accrued benefits at some point in time. Ninety-six per cent of DB plan participants have cliff-vesting, versus 29 per cent of DC plan participants. Eighty per cent of DB plan participants become entitled to all accrued benefits after five years, another 12 per cent after 10 years.

10.4   SUSTAINABILITY OF THE PUBLIC SYSTEM

As noted in Section 10.1, the US social insurance system is not in long-run fiscal balance. Over the last years the OASDI system has been accumulating surpluses. At the beginning of 1997 the combined level of the OASI and DI funds was US$567 billion. Nevertheless, faced with the ageing of the population, the system is expected to run into financial problems in the medium and long run. The increase in the dependency ratio of elderly people as a proportion of those of working age, from 21 per cent to 37 per cent between 2000 and 2050, is a good summary measure of the dramatic demographic change that the system has to face.

The financial problems of the social insurance system are not confined to any single programme. The present section focuses primarily on the public OASDI system. Without any further change to the benefit formula, the costs of the OASDI system are expected to grow from an approximate 4.6 per cent of GDP in 1997 to about 6.3 per cent in 2050. The OASDI system is projected to generate sufficient tax receipts to cover its current commitments until 2015. After that time the system will have to start running down the accumulated reserves. In the long run the outlook is hardly improved, as the programme's deficit is expected to grow further (see Leimer (1994 and 1995) and Lee and Skinner (1999)).

Notice however that the financial problems of the US social security system are much smaller than those of its continental European counterparts. Germany is again a striking example. The OECD projects an increase there in the share of public pension payments from 11.1 per cent of GDP in 1995 to 18.4 per cent in 2040 as a reaction to the steep increase in the old-age dependency ratio from 23.8 per cent in 2000 to 49.2 per cent in 2030 (Roseveare et al., 1996).

The Hospital Insurance (HI) system's problems are more imminent and more severe: its insolvency is projected for 2001 and its expenses are expected to grow even faster than those of OASDI. Expressed as a percentage of the payroll, OASDI and HI payments would rise from 15.2 per cent in 2000 to 23.8 per cent in 2025. For OASDI alone, the gap between the costs and revenues expressed as a percentage of payroll is expected to attain approximately 5 per cent in 2030, and stay at this high level thereafter.

Table 10.5 summarises the expected evolution of some key variables until 2050 under 'intermediate' growth assumptions for economic and demographic variables.

Faced with these medium- and long-term problems, there has been a good deal of discussion both among the public and among decision-makers about potential changes to the OASDI programme. None the less the outcome of these discussions has been rather limited: there has not been any major change to the system since the amendments in 1983. In an attempt to explore different potential solutions to the well-publicised financial problems of the system, the Quadrennial Advisory Council on Social Security was charged in 1994 with finding ways of reforming the system to make it break even. After two years' work the Council was unable to find a consensus among its members. Instead it came forward with three different plans for reforming the

Table 10.5   Future Projections of Costs of OASDI and HI

	Financial year starting:					
	2000	2010	2020	2030	2040	2050
Dependency ratio[a] (%)	21.1	21.4	27.5	35.5	36.9	37.2
US$ billion						
OASDI spending	391	489	665	846	963	1 078
OASDI trust fund assets	824	1 379	1 293.5	0	0	0
As a % of payroll						
OASDI cost	11.7	12.5	15.1	17.5	17.8	18.0
OASDI revenue[b]	12.6	12.7	12.9	13.1	13.2	13.2
As a % of GDP						
OASI	4.1	4.0	4.9	5.5	5.5	5.4
DI	0.7	0.8	0.9	0.9	0.9	0.9
OASDI	4.7	4.9	5.7	6.4	6.4	6.3
HI	2.0	2.4	3.1	3.9	4.4	4.6
Total	6.7	7.3	8.9	10.3	10.8	10.9

Notes:
Projections based on 'intermediate scenario': real GDP growth 2 per cent per annum in medium run declining to 1.3 per cent by 2050; real earnings growth approximately 1 per cent per annum over whole period; growth of female participation to level out while decline in male participation rate continues. Ultimate total fertility rate 1.9 per cent in 2021 from 2.1 per cent in 2000. The age- and gender-adjusted death rate to decrease by 35 per cent from 1996 to 2071. Total net immigration to grow to steady-state level of +900 000 per annum.
[a]Defined as population aged 65 or over divided by population aged 20–64.
[b]Income of OASDI (contributions plus income taxes on OASDI benefits) / taxable payroll.

Source: Author's computations using various tables from the OASDI Trustee Report (1997).

current system (Advisory Council on Social Security, 1997). The three alternatives not only differ in detail but also reflect widely different perspectives on the reform potential of the existing retirement income system.

The 'maintenance of benefits' proposal essentially wants to keep the present DB structure of the system. To solve the financing problems, its authors suggest a combination of tax increases and changes in the benefit computation formula. The 'individual accounts' proposal supplements the current PAYG system with government-administered individual retirement savings accounts that invest in a relatively small number of government-managed investment funds. The 'personal security account' proposal wants to bring about a more radical shift from the present-day PAYG system in the direction of a basic pension financed by a flat payroll tax supplemented with individual savings in private retirement savings accounts. The financial burden of the transition would be spread over a 72-year period through an additional payroll tax. Summarising, the main differences between the three suggestions are: what role the public sector has to play in the area of retirement income provision; whether to have a DC or DB set-up; and what the benefits of added savings to the economy are. Other issues discussed in the debate include the implications of the higher rate of return in stock markets rather than bond markets, as well as the question of who bears the risk in the economy.

10.5   ACTIVITY RATES

Aside from population growth and the overall generosity of the retirement system, economic activity rates play an important role in determining the financial status of the retirement system at the macro level, as well as the economic status of the elderly at the micro level. Here the main interest is in activity rates for the population just under the official (early) retirement age. Although social security old-age benefits are only available at the earliest at age 62, many people withdraw from the labour market earlier. Table 10.6 depicts the proportion of men and women in work in the age ranges 55–59, 60–64 and 65–69 and illustrates this earlier withdrawal.

As previously noted when discussing the DI system, there are substantial financial incentives for people below the NRA to get onto the DI rolls, as benefits are available before the NRA and their amount is equal to the unreduced value of the PIA. In the US there is a substantial empirical literature that focuses on the question of what the influence of the DI programme is on labour force participation.[16] Table 10.7 shows the proportion of men receiving different forms of social insurance and social assistance payments for three different age-groups.

Table 10.6   Percentage of Economically Active Men and Women, by Age-group, 1995 (%)

	Age-group		
	55–59	60–64	65–69
Men	77.4	53.2	16.8
Women	59.5	28.0	8.8

Source: US Congress, 1996.

The evolution of activity rates over time is illustrated by Figures 10.3 and 10.4, which show male and female activity rates over the period 1976–97. Male activity rates display a downward trend, which is the most pronounced for the 60–64 age-group. Between 1970 and 2000 this cohort's activity rate has fallen by more than 20 percentage points in spite of the fact that early retirement provisions were not changed over this period. The trend in female activity rates looks very different as the effect of increased labour force participation more than outweighs any trend toward earlier retirement.

Table 10.7   Percentage of Men Receiving Social Insurance or Assistance, by Age-group, 1997 (%)

Benefit	Age-group		
	55–59	60–64	65–69
None	88.8	63.3	16.5
OASDI	6.7	32.9	82.3
SSI	2.4	2.5	2.6
Food stamps	4.1	4.3	3.6
Housing	0.5	0.6	0.3
Public assistance	0.3	0.8	0.1

Source: Author's computations based on the March 1997 CPS.

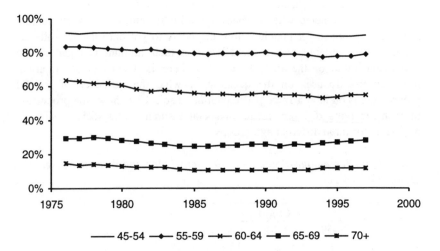

Source: US Bureau of Labor Statistics, various years.

Figure 10.3   Male Activity Rates

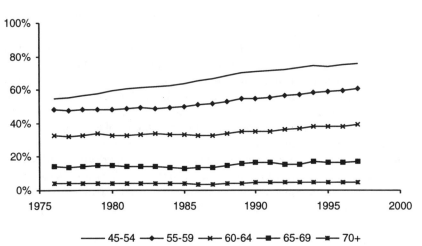

Source: US Bureau of Labor Statistics, various years.

Figure 10.4   Female Activity Rates

10.6   INCOME DISTRIBUTION

All tabulations in this section use data from the March 1997 Current Population Survey (CPS). The sample size is approximately 120 000 people, corresponding to roughly 50 000 households, among which there are 12 092 pensioner households. The sample does not contain any institutionalised individuals. A person is part of our pensioner sample if he or she is either over the NRA, or in the 60–64 age-group and not employed or self-employed. This has the effect of including as pensioners those still working beyond the NRA as well as those aged 60–64 who are out of work but actively looking for a job. For couples we have based the classification on the status of the husband. As a result some working wives are included, as are some retired below the age of 60.

Total income is defined as gross income net of state and federal taxes. The money value of food stamps received by the household is included as income. When breaking income down by source, only pre-tax figures are considered, as it is impossible to assign taxes correctly to any single income source. When comparing incomes of families and households of different sizes, a simple equivalence scale is used: the first adult is assigned 1, any additional adult 0.7 and any children 0.5. The figures are also presented for an alternative equivalence scale of 0.5 for additional adults and 0.3 for children. Housing costs are not included.

Table 10.8 presents net annual mean income in US dollars for three different demographic groups – namely couples, single men and single women – as well as for five different age-groups and for the two equivalence scales. Given the definition of the term 'pensioner' for people under 65, it is not surprising that their average income is rather low. Focusing on those aged 65 or over, income is higher for younger households than for older households. This is partly due to lower participation in the labour force of earlier cohorts (i.e. older pensioners) and also due to a pure cohort effect, i.e. the older cohort being poorer than the younger one. This difference arises because private investment income decreases as older individuals deplete their stock of wealth and because older individuals have lower private pension benefits.

Single women are universally worse off than their male counterparts, the biggest differences stemming from lower private pension benefits and from lower earnings. Levels of social security benefits are less disparate between the two sexes.

Table 10.8   Average Income of Pensioner Households, by Age-group, 1997 (incomes in $US p.a.)

	Age-group				
	60–64	65–69	70–74	75+	60+
Couples					
Annual income	32 741	38 505	34 514	30 177	34 131
Ratio 1	(0.81)	(0.95)	(0.86)	(0.75)	(0.85)
Ratio 2	(0.83)	(0.97)	(0.87)	(0.76)	(0.86)
Single men					
Annual income	16 289	21 707	20 667	18 107	19 262
Ratio 1	(0.68)	(0.92)	(0.88)	(0.78)	(0.82)
Ratio 2	(0.61)	(0.82)	(0.79)	(0.70)	(0.74)
Single women					
Annual income	11 915	16 185	14 575	13 668	14 029
Ratio 1	(0.49)	(0.67)	(0.61)	(0.56)	(0.58)
Ratio 2	(0.44)	(0.60)	(0.55)	(0.50)	(0.53)

Note: Numbers in parentheses are the ratios of average income in each cell to the average income of an identical family type in the general population, ratio 1 being computed with the (1, 0.7, 0.5) equivalence scale and ratio 2 with the (1, 0.5, 0.3) equivalence scale.

Source: Author's calculations from March 1997 CPS.

The proportions in parentheses in Table 10.8 are the ratios of average income in each cell to the average income of an identical family type in the general population, using the two equivalence scales. For the comparisons a pensioner family is defined as the pensioner, his spouse and any children under the age of 18. Notice the relatively high ratios for both couples and single men. Single female pensioners on the other hand have a substantially lower income level than the active population. This is especially true for the group of early retirees, which is essentially composed of involuntary early retirees.

Tables 10.9 and 10.10 compare measures of income inequality across the non-pensioner and pensioner populations. Table 10.9 gives an idea of the distribution of the total equivalised net income across different demographic groups in the non-pensioner population. Couples are substantially wealthier than single people, even when incomes are adjusted for the size of the family. Further, single women are much poorer than single men.

Table 10.9   Moments of the Income Distribution and Inter-decile Ratios for Different Groups of the Non-pensioner Population, 1997 (incomes in US$ p.a.)

	Mean	Median	90th percentile	10th percentile	90/10 ratio
Couples, no children, head aged <40	48 081	43 349	78 026	19 610	3.98
Couples, no children, head aged ≥40	56 275	48 659	91 738	20 444	4.49
Couples with children	52 591	45 404	85 464	19 653	4.35
Single parents	19 192	15 024	37 367	3 600	10.38
Single men aged <40	24 197	20 808	42 249	5 964	7.08
Single men aged ≥40	32 988	25 752	56 722	7 000	8.10
Single women aged <40	20 220	18 019	36 341	4 281	8.49
Single women aged ≥40	24 375	19 887	45 560	5 676	8.03

Source: Author's calculations from March 1997 CPS.

Table 10.10   Moments of the Income Distribution and Inter-decile Ratios for Different Groups of the Pensioner Population, 1997 (incomes in US$ p.a.)

	Age-group				
	60–64	65–69	70–74	75+	60+
Couples					
Median	28 101	31 972	28 040	24 660	27 926
90th percentile	62 587	69 111	62 040	53 971	61 859
10th percentile	8 856	13 069	13 500	9 420	12 043
90/10 ratio	7.07	5.29	4.60	5.73	5.14
Single men					
Median	10 708	15 653	16 008	13 941	14 223
90th percentile	35 162	39 991	36 370	31 949	34 735
10th percentile	3 733	6 168	7 344	6 510	6 300
90/10 ratio	9.42	6.48	4.95	4.91	5.51
Single women					
Median	8 318	12 253	11 681	10 374	10 782
90th percentile	27 330	29 367	26 641	24 262	26 235
10th percentile	255	5 135	5 910	5 384	5 240
90/10 ratio	107.18	5.72	4.51	4.51	5.01

Source: Author's calculations from March 1997 CPS.

Table 10.10 examines pensioners. Notice the very low level of total net income at the 10th percentile for women in the 60–64 age-group displayed in the table and also the extremely high income for the highest income decile. The 90/10 ratios are extremely high for those in the 60–64 age-group, due to considerable heterogeneity of this population group. One reason for the low incomes of women at the 10th percentile of single women in the 60–64 age-group is that some of them are simply not eligible for survivor benefits under the husband's pension plan and hence report zero incomes. Another reason is that among these women a substantial fraction live in households where other household members have more substantial incomes, hence excluding the pensioner from any kind of means-tested benefit such as SSI. There is also evidence of widening disparities among the oldest couples, which may illustrate differential mortality by income group, although a similar feature is not apparent for single people.

A further illustration of the heterogeneity in the pensioner population is summarised in Table 10.11. In addition to the wide variety in total net pensioner incomes, the composition of income is very different across demographic groups. The table contains the breakdown of gross pensioner

Table 10.11   Composition of Pensioner Income, by Marital Status and Age-group, 1997 (% of total)

	Age-group				
	60–64	65–69	70–74	75+	60+
Couples					
OASDI	17.4	25.6	36.7	45.6	32.5
Means-tested benefits	1.0	0.3	0.3	0.3	0.4
Other benefits	4.7	2.6	1.9	1.7	2.5
Private pensions	29.0	19.7	20.9	20.2	21.4
Investment income	12.7	15.0	18.4	19.9	16.8
Earnings	35.2	36.8	21.8	12.3	26.4
Single men					
OASDI	28.2	28.9	36.1	45.0	37.1
Means-tested benefits	3.5	0.7	0.9	1.0	1.1
Other benefits	5.8	4.0	2.8	3.2	3.6
Private pensions	29.8	17.6	26.9	19.7	21.9
Investment income	14.0	11.4	15.7	18.8	15.7
Earnings	18.7	37.4	17.5	12.4	20.6
Single women					
OASDI	31.1	36.7	49.4	56.1	48.5
Means-tested benefits	7.2	1.7	1.6	1.5	2.0
Other benefits	5.9	2.6	2.4	1.9	2.5
Private pensions	26.7	15.0	18.0	15.4	16.7
Investment income	12.7	16.5	18.9	20.1	18.5
Earnings	16.4	27.5	9.6	4.9	11.9

Notes:
Means-tested benefits are composed of SSI payments and of public assistance payments, i.e. general assistance, emergency assistance, Aid for Families with Dependent Children (AFDC), Aid to Dependent Children (ADC), refugee assistance, Indian assistance and income from the WIC (Women, Infants and Children) Nutrition programme.
Other benefits include unemployment and workers' compensation as well as disability and veterans' benefits.

Source: Author's calculations from March 1997 CPS.

income (including the value of food stamps). Not surprisingly OASDI income is lower for the 60–64 age-group, as some of this group are ineligible for benefits. The natural complement to this finding is that means-tested benefits are much more important for this population group than for the 65+ age-group. The role of OASDI benefits increases with age, both for single people and for couples. Notice the relatively high proportion that OASDI represents for the 75+ age-group and the importance of income from earnings even for the 65–69 age-group.

Another way of arranging the data is to consider the share of income a couple receives that is due to the husband and that due to the wife. Across all age-groups the pattern is essentially that two-thirds of the income is obtained by the husband (see Table 10.12).

Aside from substantial variation in the composition of pensioner income across different demographic groups, as illustrated in Table 10.11, there is a wide variation across different income groups. Equivalising the income of couples and single people using the (1, 0.7, 0.5) equivalence scale, we take the average incomes of pensioners across the five quintiles. Table 10.13 shows the enormous differences in income composition across these income quintiles. Notice the substantial difference in total income from the lowest to the highest income quintile: average annual income levels are almost 10 times higher in the top quintile than in the lowest one.

Table 10.12   Shares of Couples' Total Income Received by the Man and by the Woman (% of total)

	Age-group				
	60–64	65–69	70–74	75+	60+
Share received by man	63.35	66.56	67.08	65.94	66.10
Share received by woman	36.65	33.44	32.92	34.06	33.90

Source: Author's calculations from March 1997 CPS.

Table 10.13   Gross and Net Pensioner Income, by Composition and Income Quintile (US$ p.a.)

Source	Quintile of annual income				
	1	2	3	4	5
OASDI	4 218	7 647	8 273	8 395	8 503
Means-tested benefits	530	129	84	42	46
Other benefits	137	228	395	574	1 267
Private pensions	208	962	2 938	5 753	10 773
Investment income	192	581	1 399	3 080	12 057
Earnings	153	542	1 528	3 822	16 714
Average gross income	5 438	10 087	14 616	21 666	49 359
Average net income	5 435	10 049	14 418	20 576	40 366

Source: Author's calculations from March 1997 CPS.

For the lowest two quintiles, OASDI accounts for approximately 75 per cent of income, whereas for the highest income quintile the number is less than 20 per cent. The importance of private forms of income provision in a pensioner family's total income increases dramatically with total income. Similarly the total money income from private sources is highly concentrated at the top of the income distribution. Private pensions and especially earnings and investment income are distributed quite unequally across income levels. Table 10.14 illustrates these points as ratios of total income.

Table 10.14   Gross Pensioner Income, by Composition and Income Quintile (% of total)

Source	Quintile of annual income				
	1	2	3	4	5
OASDI	77.6	75.8	56.6	38.8	17.2
Means-tested benefits	9.7	1.3	0.6	0.2	0.1
Other benefits	2.5	2.3	2.7	2.7	2.6
Private pensions	3.8	9.5	20.1	26.6	21.8
Investment income	3.5	5.8	9.6	14.2	24.4
Earnings	2.8	5.4	10.5	17.6	33.9

Source: Author's calculations from March 1997 CPS.

Table 10.15   Percentage of Pensioners in Each Income Decile Band of the Population (%)

Income decile	% of all pensioners	% of pensioner couples	% of single male pensioners	% of single female pensioners
1	10.4	7.0	9.5	16.9
2	16.5	12.0	17.1	24.7
3	14.4	13.6	13.8	16.0
4	12.3	12.5	13.4	11.5
5	11.1	12.3	9.4	9.3
6	8.9	10.3	8.9	6.5
7	8.2	9.9	8.3	5.0
8	6.4	7.6	6.6	4.1
9	6.2	7.8	5.8	3.3
10	5.6	6.9	7.2	2.8

Source: Author's calculations from March 1997 CPS.

Finally Table 10.15 determines the pensioner population's situation in the overall income distribution using the $(1, 0.7, 0.5)$ equivalence scale.[17] Pensioners are more likely to be in the bottom half of the income distribution, but there are still a substantial number of pensioner households in the highest income deciles. Notice that the proportion of single women in the bottom deciles of the overall income distribution is much higher than the proportions for couples and for single men. The proportion of pensioners in the 1st decile is relatively low, at least compared with the 2nd decile. A partial reason for this finding is that incomes are equivalised, and single non-pensioner mothers for example represent a substantial proportion of the lowest decile.

10.7   CONCLUSIONS

The US social security system is a substantial benefit programme which provides an important source of income to the elderly. But the system is also a system in fiscal imbalance: major reforms will be necessary to keep it solvent in the medium and long run. One natural solution is to increase the importance of private forms of income provision, be it through individual retirement arrangements, such as IRAs and Keogh plans, or through occupational defined benefit or defined contribution plans, with the fastest-growing example being the 401(k) deferred taxation arrangements.

Such a change from public to private sources will not be without distributional implications. We have illustrated that private pension receipt as well as income from investments is distributed highly unequally across different income groups. Further, private pension plans generally do not provide the same high level of income to survivors as the social security programme does, which implies a potentially serious threat of further worsening of the relative financial situation of divorced and widowed women.

NOTES

1. i.e. thousand million.
2. With the assumption of a constant benefit formula, social security payroll taxes would have to rise from 12.4 per cent to almost 20 per cent in 2070 to keep the programme solvent.
3. Similarly to what had become the rule for old-age benefits, the eligibility for benefits was extended to dependants and survivors of disabled workers.
4. More recently some politicians and economists have proposed speeding up the scheduled increases in the NRA and lifting the NRA to 70. However none of these proposals was close to implementation early in 2000.
5. Originally the credit was only 1 per cent a year. It was then raised to 3 per cent by the 1977 amendment.

6. Nevertheless EBRI (1997, Table 7.12) estimated the tax expenditure due to the continued non-taxation of some social security benefits to be approximately US$29.7 billion in 1997.
7. For workers with a dependent spouse the corresponding replacement rates are distinctly higher because of the dependant and survivor benefits.
8. In all other scenarios benefits can be claimed at the earliest at age 62 but facing a reduction factor that is slightly higher than the corresponding one for workers' benefits.
9. The maximum family benefit depends on the PIA level but is approximately equal to 175 per cent of the PIA.
10. Some legal immigrants are also eligible if they have more than 40 quarters of social-security-covered employment.
11. Eligibility depends on an income test, with the precise level of the cut-off varying by county or metropolitan area.
12. The limit is US$35 000 for single taxpayers and US$50 000 for married taxpayers filing jointly.
13. Between US$25 000 and US$35 000 of adjusted gross income for single taxpayers and between US$40 000 and US$50 000 for married joint filers.
14. For an analysis of the rapid shift in the late 1980s see Gustman and Steinmeier (1992).
15. All employee contributions are immediately vested.
16. See for example the Bound (1989 and 1991) debate with Parsons (1991) in the late 1980s and early 1990s and the recent discussion of incentives for early retirement in Gruber and Wise (1999) and in Diamond and Gruber (1999).
17. Similar results can be derived using the (1, 0.5, 0.3) equivalence scale.

REFERENCES

Advisory Council on Social Security (1997), *Report of the 1994–1996 Advisory Council on Social Security, Volume I: Findings and Recommendations*, Washington, DC: US Department of Health and Human Services, Social Security Administration, Advisory Council. This document can be found on the web at http://www.ssa.gov/history/reports/adcouncil/report/toc.htm.

Bound, J. (1989), 'The health and earnings of rejected disability insurance applicants', *American Economic Review*, **79** (3), 482–503.

Bound, J. (1991), 'The health and earnings of rejected disability insurance applicants: reply', *American Economic Review*, **81** (5), 1427–31.

Diamond, P. and J. Gruber (1999), 'Social security and retirement in the US', in J. Gruber and D.A. Wise (eds), *Social Security and Retirement around the World*, Chicago: Chicago University Press for National Bureau of Economic Research, pp. 437–74.

EBRI (1995), *EBRI Databook on Employee Benefits*, 3rd edition, Washington, DC: Employee Benefit Research Institute.

EBRI (1997), *EBRI Databook on Employee Benefits*, 4th edition, Washington, DC: Employee Benefit Research Institute.

Executive Office of the President (1997), *Economic Report of the President*, February, Washington, DC: US Government Printing Office.

Gruber, J. and D.A. Wise (eds) (1999), *Social Security and Retirement around the World*, Chicago: Chicago University Press for National Bureau of Economic Research.

Gustman, A. and T. Steinmeier (1992), 'The stampede towards defined contribution pension plans: fact or fiction?', *Industrial Relations*, **32** (2), 361–9.

Lee, R. and J. Skinner (1999), 'Will aging baby boomers bust the federal budget?', *Journal of Economic Perspectives*, **13** (1), 117–40.

Leimer, D.R. (1994), 'Cohort-specific measures of lifetime net social security transfers', Social Security Administration, Office of Research and Statistics, Working Paper no. 59.

Leimer, D.R. (1995), 'A guide to social security money's worth issues', Social Security Administration, Office of Research and Statistics, Working Paper no. 67.

OASDI Trustee Report (1997), *Annual Report of the Board of the Federal Old-age and Survivors Insurance and Disability Insurance Trust Funds*, US Department of Health and Human Services, Social Security Administration, Office of the Chief Actuary, Washington, DC: US Government Printing Office.

Parsons, D. (1991), 'The health and earnings of rejected disability insurance applicants: comment', *American Economic Review*, **81** (5), 1419–26.

Roseveare, D., W. Leibfritz, D. Fore and F. Wurzel (1996), 'Ageing populations, pension systems and government budgets: simulations for 26 OECD countries', Organisation for Economic Co-operation and Development, Economics Department, Working Paper no. 168.

US Bureau of Labor Statistics (various years), *Employment and Earnings*, Washington, DC: US Bureau of Labor Statistics.

US Congress (1996), *Green Book: Background Material and Data on Programs within the Jurisdiction of the Committee on Ways and Means*, House of Representatives, Committee on Ways and Means, Washington, DC: US Government Printing Office.

US Department of Labor (1997), *Private Pension Plan Bulletin: Abstract of 1993 Form 5500 Annual Reports*, Washington, DC: Pension and Welfare Benefit Administration.

US Department of the Treasury, Internal Revenue Service (various years), *Statistics of Income Bulletin*, Winter 1984–1985, 1986–1987, 1990–1991, 1993–1994 and Summer 1994, Washington, DC: US Department of the Treasury.

Index